Julian S. Corbett

Drake and the Tudor Navy

With a History of the Rise of England as a Maritime Power, Vol. I

Julian S. Corbett

Drake and the Tudor Navy

With a History of the Rise of England as a Maritime Power, Vol. I

ISBN/EAN: 9783743400122

Manufactured in Europe, USA, Canada, Australia, Japa

Cover: Foto ©ninafisch / pixelio.de

Manufactured and distributed by brebook publishing software (www.brebook.com)

Julian S. Corbett

Drake and the Tudor Navy

DRAKE

AND

THE TUDOR NAVY

WITH A HISTORY OF THE
RISE OF ENGLAND AS A MARITIME POWER

BY

JULIAN S. CORBETT

IN TWO VOLUMES—VOL. I.

'Whosoever commands the sea commands the trade; whosoever commands the trade of the world commands the riches of the world, and consequently the world itself.'—SIR WALTER RALEIGH.

NEW IMPRESSION

LONGMANS, GREEN, AND CO
39 PATERNOSTER ROW, LONDON
FOURTH AVENUE & 30TH STREET, NEW YORK
BOMBAY, CALCUTTA AND MADRAS
1917

All rights reserved

BIBLIOGRAPHICAL NOTE.

First printed, 2 vols. 8vo., *February* 1898.

New and Cheaper Edition, 2 vols. crown 8vo. *September* 1899; *reprinted September* 1912 *and April* 1917.

PREFACE
TO
THE SECOND EDITION

IN the present edition I have been able to remove a few errors and inaccuracies which have been pointed out to me by the care and kindness of friends both known and unknown, and to add in the notes here and there some additional evidence in support of the views expressed on controversial points. Otherwise the work remains substantially the same. Although I have to thank many serious critics for most careful and often too generous treatment of the book, I have seen no reason to modify its main conclusions. On only one important point do I seem to be at variance with any recognised authority. In the *English Historical Review*, 1898, p. 582, Professor Laughton disputes the view that Drake invented or introduced the close-hauled line-ahead in 1588, because if he did it was certainly forgotten by 1653. The criticism seems to be due to a want of clearness on my part. In avoiding the expression 'line of battle' and in saying that the Elizabethan tactics were very different from the attack line-ahead as it was afterwards developed, I hoped it would be clear that I did not wish to attribute to Drake a tactical formation which certainly was not fully understood till nearly a century later. All I attribute to him and his school is the first real appreciation of the broadside and the definite adoption, as a fundamental tactical idea, of the line-ahead, as opposed to the line-abreast of mediæval and galley warfare. Professor Laughton considers that the actual system in vogue in Elizabethan times was one of groups. I am of the same opinion; but the point is that they were groups in line-ahead and not in line-abreast. This was the great revolution. It contained in itself the active germ of the full fledged battle order of the eighteenth century; and as it first appeared in the fleet of which Drake was the Vice-admiral and real commander, there seems nothing extravagant in regarding him as the father of 'a rational system of sailing tactics,' unless indeed it can be shown that some other admiral used the formation before him.

I have again to thank Dr. Tilton and Mr. Oppenheim for much invaluable help in detecting and amending errors.

J. S. C.

THAMES DITTON:
January 1899

PREFACE

TO

THE FIRST EDITION

IN the present work an attempt is made to give a general view of the circumstances under which England first became a controlling force in the European system by virtue of her power upon the sea. In centering the history of such a movement upon the life of one of its leaders, there must be almost inevitably a tendency to present him too much as its author, where he was in reality only the foremost of men similarly inspired who determined its direction and extent.

Still, for the adoption of the method in the present case history affords ample justification. Not only was Drake intimately connected, in all the various phases of his life, with every aspect of the Elizabethan maritime upheaval, but throughout Europe he was recognised and applauded, even in his lifetime, as the personification of the new political force. Nor has recent research disclosed any reason for reversing the verdict of his contemporaries. The romantic fascination of his career as a corsair and explorer began, it is true, very shortly after his death to overshadow his work as an admiral and a statesman, but in his own time it was not so; and a principal object of the present work is to restore him to the position he once held as one of the great military figures of the Reformation.

The most graphic picture of him, as he then appeared to judicious observers, is from the pen of Stowe. 'He was more skilful,' he writes, 'in all points of navigation than any that ever was before his time, in his time or since his death. He was also of perfect memory, great observation, eloquent by nature, skilful in artillery, expert and apt to let blood and give physic unto his people according to the climate. . . . His name was a terror to the French, Spaniard, Portugal, and Indian. Many princes of Italy and Germany desired his picture. . . . In brief, he was as famous in Europe and America, as Tamberlane in Asia and Africa.'

Still, great as was the part he played as the moving spirit of the English maritime power, the significance of his career as a corsair must not be minimised; and with this the first volume is mainly occupied. It will be seen how during this part of his life he was brought into intimate contact with all that went to make up what we know as the Elizabethan period of maritime history, and how the part he played in each phase of the development went to make up the man who led and dominated our first great bid for the command of the sea. Yet in this work he was but one of many, emphasising and developing what others had begun before him. It is in his career as an admiral and administrator, with which the second volume is concerned, that he stands alone as the creator and inspiration of a force that was new to the world. As the perfecter of a rational system of sailing tactics, as the father of a sound system of strategy, as the first and unsurpassed master of that amphibious warfare which has built up the British Empire, as an officer always ready to accept the responsibility of ignoring unintelligent orders, he has no rival in our history but Nelson. Never once when in sole command of an expedition did he fail to achieve success. The miscarriage of the Portugal expedition which brought him into disgrace was in no way his fault, and his colleague Norreys was almost as little to blame. Drake was denied the consummation of his work and his renown by the inherent and abiding vice of our system of national defence. The idea of following up the victorious Armada campaign by the capture of Lisbon and the liberation of Portugal was as obvious as it was sound. The navy had laid the way open, and all that was required to deal Spain a mortal blow was a small compact military force properly equipped and organised. Drake knew this perfectly well. He and Norreys asked for such a force; it was promised them, and the promise could not be fulfilled. The attempt was made without the perfected weapon, and it failed. It was not only Drake's reputation that was lost, it was the hard-earned fruits of what the navy had achieved. For want of a mobile military force the blow to which Spain was exposed by her naval defeat could not be struck—her discomfiture could not be completed. The result was that she assumed the defensive, and we could barely touch her. While she rapidly recovered all she had lost, the war necessarily sank into that hopeless form of hostility—a war on commerce, which sooner or later degenerates into a scramble for prize money, demoralises the navy, and leads to no decisive result. Yet the lesson is still to learn, and for us to-day the moral of Drake's marred career is to beware the heresy which the 'martialists' of his day called the 'Idolatry of Neptune.'

Unfortunately for Drake, in the Elizabethan age the principles of naval warfare were as little understood as its limitations. He could convince the Government of neither the one nor the other, and was made to suffer for their inability to grasp his teaching. In a later age, under almost any other sovereign, his unexampled services must have received the same recognition which the instructed opinion of all Europe awarded him, and he would have been permitted to spend for his country the whole of that genius and energy which in so large a measure exhausted itself in working with inadequate materials and in breaking through the obstacles that encumbered his path.

The research involved in the attempt to reconstruct

budding moustache and no beard. It is finely executed, but in too bad a condition for reproduction.

Drake relics are fairly numerous. At Nutwell Court are preserved the following: A bundle of flags said to have decorated his ship when he was knighted, containing amongst others two silk banners (England ancient) and a number of red silk flags with a white cross, and in the corners various devices in gold—a hawk, a globe, a pole-star, a flame, &c.; a great Bible, 'which he had about the world with him;' a green silk scarf embroidered in bullion with globes and compasses, and a purse to match, given him by Elizabeth and worn by him when Zucchero painted his portrait; the jewel above mentioned; and another, in the form of a pole-star, set with opals, and containing a portrait of the queen; a fine cocoanut cup set in gold, and surmounted with the ship and globe crest and engraved with incidents of the circumnavigation voyage; a panel from his ship carved with his new arms; and a splendid carved wood bedstead, highly coloured and gilt, which was taken from the cabin of Don Pedro de Valdez: arms, *barry*; crest, a demi-boar *rampant*. At Buckland Abbey is a State drum decorated with Drake's arms, on which it is probable his last salute was beaten as he was committed to the sea, and upon which the legend says he may still be summoned when England is in danger.

J. S. C.

CONTENTS

OF

THE FIRST VOLUME

CHAPTER		PAGE
	INTRODUCTION. THE NAVAL ART IN THE MIDDLE OF THE SIXTEENTH CENTURY	1
I.	DRAKE'S EARLY YEARS	60
II.	JOHN HAWKINS	74
III.	SAN JUAN DE ULUA	101
IV.	DRAKE'S FIRST SERVICE IN THE NAVY	120
V.	NOMBRE DE DIOS	144
VI.	THE SPANISH MAIN	169
VII.	DRAKE AND THE WAR PARTY	190
VIII.	THE VOYAGE OF CIRCUMNAVIGATION	216
IX.	THE VOYAGE OF CIRCUMNAVIGATION—(*continued*)	248
X.	THE VOYAGE OF CIRCUMNAVIGATION—(*continued*)	278
XI.	KNIGHTHOOD	306
XII.	THE NAVY OF ELIZABETH	342

[APPENDICES

APPENDICES

		PAGE
A.	BIRTH, PARENTAGE, AND EARLY YEARS	391
B.	AUTHORITIES FOR HAWKINS'S THIRD VOYAGE, WITH A TRANSLATION OF THE SPANISH OFFICIAL REPORT ON THE AFFAIR OF SAN JUAN DE ULUA	397
C.	DRAKE'S DESERTION OF HAWKINS	400
D.	THE AUTHENTICITY OF 'SIR FRANCIS DRAKE REVIVED'	401
E.	AUTHORITIES FOR THE VOYAGE OF CIRCUMNAVIGATION	403
F.	AMOUNT OF DRAKE'S PLUNDER	408
G.	DRAKE'S ARMS	410

REFERENCES IN THE NOTES

'S. P. Dom.' = State Papers, Domestic Series; 'S.P.' followed by the name of a country refers to that special series of State Papers. All these are in the London Record Office. 'Lansd. MSS.,' 'Harl. MSS.,' 'Eg. MSS.,' and 'Add. MSS.' = the Lansdowne, the Harleian, the Egerton, and the Additional Manuscripts in the British Museum. The Sloane and Stowe MSS. are in the same place. The Ashmolean and Tanner MSS. are at Oxford. 'Hist. MSS. Comm.' refers to the series of calendars issued by the Royal Commission on Historical Manuscripts. 'Hatfield Papers' refers to their special calendar of Lord Salisbury's MSS. at Hatfield House. 'B. M.,' followed by figures, gives the press mark of the work cited at the British Museum. 'Hakl. Soc.' denotes the publications of the Hakluyt Society, 'C. S.' or 'Cam. Soc.' those of the Camden Society. 'Cal.' or 'Calendar' refers to the various series of calendars (Domestic, Spanish, Venetian, Foreign, Colonial, &c.) issued from the Record Office by the Master of the Rolls.

ILLUSTRATIONS

IN VOLUME I

PLATES

SIR FRANCIS DRAKE . . . . *Frontispiece*		
From the original oil painting at Buckland Abbey.		
THE GALLEASSE 'ANNE GALANT'	*To face p.*	24
Reduced from Anthony's Second Roll (British Museum, Add. MSS. 22047).		
THE GALLEASSE 'HART'	,,	84
Reduced from Anthony's Second Roll (British Museum, Add. MSS. 22047).		
THE PINNACE 'ROE'	,,	38
Reduced from Anthony's Third Roll (Magdalene College, Cambridge).		
THE ROW-BARGE 'CLOUD-IN-THE-SUN'	,,	42
Reduced from Anthony's Third Roll (Magdalene College, Cambridge).		
THE GREAT-SHIP 'JESUS OF LUBECK'	,,	84
Reduced from Anthony's First Roll (Magdalene College, Cambridge).		
THE GREAT-SHIP 'MINION'	,,	102
Reduced from Anthony's First Roll (Magdalene College, Cambridge).		
A PINNACE UNDER FIGHTING SAILS (*circa* 1586). . .	,,	338
AN ELIZABETHAN GALLEON	,,	352
From Visscher's Series, circ. 1588.		
A 'RACE-BUILT' SHIP, PROBABLY A 'GALLEASSE' . .	,,	358
From Visscher's Series, circ. 1588.		
AN ELIZABETHAN GREAT-SHIP OR GALLEON	,,	374
From Visscher's Series, circ. 1588.		

IN TEXT

	PAGE
CHART OF DARIEN	160
CHART TO ILLUSTRATE DRAKE'S OPERATIONS ON THE AMERICAN COAST IN 1577-8	229
CHART FROM FLETCHER'S 'NOTES' TO ILLUSTRATE THE VOYAGE TO THE STRAITS OF MAGELLAN AND THE DISCOVERY OF AN OPEN SEA SOUTH OF THEM (SLOANE MSS. 61)	233
THE SOUTHERN EXTREMITY OF AMERICA, AS DELINEATED BEFORE AND AFTER DRAKE'S CIRCUMNAVIGATION	258
CARRIAGE OF BREECH-LOADING PIECE, SHOWING PIVOT-MOUNTING . .	367
BREECH-LOADING PIECE, SHOWING THE DETACHED CHAMBER WITH 'SHOULDERING' OR 'WATER-PIPE' JOINT, AND THE 'WEDGE' OR 'COIN' FOR LOCKING IT IN POSITION	367
RANGE-FINDING BY MEANS OF THE GUNNER'S 'HALF-CIRCLE' . . . *From Tartaglia's 'Colloquies,' 1588.*	379
DEPRESSION RANGE-FINDING . . . . *From Tartaglia's 'Colloquies,' 1588.*	381

DRAKE AND THE TUDOR NAVY

INTRODUCTION

THE NAVAL ART IN THE MIDDLE OF THE SIXTEENTH CENTURY

THE conspicuous technical feature of the maritime revolution which in the sixteenth century transferred the focus of the naval art from the Mediterranean to the Atlantic is the transition from galley warfare to warfare under sail; and the history of that transition, of its causes, its development, and its results, is the history of the rise of the English naval supremacy.

The whole of maritime warfare falls naturally into three periods, each sharply characterised by a generic difference in the 'capital ship,' as in the seventeenth century it was happily called—the ship, that is, which formed the backbone of a fighting fleet and which had a place in the fighting line. The first period is that of the galley, beginning in prehistoric times and culminating in the year 1571, at the battle of Lepanto; the second is that of the 'great-ship,' or 'ship-of-the-line,' which was established in 1588 with the campaign of the Great Armada, and reached its highest development at Trafalgar; the third is that in which we now live, the period of the 'battleship.' Or, to state the classification in terms of its real basis, there is a period of oars, a period of sails, and a period of steam.

The classification, it will be seen, is no arbitrary device invented for the clearer exposition of naval history, but one that is natural and inevitable. Not only do the divisions lie between well defined chronological limits, but they are rooted in the essentials of the art. The essence of naval strategy is sea endurance, by which is meant the degree of a fleet's capability of keeping the sea. The essence of naval tactics is the nature of the motive power; that is to say, tactics primarily depend upon how far the movements of the fleet or ship are under human control, and how far dependent upon conditions that lie beyond it, or, in other words, whether the units of the fleet are of free or of subservient movement.

To these essential elements of the art each of the three periods has its own distinct relation. Each of them is measurable and determined by the degree of sea endurance and the degree of mobility exhibited by its characteristic type of capital ship. The galley was a vessel of low sea endurance but of highly free movement. The great-ship, or ship-of-the-line, was of large sea endurance but entirely subservient to the wind for its power of movement. The steam battleship, while far surpassing the galley in mobility, approaches the ship-of-the-line in sea endurance. In the first period, the period of oars, when the focus of empire lay within the confined waters of the Mediterranean, we see mobility taking precedence of sea endurance; in the second, the period of sails, when the arena of history widens out into the ocean, sea endurance becomes of the first importance; in the third, the period of steam, when the area of naval action is greater and the demand for extreme mobility more pressing than ever, we have the effort to combine both qualities in one type of ship, and in this type the possibility of securing the one essential without sacrifice of the other has most nearly reached attainment.

It is the solution of this problem that is the eternal

pre-occupation of the naval art. Its two factors are necessarily antagonistic. Sea endurance depends mainly on two considerations : it depends on the degree of bad weather the vessel can support and on its capacity for carrying provisions and material of war. Sea endurance, therefore, has two limits, the limit of seaworthiness and the limit of supply. In the galley both limits were low. The weakness of its method of propulsion required lightness of construction, fine lines, and a low freeboard, all of which tended to unseaworthiness. The same inherent defect demanded that its tonnage should be small in relation to the number of the crew, so that the point of extreme mobility had to be sought in reducing storage space to a minimum and increasing to a maximum the number of mouths to feed. In the great-ship the conditions were reversed. The sacrifice of free movement gave a largely increased storage space with a largely diminished crew, and at the same time permitted construction on lines essentially seaworthy, so that in time the sea endurance of the line-of-battle ship for strategical calculations became practically limitless. In the battleship the same conflict is apparent, and the final abandonment of subservient movement and reliance on free movement alone, while highly increasing mobility and tactical value, has in some degree decreased strategical value ; that is to say, the increased engine power, while increasing the capacity for exercising free movement, decreases the capacity for sustaining it. This, then, is the main problem which lies at the root of all naval history, the problem of reconciling sea endurance with free movement ; and to understand the transition in which the English naval power was founded its factors must be clearly apprehended and continually borne in mind.

The problem, however, has not yet been stated in its full complexity. There are other factors as important as sea endurance and mobility, since the effectiveness of a warship must be estimated also by the offensive power of its armament. For the present purpose its defensive power may be ignored; for though isolated attempts to protect ships were made in early times, they had no effect upon the transition of the sixteenth century. The offensive power, on the other hand, influenced it profoundly. The weakness of the galley was that it could only deliver the weight of its attack and its fire end-on and forward, and the weakness was inherent in the type. The system of propulsion, necessitating as it did a low freeboard, lightness of burden, and fine lines, practically excluded the possibility of broadside batteries, and though in the period of transition attempts were made with some success to combine broadside fire with oar propulsion, the defects developed were too great for continuance. After Lepanto the galleasse, as the new type was named, seemed to be the battleship of the future; with the defeat of the Armada it began to be obsolete.

In considering, then, the first two periods, we must think of a period of free movement, of low sea endurance, and of end-on fire, followed by a period of subservient movement, of high sea endurance, and of fire mainly broadside. For though the earlier great-ships could deliver a powerful fire both fore and aft, as well as abeam, it was not till the present period that the battleship could deliver anything like an all-round fire, and practically develop the bulk of its gun power in any direction at any moment.

At the middle of the sixteenth century the vessel of free movement, notwithstanding its defects, still held its own in the Mediterranean. During the long naval struggle with the Turks and the incessant warfare between the Italian states the art of handling galleys had reached a high degree of perfection. A great school of Italian admirals had grown up whose services were sought by all the Mediterranean powers, and since Italy had resumed her old position as the school of arms for all Europe, their influence was strong enough, supported, as it was, by classical tradition, to outweigh the oceanic experience of Spanish and Portuguese seamen. In the scientific spirit of the age the art of commanding a fleet had become akin to a branch of mathematics, and an admiral of the Italian school would manœuvre a squadron with almost as much pedantic intricacy as a *maestro di campo* could handle his *tertia* of infantry.

In 1532, as the Venetian fleet was lying at Zante, that of the Holy League under Andrea Doria, the greatest of the Italian admirals, appeared in the offing. The Venetians put out to receive them in three divisions, each of twenty galleys line abreast. The Leaguers were proceeding in column of divisions, each division being formed in three ranks with six galleys abreast. In the rear came the sailing ships. By the custom of the sea, which Drake followed at his memorable junction with Howard off Plymouth in 1588, Doria, when at a convenient distance, gave the signal to form line of battle in honour of the fleet he was approaching; whereupon his vanguard inclined to the right and extended itself as a right wing, the *battaglia* or 'main battle' continued its course and formed the centre, while the rearguard under press of oars inclined to the left and rapidly extended to form the other wing; and so in perfect order the two fleets exchanged salutes with oars, ordnance, flags, and trumpets.[1] Again in 1538, when Doria was in command of the allied Christian fleet, the Turks were seen advancing under sail in the form of an eagle. The head was formed by an advanced squadron of twenty galleys; the neck, of a column of lighter vessels of the same class. The body was a rhombus of twenty-six galleys, in the midst of which towered the flag of Barbarossa, the great Turkish admiral. To the right and left of him were extended wings of twenty-four galleys each, and in rear, like a tail, came ranks of brigantines and smaller vessels. Doria formed his fleet into the usual line abreast, with the three divisions echeloned from port to starboard and a squadron of sailing ships and galleons covering each flank. Thereupon Barbarossa struck sail, and with his

[1] Guglielmotti, *Storia della Marina Pontificia*, iii. 294. Roma, Tipografia Vaticana, 10 vols. 1886-93.

oars developed from his eagle formation a line of battle in a half moon edging in shore of Doria to get the weather gauge, and the disastrous battle of Prévésa was fought.[1] For a bombardment galley manœuvres were even more complex. A fighting line was formed of detached groups, so that each group could be constantly shifting its position to avoid giving a fixed target. Each group, moreover, in order to economise space and sustain the flow of fire, was formed of galleys lashed stern to stern in pairs, and as one delivered its fire the two turned together on their axis and so brought the battery of the other to bear. When space did not permit of a line, they would form column of 'quadrilles'—that is, four abreast—and by executing an endless countermarch keep up an almost uninterrupted fire.[2]

When manœuvres so formal were regarded as a measure of the admiral's skill, it is easy to understand how impatient an officer of the Italian school must have been of the defects of a ship of subservient movement. His desire was to handle his fleet with the precision of an army ashore, and the comparative uncertainty of the movements of sailing vessels seemed to him incapable of being reduced to scientific tactics. It must not be supposed, however, that sailing warships did not exist, or had no place in the naval art. From very early times they had been regarded as necessary adjuncts to a navy, and had reached a considerable degree of development even in the Mediterranean. During the Crusades ships of very large size were used. As early as the twelfth century there is notice of one capable of carrying 1,500 men and 100 horses.[3] The 'Paradise,' in which St. Louis sailed on his last Crusade in 1269, was large enough to carry a mainmast forty-six cubits high and a mainsail measuring sixty-three cubits. By the end of the fourteenth century, Ancona had a number of vessels of 300 tons armed with bombards and lighter guns. Indeed, it

[1] Guglielmotti, *Storia della Marina Pontificia*. iv. 51 *et seq.*
[2] *Ibid.* iii. 300, 400; iv. 80.   [3] *Ibid.* i. 326 *et seq.*

became a standing order of all the maritime republics that no merchant vessel must go to sea without an armament of guns in proportion to its tonnage, and so was formed in each case the nucleus of a sailing war fleet. As the use of artillery grew the armament of sailing vessels continually increased, but still it was rather with a view to their individual safety from pirates than to create a regular sailing navy. It is true that the great Doria on several occasions made use of galleons, not only as flankers, but also in advance of his line to break the enemy's attack formation. It is by no means certain, however, that these galleons did not have oars. In any case little came of Doria's experiment, and in the Mediterranean sailing ships continued to be thought incapable of contending against galleys. The advantage which an oared vessel had in calms or light airs was deemed to outweigh every other consideration, and it became a fundamental rule of naval warfare that sailing vessels were unfit to take their place in the line of battle. For transport purposes, for hospital and supply ships, for use as a siege train, they came to be an essential part of a complete navy, but only as auxiliary to the galleys. For the galleys the fighting line was reserved. Sailing vessels might be of use to protect flanks and rear, and even to afford a rallying point for worsted galleys, but to the last the great Italian admirals considered that their admission to the line of battle was impossible, and even that for strategical purposes it was hardly practicable to handle with advantage a fleet of the combined types. The auxiliary fleet, if unable to follow the galleys, would be left behind without hesitation, and in the last great day of Lepanto not a single sailing vessel was present to take part in the action.[1]

[1] These principles were clearly laid down by Antonio Doria in his *Discorso* about the middle of the century. (See Guglielmotti, iii. 281.) When Alvaro de Bazan, the famous Marquis of Santa Cruz, was going to the relief of Malta with a fleet of galleys and ships in 1565, a council of war held at Messina decided to leave the ships behind, although Santa Cruz was inferior to the Turks in galleys. 'From the little I saw of the

The vessel on which the Italian school relied for the bulk of the fighting line—the vessel, that is, which corresponded in tactical values to the seventy-four of Nelson's time—was the *galea* or galley proper. The normal type was a vessel about 160 feet long with a beam of one-seventh of its length. It was covered by a single deck sloping upwards from close to the waterline to the *corsia*. This was a well about six feet wide rising above the deck and running fore and aft. It was designed to give access to the various chambers in the hold, and being covered in, formed a gangway from the poop to the forecastle. On each side of the *corsia* were the benches for the rowers, under whom, as they sat raised above the deck, the water in choppy weather had free play through the scuppers. Forward was a solid platform athwart the ship which was called the *rembata*, and carried the battery or forecastle. Aft was another platform, called the *spalliera*, which carried a deck house, and from here the officers fought and navigated the ship. Both platforms were closed in below, so as to form quarters for the soldiers forward and the officers aft. The galley slaves lived entirely on the benches, with nothing to cover them except an awning, and that only when in port. Between the *rembata* and *spalliera* ran low bulwarks to afford some protection to the galley slaves from fire and the weather, and to carry a kind of protected fighting gallery for musketeers. The motive power was provided by fifty oars, twenty-five a side, each manned by a bench of from three to five rowers. There were also two, and sometimes three, masts, each bearing a large lateen sail, and to manage these and perform the ordinary work of the vessel a crew of sailors had to be provided. A complement of artificers was also necessary, so that the space left for the fighting crew was necessarily very small. In the sixteenth century the normal navigating crew consisted of

battle of Prévésa,' said one of its members, 'a combination of ships and galleys is not worth much, for ships support galleys badly.' (Jurien de la Gravière, *Chevaliers de Malte*, ii. 176.)

INTRODUCTION

a master and his mate, a pilot and two mates, eight helmsmen, and twenty-four mariners—that is, forty hands all told. The rest of the non-effectives—such as surgeons, clerks, cooks, artificers, apprentices, and boys—amounted to twenty besides the overseer of the slaves. The actual fighting force consisted of the captain and three 'gentlemen of the poop,' two gunners with their mates, one sergeant, four corporals, and forty-five soldiers, or fifty-eight in all, as against at least over two hundred non-effectives. With a full rowing crew the disproportion was much greater, but varied in different services, the Spaniards tending towards increasing the soldier element, the Venetians to reducing it.

The normal armament consisted of eleven guns, five of which were in the *rembata* or forward battery. The most heavily armed carried amidships directly over the prow a 'cannon serpentine' or long fifty-pounder, which was called from its position the *corsia*. On each side of it was a 'demi-cannon serpentine,' or long twenty-four pounder. These three guns were the main armament. They were all mounted on fixed carriages, so that they could be neither trained nor traversed, except by the motion of the galley. To hit an enemy between wind and water the gunner had to trust to the rise and fall of the sea, and in a calm he could only depress his pieces by moving a lot of gear or a number of the crew forward.[1] To traverse them to right or left he must signal to the helmsman. Outwards of these three bow-chasers were two 'quarter-cannons,' or short twelve-pounders, which, unlike the chasers, could be fired in broadside and were intended for close quarters.[2] The galleys of Malta appear sometimes to have carried similar pieces in broadside upon platforms over the after benches, but this was unusual. In the typical galley the five forward guns formed the whole main battery, and the tendency as time went on

[1] William Bourne, *Arte of Shooting in Great Ordnance*; p. 561. London, 1587.
[2] Guglielmotti, iii. 421.

was to reduce rather than increase the size of the guns on each side of the *corsia*. There was also, as in a modern battleship, an auxiliary armament. It consisted, as a rule, of small breech-loading or quick-firing pieces, called *smerigli*. They were usually four-pounder guns, mounted on a non-recoil system, and provided with two or more *mascoli* or 'chambers,' which, like a modern quick-firing cartridge, held a powder charge and could be inserted in the breech in succession.[1] Sometimes, however, for one or two of them was substituted a short gun, similar to a carronade or a modern howitzer. Two pieces of this auxiliary armament were carried in the fighting gallery and four on the poop, and the whole of it was intended for very close quarters, for clearing the galley when boarders had entered and for overawing the slaves.

Besides the *galea* a number of other types were in use. For the flag officers galleys of larger size but of identical pattern were provided, while a host of smaller types did the light work of the fleet, acting as cruisers, despatch boats, and tenders. Foremost among them was the 'foyst,' so called because it was so long in proportion to its beam as to resemble a *fusta* or canoe hollowed out of a tree. It had two masts, rowed from eighteen to twenty oars aside, and had a crew of about a hundred men, all of whom were free and did the rowing and fighting indifferently. Next came the *brigantina* (so called from *briga*, an old word meaning 'hunt' or 'chase'), which was manned, rigged, and moulded like a foyst, and had from twelve to sixteen oars aside. The *saettia*, or 'arrow,' was a smaller type still, a kind of launch with three lateen sails. Another form which grew into great favour was the *fregata*, but how precisely it differed from the other light vessels is not clear. Normally it rowed fourteen oars aside, had one mast only, was peculiarly swift and of small draught, and could carry two *smerigli* in the bows; but the word soon came to be used, like the English 'pinnace,'

[1] Cf. *post*, pp. 383 *et seq.*, where details of the various patterns of these guns as used in the English service will be found.

as a generic term for all the classes of small swift sailing vessels with auxiliary oar propulsion.[1]

Of the *galeazza*, as a bastard type designed to reconcile oar propulsion with broadside fire, mention has been made already. It was about two hundred and twenty feet between uprights, and its other dimensions were in the same relation as those of a galley. It had thirty oars a side, worked by a crew wholly under cover. On the deck above them was a tier of guns, and fore and aft two great square castles of several tiers. It had three masts, and the whole ship's company, including slaves, sailors, and marines, numbered about a thousand. Their great day was at Lepanto, where thrown forward in couples well in advance of the galley line, as Andrea Doria had used his galleons, they entirely broke up the Turks' attack formation, and were the chief element that decided the victory for Don John. Still they were but a compromise, and though introduced in another form perhaps a hundred years before, they had in no way influenced the naval art.[2]

Naval tactics still turned on an attack directly forward. Not only was this the only way in which a galley could deliver her fire, but she still retained her ancient characteristic weapon. Some twenty feet or more from her bows projected a massive beam which carried her metal spur or 'beak,' and with this her most deadly

[1] In 1574 Pero Menendez, the great Spanish admiral, suggested the construction of a permanent force of 'galliots' for operation in the Channel, because they were good sailers and because a galley would cost as much as 'four of that kind of frigate.' See 'Letters of Menendez,' Aug. 15, 1574, in Ruidiaz y Caravia, *La Conquista de la Florida*, vol. ii. His *gallizabras* were also called 'frigates.' In the museum of the arsenal at Venice are models of these various types, but they do not correspond with Guglielmotti's descriptions. The date of their design seems uncertain.

[2] Galleasses, like all compromise types, differed greatly in form. Some are described as being merely large galleys. The model in the Venice arsenal is like a galley made on galleon lines. It has no upper deck, but instead of it massive outrigged superstructures carrying broad fighting galleries. Beneath these galleries are placed the broadside guns. They are all quick-firing pieces mounted on the ends of the rowing benches, which broaden out so as to afford platforms for the gun crews. Where galleasses were thus armed, their broadside fire must have been very weak.

stroke was still delivered. The ultimate aim of a galley captain was to ram, and all galley tactics were based upon delivering a blow with the greatest possible momentum and avoiding a similar attack.[1] For this reason a fleet of galleys meeting an enemy would manœuvre for the wind as assiduously as a fleet of great-ships. Engagements, however, seldom took place in the open. One commander or the other would usually seek a position where his flanks were covered by the land. A well-delivered flank attack was necessarily fatal, and the tactics of the fleet which had to take the offensive were as a rule chiefly designed to draw the enemy from his position and expose him to a flank attack from a masked reserve squadron. The whole system, indeed, differed little in principle from contemporary cavalry tactics. Artillery fire played but a minor part in a battle, except to emphasise the shock at the moment of impact. An action almost always began with a charge of the opposing centres prow to prow which rapidly degenerated into a confused *mêlée* round the opposing admirals. The wings, in endeavouring to carry out or frustrate the inevitable flanking movement, soon lost all formation, and broke up into contending groups round the contests of their flagships, while detachments of unengaged vessels scoured the scene of action in all directions, like squads of lances, to bring succour where it seemed most needed. To close and board an opposing ship, or to throw a reinforcement into one severely pressed, was then the only aim. It was a land fight fought at sea.

That sea fights of this time were mainly a series of Homeric contests between the opposing admirals and their supports is no illusion, as might fairly be objected, born of the fancy of picturesque chroniclers, or of the egoism of the admirals' despatches. It must have been necessarily so from the tactics in vogue. The standing rule was that

---

[1] It should be noted, however, that before Lepanto, Don John is said to have ordered the 'beaks' of his galleys to be cut away. The projection of the beak seems sometimes to have made boarding from the bows difficult.

every ship should seek to engage an enemy of its own size, and that no captain should presume to engage the enemy's admiral until his own admiral had had a fair chance of doing so himself. More than this, the fleet formations could hardly produce any other result. Of naval tactics as we understand the phrase, at least after battle was fairly joined, there were none. The formations were modelled on those of an army, and were organically focussed on the flagships. The disposition of the Christian fleet which Don John of Austria and his council of war drew up for the battle of Lepanto gives the last word of the art. The structure of the order of battle is fundamentally the usual single line abreast, composed solely of galleys, which were spaced so that while they had room to row, it was impossible for an enemy to pass between them. The formation was according to rule in three divisions, the main-battle in the centre, the vanguard on the right, and the rearguard on the left, each with its distinctive colour; and between the divisions was an interval wide enough to allow of any of them manœuvring independently. The root idea was an impregnable centre, and here in the midst of the main-battle of sixty-two galleys Don John had his place with the four flag officers of his division on each hand, thus concentrating his most powerful ships at the vital point. The two wings seemed to have been in conception what were then called 'flankers' of the main-battle. Each contained fifty-four galleys, and, unlike the main-battle, they were organised with their respective flagships on the flanks. The reason for this was that their weakness lay in the enemy's attempting either to turn their outer flank, or to penetrate the intervals that divided them from the main-battle. By placing the flagships at each end of the divisions instead of in the centre, the greatest strength was obtained at the points most likely to be threatened. Such was the backbone of the formation, but it was emphasised and supported in a way that marks still more clearly the high development the art had reached. In rear of the main-battle was placed under the famous Spanish admiral, the Marquis of Santa Cruz, a reserve division of thirty galleys, ready either to support the centre or to frustrate any attempt to break the line at the divisional intervals; and in rear of the outer ends of each wing was a small squadron of four galleys to support the flagships on the exposed flanks. Besides this each of the four squadrons had its own proper supports. In rear of Don John's flagship were stationed two galleys, while each of the other admirals had two foysts in attendance, and thus a supernumerary rank of ten or twelve sail was formed behind each division, not as repeating ships, but as reinforcements at points of dangerous pressure. The front of the whole formation was covered, as has been said, by the great galleasses which were arranged in pairs a mile in advance of each division, with the intention of breaking with their fire the attack formation of the enemy, like advanced posts in front of a military position.[1] On the day of battle the design was somewhat modified by force of circumstances, but as far as time and weather permitted this elaborate formation was actually taken up in presence of the enemy. No sailing vessels, it will be observed, had any place in the scheme, and the powerful auxiliary sailing squadron which was attached to the fleet had to be content with vague orders to work to windward and endeavour to annoy the Turks in flank; but so little were their movements regarded that, as has been said, they were not able to be present at the action at all.[2]

One example of the flexibility of such a galley formation will suffice. At the outset of the action the left wing

[1] So says Guglielmotti; but Don John's plan shows them at equal intervals. Savorgnano, in his *Arte Militare Terrestre e Maritima* (Venice, 1599, but written several years before), says they were in pairs, one in front of the centre and one in front of each of the extreme flanks.

[2] Guglielmotti, vol. vi. lib. ii. c. 14; Farochon, *Chypre et Lépante*, p. 227, where Don John's sketch is reproduced. For the actual formation when the action began, see Jurien de la Gravière, *La Guerre de Chypre et la Bataille de Lépante*, tom ii., where detailed plans will be found.

of the Turks threatened the right or seaward wing of the League with a turning movement. Gian Andrea Doria, the Italian admiral who commanded the Spanish contingent and the threatened wing, fell into the trap, and without orders led his whole division to the right, leaving the right flank of the main-battle uncovered. The Turkish vice-admiral at once made for the gap, but arrived to find it filled up by Santa Cruz with part of his reserve division and one of the galleasses. With the sailing vessels of the time and such seamanship as then existed no manœuvres so precise and rapid could have been made, and hence the distrust of subservient movement felt by all the Italian admirals.

But while in the Mediterranean they were thus abandoning as hopeless the problem of bringing sailing ships into the line of battle, on the Atlantic seaboard a new school was arising that was approaching the solution; and the home and heart of that school was England. To apprehend the revolution more clearly it is necessary to remember that from all time ships had been divided into two great classes—the 'long ship' and the 'round ship.' It was to the former class exclusively that in the old days belonged the man-of-war, the *navis longa* of the Romans, the 'long-ship' or Drakar of the Norsemen, vessels which were constructed primarily for speed and for fighting, and which used sails only as an auxiliary means of motion. To the second class belonged the merchant ship, the *vaisseau rond* of the French, the *vascello* of the Italians, which was constructed primarily with a view to capacity for cargo, to seaworthiness, and to sail propulsion only. The round-ship was the merchantman, the long-ship, the man-of-war; and while the Italians were absorbed in developing the highest capabilities of the long-ship, the process upon which the English seamen were engaged was the gradual development of a new type of man-of-war out of the round-ship.

Like most other things English, the growth of our school of naval warfare was slow, eminently unscientific, and extremely complex in its determining forces. It was a process of almost blind evolution shaped partly by the national character, partly by geographical position, partly by the nature of the wars in which we were chiefly engaged. Its origin is not to be traced even approximately. There is no epoch in which it can be said the long-ship of the Vikings ceased to be the typical warship of the English. All we can observe is that throughout the maritime history of the middle ages no feature is more remarkable or more constant than the inferiority of the English to their enemies in ships of the galley type. One cause of this lay inherent in the national system. Of a navy, as we understand it, there was little more than a trace. The navy of England, as appears from continual petitions of Parliament, was synonymous with the English marine. The royal navy was merely that part of it which belonged to the king, and which was used by him in time of peace as his subjects used theirs. When a fleet was required for national purposes, it necessarily was composed mainly of merchantmen, and the fact that it was usually required for transporting a land force to the Continent, and that the most serious danger it had to encounter was bad weather, made a fleet so composed the best that could be had.

The geographical position of England must have emphasised in a great measure the advantages of the round-ship. But this influence, at first sight the most obvious and weighty, must not be exaggerated. The great invasions of the Norsemen had all been carried out with oared long-ships. As late as 1259 Eric XII. of Norway undertook to furnish Philippe le Bel with two hundred galleys for his war with England, and throughout the middle ages, when naval warfare had not emerged from the primitive condition of cross-raiding between adjacent coasts, galleys were hardly if at all less suitable to the narrow seas than they were to the Mediterranean.[1]

[1] Jal, *Glossaire nautique*, p. 753. *Cf.* Proposal made by the Genoese Admiral, Benedetto Zaccaria, in the same year, for a fleet of galleys, Guglielmotti, iv. 345.

INTRODUCTION

The obscurity of the subject is due in a great measure to the difficulty of determining the nature of the vessels in use. English and indeed most northern war fleets of the later middle ages were composed mainly of ships (*niefs*), cogs, barges, and balyngers, with sometimes 'spynes' or pinnaces attached. The first two were certainly sailing vessels, though how the cog differed from the ship it is needless for the present purpose to inquire. Of barges and balyngers there is some difference of opinion, but there can really be no serious doubt that in these types we see the tradition of the long-ship surviving in a fixed naval idea that no war fleet was complete without its contingent of oared vessels. In 1301 an English barge is mentioned as having thirty oars. When Arnoul le Maire, in 1386, heard of the battle proceeding between the English and Flemish fleets, Froissart tells us 'il entra en une sienne barge que il avoit bonne et belle . . . et nagea a force des rames jusques à la battaille.' Though sometimes used of large ships' boats or tenders, the word 'barge' certainly meant in English fleets something more important. In 1415 the barges provided by the Council as part of the Channel guard were of a hundred tons, and carried a complement of forty-eight mariners, twenty-six men-at-arms, and twenty-six archers. Their ordinary burden at this time was from sixty to eighty tons.[1] It may be taken, therefore, that they roughly corresponded to the larger brigantines of the Mediterranean, or to the lesser foysts of the later English service.

The balynger presents greater difficulties. The derivation of the name is certainly from *balæna*, a whale, and most authorities, for this reason and from apparent misreadings of passages where the balynger is mentioned with great-ships, have regarded it as a 'whaler' and classed it with the larger sailing vessels. Jal himself fell into this error, but subsequently altered his opinion, and,

---

[1] Nicolas, *History of the Royal Navy*, i. 305; ii. 407; Froissart, *Chron.* lib. iii. c. 53; Jal, *Glossaire nautique*, p. 247; Oppenheim, *History of the Administration of the Royal Navy*, i. 13.

summing up all that could be ascertained about the vessel beyond doubt from contemporary authority, held that it was small and fast, the favourite craft of pirates, and sometimes employed as a light vessel in fleets from the fourteenth to the sixteenth centuries.[1] Froissart also distinctly says a special character was that it drew very little water.[2] Such a craft cannot possibly have been a 'whaler,' but it may very well have been a 'whale boat' —a boat, that is, attached to a 'whaler' and used for harpooning. A 'whale boat,' as defined by Admiral Smyth, is a 'boat varying from 26 to 56 feet in length and from 4 to 10 feet in beam, sharp at both ends . . . combining swiftness of motion, buoyancy, and stability.' These are exactly the prominent characteristics of the Viking ship preserved at Christiania, and any doubt as to the antiquity of the use of such a boat in whaling is set at rest by a seal of the thirteenth century whereon is engraved a representation of men harpooning from a craft precisely of this type.[3] The presumption, then, is that there did exist in the later middle ages a whaling-boat on the lines of a Viking ship and of the ordinary Norwegian sea boats of the present day, which was used for harpooning and therefore a rowing-boat. Could it now be shown that the balynger had oars, we need have little hesitation in identifying it with this boat and forming a fairly clear picture of what it was. Fortunately this evidence, though overlooked by Jal, exists. An order to the Cinque Ports of 1401 requisitions three balyngers with the requisite sailors to row them. We are also told on high authority that the Spanish *ballenere*, introduced by the Biscayan shipwrights in the fourteenth century, was a long low vessel for oars and sails.[4] This fairly sets the matter at rest, and explains why they were always classed with

---

[1] *Glossaire*, p. 224.   [2] Nicolas, ii. 327 n.
[3] Figured by Jal, *Glossaire*, p. 224.
[4] Nicolas, ii. 348, quoting *Fœdera*, viii. 205; *Proc. Privy Council*, i. 142. Duro, *La Marina de Castilla*, p. 158. Mr. Oppenheim (*op. cit.* p. 13) quotes this as the origin of the balynger. It no doubt was the origin of the word, but the thing almost certainly was a North Sea type of high antiquity

barges, why Conflans in 1515 places them between *pinnaces* and *garbares* (a kind of small barge), and why Duez in 1674 defines them as 'une sorte de pinnace.'[1] As to their normal size we know from the order of 1415 above mentioned that their complement might be forty mariners, ten men-at-arms, and ten archers. We may therefore safely conceive the balynger, although latterly under Henry V. it ranged from one hundred and twenty to twenty tons, as normally a rowing vessel corresponding in tactical value to the smaller *brigantina* or the *saettia* of the Mediterranean, and deriving the special form which fitted it peculiarly to the North Sea by direct descent from the oared long-ship of the Norsemen.[2]

But it is not only in these middle and small types, the barge, the balynger, and the spyne, that we see the survival of the old ideas. Until late in the middle ages galleys of large size continue to be found sometimes in the possession of the king and sometimes hired on the outbreak of a war; but by the beginning of the fifteenth century it may be taken that they were no longer considered in England as indispensable. When Henry V. laid what are usually regarded as the foundations of a true Royal Navy, the bulk of it was great-ships. In 1417 he had six 'grands niefs,' eight barges, and ten balyngers. In the next year the 'Navy List' shows eleven great-ships and carracks, five of a class called 'niefs,'

[1] Jal, *Glossaire*, p. 226.
[2] Oppenheim, *op. cit.* p. 12. Monsieur Chas. de la Roncière, of the Bibliothèque Nationale, the highest French authority on Mediæval shipping, classes balyngers with carracks and nefs as sailing vessels (Jusserand, *English Essays*, App. i.), and this in spite of admitting the fact that they had oars. These, however, as he has kindly explained to me, he regards as auxiliary only, since balyngers both on voyages and in action are often spoken of as under sail. But it is submitted that all rowing vessels from the drakar to the galley sailed whenever they could and used their oars only in calms, or when the wind was contrary, or when extra speed was required. The point is, that—whether we call balyngers sailing vessels or not—for tactical purposes their oars and shape made them distinctly vessels of free movement. They could freely take up their position in action independently of the wind, and were therefore as naval units of an essentially different class from the carrack and nef.

only one barge, and nine balyngers. A complete list of his Navy gives seventeen ships and cogs, seven carracks, and fourteen barges and balyngers.[1] A curious letter exists, written by an English agent at Valencia in Spain to one of Henry's Ministers, saying that he may have ten or twelve armed galleys and even more from Barcelona if he wants them, and that one of the galley captains is coming to England to treat about them.[2] It does not appear, however, that Henry ever took them into his service, and in any case we may conclude that from its very infancy the English Navy showed a marked preference for great-ships over galleys, or at least a marked distaste for keeping galleys as part of a standing fleet, and a tendency to reduce the type to a subordinate position in its tactical system.

It must not be supposed, however, that anything like true sailing tactics had yet been introduced. Though the English seaman loved his great-ship he fought it like a galley. His only idea of an attack was to work to windward and then run his enemy down and board if he did not sink her with the collision. 'Set me against yonder Spaniard that is coming, for I wish to joust with him,' was Edward's order to his pilot at the famous victory of 'Les Espagnols sur Mer' in 1350 which won him the title of 'King of the Seas.' Even when gun-fire began to be better understood there was little change. When in 1416 the Duke of Bedford on his way to Harfleur encountered the French fleet, there was nothing, so far as can be learnt from the chroniclers, but a general charge in which the great-ships met with a violent shock and then grappled. In the following year, when the Earl of

---

[1] Nicolas, *Agincourt*, App. p. 21; *History of Navy*, ii. 514, App. x.; Ellis, *Original Letters*, 3rd series, i. 72; Oppenheim, i. 12. The relative importance of the classes may be gathered from the annuities of the masters. The great-ships and carracks were allotted 6*l*. 13*s*. 4*d*.; the 'niefs' 5*l*.; the barge and the balyngers 3*l*. 6*s*. 8*d*. A *carracca* was the largest kind of merchant ship which, when armed and fitted with 'castles,' was constantly used as a 'great-ship.'

[2] Ellis, 2nd series, i. 69 n.

Huntingdon was sent out to clear the way for Henry's expedition to France, the same thing happened. 'Some of the ships,' says Nicolas, 'came in contact with such violence that their prows or, mcre properly, forecastles were carried away and the men in them thrown into the sea. The vessels fastened themselves to each other by chains and cables in the usual manner, when another hand-to-hand fight took place, which lasted nearly the whole day.'[1]

For another century these land fights at sea continued to be the only possible form of engagement between fleets, and great-ships continued to be attended by fighting vessels of the galley type. The proposal of Parliament to Henry VI. in 1442 for a permanent naval force for the defence of the Narrow Seas suggests eight great-ships with castles, eight barges, eight balyngers, and four spynes or pinnaces. The policy of the succeeding reigns, which tended towards the abandonment of Henry V.'s idea of a Royal Navy in favour of securing warships by contract with private citizens, shows no signs of change. Henry VII. continued to work on much the same lines, and the policy he introduced of subsidising the building of large merchantmen only emphasises the vitality of the old ideas. Henry VIII., too, in the early part of his reign was still under the same mediæval influence. The fleet which he prepared in 1512 for his first war with France consisted entirely of carracks and other sailing vessels, and as yet the only sign of a change is one rather of retrogression than advance. During the progress of the war the whole energies of the dock-yards seem to have been devoted to turning out vessels with a tendency towards the galley type. In 1513 the 'Great Galley' appears, which was of 700 tons, carried over 200 pieces of artillery great and small, rowed 120 oars, and could carry from 800 to 1,000 men. Besides this in the same year the 'Katherine Galley' of 70 tons takes its place in the lists,

[1] *History of Navy*, ii. 431.

and in the summer of the same year others were on the stocks at Woolwich.[1]

Though these vessels, as we shall see, were certainly not ordinary galleys, and indeed contained the germs of the coming change, it is clear that Henry's first experiments in the naval art led him to cast back towards vessels of free movement. This was but natural. The events of the war show their moral effect was as great as ever. Prégent, a knight of Rhodes in the service of France, was known to be bringing six galleys and four 'foysts' from the Mediterranean to join the French sailing fleet at Brest.[2] Sir Edward Howard, the Lord Admiral, to prevent the junction taking place, put to sea and succeeded in blockading Brest—for the first time, it is believed, on record. Prégent, fearing to face Howard's great-ships alone, put into Conquêt at the north of the entrance to Brest, and took up a position in Blanc Sablon Bay, where his flanks were protected by two fortified islands. In this almost impregnable position Howard, leaving his main-fleet to watch Brest, attacked him with two galleys, two row-barges, and two 'crayers,' and lost his life fighting heroically on Prégent's flagship. The defeat went far to paralyse the English strategy. Sir Thomas Howard, Sir Edward's successor, 'wisely considering the advantage of the French galleys in a calm,' begged for reinforcements of men, since with the galleys where they were he dared not weaken his fleet by landing a force sufficient to take Brest and destroy the blockaded fleet, and while he lay incapable of striking a blow Prégent began raiding the Sussex coast.[3]

---

[1] See Navy Lists in Brewer's *State Papers*, I. 455, 551, 552, 811. Also, *ibid.* II. ii. 1462. 'Wm. Bonde for making the King's great-ship and 4 new gallies at Woolwich, £600.' Mr. Oppenheim is doubtful about the 'great galley,' and inclines to think from its fitful appearance in the lists it was a designation applied to various ships. But in any case it is clear there was at least one large vessel of the galley type with powerful oar propulsion.

[2] Hall says 'three galleys of force with divers Foists and Row-galleys.' *Chronicle*, p. 535.

[3] Lord Herbert in Kennet's *Complete History of England*, vol. II. i.

The Lord Admiral was probably justified in his caution. The great-ship for tactical purposes must still have been, as before, little better than a more seaworthy and less mobile galley. In the early part of Henry VIII.'s reign, the Navy was armed mainly with small breech-loading pieces for use as mankillers in repelling boarders or preparing an enemy's decks for a counter attack. In Elizabeth's time such pieces were regarded as merely a secondary armament. A few only of the newer vessels carried heavy ordnance, and that in little higher proportion than galleys. The real secret of the great-ship's power was yet undiscovered. Besides its sea endurance, as we have seen, the true value of the great-ship lay in its broadside fire, and the development of broadside fire was a question of gunnery, of naval architecture, and of seamanship. With Henry's introduction of heavy guns on board his larger vessels, however, the true note had been struck, and by the end of his reign the first two arts had made great strides. Guns of all patterns and sizes were being cast in England, both in bronze and iron, which were little inferior to those Nelson fought with, and numbers of small wrought-iron breech-loading pieces of the *smerigli* type were turned out for rapid firing from the tops and cage-works.[1] Naval architecture had perfected the port-hole, whereby ships were able not only to carry two tiers of ordnance, but also to bear in broadside much heavier guns by having them closer to the water line.[2]

[1] See *post*, p. 367. 'Cage-works' was the name given to the superstructures fore and aft, the *opere morte* of the Italians.

[2] The armament of Henry's VIII.'s ships at first consisted mainly and sometimes entirely of small quick-firing or secondary pieces, for use at the closest quarters and in boarding. These were *serpentines*, *slings*, and *murderers*. Serpentines were 'double' or 'single' (i.e. large and small), and from their name were presumably 'long' guns—i.e. of the 'culverin' or 'serpent' type. They disappear with the introduction of the *bases*, which were small quick-firing culverins. *Slings* and *half-slings* were of the 'Perier' or short (howitzer) type, and though they survived longer were replaced by *port-pieces* and *fowlers*, which were small quick-firing periers. *Murderers* were small quick-firing mortars and remained in use till the end of the century. The heavy guns of the time were mainly wrought-iron breech-loading *bombards*, the earliest form of ordnance. Henry introduced

But important as were these improvements it was not in them that the solution of the great problem was found. The thing that finally changed the naval art from its mediæval to its modern state was an achievement of marine achitecture. This was the development of the galleon, the typical ship of the great transition and the immediate parent of the ship-of-the-line.

Though a loose habit of thought has made us picture it as an old-fashioned craft essentially cumbrous, slow, and unwieldy, it was in its inception and by comparison with pre-existing types exactly the reverse. By a similar misconception, and one that is almost universal, it has been regarded as a type that specially belonged to Spain, whereas the truth is that Spain was probably the last of the oceanic powers to adopt it and the last by perhaps half a century. These two errors lie at the root of most of the misunderstanding which has obscured the naval history of the sixteenth century, and it is not till we have obtained a clear conception of what the galleon was and how it became established as a typical sailing war-ship that we can hope to see the period in its true light.

To the north the galleon came not from Spain, but from Italy. There the name occurs very early, but only as a slightly modified galley. It was not till the fifteenth century that the true galleon began to appear. Two influences were then at work. One, we have seen, was the desire to produce a sailing warship that could act with galleys, the other perhaps still stronger, the desire to produce a merchant ship fast and powerful enough to be secure from the growing boldness of the pirates and at the same time able to carry a large cargo and endure the

into the sea service ' curtals,' the new form of siege gun. They weighed about 3,000 lb., but no further details are given of them. ' Curtal ' meant a docked horse or dog, and presumably, therefore, they were short guns. Doubtless they were of the same type as the Italian *Cortaldi*, an early form of muzzle-loading stone-gun or perier. They are thus scheduled by Tartaglia in his *Commentaries concerning Artillery*, which he dedicated to Henry VIII. (Lucar's edition, 1588, p. 30). His 3,000-lb. stone-guns fired a 100-lb. shot, and were 9½ feet long.

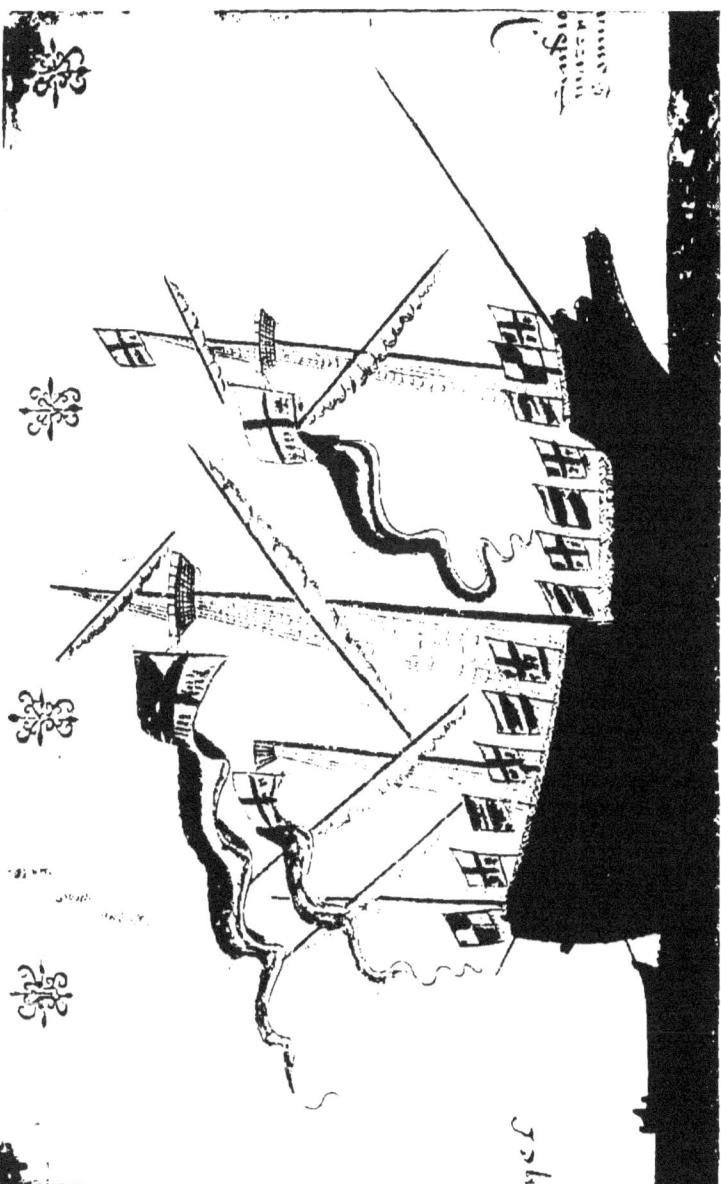

THE GALLEASSE 'ANNE GALANT.'

Reduced from Anthony's Second Roll (British Museum, Add. MSS. 22047).

seas of the Atlantic for voyages outside the Straits. The result was a compromise between the long-ship and the round-ship, a *vascello* designed as much like a galley as was then thought possible for a sailing ship. The normal type eventually evolved was a vessel of about three times the length of its beam, the normal round-ship or 'hulk' being only twice the length of its beam. It had also a long flat floor like a galley, and was of lower free-board than an ordinary round-ship. It was also like a galley flush-decked, and would seem always to have had the half-deck carried across the waist so as to make one flush deck with the old forecastle. In the larger types the quarter-deck was also carried flush from stem to stern, so that latterly at any rate a true galleon had at least two decks and sometimes three. On the upper deck in the earlier types were erected both fore and aft high-castles as in a galleasse, but usually on curved lines, which gave the hull of the old-fashioned galleons the appearance of a half moon. Originally they certainly had auxiliary oar propulsion for working them in harbours, rivers, and confined waters. But the increasing height of freeboard, and weight of construction, to which the desire for higher sea-endurance led, must have continued to make them less and less adapted for rowing, and eventually in the true galleon, in accordance with the invariable tendency of bastard types to shed their means of free movement, oars were entirely eliminated. In one class of galleon, however, the original low freeboard was long retained, so as to permit the use of oars in the waist. A vessel of this type was called in Italy a *galleazza di mercantia*, or merchant-galleasse, to distinguish it from the true war-galleasse. It was in this type of galleon that the whole of the Venetian trade with London and Antwerp was carried on, and it therefore assumes for us a very special interest, as the latest effort of Italian naval architecture presented to English experts at the time Henry VIII. was creating the new Navy. Coronelli describes the *galleazza* or *galéa di Londra* as generally upon the lines of a war-galleasse, but with a length of over three and three-fifths its beam. Further, he says that in order to enable them to work in and out of confined waters and rivers, but as an auxiliary means of movement only, they were furnished with oars. But instead of thirty aside, like the war-galleasses, they carried but seventeen, and these were rowed between the *fuocone* or cooking place amidships and the forecastle, so that the vessel was in type a *mezzo galera*. The rest of the ship was devoted to cargo. They were rigged with three masts, the foremast carrying square sails, the main and mizen lateens.[1]

The fact that in the later seventeenth century the galleon became the ordinary ocean trader of the Spaniards and its obvious fitness for the purpose have led to an unquestioned belief that they at once adopted it. But this was not so. Throughout the sixteenth century they continued to use for their Indian commerce caravels and ordinary ships. Even the Portuguese, though they soon adopted the galleon as a warship, continued to use the carracks for the Indian voyage. Long after the French had adopted the new invention and were using it to make havoc with the trade of Charles V. there is no

[1] Coronelli, *Atlante Veneto*, i. 141, Venice, 1691. Cataneo (*Dell' Essamini di Bombardieri*, p. 831. Brescia, 1564) calls them *galée di mercantia*. As to what a galleon was, Simoneta, describing those used on the Po in 1447, says: 'Sunt autem galeones triremibus breviores sed latiores et sublimiores'—that is, 'shorter than galleys but of broader beam and higher freeboard.' He also says they had a high prow and stern, and sailed. In 1495 a Frenchman (Du Parc) describes some galleons in the king's service as 'a kind of vessel bearing some resemblance to a small cargo ship or to a high and broad galley which uses sails and sometimes oars.' In 1526 another Frenchman (Lazare Baïf) writes 'Forma erat mixta ex nave oneraria et longa triremi,' and calls them galleasses. All the above are cited by Jal in his *Glossaire nautique*. William Borough, controller of the Navy in 1593, gives the typical proportions of the galleon as three times its beam in length, with a depth in hold of two-fifths its beam (*S. P. Dom.* ccxliii. 110). Crescentio in 1607 gives the same proportions as an ideal form. Pantero-Pantera, in 1614, says small galleons had two decks and large ones three, all being flush decked. (Jal.) Numberless other authorities could be quoted to show they were a compromise between a galley and a round-ship, and that their special advantage was that they were more weatherly and faster than the old types. See especially, Pantero-Pantera, *ubi supra*.

sign amongst the Spanish naval orders of any galleon existing to withstand them. The first appearance of a galleon in Spain seems to be in 1540, when Santa Cruz offered to undertake the police of the Straits with two galleasses and two galleons, but even these were galleons of his own invention and as would seem mere modifications of the war-galleasse. In any case little came of it, and four years later, when the French had nearly paralysed his Indian trade, Charles V. had to beg the King of Portugal to send out some of his galleons and clear the way for the homeward bound West Indian fleet. It was not till the second half of the century, as we shall see, that anything like a regular squadron of galleons appeared in the Spanish service, and then only as convoy ships for the Indian trade.[1]

Meanwhile in the North, in France, in Scotland, and above all in England, the new type had been seized upon greedily. A natural aptitude for the sea had shown them quickly that here was the model for the sailing warship to which they had so long been groping their way instinctively. Who was the first in the field it is needless to inquire—probably France, for in 1495 the king is known to have had three galleons which resembled small cargo ships, or high and broad galleys, and which used their oars as auxiliary only, principally for getting to sea.[2] The probability is that all three nations adopted them about the same time from the special Venetian model, the *galleazza di mercantia*; but if there is any one man to whom the revolution is to be attributed it is above all our great sea-king, Henry VIII. As by his religious policy he definitely cut himself free from the mediæval dream of a European system, he seems to have felt that henceforward the greatness of his kingdom must rest upon

---

[1] Duro, *Armada Española*, vols. i. and ii., Appendices, containing calendars of documents relating to the Navy and the Indian trade *passim*. In the *Vocabularia nautica* attached to Dr. Diego Garcia de Palacio's *Instrucion Nauthica* (Mexico 1587) the word *galeon* is not given at all.

[2] *Supra*, p. 29 n.

the sea. While the continental princes were absorbed with the problems of establishing standing armies, Henry devoted himself to the creation of a standing Navy. It was thus that under his guidance the English genius for maritime warfare took possession of the new idea, and without a pause worked it out until it developed a type of galleon peculiarly its own and a Navy such as the world had never seen before. To the French seamen of the Atlantic seaboard during the incessant wars with Charles V. the advantages of the type were thoroughly clear, but there it ended. For them the problem of national defence was neither so simple nor so clear as our own, and in spite of their long experience against the Spaniards, when it came to the final trial of strength between Francis and Henry it was the English king who remained undisputed master of the seas.

Although throughout his whole reign, and especially in its early part, Henry, like his predecessors, continued to hire and purchase large merchant vessels abroad for the purpose of turning them into men-of-war, in his earliest Navy List several of the new type of war-ship appear.[1] At each successive period of naval activity, which the necessities of his ambitious foreign policy called forth, others made their appearance, till at the close of his last struggle with Francis he possessed fifteen vessels of this class averaging nearly 250 tons. At first like the 'great galley,' which was undoubtedly of this class, they were probably intended to be used with a powerful oar-propulsion, but by the end of the reign it would seem that the extraordinary sailing powers which the ocean

---

[1] The 'Swallow' is classed by Anthony as a galleasse (see *post*, p. 32). The 'Anne Gallant,' though called a 'schippe,' was possibly also of this class. She was wrecked on the coast of Galicia in 1518 (*Oppenheim*, pp. 66 and 68) and replaced by a galleasse. The 'Swallow' was also replaced by a galleasse. Besides these, Henry had in 1512 other vessels described as 'galleys,' which were almost certainly sailing vessels. Till the middle of the century 'galley,' 'galleasse,' and 'galleon' seem to have been used almost at haphazard to describe the new class of ship.

seamen had brought out of them had caused them to be regarded as essentially sailing vessels.[1] Anthony Anthony, an officer of the Ordnance Department, has left us a complete picture of what the Royal Navy had become at this time. According to him it consisted of forty-five sail divided into four classes. They were named respectively 'ships,' 'galleasses,' 'pinnaces' and 'row-barges.'[2] Cogs, barges, and balyngers have all disappeared, and it is only in the first class that we see the relics of a mediæval Navy. This class of 'great-ships' proper is made up almost entirely of the remains of Henry's original fleet and four large vessels purchased from the Hanse Towns. At its head is the 'Great Harry,' an unwieldy over-gunned vessel of a thousand tons, seemingly devised in the mediæval spirit rather with a view to the dignity of the king's banner than for a fighting ship, with two tiers of ordnance on the lower decks, a third tier on her half deck and forecastle. Fore and aft her massive superstructures towered still higher, so that astern she had actually five tiers of guns, and eight decks.

It is in the new second class of 'galleasses,' or 'galleys,' as they were called indifferently, that the real interest of Henry's fleet lies. How exactly they differed from ordinary ships Anthony's rolls unfortunately do not show very clearly. Most of them appear to be flush-decked and all are of comparatively low freeboard and without high superstructures or 'cage-works.' Still we know there was a further difference. In Elizabethan times the main distinction between galleasses or galleons and ships was the proportion of length to beam. This is

[1] The 'great galley' cannot have been a true galley, though it had 120 oars, for it carried 200 guns and must therefore have been a broadside ship, even if we assume the total included 'hand guns.'

[2] Anthony's list consists of three rolls of parchment, upon which is depicted in watercolour every ship with details of its armament, crew, &c. Roll 1, containing the 'ships,' and Roll 3, containing the 'pinnaces' and 'row barges,' have been bound in a book which is preserved in the Pepysian Library at Magdalene College, Cambridge. Roll 2, containing the 'galleasses,' is in its original state in the British Museum. (*Add. MS.* 22,047.)

just the one distinction that Anthony's broadside sketches cannot show. From a naval programme of 1588 we know that a vessel a hundred feet long with a beam of thirty feet was regarded as 'a bastard betwixt a galleasse and a galleon.'[1] In the same paper the dimensions of galleons are given as rather under three beams long, and those of the bastard galleasse three and a-third beams long. A 'galleasse,' therefore, on this progression must have been rather over three and two-thirds beams long, or very near the proportions of a *galleazza di mercantia*, which had a length of over three and three-fifths of its beam. In every respect, indeed, allowing for experimental differences of detail, they closely correspond in type to all we know of the *galea* or *galleazza di Londra*, even to the alternative name. There can be little doubt then that Henry's second class of capital ship was in the wide sense a galleon, which got its special name and form from the Venetian model.[2]

Examining them in detail we see traces of a gradual development, for they are by no means all of identical type. First on the list are the 'Anne Gallant' and the 'Grand Mistress' given by Anthony as sister-ships of 450 tons. Both were new in 1545, and probably represent the latest ideas of Henry's naval architects. The 'Grand Mistress' apparently had been built at Rye, where the Sussex shipwrights with the famous Mr. Fletcher at their head were revolutionising the art of sailing on a

[1] *S. P. Dom. Eliz.* ccxviii. 31.
[2] If any doubt remained that the type was a new one, it would be removed by the uncertainty Navy men displayed in fixing a name for the class. At the end of Henry's reign two of Anthony's galleasses are called 'galleons;' and another smaller one a 'galliot' (see Oppenheim, i. 51 n). In an account of 1550 amongst the Harfleur Archives two vessels in the same sentence are called 'galliotz' and 'gallions' (Jal, p. 764). The main characteristic of the true 'galleota' was that it had no *rembata* or forward gun-platform. Like 'galley,' the name seems to have been eventually applied to a ship's boat. Mr. Oppenheim gives the forms 'galley-watt' and 'joley-watt' for a ship's boat. In galliot, then, we perhaps have the real origin of 'jolly-boat,' which hitherto has defied the ingenuity of etymologists.

wind.[1] Next came two vessels of 'notable fairness' called the 'Salamander' and the 'Unicorn,' which were captured from the Scots during Lord Lisle's expedition to Leith in 1544, the second year of Henry's last war with France, when he took or destroyed everything that floated from Stirling to the Bass. The 'Salamander' was a vessel of 300 tons which had been presented to James V. by Francis I., as part of the dowry of his daughter, the Princess Madeleine.[2] The 'Unicorn,' which was of the same type but of 240 tons only, had been built by James V. himself, probably on the lines of his father-in-law's present. The rest seem all new and show a still further improvement in design. Four of them, all named after animals, the 'Hart' and 'Antelope' of 300 tons and the 'Tiger' and 'Bull' of 200, appear distinctly flush-decked and are without any lofty cage-works on the half deck or forecastle. The others, the 'Greyhound' of 200 tons the 'Jennet' of 180, and the 'Lion' and 'Dragon' of 140 approach near the ship type, though with lower cage-works both fore and aft, and have only three masts. Amongst them is one true galley and this is represented with oars. None of the others are. In spite of the original design of the English type and notwithstanding, as will presently be seen, that under the influence of a passing reaction they were actually furnished with oars, it is therefore certain that when the war broke out the tendency of the English school had brought them to be regarded purely as sailing ships.

In the third class of 'pinnaces' we see the same tendency at work—the tendency to seek fast and handy sailing vessels in modifications of the old rowing types. Originally the pinnace or spyne was certainly regarded as a vessel of free-movement. Under Henry VI. we have seen it placed after the barge and the balyngers, both auxiliary rowing types. The general opinion is that it

[1] Lord Lisle's despatch, August 20, 1545, *State Papers*, Henry VIII. i. 820.
[2] *Holinshed*, sub anno 1544.

was then a long open boat. But in Anthony's rolls it is a sailing vessel with half deck and forecastle, and with three masts carrying lateen sails, differing little except in rig and size from the galleasses. Judging from what they became in Elizabeth's time we may assume they were longer in proportion, approaching four beams in length. The absence of oars in Anthony's sketches does not necessarily mean that they were not intended to be rowed. Indeed we know that in the latter half of the century and onward the essential characteristic of the pinnace was its power of free-movement: but we may with certainty conclude that under Henry VIII. it began to be regarded primarily as a sailing vessel. In one list of Mary's time these vessels are actually classed as greatships, but this is certainly a blunder. In burden they ranged from eighty to fifteen tons, the majority being forty tons, and setting aside certain special functions in general actions and landing operations they were to the capital ships exactly what the frigate was to the ship-of-the-line.[1]

We thus see the two mediæval types of barges and balyngers superseded by vessels of a new kind, trusting mainly to their sails for mobility in action. Naval ideas, however, were still conservative enough to cling to the rule that purely oared vessels were a necessary adjunct to a fighting fleet. The old oared tender was the 'spyne,' and now that it had developed into a sailing vessel we see it replaced by an entirely new type. This was the row-barge, which formed Henry's fourth class. Of these light craft, there were thirteen named all alike after well known

---

[1] There were ten in the class. Two of them, the 'Saker' and the 'Falcon,' were named after birds; four or five others, like the smaller 'galleasses,' after animals; one with the curious name, 'Trego-Ronnyger,' apparently Spanish; and lastly one known as the 'Brigantine,' which as we have seen was originally the same thing as a barge. Two were very probably the 'zabras' or pinnaces which Henry procured in Spain in 1542 as despatch vessels to carry his correspondence with the Emperor (*Spanish Calendar*, 6, ii. 'Chapuys to the Queen of Hungary, July 3, 1542'). One of these pinnaces is sometimes called the 'Spanish shallop.'

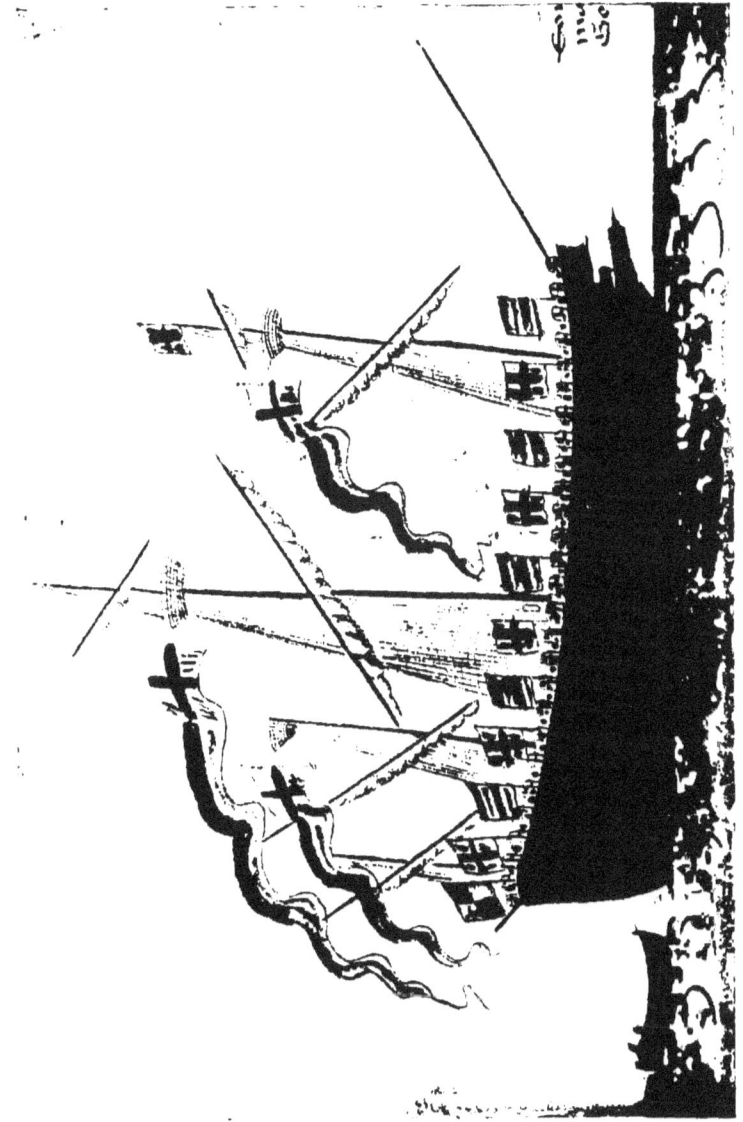

THE GALLEASSE 'HART.'
Reduced from Anthony's Second Roll (British Museum, Add. MSS. 22047).

heraldic badges: 'Cloud-in-the-Sun,' 'Rose-in-the-Sun,' 'Sun,' 'Harp,' 'Maidenhead,' 'Gilly-flower,' 'Ostrich-feather,' 'Rose-slip,' 'Flower-de-luce,' 'Portcullice,' 'Falcon-in-the-Fetterlock,' 'Hawthorn,' and 'Double Rose.' These dainty names occur in no early list, and Marshal du Bellay, who saw them in action at Spithead in 1545, particularly says these 'ram-berges,' as he calls them, were peculiar to the English service. He describes them as very long in proportion to their beam, longer even than galleys, and as being extraordinarily handy in strong currents and tideways and as rivalling galleys in swiftness. From Anthony's third roll they appear very like the pinnaces, but show sixteen oars aside rowed in the waist. Most of them seem to be armed with a bow chaser and two short guns in broadside under the half deck; four only have stern chasers. The survey of 1548 puts them all at 20 tons.[1] From a letter of Chapuys to the Emperor it would seem they were laid down in 1541, and were Henry's own design. 'The King,' he says, ' has fetched from Italy three master ship-wrights expert in making galleys, and I think he will not even set them to work since he has begun to have built vessels with oars of which he himself is the designer and inventor.'[2]

The letter is of peculiar interest not only as throwing light on the 'row-barges' and showing the king's keen interest in naval science, but also as hinting at a very precise date for Henry's final conversion to the theory that the proper function of oared vessels was to be secondary and not 'capital' ships. It was when Lord Russell, the great Devonshire magnate and patron of the western seamen, had become Lord Admiral: and thus perhaps we may see in the change the influence of men like William

[1] Derrick, p. 11.
[2] *Spanish Calendar*, 6, i. 342, July 16, 1541. The word translated 'oars' is in the original '*environs*,' but this is almost certainly a slip for '*avirons*.' Henry's 'row-barges' were certainly something quite different from the French 'roberge.' Some of these designed in 1576 were of 80 tons, being 45 feet on the keel, 18 feet beam, 18 feet overhang fore and aft, 11 feet in depth (Bréard, *Documents relatifs à la Marine Normande*).

Hawkins of Plymouth, who by his recent voyages to Guinea and Brazil had made himself the father of English oceanic navigation, and, as Hakluyt says, for his wisdom, valour, experience, and skill in sea causes was much esteemed and beloved by the king; and of men like Robert Reniger who followed in Hawkins's steps in 1540, and whose influence we may perhaps see in the queerly named royal pinnace the 'Trego Ronnyger.'[1] But however this may be, it is abundantly clear that under Henry VIII. the English Navy was becoming an entirely new thing, a thing the world had never seen before. With ample resources to have anything he wanted, in face of Italian, Spanish, and even French opinion, he chose to create a Navy which ignored the vessel that all ages had regarded as the ideal capital ship, and to reduce the rowing vessel to entirely subordinate functions, to place it in fact in much the same position as that which a torpedo-boat holds to-day.

To understand the meaning of Henry's four classes it now becomes necessary to consider the point to which sailing tactics had reached. It is a subject that has lain long in deep obscurity. Hitherto, indeed, it has been an almost axiomatic proposition that sailing tactics had practically no existence till the end of the seventeenth century; indeed, until recently their birth was usually assigned to the eighteenth. The old actions of our early Spanish and Dutch wars were treated of as though they were mere mêlées without thought or order, and no trace of naval science was held to exist. This view is no longer tenable. The 'Espejo de Navigantes' or 'Seaman's Glass' of Alonso de Chaves leaves no room to doubt that regular sailing formations existed as the result of elaborate and

[1] The *Hawkins's Voyages*, Hakluyt Society, 1878, pp. 2 and 3. A man's name appearing thus usually means that the vessel was chartered or bought of the person whose name it bears. Two Ronnygers served as Captains in 1545 and furnished ships. One of them seems to have been the first Englishman to capture an 'Indian ship.' It was under Edward VI., and restitution was made to the Emperor (*Spanish Calendar*, 1580 &c., pp. 55 and 94).

THE PINNACE 'ROE.'
Reduced from Anthony's Third Roll (Magdalene College, Cambridge).

sagacious study by experts at the time the treatise was produced, and this was in the first half of the sixteenth century.[1]

That it is to Spain we have to go for our origins is only natural. Though the English had been the first to perfect a sailing warship, there is little or no reason to expect from the same source the best system of tactics for its employment. Men practically acquainted with the handling of single vessels or even of small squadrons may instinctively see the best form for a ship, but a genius for devising a system of working large fleets of them is quite a different thing. Tactics is essentially a soldier's art; it was to men trained as soldiers that the command of large fleets was always given. Until some great genius arose to break through the military traditions, it was inevitable that naval tactics must remain under military influence. Henry could look to his practical seamen and shipwrights to develop from foreign models an ideal warship, but of fleet manœuvres they knew nothing. As an advanced military student he would naturally regard tactics as his own affair, and would found his system on the practice of the great military power of his day. Thus it was that, although Spain was far behind him in her naval weapons, she still, as we shall see, dominated the art of using them.

As his text De Chaves enunciates that a fixed order of battle is as necessary at sea as on land. With a suggestive admission of where it was that naval tacticians found their model, he goes on to say, that as in an army the men-at-arms and the light cavalry are separately marshalled for the discharge of their respective functions, so should a naval commander 'bring together in one part his strongest and largest ships to attack, board, grapple

[1] For the discovery of this manuscript we are indebted to the indefatigable industry of Captain Duro. He recently discovered it in the Library of the Spanish Academy of History, and reproduced it in his *Armada Española*, vol. i. app. 12, Madrid, 1895. See also his *De algunas obras desconocidas de Cosmografía y de Navegacion*, &c., reprinted from the *Revista de Navegacion y Comercio*, Madrid 1894-5.

and break the enemy, and his middle sized and weaker ships in another part, so as from where they are they may with their guns and munitions harass [1] and also follow and give chase to the enemy, if he flies, and come up to support wherever they see the greatest necessity.' He also advises that a fourth part of the smallest and lightest vessels should be told off to act as observation squadrons on each flank. Each ship is to endeavour to board its enemy, taking care that it does not get between two of them so as to be boarded on each side. A fourth part of the 'barks' is also to be told off, the largest that are with the fleet to be chosen, as special supports to the main ships. Their duties were when an enemy was grappled by a great-ship to attack it on the opposite side, provided the conditions of the action were favourable. Otherwise they were to remain in the rear, or with the rest of the general supports, to assist distressed vessels and to endeavour to scuttle the enemy's ships already engaged or disable their rudders.

Having thus organised his fleet the admiral must draw it up according to the scene of action, the wind, and the enemy's disposition. This leads the writer to an exceedingly valuable exposition of the various battle formations that might be expected in his time. The enemy, he says, might be all massed together, or one behind the other in file [2]; they might be disposed in squadrons or in line [3]: the great-ships might be in the centre or on the flanks; and it was also necessary to observe where the flag-ship sailed. If the enemy formed his fleet into squadrons, you ought to do the same, always placing the largest ships by themselves in the vanguard or so as to be the first to grapple

---

[1] *Entrar y salir*, a technical military expression used of light cavalry. The exact meaning is difficult to determine. It seems generally to signify sudden short attacks on weak points.

[2] *Unos en pos de otros á la hila.* This may mean line ahead, in single file, but more probably, from the plural being used, it means in several files.

[3] *Puestos en escuadrones ó en ala.* 'Escuadrone' in the technical military phraseology of the sixteenth and seventeenth centuries meant a separate body of troops in square formation, the battle-column of the eighteenth century, as opposed to the *ala* or 'line.'

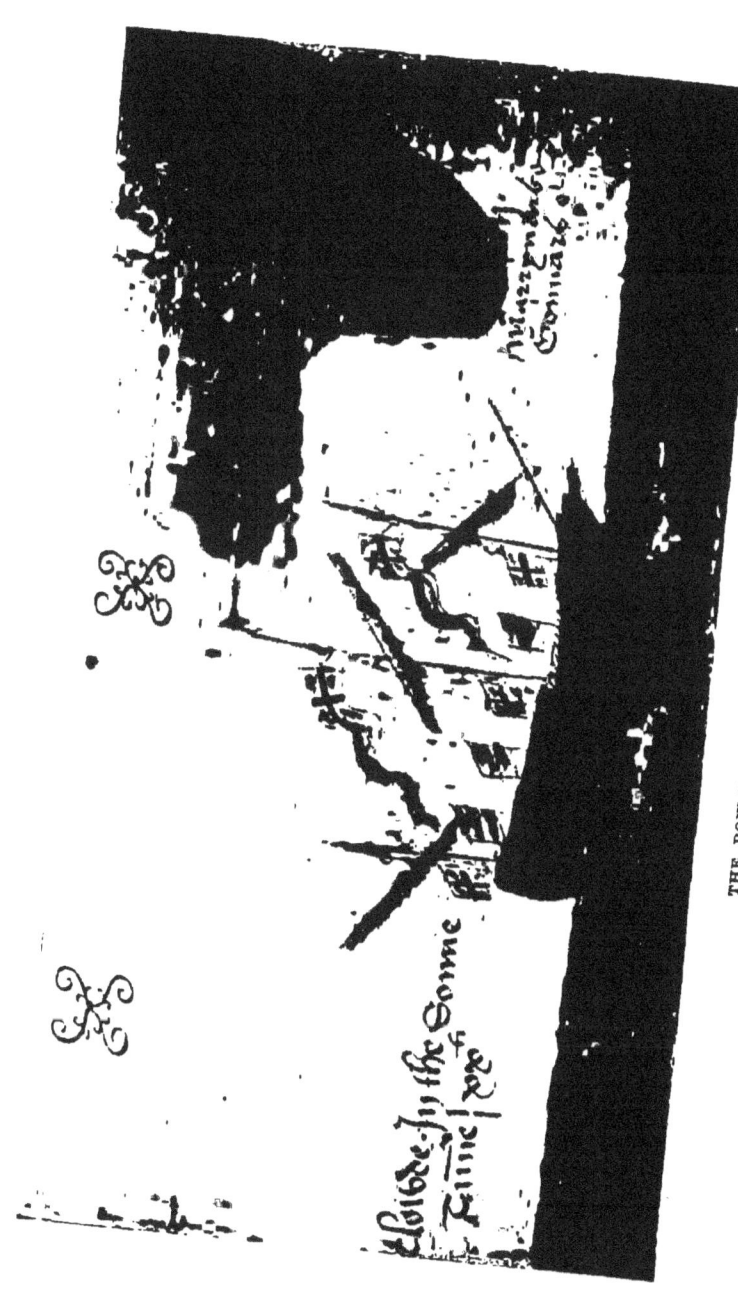

THE ROW-BARGE 'CLOUD-IN-THE-SUN.'
Reduced from Anthony's Third Roll (Magdalene College, Cambridge).

and to receive the first shock; and the Admiral ought to take his station in the squadron which is in the middle, so that he may see those in front of him and may be seen by those who follow him. 'Each of the squadrons ought to sail in single line [en ala], so that all can see the enemy, and work their guns without getting in each other's way, and they ought not to sail in several ranks [á la hila] one behind the other, because in such wise will come great harm, since only those in front can fight, seeing that a ship is not so nimble as a man that it can wheel and do as it will.'[1] The rear-guard, he adds, which is to consist of the vessels told off as supports, is not to remain in rear of the 'anti-guardia' or fighting squadrons, but to get on each flank, or, if on one only, then on the windward flank.

So much for a squadronal battle formation. If, on the other hand, the enemy be formed in one body in line[2] he advises that the same order be taken with the strongest and largest vessels in the centre and the lightest at the flanks of the line, 'since the centre ships always receive the greatest hurt, because of necessity they will be engaged on both sides.'

If the enemy come on in a pointed or triangular order, he is to be met with two lines not parallel to each other but rather V-shaped, with the advanced ends wide apart and the rear ends close together, so as to take him between two fires. In this case the strongest ships are to be in the rear and the lightest at the advanced ends, so that each may more quickly close with the enemy opposite to it.

If the enemy, on the other hand, be in two lines, he enjoins that their formation must be imitated with your own largest ships opposite the largest of the enemy. Your

[1] The writer is clearly thinking of the counter march by files, which was the method of delivering fire ashore both for musketeers and cavalry, showing that the expression *los unos tras los otros á la hila* which he uses in this p'ace does not mean 'single file' but in ranks 'two or more deep.'

[2] *To la junta puesta in ala.* Here again we have *ala* contrasted with *escuadrone*.

object then will be to take the enemy between your two lines, and on no account must you enter the enemy's formation, for then it will be impossible for the supports to reach you.

In every case and as a matter of the first importance he insists on getting the weather-gauge. The reason he gives is very significant, for it is a soldier's reason. For a seaman the advantage of the weather-gauge is in the first place the facility of manœuvring. For De Chaves it is that your smoke will blow clear of you and enable you to see to keep your formation, while at the same time it will confuse the enemy and prevent him seeing what he is doing. It is for this reason also that he recommends the supports to act on the weather flank.

Having completed his formation and arranged his signals, the Admiral may sound to battle. It must be opened by the largest guns, first by those on the side towards the enemy and then the extraordinary manœuvre is to be performed of dragging across those on the opposite broadside which are mounted on carriages, and firing them. Only at very close quarters are the smaller guns to be fired; and at the moment of boarding the stones, lances, and other engines in the tops and castles are to be brought into play. The whole of the tactics, it will be seen, are designed for closing with the enemy as quickly as possible, and to doing him the utmost injury with the guns as he is approached. Anything like an artillery action is clearly not yet contemplated, and every disposition has immediate regard to boarding the enemy under favourable conditions. The whole system still bears the mediæval taint of the typical galley formation line-abreast. In no case, not even in the V-shaped order for receiving the triangular formation, does the line ahead appear as a fighting order. Yet it is sufficiently clear that deep attention had been paid by the Spaniards to sailing formations, and that the greatest importance was attached to them. De Chaves strictly enjoins the revolutionary rule that the Admiral should, if possible, avoid boarding, so that he may keep control of the fleet movements. That he was the exponent of a school is certain; for he concludes by controverting the opinions of men who hold that regular orders and movements under sail are impracticable—opinions, as we have seen, which were almost universally held by the Italian admirals. Still it is to be demonstrated he was no mere theorist, and that his opinions were shared by practical men, and amongst them some of the first authorities of their day.

For this we have but to return to the English school. Sometime probably before 1532, Thomas Audley, afterwards Lord Chancellor, was instructed by the king to draw up a set of general orders for the regulation of the royal forces both by land and sea.[1] This he did in consultation with all the experts he could approach, and the result gives us a fair view of what English naval tactics were at the time De Chaves produced his treatise. The main idea was still confined to getting the weather-gauge and boarding, and as yet there is little or no sign of any appreciation of the value of artillery. 'If they chase the enemy,' he says, 'let them that chase shoot no ordnance till he be ready to board him, for that will let [hinder] his ship's way.' For a general action his rule is: 'Let every ship match equally as near as they can, leaving some pinnaces at liberty to help the overmatched, and one small ship when they shall join battle to be attending upon the Admiral to relieve him: for the overcoming of the Admiral is a great discouraging of the rest.' For boarding he emphasises the importance of reserving your fire till the last moment. 'In case you board,' he lays it down, 'enter not till you see all the smoke gone, and then shoot off all your pieces, your port-pieces, the pieces of hailshot and cross-bar shot to beat his cage-deck; and if you see his deck well rid, then enter with your best men, but first win his top in any wise if it be possible.' If the ship cannot be held it is to be scuttled with all its crew after removing the captain and other prisoners of value. The

[1] Oppenheim, p. 63, n. Audley's regulations are in *Harl. MS.* 309.

tactical importance of the dense smoke which the gunpowder of the time produced is very remarkable. 'A stratagem,' he suggests, 'for getting the wind if you are to leeward of a superior fleet is to fly till they begin to shoot and then shoot again.' 'And make all the smoke ye can,' he goes on, ' to the intent the enemy shall not see the ships, and then suddenly haul up your tackle aboard and have the wind of the enemy. And by this policy it is possible to win the weather "gaige" of the enemy.' Of the elaborate formations to which De Chaves devotes so much attention there is little or nothing; but by the end of the reign they were well understood, and during Henry's last struggle with France we see his naval ideas profoundly influenced by those of De Chaves. The Spanish document is known to have been kept secret, but in the king's conduct of the war appear manifest signs that he had obtained a copy of it, perhaps through spies, perhaps from Charles V. himself while their alliance lasted.

For England the war opened well. With the Emperor's alliance she was in complete command of the sea. Though war was declared too late in 1543 for any serious move to be made, during the whole summer English vessels had been sweeping the seas under colour of reprisals and the French commerce was almost destroyed in the Narrow Seas. In the following year a sudden descent of the fleet upon Leith in support of a cavalry column thrown across the border paralysed at a stroke the trouble which the French were seeking to organise in Henry's rear, and the fleet was free to cover the English invasion and keep communications open. The real naval interest of the war begins with the campaign of 1545, when Francis had had time to gather a navy, and Henry by Charles V.'s desertion was left to match his strength against his rival single-handed. The conditions of the war were now reversed. In the previous campaign Henry, taking the offensive, had invaded France and captured Boulogne. Now Francis resolved to retaliate with operations against Portsmouth and the Isle of Wight. By the end of spring he had gathered in Havre and the adjacent ports a fleet of some hundred and fifty large merchant vessels (*gros vaisseaux ronds*), and sixty oared coasters (*flouins*).[1] These were joined by some twenty-five galleys which Paulin, Baron de la Garde, had fetched from the Mediterranean, and among them was a contingent under Leone Strozzi, Prior of Capua, and Admiral of the galleys of Rhodes, one of the most famous galley commanders of his time.[2] Upon the whole was embarked a force of sixty thousand men. So great a host had not appeared upon the Narrow Seas for centuries; in power of offence it was scarcely, if at all, inferior to the Invincible Armada itself, and much of the confidence of 1588 must have been due to the memory of this campaign.

The English Navy, to the number of over a hundred sail of fighting ships, both royal and auxiliary, was being concentrated at Spithead; but with a glimmering of what the command of the sea really meant, and of what the true defensive strategy of a sea power should be, Henry did not wait to be attacked, and repeating his move of the previous war he sent out Seymour with a strong division to disturb the enemy's concentration. The design was to destroy the main body of the French fleet by fire-ships. It did not succeed. Boisterous weather set in. Seymour's power of handling a squadron and the immature seamanship of his captains were insufficient either to hold the coast or bring the enemy to a decisive action, and with his storm-beaten ships he returned to Spithead without having effected anything.

---

[1] The *flouin* is thus described by J. Nicot, *Thrés. de la lang. franç.* 1606: 'It is a kind of vessel resembling the row-barge, but a little smaller. It goes by oar or sail like a galley, but has no benches, the rowers pulling on the deck and standing. It is of higher freeboard than the galley and lower than the ship. . . . The ordinary burden is from forty to fifty ons more or less. . . . The fashion came from Rye in England. It is the best sailer there is on a bowline,' &c. (Jal, *Glossaire*, p. 705.)

[2] Jal, *Glossaire*, p. 342; *Guglielmotti*, iv. 268, 315, 340.

The fleet was still lying in Portsmouth busy repairing damages when D'Annibault, the French Admiral, put to sea. On July 17 the French advanced guard of four galleys under Paulin appeared off St. Helen's Bay. A land wind was blowing, and fourteen English vessels stood out to meet them, and that, says the admiring Du Bellay, 'with so great a promptitude and in so fair an array that you would have said they meant to stand resolutely and engage our whole fleet.' D'Annibault moved up the rest of his galleys in support, and Lord Lisle, who was now in command of the English fleet, put out with the bulk of his force. A desultory action at long range ensued, and continued for a considerable time until towards sundown, as Du Bellay says, the English began to draw away. Retiring to the left they took up a position where they were covered on the one flank by some batteries that had been erected upon the beach, and on the other by sand-banks and sunken rocks, which lay athwart the Channel and left only an intricate fair-way too narrow for more than a few ships to pass abreast. Where exactly this position was is not clear from Du Bellay's description, but it was evidently chosen with sufficient skill according to the science of the day to cause the galleys to retire to the anchorage at St. Helen's and to bring the engagement to an end.[1]

In the face of the hostile fleet nothing was attempted against the Isle of Wight, but on the following day an elaborate effort was made to draw the English from their position. D'Annibault formed up his fleet line-abreast in three 'battles' or divisions, with the galleys under Paulin,

[1] The famous Cowdry picture, painted at the time and engraved by Basire in 1778 for the Society of Antiquaries, throws little or no light on the point. It was apparently painted mainly for the sake of showing the Camp Royal at Southsea. In the background are the two fleets, the French at St. Helen's, the English seemingly on the Spit Sand. The incidents of the various days are confused. The 'Great Harry' is shown in action with the four advanced galleys, as on the first day, while at the same time is represented the loss of the 'Mary Rose,' which took place subsequently, but on which day authorities differ.

taking the place of De Chaves's light supports, as a detached wing-squadron independent of the line of battle. The great-ships, it would seem, took up a position approximately facing the English front. . Each division consisted of thirty-six sail, while the galleys were formed into an advanced guard corresponding to the military 'forlorn.' Their orders were to engage the enemy as closely as possible and to fall back as they fought in order to tempt the English into the open.[1] The conditions were exactly suited to a galley attack. It was dead calm and slack tide, and they were able to carry out their instructions under every advantage. Indeed they seem to have been handled very brilliantly, and for about an hour to have made excellent practice upon the great hulls of the English as they lay motionless at their anchors. At last, however, the land wind sprang up again, Lisle suddenly slipped his cables, and so boldly had the galleys' attack been pushed home that they found themselves in present danger of being rammed. Of this, as we have seen, a galley captain lived in terror: it was defensively the weak point of the type of ship. From its great proportionate length a galley was necessarily slow in turning, and during the whole time the manœuvre was being executed she was exposed to being taken abeam by an enemy. In such a case not only did her low freeboard present itself to be overborne with impunity by the towering stems of the great-ships, but even the glancing shock of a comparatively small vessel ploughing through the oars was enough to break off the blades and so destroy her power of locomotion.[2] On the present occasion, however, all the galleys were well enough handled to get clear before the leading ships could close. So far all was well, and they leisurely continued the retreat in pursuance of their orders to tempt the enemy to follow.

[1] This is the kind of operation which De Chaves probably intended to indicate by his *entrar y salir* ; see *ante*, p. 42.
[2] The oars of galleys seem to have had a comparatively slender blade spliced on the stock, so that in case of collision they easily broke off without injuring the galley slaves.

But now a new surprise awaited them. Instead of the great-ships pursuing them as they hoped, out of the English ranks shot Henry's little swarm of row-barges. Their daring filled Du Bellay with amazement. A galley, it will be remembered, could deliver no fire aft, and taking advantage of this weakness the row-barges, with incredible swiftness, followed close on their heels and began firing into their unprotected poops. Turn they dared not, so great was their dread of being rammed even by these small fry. But at last Strozzi, whose high naval reputation could no longer brook the ignominy of the position, managed to get room to turn his own galley on his tormentor. In a moment the row-barges had gone about, and before the galleys could bring their guns to bear they were well out of danger.

D'Annibault's next move in order to draw Lisle from his position was to land troops upon the Island; but Lisle was not to be tempted, and after considerable loss from the garrison the landing parties were recalled. Lisle—or perhaps it should be said the king, for he was present in person directing the operations—was too good a commander to be enticed into an action against galleys in confined waters and calm weather. D'Annibault saw his only chance was to attack the English fleet where it lay; but after spending the night in a personal examination of the Channel he was convinced of the hopelessness of the operation, and eventually retired to an anchorage off Bricklesome Bay.

The same night a fresh westerly wind sprang up and Lisle saw his opportunity. Under D'Annibault's lee were the shoals that lie off Selsea, and Lisle called his pilots to council. How mediæval sailing tactics still were his questions and their answers reveal to us. His idea, if the wind held strong at west, was to attack the enemy where they rode, and he asked the pilots if they thought in that case the French would abide them at anchor. The pilots answered 'that if they did bide us at anchor they were cast away, for we coming with a fore wind should bear over whom we listed into the sea, and therefore they would not sure bide that adventure, but rather come under their small sails to bide us loose, for that were their most advantage.' Here still we have the mediæval idea of a great-ship ramming to leeward, but it is accompanied by a suggestion of something more modern. For Lisle contemplated, if they weighed, attacking them and endeavouring to force them upon the Owers, a manœuvre which Drake seems to have attempted in the same place when the Armada lay there. The wind did not hold, however, so that the design was not put into execution.[1]

In spite of the urgent counsels of the French soldiers that they might be allowed to land in force on the Wight and entrench themselves there, D'Annibault now decided to return to his own coast. Victuals were running short, sickness as usual had broken out, and with the instinct of a great captain he seems to have seen the futility of attempting offensive operations ashore until the English fleet had been beaten. Lisle did not follow him, principally it would appear because through some carelessness the 'Marie Rose,' one of the finest of the royal ships, had been sunk after the first day's action, and it was hoped she might be speedily floated, and also because reinforcements were expected from the West. But there was without doubt another reason, perhaps the most weighty, certainly the most interesting.

The complete advantage which D'Annibault's galleys had given him in the Solent and the helplessness with which Henry had been compelled to sit idle and see his rival's flag flouting him defiance at his very gates had had a reactionary effect upon the royal mind. Lisle was ordered to organise an oared squadron that he might be on equal terms with the French Admiral.[2] The work

[1] Lisle to the King, July 21; *Burghley State Papers*, ed. Haynes, p. 51. The letter is one of apology to the king for having contemplated acting without his orders and is of additional interest as showing how Henry was keeping the reins in his own hand.

[2] 'Whereas the King's Majesty's pleasure is to have certain of his ships brought to pass to row, to keep company with others of that sort to attend

took some time, for there was hardly more than a nucleus to go upon. The row-barges, it would seem, had been found unfitted to accompany a sea-going fleet; they at least formed no part of the new squadron; and besides this, as Lisle complained, all the shipwrights were occupied in the preparations for raising the 'Marie Rose.' Still by the middle of August the new squadron was ready. As 'Admiral' and 'Vice-Admiral,' as the two flagships of a fleet or squadron were then called, appear the 'Grand Mistress' and the 'Anne Gallant,' the largest and latest in design of the galleasses. Next come the 'Galley Subtil' and the 'Greyhound,' another of the galleasses, and then nine of the ten pinnaces, the tenth being probably reserved to attend the Admiral. To these royal ships were attached from the auxiliary fleet twenty pinnaces, which had now joined from the Western Ports, and seven of the famous boats of Rye. In command of the whole was Captain William Tyrrell, with Captain Robert Legge as his Vice-Admiral.[1]

In the light of the De Chaves treatise the tactical idea which underlay the reorganisation is clear. According to the original scheme the whole fleet was to be organised, as the Spaniard advises for large fleets, into four divisions, a 'vantward' and two 'wings,' with a rear-guard of some fifty sail of armed hulks or round-ships.[2] The 'vantguard,'

---

upon the French galleys, there shall be as much done unto it as stuff and time will serve to perform the same.' 'Lisle to Paget;' *State Papers*, i. 805.

[1] Neither the 'Great' nor the 'Less Galley' was attached to this squadron, but found a place in the main division of great-ships, which is almost conclusive that they were really 'galleons' of some kind.

[2] *Le Fleming Papers*: Hist. MSS. Comm. XII. vii. 8. The paper is dated 1545, so that we do not know for certain whether it contains the original scheme, but internal evidence seems to show it was anterior to the scheme in the *State Papers*, Henry VIII. (i. 816), which purports to contain a list of the fleet as it actually sailed. In the Le Fleming Paper the 'rowing pieces' are less numerous than in the State Paper, and only include four private 'boats,' so that probably it was drawn up before the rest joined. It also includes all the eight 'galleasses' that were then available, although it seems certain that eventually it was found impossible to equip them all as 'rowing pieces.'

exactly in accordance with the plan of De Chaves, was to be formed in three divisions or ranks with the strongest ships leading and the Admiral in the centre, the rear rank being longer than the middle and the middle than the front, so as to form with the whole the blunt wedge. In the first line were placed the 'Great Argosy' and seven of the largest great-ships; in the second, the 'Great Harry' and ten great-ships and galleons :[1] and in the third nineteen lesser great-ships. Half a cable's length was to be allowed between the ships, and the ranks were to keep such order in sailing that none touched another and no ship passed its fellows. On meeting the enemy, the first rank was to make sail straight to its front, pass through the enemy's line, and 'make a short return to the midwards, having special regard to the course of the second rank.' 'The ships of the second and third ranks,' the instructions proceed, 'are to lay aboard the principal ships of the enemy, every one chosing his mate, reserving the Admiral for my Lord Admiral.' Here we have quite clearly the conception of a blunt wedge-shaped formation intended to break through the enemy's centre, and to concentrate the whole force of the attack in the region of his principal ships. The two 'wings,' each consisting of twelve rowing-pieces, were primarily intended, as we have seen, to protect the great-ships from a galley attack in a calm. In case of a general engagement in a wind they were to hold aloof to windward just as De Chaves directs, and to act as a reserve. 'Neither of the wings,' continue the instructions, 'shall enter into the fight, but having advanced as nigh as they can of the wind, shall give succour as they see occasion. They shall not give succour to any of the small vessels, so as not to weaken our force.' To the rearguard of armed merchantmen no instructions are given, unless these were the 'victuallers' which were to follow the third rank, with the

---

[1] It included the 'Venetian' (which was probably the requisitioned 'Galleazza di Londra'), the 'Great Galley,' and the galleasses 'Swallow' and 'New Bark.'

idea probably, as they carried a strong force of soldiers, of providing a reserve of men for hard pressed ships.

Another paper, which purports to be a list of the fleet as it actually sailed from Portsmouth, shows a considerable modification of the original idea to an even closer conformity with the ideas of De Chaves.[1] Here we have a 'vantward' of twenty-four great-ships and a 'main battle' of forty including the Great and Less Galleys, and a 'wing' of forty 'galleasses, shallops, and boats of war' constituted as already described. In this case the instructions were that the 'vantward' was to attack the enemy's 'vantward' if they had one. 'If they be in one,' they proceed, 'our vantward, taking advantage of the wind, shall set upon their foremost rank, setting them out of order.' Here then we still have the idea of a blunt wedge formation with a front rank preparing the enemy's line for the attack of a second. Again each ship is to choose one of its own size, and 'the Admiral of the "wing" shall always be in the wind.' This time, however, it is not said as a reserve, but 'so as better to beat off the galleys from the great-ships,' which would look as though some one had pointed out that the weakness of the three-rank formation was that it gave too wide a flank-face exposed to a galley attack.

From these general orders we are able to see in the clearest way the military origin of the naval tactics of the time. In his chapter on 'The Modern Way of Embatteling and Marshalling Armies' Sir James Turner describes the typical formation which had subsisted from Charles V.'s time to his own, as an order in three bodies, the vanguard, the battle, and the rear-guard, with two 'wings' of horse.[2] It was this form of 'embatteling' that came in at the end of the fifteenth century when Gonsalvo de Cordova the 'Great Captain' had re-established infantry as the backbone of a fighting formation, and we thus see both in the De Chaves treatise and Lisle's orders the dominating tendency of the great military tradition. For them the

[1] *State Papers*, Henry VIII. i. 810.   [2] *Pallas Armata*, 1683, p. 269.

great-ships were their infantry—the primary strength of their formation—and the light oared-ships their cavalry, disposed in mobile wings for flank-defence and pursuit.

Meanwhile, during the progress of the English re-organisation D'Annibault having discharged his pioneers and a number of the soldiers had put to sea to fight the English fleet, and was parading the Channel in triumph. By the middle of August, however, Lisle got to sea with eighty-four sail. In the van under Sir Thomas Clere, Vice-Admiral of England, were twenty-four sail, consisting mainly of the heavy vessels which had been purchased from the Hansa; in the 'battle,' under the Lord Admiral, were forty sail, including the finest of the king's ships, and most of his galleasses and galleys. In the 'wing' under Tyrrell were forty sail of 'galleasses, shallops, and boats of war.'

On weighing Lisle turned westward, there being an idea apparently that the French meant to attack Dover. On the 15th the two fleets met somewhere in mid-Channel athwart Shoreham, and the wind being light and the French superior in galleys D'Annibault prepared to attack. 'The only difficulty,' says Lord Herbert, restating the problem which Henry had attempted to solve with his wing of 'rowing pieces,' 'was in regard to the currents how to use both ships and galleys together; for in calms when the galleys made way the ships could not stir, and without them they durst not encounter us.'[1]

The action seems to have begun by the two opposing 'wings' or oared squadrons manœuvring for what wind there was, and eventually Paulin developed an attack upon the English great-ships, which was encountered by the English 'oared-pieces.' '"The Mistress,"' wrote Lord Lisle to the king, 'the "Anne Gallant" and the "Greyhound," with all your Highness's shallops and rowing pieces did their parts well, but especially the "Mistress" and the "Anne Gallant" did so handle the galleys, as well with their sides as with their prows, that your great-ships in a manner

[1] In *Kennett*, p. 250.

had little to do.'[1] It is probable that Paulin did not care to press his attack until D'Annibault could support him with the great-ships. The engagement continued all day with no worse casualty on the English side than that some of Tyrrell's oars were broken.[2] It was evening before D'Annibault was able to get up, and then it would seem the wind shifted in favour of the English. Lisle, however, very properly decided not to press his advantage unless the wind increased to a point favourable to great-ships and unfavourable to galleys, and both fleets came to anchor. In the morning the French had disappeared, and though Lisle gave chase he did not succeed in bringing D'Annibault to another action. Both sides returned to port to repair damages. The 'Grand Mistress,' the 'Galley Subtil,' and the 'Foyst' or 'Brigantine' had been so shaken by the weather and the shock of their guns that they were pronounced no longer serviceable without extensive repairs, and so our knowledge of the campaign ends with a despatch from Lord Lisle lamenting how he will miss those three 'rowing pieces' if the French put to sea again. But Francis did not care to renew the attempt. Though no great action had been fought, his grand invasion had ended in a most lamentable and costly failure through his inability to defeat the English fleet, and peace was proclaimed before another campaign could elaborate the lessons of the last.

Before the conclusion of the war, however, one other action of interest was fought. Off Ambleteuse, a small seaport to the north of Boulogne, eight French galleys attacked a hybrid English squadron of four ships or perhaps galleasses and four pinnaces. The engagement seems to have been principally with guns in the growing English fashion. There was great shooting between them, says Stowe, and in the end a French galley manned with 230 soldiers and 140 rowers was captured.[3]

So much is all that can be gathered of the naval art

---

[1] *State Papers*, i. 819. [2] *Ibid*. x. 585.
[3] Stowe, *Chron.* p. 591. This was the galley 'Blancherd.'

from this forgotten war; but it is enough to show that in the middle of the sixteenth century—while Italy, in endeavouring to solve the great problem of sails and oars was still elaborating the fleet of free-movement, and almost ignoring the sailing vessel as a fighting ship—England was committed to a revolution in the opposite direction. After first attempting to ignore the rowing vessel almost as completely as the Italians were ignoring the sailing vessel, Henry's last word had been one of reaction. His latest fleet was of dual composition. Its main force was still of sailing ships, but attached to it was a light squadron of oared vessels with a distinct status as a fighting member, but yet independent of the line of battle. It was a fleet, in fact, which had a certain resemblance in idea to a modern fleet of battle ships and the attendant sea-going torpedo-squadron, and it undoubtedly points to a great advance in naval science. It is here we are at the parting of the ways: it is here we see the road opening for the great school of the Elizabethan seamen. Of all others the year 1545 best marks the birth of the English naval power; it is the year that most clearly displays the transition from oars to sails, and it was probably in this very year the first great sailing Admiral the world ever saw came obscurely into being.

CHAPTER I

DRAKE'S EARLY YEARS [1]

It was at a farm called Crowndale, close by Tavistock in Devonshire, that Drake was born. Once the property of Tavistock Abbey, it had passed at the dissolution of the monasteries into the hands of Sir John Russell, whom we have seen as Lord High Admiral, the founder of the great house of Bedford. At the beginning of the eighteenth century the farm appears from the Bedford Estate books to have been nearly two hundred acres in extent; and in Henry VIII.'s time it was probably of much the same size. For how many generations the Drakes had occupied it cannot be determined. Early in Henry's time it had been held of the Abbot of Tavistock by Simon Drake. To him succeeded his nephew John, Sir Francis's grandfather, and he when his grandson was born was occupying it under a lease from Lord Russell for the lives of himself, his wife Margery, and his eldest son John.[2] He had besides a younger son called Edmund, who lived in a cottage on the farm. In the early days of this century the Tavistock people could still point out the place, and in the Bedford Estate plan it was marked by a cross with a note that in the building so distinguished 'the great and celebrated Admiral Drake was born.' From a sketch made shortly before its demolition it would appear to have been a cottage of the better sort, such as a small farmer might occupy to-day, and such as at that time a well-to-do yeoman's son might live in without losing

[1] For authorities, &c., see Appendix A.
[2] These two leases are still in possession of the family.

caste. Edmund Drake, so Stowe tells us, was by trade a sailor, and there is no reason for doubting his statement.[1] At any rate he does not appear upon the Subsidy Rolls as an inhabitant of Tavistock until 1544. His goods were at that time assessed at 4*l.*, which indicates a certain prosperity as things went then. It may well have come from the sea, and since his first child Francis was probably born in the following year it would look as though he had thought it entitled him to marry and settle down. John Drake the elder was assessed at 20*l.* and John the younger at 5*l.*, so that they may be regarded as fairly well-to-do people, who adequately upheld the position of the family.

There had been Drakes of Tavistock from time immemorial, and moderate as were the circumstances of the Crowndale family it would seem they had come of gentle blood. What precisely was the connection with the higher branches of the family is not clear, but in the days of Francis Drake's renown they were glad to call him cousin, and to admit his claim to bear the Wyvern or Waver-Dragon *gules*, which was the ancient cognizance of the house. The well-known story to the contrary which Prince has to tell in his 'Worthies of Devon' was perhaps never meant to be taken seriously. He relates that Sir Francis upon receiving his knighthood from the queen in 1581 assumed the family arms without authority, and that Mr. Bernard Drake of Asshe, who claimed to be head of the name, boxed his ears at Court for the impertinence. The queen thereupon, to soothe her favourite's feelings, gave him that 'new coat of everlasting honour' and preposterous crest which Clarenceux devised for him to commemorate his voyage round the world, and as an additional punishment to Bernard ordered that the Wyvern *gules* was to be represented hanging by the heels from the ship that served Sir Francis for his new crest. The jest hardly deserves refutation. Prince was a client

---

[1] Barrow, who overlooked the obvious error of Camden's account, preferred it to Stowe's, and for reasons which now seem inadequate rejected this account of Edmund Drake's trade.

of the Drakes of Asshe, and one of them probably told him the tale at the time when the two branches of the family were quarrelling over the Admiral's property. The original draft of the new coat of arms exists. No Wyvern appears in it hanging by the heels, but on the contrary there is attached to it a memorandum that Bernard Drake, 'chief of that coat-armour' and 'sundry others of that family of worship and good credit,' had testified that Sir Francis by prerogative of his birth and by right descent from his ancestor might bear the arms of his surname and family, to wit, *Argent*, a Waver-Dragon *gules*, with the difference of a third brother.' Sir Francis did certainly bear them and seldom used his new arms except quarterly as an augmentation of honour upon the family coat; and if we may believe the testimony of one of his Spanish prisoners he used armorial bearings of some kind upon the silver furniture of his cabin some years before the queen's grant was made.[1] Be that as it may, there were certainly Drakes living at or holding land about Tavistock from the time of Edward III. The Subsidy Rolls show them to have been men of substance and good standing. By marriage and office they were associated with the best of the neighbouring gentry, and as late as Henry VII.'s time were attaching their Wyvern seal to Subsidy Rolls like gentlemen.

But however well-founded were Sir Francis's subsequent pretensions to gentility, at the time of his birth his own family was rather of the yeoman than the gentry class. By the actual position of his father he was born into the revolutionary ranks. He even would seem to have had a kind of pride that this was so. Camden, who says he had the information from Drake's own lips, actually uses the words 'middle class,' *natus est loco mediocri*.[2] It was the class that was fast becoming the

---

[1] See *post*, p. 264, and Appendix G.
[2] The use of the word 'mean' to translate *mediocri* in the English edition led to an impression that Drake must be of lower birth than he really was. For though at the time 'mean' would bear the sense of 'middling,'

controlling power in the State, as it was already the great moving force. Fostered in the towns during the decay of feudalism and constantly fed upon the new liberalism of the Renaissance with which foreign commerce brought it in contact, it found itself with the advent of the Tudors given an ever increasing liberty of growth. The domination of the old territorial nobility was disappearing under the crushing blows it had received; and freed from its shadow and restraint the rising order found light and air, and like the vigorous underwood of a forest, when the old timber is cleared, it was pushing forth a new and healthier growth that was spreading far and wide over the face of the country. It was on this class that the Tudor monarchy rested; it was upon their ripe support that Henry relied when he finally threw in his lot with the Reformation, and it was from the higher grades of the order that he chose the 'New Men' who were his most trusted councillors.

But not only was Francis Drake born into the new order, he was made its son also by adoption. Chief of the 'New Men' was Lord Russell, his grandfather's landlord. From the first he and Cromwell had been the leaders of the reforming party, and now that Cromwell was gone he remained throughout the great quarrel with the Bishop of Rome, both in camp and council the king's right hand. Of all the men Henry raised up about him there was not one who showed himself more worthy of his position and whose elevation was more widely approved. In the west he ruled with something of the authority of a proconsul, and towered above his fellows till in the people's eyes he rose to proportions second only to the king in power, worship, and popularity. But great and

it even then was getting something of its present value. The word is used in the draft apology to Spain for his piracies in its modern sense. It is also so used by his nephew in his preface to the *English Hero Revived*. In this case, however, it should be remembered that a literary contrast is being aimed at, and that the author was writing after his family had quarrelled with the Drakes of Asshe, and refused to trace their descent beyond the great Admiral.

honoured as Lord Russell was, Edmund Drake had succeeded in winning more than ordinary favour in his eyes. How he had done so can only be surmised from his character and his opinions. Through his will we get a glimpse of them—of his faith in his own redemption, of his love for 'the beginning of Romans,' and from this as well as from his subsequent career it is hard to doubt that there was something in him of what was called in the slang of the day 'a hot gospeller.' We can picture him as a layman who, with a taste for preaching and hot for the new opinions, felt he had mistaken his vocation; and it may have been as an earnest and active local politician, as we should now say, that he came under the great man's patronage. But, whatever the cause, it is certain he was on so happy a footing with his patron that when his first child was born Francis Russell, Lord Russell's eldest son, stood godfather and gave the baby his own baptismal name.

In days when patronage meant so much and baptismal relations were still a reality, such a start in life promised at once a career beyond what a boy born in such a position could reasonably hope. Yet even here his good fortune did not end. In the neighbouring port of Plymouth the Hawkinses were now one of the most prominent families. For generations they had been established like the Drakes about Tavistock; but early in the century in sympathy with the new spirit, they begin also to appear as well-to-do freemen of Plymouth. Here they would seem soon to have made themselves a name in the sea-faring world, and from the first to have been connected with Henry's resolve to create a Navy. John Hawkins, who is described as 'of Tavistock, gentleman, captain and shipowner,' was in the king's service from 1513 to 1518 and was perhaps the man who was 'master of the Great Galley' in 1513.[1] With the cessation of Henry's early efforts he probably returned to his own business, and would seem to have prospered. At

---

[1] Brewer, *State Papers*, ii. 1369.

the time of Drake's birth the family was represented by his son, the famous old William Hawkins, the man whom we have seen as one of the experts in maritime matters consulted by Henry VIII. while he was forming his later Navy. The king's favour and the reputation of his own adventurous voyages to America had won him the most prominent position in the town. Twice he had been mayor and three times member for the borough, and by his marriage with Joan Trelawney had allied himself with the great brotherhood of western families that was to play so wild a part in the Protestant cause. Edmund Drake was probably his first cousin, or perhaps his brother-in-law, for here again the exact relationship is not ascertained. It was at any rate near enough for John and William, the old captain's sons, now some twelve or thirteen years old, to regard Francis as a close relation and call him cousin.

So Drake was born with the English revolt against Rome; and so the side he was to take and the career he was to devote to it were settled inevitably by the surroundings of his birth; nor can it well be doubted that he would have become what he did even if there had not fallen on him the rude change of fortune that was to score still more deeply the lines of his destiny.

Henry had been in his grave little more than two years when the Protector Somerset's efforts to force the English Reformation to its logical perfection drove the west country into insurrection. As England was becoming more and more a commercial and manufacturing country, an agrarian revolution was going forward which pressed heavily upon the peasants. Outbreaks had occurred already in various parts of the country, directed against the increasing tendency towards the enclosure of common land and the formation of large grazing estates. With the suppression of the monasteries the troubles of the poorer and less provident peasantry increased, and it was easy for the priests of the old faith, themselves convinced of what they taught, to persuade a people ripe for revolt that it was to the change of religion their troubles were due. To the smouldering force of a new Jacquerie they were able to add the fire of a crusade. The new Prayer Book—the first of Edward VI.—which was designed as the initial step towards clearing the new faith of all taint of the 'idolatrous rite' of the Mass, was ready, and on Whit Sunday in the year 1549 it was ordered to be used. In a week the west country was in a blaze, all favourers of the new book were flying for their lives, the gentry were hiding in woods and caves, and Lord Russell, who was sent down to restore order, found he could not move nearer to his home than Honiton.

Edmund Drake and his family fled like the rest. It was to Plymouth they probably betook themselves, to secure the protection of their kinsmen and their Protestant friends, who were always numerous in the sea-ports. But even here security was denied them. For years the dispossessed agriculturists had been flocking into the towns, and when the rebels appeared before Plymouth the mayor, either from inclination or distrust of the people, opened his gates. It would seem, however, that some of the more sturdy Protestants held their ground, perhaps on the Island of St. Nicholas, afterwards called 'Drake's Island,' where according to local tradition the refugees took shelter; and no sooner did the news of the mayor's treason come to the Council's ears than they took immediate steps to relieve the loyal minority and place them in power again. In the spring a squadron had been fitted out under Sir Thomas Cotton to clear the Narrow Seas of French and Scottish pirates. It was composed as follows:

Ships.	Tonnage.	Commanders.
The 'Antelope'	300 tons	Sir Thomas Cotton, Vice-Admiral
The 'Hart'	300 ,,	Captain Richard Bethell
The 'Salamander'	300 ,,	?
The 'Jennet'	180 ,,	Captain William Hall
The 'English Galley'	—	Captain Richard Drake
The late 'French Galley' and six shallops.[1]	—	Captain Sir William Tyrrell

[1] *S. P. Dom.* Edward VI. 1552, vii. f. 9.

As was natural in a squadron intended for pirate catching, the 'oared pieces,' it will be seen, largely predominated, if indeed all the vessels were not intended for rowing. The first four are all 'galleasses,' the first of which we know had been fitted with oars in 1545. The French galley that was captured at Ambleteuse, we see, had been added to the Navy, and all the 'shallops' were probably pinnaces, but certainly oared. Cotton's instructions were to pay particular attention to the advice of Tyrrell and Drake, and to communicate with them whenever it was possible. Tyrrell, we know, was the man who had so brilliantly commanded the 'wing' of 'oared pieces' in 1545, and he seems to have been knighted for his services.[1] But how Captain Richard Drake had won his reputation is not known. His name does not even occur among the captains of 1545. Nothing indeed is to be learnt of him. Even whether he was any relation to the Crowndale family is quite uncertain.[2] All we know is that it was the squadron to which he was attached that was sent to relieve the Plymouth Protestants with orders as a first step 'to attempt by all good means to win possession of the castle and place Hawkins with some other men there to apprehend the mayor and to give good order for the town.'[3] Whether Cotton arrived in time to be of service we do not know, for the French had seized the opportunity to declare war, and his squadron had to be diverted to re-victual Alderney on its way. The subsequent movements of Cotton do not appear nor how far they influenced those of Edmund Drake. Whether it was that he availed himself of this or some

[1] In a minute of the Privy Council of September 1551 he is called Sir William Tyrrell. (See *Naval Extracts from Clarendon's Copy of the Council Book*, MS. in the Pepysian Library.)

[2] The lay Subsidy Rolls show two Richard Drakes, senior and junior, in Tavistock parish, but there is nothing to identify either of them with the naval officer.

[3] 'Somerset to Lord Russell,' July 22, 1549, printed in Pocock's *Troubles connected with the Prayer Book in 1549*, Camden Soc. N.S. vol. 37, 1885, p. 33. 'Council to same,' *ibid*. p. 61.

similar chance of placing his family in security, or whether it was that he felt Tavistock was too insecure an abode, Edmund Drake never returned to his old home. Though his father would seem to have remained in Devonshire, the family disappears from Tavistock entirely. It is probable that they had lost everything in the insurrection, and that Edmund was only too glad to accept the asylum which Lord Russell, Hawkins, Captain Richard Drake, or some other naval friend and sympathiser was able to procure him. The result of his persecution, so Sir Francis Drake the younger tells, was 'that he was forced to fly into Kent and there to inhabit in the hull of a ship.'[1] It must have been these words that raised in Motley's mind the picture of 'an old boat turned bottom upwards upon a sandy down,'[2] but in view of Drake's good connections it is impossible to accept it. In any case the younger Sir Francis's words clearly imply that the new home was afloat and not ashore, and this fact suggests a possible explanation. At this very time the Government was engaged in establishing Gillingham Reach, just below Chatham, as the eastern headquarters of the Navy, and here it was ordered that the king's ships were to be laid up when out of commission.[3] To a Government like the Protector Somerset's no new scheme could be perfect without due provision for the spiritual welfare of the men who were to work it. Now it was about this time, as Sir Francis Drake told Camden, his father got a place among the seamen in the king's Navy to read prayers to them. It is not impossible, therefore, that it was Edmund Drake who supplied the spiritual element of the Protector's new scheme; and if this was so nothing could be more natural than that, for the convenient

[1] See 'Sir F. Drake Revived.' Introd. in Arber's *English Garner*, vol. v.
[2] *United Netherlands*, cap. xi.
[3] See Report in *Harl. MS.* 354, ff. 90 b and 91. Oppenheim, p. 102. The first order for harbouring paid-off ships at Gillingham is dated June 8, 1550.

discharge of his duties among the ship-keepers, quarters should be found for him on board one of the Navy hulks. Be that as it may, it was upon Edmund Drake's floating home, so the younger Sir Francis writes, 'many of his younger sons were born: he had twelve in all, and as it pleased God to give most of them a living on the water, so the greatest part of them died at sea.' From the fact that all the sons were not born afloat it is to be gathered that other children besides Francis shared the flight. Of the eleven brothers we know the names of four only:—John, who was killed during the Nombre de Dios expedition; Joseph, who died upon the same voyage; Edward, who was buried at Upchurch; and Thomas, the youngest, father of Sir Francis, the first baronet. It is also to be inferred, since most of them were born upon the water, that the hulk was the family home for several years; so that we may picture with certainty the boyhood of the great sailor and see how the seeds were sown that brought forth so exuberantly.

It must have been a life by its nature almost amphibious, where the old Navy hulks were like playfellows and the river a taskmaster to be learned and humoured. We can see him, the eldest and ringleader of a band of urchins as adventurous as himself, growing always more familiar with the forces that were to be his servants, till the rushing tideways, the intricate channels, the treacherous banks, and the shifting winds that were the surroundings of his home had no dangers or secrets he had not mastered. We can see him in his very pastimes acquiring that confident familiarity, that alert intuition, which are only to be stored up in boyhood and are the soul of seamanship; and we understand how he laid the foundations of a power which enabled him to carry out the great naval revolution, and make of maritime warfare a sailor's art.

Of education he must have had the elements from his father. It never at least showed any mark of neglect; and for the rest there was the Bible on his father's knees,

which for such men was then the fountain of all wisdom.
As we read the old man's will we can almost see the
volume, dog-eared and thumbed and loose in the binding
with constant use. 'Remember,' he wrote, addressing his
youngest son, 'remember my wish to be new set in the
beginning of the Romans, and so trim the book and keep
in bosom and feed upon. Make much of the Bible, that
I do here send thee with all the rest of my godly books.'
We cannot doubt that Francis received the same instruction, nor how it was he learned where to look when he
would know right from wrong. We can see the making
of the man in whose hatred of Spaniard and Papist there
was always a sweetening of the love of God, in whose
most high-handed and least defensible exploits there
sounds a note of piety that rings sincere, and with whose
moods of most reckless daring was always mixed some
sober calculation and something of a child-like faith
that Heaven was listening to his prayers.

How long Francis was subject to the influences of his
home is again a matter of inference, but certainly it must
have been long enough to leave a lasting impression
upon his character. The next ray of light is from
Camden. He tells us that Edmund Drake 'by reason of
his poverty put his son to the master of a bark, which he
used to coast along the shore, and sometimes to carry
merchandise into Zeeland and France.' If the Navy prayer
reader, the client of Lord Russell and kinsman of Hawkins,
was reduced to apprenticing his eldest son to the skipper
of a Channel coaster, it could only have been because
his influential friends were in disgrace and unable to
assist him. We must conclude then that young Francis's
apprenticeship began not only after Edward's death, but
after the failure of Wyatt's rising had exposed the Protestant party to a relentless persecution. In all probability, therefore, about the age of nine or ten he was in the
midst of one of the most violent religious movements this
country has ever seen. The news was that Mary meant
to marry the Prince of Spain, and the new faith, the very

independence of England, seemed at stake. Every principle
that underlay the English Reformation was in peril. So
clear was the issue, so intense the party feeling, that
children forgot their games to play at politics. They snow-
balled the suite of the Spanish Ambassador, they fought
mock combats between Wyatt and the Prince of Spain,
and once were barely prevented from hanging the lad
who played the part of Philip.[1] It was in Rochester
Castle that Wyatt made his headquarters ; it was at
Rochester bridge he had his first encounter with the
queen's troops and drove them back on London. It was
Wynter's squadron in the Medway that supplied him
secretly with guns and ammunition, and it was the
queen's ships in Gillingham Reach that the insurgents
seized and openly spoiled of their warlike stores. These
scenes may well have been Drake's earliest memories of
public affairs, and his next the gibbets on which men
he had perhaps known were swinging. In Kent alone
twenty-two of Wyatt's followers were hanged. The
Russells were found to have been in correspondence with
him ; Edmund Drake can hardly have been guiltless. At
any rate we may be sure he was not allowed to retain
his post; and in the bottom of his fortunes, a marked
man and probably penniless, it is easy to understand how
gladly he clutched at any opening for his son.

In his new situation, as Fuller says, the boy 'under-
went a hard service.' Indeed the roughness of an
apprentice's life on board a Channel coaster in those days
must have been something we can hardly conceive now.
And yet he might have fared worse. The school of seamanship in which he found himself, if severe, was sound
and he availed himself of his chances to the utmost. Nor
was it without reward. The promise he showed entirely
won the skipper's heart. 'The youth,' says Camden,
'being painful and diligent, so pleased the old man by his
industry, that, being a bachelor, at his death he bequeathed
his bark unto him by will and testament.' With the

[1] De Noailles, *Ambassades*, iii. 128. March 12, 1553.

accession of Elizabeth fortune smiled again on the father too. As the reformed religion was quietly re-established, it proved not too easy to find adequate ministers to serve the vacant churches. Edmund Drake was certainly not below the average of the class of men from whom the new clergy were chosen, and there is nothing surprising in finding him taking orders and getting preferment. In January 1561 he was inducted to the Vicarage of Upchurch, a lonely parish down on the Medway marshes with a fine church and a decent stipend. So here was the family re-established in respectability and their sufferings for religion were at an end.[1]

Such then was Francis's boyhood as fully as we can see it by the few rays of light that have reached us, a boyhood by no means spent, as it has often been pictured, in dreams of the West and the fables of the New World. After the first start of wonder, the discoveries of Columbus and the conquests of Cortez had made but little impression on the English mind. Since William Hawkins came home the last time from Brazil, little or nothing had been done to the westward.[2] Even when in Edward's last days Cabot had succeeded in rousing the London merchants, it was to a venture eastwards to find Cathay that their energy was directed, and not to America. All through Mary's reign and the first years of Elizabeth the tide of enterprise continued to flow the same way. It was from the Thames that the successive expeditions sailed, and if young Drake had dreams they were more likely to have been of Muscovy and Cathay. But born and bred as he was, and by his calling brought into contact with Alva's inhuman persecutions across the sea, and himself of the party that was suffering in Mary's fires at home, it is more natural to conceive of his youthful ardour being spent in the formation of a fanatic and

---

[1] For authorities and further details of Drake's family and early years see Appendix A.
[2] The only other voyage which Hakluyt could hear of was that of Robert Reniger or Rennyger about 1540; *Hawkins' Voyages* (Hakluyt Soc.), p. 4.

lasting antipathy to the Church of Rome. Far from any thoughts of the golden West, the most adventurous and capable of our Protestant seamen—gentle and simple alike—were fiercely preoccupied with reprisals upon their Catholic enemies, and there is no reason to think that Drake was different from the rest. The exploits of the pirates were in everyone's mouth, the cruelties of Catholic officers ashore were almost outdone by the savage retribution of Protestant rovers at sea, and trading as he did to Zeeland and France, Drake was in the midst of it, till with the restoration of his father's fortune a change came in his own.

CHAPTER II

JOHN HAWKINS

IN tracing the causes which led to the rupture of our ancient friendship with Spain and the House of Burgundy, we perceive three great streams of national sentiment, which, gathering volume as they flowed, at length joined in one irresistible flood and swept the country into war.

Hitherto the story of Drake's life has led beside but one of them—the most violent of the three—the stream of religious passion. Until recent times it was generally regarded as the one great determining force of the situation, and the Elizabethan war lived in the popular mind as a war of religion. Lately the tendency has been to minimise its theological aspect and to make it appear as mainly political. But, however laudable the desire of historians to remove by this means the bitterness with which the long struggle impregnated the national sentiment, however expedient it may be to obliterate the last traces of the old animosity between men of Protestant and of Catholic proclivities, such a representation of the spirit in which the great war was waged cannot be made without sacrifice of historic truth. As with the Great Rebellion, the more deeply research is carried the clearer grows the religious character of the upheaval, so is it impossible to conceal the passion which underlay the Elizabethan war. In England contemporary popular literature is full of Antichrist and the idolatry of his followers, of execration of the Mass, and cries for vengeance upon the Inquisition. In Spain the ballad writers sung of nothing but a holy strife of Christians against the Lutherans who had declared war upon God's Church. For the mass of the people of both sides it was a new crusade.[1]

On the other hand, to represent the struggle as purely religious would be almost as wrong as to conceive it as purely political. The truth is, its causes were threefold, each having its special influence on the three great classes of the State. For the people it was mainly religious, for the Government it was mainly political, for the merchants it was mainly commercial. Each class no doubt was more or less conscious of all three motives for its attitude; but for the people it was a struggle of the Reformation against the Papacy, for the statesmen it was a defence of the new idea of British nationality against the idea of a dominant Spanish Empire, and for the merchants it was an aggressive determination to break down the barriers with which Spanish policy sought to inclose the New World and to shut the way to the Indies. It was the last movement, perhaps, which was really the most actively important of the three. It was the aggressive policy of our commerce which finally made war inevitable, and it was that too which furnished the men and the means for carrying it on. But for the blows it gave to Spanish finance Parma must have completed the reduction of the Low Countries, and with the Low Countries reduced Philip could easily have forgiven England her heresy. For the incorporation of the kingdom into his system he could well have been willing to wait till it came, as so much else had come to his house, by the peaceful operation of dynastic causes. But the intrusion of foreigners and heretic foreigners into his Indies he could not endure. Whether they came for honest trade or for piracy, it was all one to him, and with a true instinct for the insidious danger, he used from the first every means in his power to repel the fatal movement.

It is with this, the latest born of the tendencies that

[1] See especially Lope de Vega's *Dragontea* and the pieces collected by Captain Duro in his *Armada Invencible*.

made for war, that we must now deal. For as the track of Drake's boyhood carried us along the flood of religious passion, so the study of his youth launches us upon the more silent but no less deep and powerful flow of an aggressive and expanding commerce in search of new markets.

The old channels of English sea-borne trade had led mainly to Holland and Spain: even the Mediterranean was as yet but seldom penetrated, and with these openings our commerce had long been satisfied. With the awakening of Tudor times came a new spirit of enterprise. Merchants began to feel discontented 'with the short voyages commonly then made to the known coasts of Europe.' The elder William Hawkins had ventured to break the old traditions with his famous voyages to the Guinea Coast and Brazil, and others followed from time to time in his steps, at least as far as Guinea, but it was not till the reign of Edward VI. that the new force began seriously to show itself. The obstacles in the way were enormous. To the North and East the road was barred by the gigantic monopoly of the Hansa; to the South and West by the Spaniards and the Portuguese taking their stand upon the Papal Bulls of Partition, which had apportioned the new worlds between them. In face of the difficulty two schools of opinion seem to have formed themselves. The one more peaceful, though none the less adventurous, was in favour of seeking new outlets in the undiscovered and unappropriated parts of the earth; while the other, more unruly, inclined to disputing the new monopolies. The earliest outcome of the first was Sir John Willoughby's ill-fated attempt to reach Cathay by the North East, and so on this side the new movement continued for a while to be occupied in genuine voyages of discovery, until here too the growing forces of necessity began to confound the two schools, and under such men as Chancellor and Jenkinson exploration gave place to a fight with monopoly. How the northern barriers broke under the pressure is the story not only of our first Arctic martyrs, but also of how, with our help and countenance, Russia became a European Power and first made herself felt in Central Asia; a story beyond measure romantic, and one which every child would know had it not been overshadowed by what happened in the West and South.

It was in 1553 that Willoughby sailed, and the same year there started for the Guinea Coast the first English expedition that tried to dispute the Portuguese claim to treat the African Seas as their own. When the discoveries of the Spaniards in the West threatened to bring them in conflict with the Portuguese in the East, the Pope had assigned to each its sphere of influence on each side of a line drawn vaguely between the 41st and 44th meridian west of Greenwich. Under this award Portugal claimed the Coast of Brazil, the East Indies, and all of Africa that lay to the South of the Canaries, and Spain the rest of America and everything else to the westward of the line of partition. It was a claim that commerce, and above all Protestant commerce, was little likely to recognise; and in spite of all the Portuguese could do by violence or artifice, English vessels continued to penetrate their sphere and trade upon the Guinea Coasts. The Portuguese affected to confound them with the French corsairs who infested those waters, and to treat them as pirates. For this there was no shadow of ground beyond the Pope's award. The men who sent them out were the merchant princes of London, with Sir William Garrard at their head, a man who in 1556 was Lord Mayor and who continued to be one of Cecil's most trusted advisers and agents in the financial operations of the Government. But, bold and persistent as he and his fellows were in their determination to expand the area of English commerce, as yet they had not ventured into the Spanish sphere. Spain was too powerful, trade to the Netherlands and the Peninsular ports too valuable to be risked, the old tradition of commercial friendship with the House of Burgundy perhaps too strong. Sooner or later of course it was bound to come, but it was Drake's new master who first tempted them to take the daring step.

This man was John Hawkins, old William's younger son. Since their father's death in 1555 the two brothers had been following steadily the traditions of the house, trading as far as the Canaries, and with so much success that within a year or so of Elizabeth's accession John Hawkins was thought a good enough match for the daughter of Benjamin Gonson, Treasurer of the Navy.[1] For his father-in-law's ear the young bridegroom had a portentous secret. 'Having made divers voyages,' says Hakluyt, 'to the Isles of the Canaries, and there by his good and upright dealing being grown in love and favour with the people, he informed himself among them by diligent inquisition of the state of the West India: whereof he had received some knowledge by the instructions of his father: but increased the same by the advertisements and report of that people. And being amongst other particulars assured that negroes were very good merchandise in Hispaniola; and that store of negroes might easily be had on the Coast of Guinea, he resolved with himself to make trial thereof.'

The slave trade was no new thing. Already it was half a century old, and as early as 1517 it had received the sanction of Charles V. Far from being stigmatised as it is now, it had been favourably regarded even by the most philanthropic and far-sighted Spanish colonists as a means of stopping the process of extermination with which forced labour was overwhelming the American Indians. The saintly Las Casas himself, 'the Protector of the Indians,' had given it his support, though he lived to acknowledge his mistake. Enormous numbers had already been imported, and to stop the abuses, which had shocked

---

[1] His position is further evidenced by an unrecorded incident in his early career. 'At the last peace with France,' wrote his son Richard in 1600, 'when my father being prisoner was forced afterwards to compound for his ransom, and had paid 10,000 crowns had he not broken prison and escaped.' *Domestic Cal.* January 2, 1600.

the tender-hearted missionary, the traffic had been subjected to strict regulations. A high duty had been placed on every negro imported, and no one was allowed to engage in the trade without first obtaining a costly licence from the king. In 1551 no fewer than 17,000 of these licences were offered for sale, and in 1553 a monopoly for seven years had been granted to one Fernando Ochoa to import 23,000 slaves. The result was that negroes became very good merchandise indeed, and Hawkins could not be expected to see the immorality of the commerce. The Hawkinses were as true Reformation men as the Drakes, and the Bible was their guide. In its pages he could find no note of warning, and the reasons which had convinced the missionary were enough to persuade the sailor.

As for the temptation, it came in a well-timed hour. The Portuguese had established a fort at Elmina on the Gold Coast, and stationed galleys there to protect their mines from pirates and to drive off intruding rivals. Hostilities were constantly occurring between the Portuguese and foreign traders trafficking along the coast for gold dust. Friendly natives began to offer sites for rival stations. In 1556 an expedition had sailed from London to pursue the idea, and had obtained a definite proposal from a native chief to establish a fort at Benin. So roughly, however, had the Portuguese guard ships handled a combined squadron which the English formed with some French traders, that nothing as yet had come of it. In 1561, however, Gonson, in partnership with Sir William Garrard and the famous Captain William Wynter, Master of the Naval Ordnance, had formed a syndicate to send out a stronger expedition to establish a factory in spite of the Portuguese opposition. The queen herself, perhaps, was a shareholder; at all events she lent a ship from the Navy called the 'Minion,' and all promised well.[1]

[1] In the *Hawkins' Voyages* the 'Minion' is always spoken of as a Queen's ship, and from Hakluyt's report of the meeting at Garrard's house in 1564 it appears she was to be refitted 'at the Queen's Majesty's charges.' It is clear from her captain's complaint of the rottenness of 'water-works and footings' that she was an old ship (see Lock to Guinea

The voyage, however, was a failure. The 'Minion' was not too seaworthy, and having encountered bad weather the commander of the expedition did not consider it safe to proceed, and he returned. Some soreness seems to have been felt at his conduct, and the syndicate was broken up.

In the following year the attempt was renewed, but neither Gonson nor Wynter had any share in it. In their place appear the names of two other leading merchants and aldermen—Sir William Chester, who had been Lord Mayor the previous year, and Mr. (afterwards Sir) Thomas Lodge, a Governor of the Muscovy Company. Why Gonson and Wynter withdrew we cannot tell for certain; but there is little doubt that they had been listening to Hawkins. They were now probably unwilling to stop at establishing a fort at Benin or to confine themselves to the old gold-dust trade. Their real desire was to take up Hawkins's project and with a cargo of negroes collected on the Guinea Coast to push their operations across the Atlantic into the Spanish sphere. The boldness of the innovation is difficult for us thoroughly to appreciate. To dispute the claims of Portugal was one thing; to challenge the monopoly of Spain was another; and if the Navy men had found it impossible to tempt old-fashioned merchants to so dangerous a venture, it was only to be expected. In Alderman Lionel Ducket, however, another city magnate, and in Garrard's new partner, Lodge, they found a more adventurous spirit, and with their help they were able successfully to set on foot the voyage upon which Hawkins was bent. Everything was done on a very modest scale. Three small private vessels, the biggest but 120 tons, were

Merchants, in *Hakluyt*). The old 'Minion,' 1523, had been rebuilt as a 300-ton ship about 1536 (*Oppenheim*, i. 50). She is not, however, mentioned in the 'Official Navy List' of March 24, 1559 ('Book of Sea Causes,' *State Papers Domestic*, Elizabeth, iii. 44), nor in any published list of the two previous reigns. Still she must have been a Navy ship; for in the rough 'List of Her Highnesses Ships,' dated February 20, 1559 (*ibid.* ii. 30), there is a note in Cecil's hand thus: '300 tons, the "Minion"—given to Sir Thomas ———' (?) [perhaps Lodge, but the word is illegible]: and she reappears in the Lists the following year (*Oppenheim*, i. 120).

all that could be provided, and, with this insignificant squadron and a stock of English goods, in October 1562 Hawkins sailed to open the great commercial struggle that ended with the downfall of Spain.

His first point was Teneriffe. There he had formed close relations with a merchant called Pedro de Ponte, who was more than suspected of having an interest in the enterprise, if not of being its actual originator.[1] This man had in readiness a Spanish pilot for the West Indies; and having taken him on board, Hawkins proceeded to Sierra Leone, where partly by the sword and partly by other means he got into his possession some three hundred negroes. With this precious cargo his pilot brought him across the Atlantic to Hispaniola, and at different ports in the island he got rid of all his English goods and most of his slaves, 'standing always upon his guard' and 'trusting the Spaniards no further than that by his own strength he was able to master them.' Commercially the voyage was an unheard-of success. So large were his receipts that he had to charter two extra vessels to carry home the proceeds of his trading. These, in bold assertion of the lawfulness of his proceedings, he sent direct to Spain for sale, and with the rest he returned to England in triumph in September of the following year.

From the details set forth it will be seen that the undertaking was essentially commercial, based on the freedom of the high seas and the reciprocal rights of trade enjoyed by Spaniards and Englishmen in each other's ports, in virtue of the old commercial treaties between England and the House of Burgundy.[2] No law had been

---

[1] 'De Silva to the King,' July 21 and 26, 1567, *Spanish Cal.*; cf. *Hawkins' Voyages* (Hakluyt Soc.), p. 11.

[2] The last formal treaty had been made in 1495, between Henry VII. and Philip of Burgundy, the father of Charles V., and although the two crowns had been at war since then, it was generally regarded and acted upon as still subsisting. Clauses x.-xiii. provide for free intercourse reciprocally. English merchants are to have free right to trade in armed ships, not only to Burgundian ports, but in all 'the countries, lands, and dominions of the foresaid Lord Archduke, and also with the ports and coasts under

VOL. I. G

broken, except a municipal restrictive law of Spain, which, as the English claimed, was a breach of their treaty rights. But the Spanish Government would not so regard it. Into the midst of the sensation Hawkins's success was causing at home, both in court and city, broke the news that the two cargoes sent to Spain had been seized. In vain the Adventurers protested. Though two of the highest officers in the Navy were engaged, though Lodge was now Lord Mayor, no redress could be obtained. When they pleaded that they had left in Hispaniola a number of negroes to cover any lawful duty the king might demand, the negroes too were confiscated. When they argued that they had done their trade by the special licence of the king's officers, orders went out to the Indies forbidding trade with English vessels on any pretence whatever. It was clear that Spain, profiting by the experience of the Portuguese, meant to take the matter in hand vigorously and nip the new growth in the bud. But Hawkins was now too big a man and the support his unprecedented success had won too powerful to be easily thwarted, and, undaunted by their failure to obtain some recognition of their claims, the Adventurers resolved to assert them once more.

In the meantime, while his kinsman was adventuring so far and high, it was not likely young Drake could sit quiet as he was. 'He soon grew weary of his bark,' says Fuller, 'which would scarce go alone but as it crept along the shore,' and it would seem that about this time he sold it, and joined the rising fortunes of his cousin. Stowe explicitly states that he was brought up under his kinsman, Sir John Hawkins, and that, when he was eighteen years of age—that is, by Stowe's date about the year 1564—he was made purser or third officer of a ship to Biscay, meaning the north-east coast of Spain. The implication is that this vessel was one of the Hawkins Brothers' fleet, and that when John's connection with the Thames naturally threw the two kinsmen together again, he, like

the authority of the said Lord the Archduke.' The ratification in 1499 was for each party's heirs and successors.

the old skipper, had recognised the lad's promise and taken him into his service.

Thus early was Drake lifted into touch with the making of Elizabethan history. Hawkins now stood at the head of the English mercantile marine, a known public character in court and city alike. Who were the actual subscribers to the new venture is not entirely ascertained. The practice of the time in forming these 'Companies of Merchant Adventurers,' as they were called, was for a small number of capitalists, usually about five, to make themselves responsible for—or, as we now say, to underwrite—definite proportions of the capital required, which they placed among their friends in shares as high as 100*l.* each, a sum equal to about 800*l.* now. The original partners formed the directorate of the Company, with power to make calls, and each, it would seem, was severally responsible to and for his sub-partners. The names of the original syndicate were the only ones that appeared officially, and this is why it is always so difficult to find out who were at their backs. In this case the queen may have been one of the sub-partners, for the flagship or 'admiral' of the squadron was provided from the Navy. As the larger merchant ships of the sixteenth century took naturally to fighting in war time, so during intervals of peace it was the custom all over Europe to make ships of war earn their tar and tallow in commerce. The best vessels, however, were seldom thus risked. The ship in question—called the 'Jesus of Lubeck'—was one which Henry VIII. had bought for his Navy from the men of Lubeck. She was of 700 tons, and no doubt had once been a fine ship, but in the Departmental Report of 1558 she was classed 'as much worn, and of no continuance and not worth repair,' and was recommended to be sold towards the cost 'of the new ships of better service.'[1] Estimates, however, were given for her repair, and the work would seem to have been carried out, for she appears in the Navy List of 1565. Some years later she was

[1] 'Book of Sea Causes,' *S. P. Dom. Eliz.* iii. 44.

valued at 4,000*l*., so that the queen must have been one of the largest shareholders. Others were found in the actual ranks of the Council, as she herself afterwards admitted to De Silva, the Spanish Ambassador. One of them was Sir William Herbert, the ablest soldier in the kingdom, who, thanks to his genius for fishing in troubled waters, was now Earl of Pembroke and a millionaire; but who were the other Councillors interested we do not know. Some one offered Cecil himself a share, but he refused, having, as he told the ambassador, no liking for such undertakings.[1]

Here we have the first note of the great minister's consistent antipathy to the new school of adventure. Till war was inevitable he set his face rigidly against a policy which he believed to be unnecessary to the development of the country and fraught with serious danger, as indeed it was; and never once, no matter how great the provocation or inducement, could he be tempted to stain his fingers with a venture that was not absolutely above suspicion. Still he took no active steps to stand in the way. As yet Hawkins had not attained the recognised position of a factor in foreign politics. The expedition was allowed to go quietly forward, and at the same time sailed the Garrard company's fleet for Guinea with the 'Minion' at its head.

After touching at Teneriffe in order to confer with his friend Pedro de Ponte, 'who gave him as gentle entertainment as if he had been his brother,' Hawkins proceeded down the west coast of Africa. Serious difficulties were encountered, and particularly those which the 'Minion's' men made for him by warning the natives; for to the gold-dust traders his slave catching operations were objectionable, as disturbing the coast and alienating friendly chiefs. Still in spite of them he soon filled up with negroes, and having escaped, as he believed by a special dispensation of Providence, a trap set for him by the Portuguese, he laid his course for the West. As for the 'Minion,' she was caught by the galleys at Elmina and

[1] 'De Silva to the King,' *Spanish Cal.* Oct. 11 and Nov. 4, 1566.

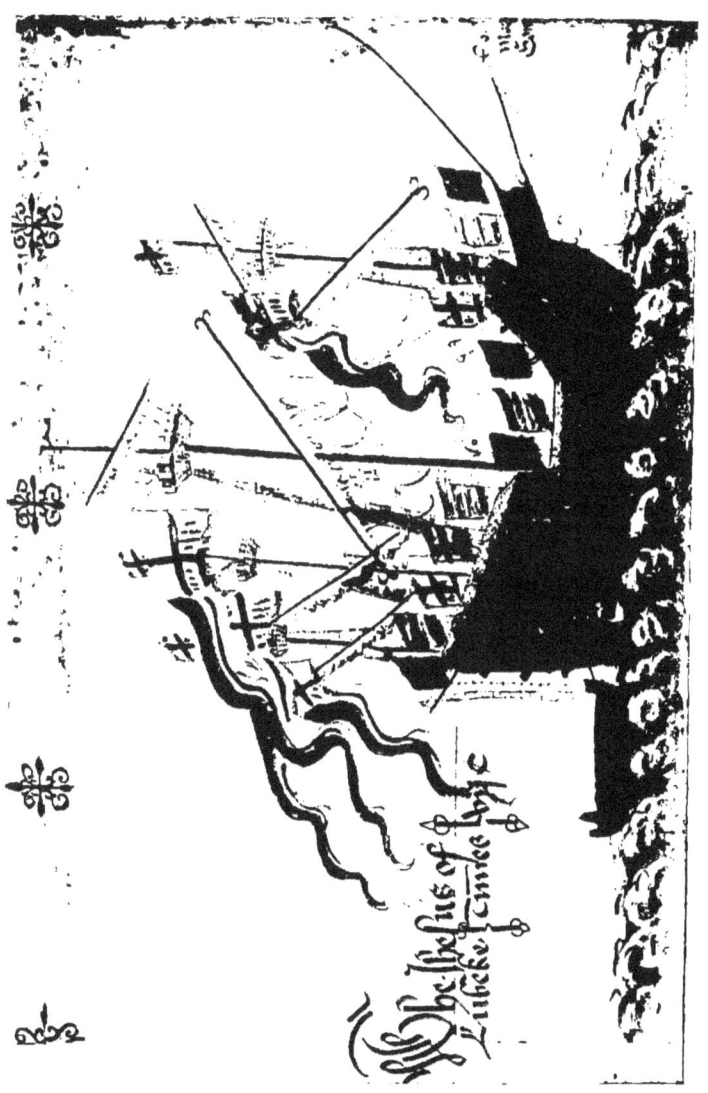

THE GREAT-SHIP 'JESUS OF LUBECK.'
Reduced from Anthony's First Roll (Magdalene College, Cambridge).

roughly handled; her captain too was taken prisoner, and she had to return discomfited.

Across the Atlantic Hawkins found things almost as bad. Avoiding Hispaniola, he this time tried Tierra Firme, the province which lay along the north coast of South America from the Orinoco to Darien. This was the famous Spanish Main of our sailors' speech, round which they were soon to hang so much of the romance of lawless daring and the glitter of untold booty that the name still tingles in the ear with a note of wild music. Already its reputation had been begun by the French privateers, who had found their way thither during the incessant wars between France and Spain and the unstable peaces that hardly intervened; and there was scarcely a settlement on the coast that had not already been plundered at their hands. For Hawkins as yet it was virgin ground, but no sooner was his presence reported to Hispaniola than the Viceroy reissued the most stringent orders against dealing with him. Everywhere he touched traffic was refused. It was a situation for which he was probably prepared, and at a place called Borburata, in the Golfo Triste, he resolved to play the part he had studied.[1]

The position was complicated by the Spaniards' experience of the methods of French corsairs, and the richer settlers had fled to the hills at his approach. For them every strange flag in those seas was a pirate, and they could never quite believe that Hawkins's sole object was fair trade. Further there was the opposite consideration, as Hawkins well knew, that they were itching to buy what he had to sell. The Spanish colonial policy, which made all trade with the Indies little better than a royal monopoly, had so highly enhanced the price not only of slaves, but of all European goods, that the temptation to welcome a

[1] Borburata, which is very variously spelt, was long ago superseded by Puerto Cabello. The *ensenada* or creek where it stood, and which still bears its name, is some four or five leagues to the eastward of the present port. See Blaeu's *Atlas Major*, 1662, vol. ii. f. 89; Lopez's *Atlas*, vol. iii. Madrid, 1736. It was known among the English seamen as 'Burborough Water.'

smuggler was almost irresistible. Still trade was denied, and Hawkins stated his case. He was there, said he, as captain of one of the Queen of England's ships and was no pirate, nor did he intend any dishonour to their prince, unless he were provoked to it by their too rigorous dealing with him. All he wanted was honest trade, which would redound to their profit as much as to his, and since their respective sovereigns were in amity there was no reason why their subjects should not have free traffic together. They still declined, and he offered them a still better excuse for yielding. He vowed he had been driven there from Guinea by stress of weather, and he and his troops were in need of many things, and that unless they would consent to buy so much of him as would enable him to supply his necessities it would show a special discourtesy to his royal mistress which their prince would resent. Still it was not till he actually landed a hundred men and began to move on the town that the Governor professed himself convinced. The only trouble was about the slave duty. Hawkins declared the king's special custom an unconscionable exaction, but offered to pay an *ad valorem* duty of $7\frac{1}{2}$ per cent., the ordinary custom for wares in all Spanish ports. To this too the Governor, after some demur, consented, and Hawkins, having received his licence, proceeded to trade, to everyone's satisfaction. On the completion of his business he demanded and obtained a certificate of good behaviour; and so continued his way westward. At the island of Curaçao no objection was raised and a large purchase of hides was made. At Borburata the Governor had given him in payment for some of his goods a bill on the Treasurer of the Indies at Rio de la Hacha. Thither he now proceeded, but only to find the special orders of the Viceroy against dealing with him already arrived, and the Treasurer bent on carrying them out. In vain he showed his certificate and presented his bill; in vain he repeated his arguments; all were unavailing till again he landed troops to enforce them. Some show of resistance was

made, but at the first sign of a charge the Treasurer's
men all ran away and Hawkins obtained his licence.
How far the official opposition was real is doubtful.
Spaniards were not in the habit of running away, and De
Silva certainly more than suspected the whole thing was
arranged as an excuse for non-compliance with the unwelcome prohibition of the Viceroy. Still it would seem
that the Treasurer did contemplate a treacherous attack
on the Englishmen, while trade was quietly going on.
This, however, was frustrated and ignored, and again
Hawkins departed with a certificate of good behaviour.
What was left of the summer was spent in improving his
knowledge of the Caribbean Sea and the coast of Florida,
where he relieved the new French colony, and so in the
autumn he returned to England with 60 per cent. profit
for himself and his owners.

So great a success could not be kept quiet, and
Hawkins became the hero of the hour. But now a new
actor was on the scene. Shortly before he sailed diplomatic relations had been resumed with Spain, and
De Silva, the new ambassador, at once began warning his
master of what had been going on and pointing out the
necessity of taking action to stop its repetition. In the
comparative innocence of the Adventurers' intentions he
had no faith. 'I do not believe,' he wrote, 'that a ship
would be safe, if they were strong enough to take it;' and
he was sure they had waited in the Indies a fortnight for
the sailing of the Plate fleet in hopes of capturing a ship.

Here for the first time we come in contact with the
abiding bugbear of the Spanish Government. As all
Europe had come to recognise, it was upon the American
trade that the whole machinery of Spanish policy depended for its motive power, and it was in what were
known in England as the 'Plate fleets' that this trade
was conducted. Since the early days of the century, when
the importance of the American colonies began fully to be
appreciated, the trade had been a government monopoly,
and its management had been delegated to a semi-official

department seated at Seville, the great Atlantic port. It was a kind of chamber of commerce, with a certain resemblance to our India House, and was known as the *Casa de Contractacion* or ' Commerce House.' In exercise of its monopoly this department regularly fitted out two fleets for the Indies. One which sailed annually was known as the 'Fleet or *flota* of New Spain,' and traded to Mexico. Once the more important of the two, it had been eclipsed by the second, which since 1564 had also sailed every year and was known as the *flota* of Tierra Firme. Originally intended, as its name implies, for the trade of the Spanish Main or north coast of South America, its real importance since the discovery of the Potosi mines was that it was also the fleet of Peru. For safety it had become the custom for both fleets, as a rule, to sail in company as far as Hispaniola, where they made their landfall. Here the Mexico fleet, after detaching the vessels bound for San Domingo and Puerto Rico, continued its way alone to San Juan de Ulua, the port of the city of Mexico; while that of the Spanish Main made for Cartagena, the capital of the Province. On the homeward voyage the latter fleet continued its way westward to call at Nombre de Dios, the Atlantic port of the Isthmus whither the Peruvian treasure was brought overland from Panama. Having there taken on board the precious cargo, it proceeded northward through the Yucatan Channel to Havana, where if so ordered from Spain it joined hands with the homeward bound Mexico fleet, and so both 'disembogued' together by the New Bahamas Channel.

It was on the protection of these two fleets, and especially during their homeward voyage, that the Spaniards began to feel their whole naval energy was being dissipated. At first neither fleet had had any kind of escort or protection beyond the few guns that every ship was supposed officially to carry; but during the interminable French wars of Charles V. the hardy seamen of Brittany, Rochelle, and Normandy had found out their enemy's

weak point, and in their smart little galleons had played
havoc with the trade. With experience their daring
increased. Not content with lying in wait at Cape St.
Vincent, or even at the Azores, the two successive
rendez-vous of the homeward bound fleets, they began to
reach out across the Atlantic and to push their depredations into the heart of the defenceless Spanish Indies.
Here their exploits grew yearly more alarming, till in 1553
a French corsair with but a single ship and eighty men,
by allying himself with escaped negroes, succeeded in
sacking the capital, and the four chief settlements of the
Spanish Main, as well as Santiago de Cuba, and finally
Havana itself, though it had at the time 1,200 inhabitants.
So at least we learn from a minute of the famous Pero
Menendez de Aviles, the greatest oceanic captain of his
time, who has come recently to be regarded in Spain as
perhaps the greatest maritime genius the country ever
produced.[1] To his energy were due the first real steps to
protect the trade. In 1555 he was serving in command
of the fleets with a small 'armada' or fighting squadron
of six sail, and the remainder of his life was one long and
thankless struggle against the growing power of the
corsairs. For this purpose he provided at his own
cost three galleons as a permanent escort, and in 1561
had so far established his position that he applied for the
official rank of Captain General of the Indian Trade.
Under his influence the new policy continued to gather
strength, and it was just as Menendez's energy was
beginning to bear fruit in checking the French operations
that the English appeared upon the scene. It was but
natural, then, that the Spaniards should see in Hawkins's
intrusion a new recruit for the corsair ranks. Already
Englishmen had been found acting with the French, and
now that their restlessness was taking the form of semi-
official expeditions the matter was growing very serious.

[1] See his minute on preventing the colonisation of Florida by foreigners.
Ruidiaz y Canovia, *La Conquista de la Florida*, vol. ii. His life and
correspondence are contained in the same work.

By this time, as the Venetian ambassadors reported, the English had earned themselves a reputation for skill and hard fighting upon the high seas above all their neighbours, and there can be no doubt that the Spanish Government, with the instinct of self-preservation and a profound disbelief in the integrity of 'Lutherans,' smelt a danger yet greater than that with which their infant sea power hardly sufficed to grapple.[1]

De Silva's remarks to the king, then, must have fallen on good ground, and if the ambassador's suspicions were unfounded, they were at least excusable. For the action he took upon them there is perhaps less to be said. Instead of making any official protest to the English Government, he proceeded, after the tortuous diplomatic method of the sixteenth century, to tamper with Hawkins's allegiance. With a view either of securing his services or of obtaining fuller information of his methods and intentions, he began asking him to dinner, flattering him, and sounding him as to his readiness to listen to offers from the King of Spain. Hawkins, whose diplomatic ability seems to have been as sound as his seamanship, was quite equal to the occasion. In order to blind the ambassador he professed himself dissatisfied with the recognition his services had met with and desirous of nothing so much as bringing his ships to serve with the King of Spain's galleys against the Turks. He protested he had had licence to trade from the colonial governors, showed the ambassador his certificates of good behaviour, and vowed he had never meant to do any wrong. He was being pressed, he said, to go out once more, but he never would again without the king's own licence.

Meanwhile a new expedition was being fitted out as secretly and quickly as might be. Its discovery severely shook the ambassador's confidence. He demanded what

---

[1] See *Correspondence and Minutes of Menendez*, *ubi supra*, and the documents calendared by Duro, *Armada Española*, ii. app. 8 and 9. Also *Galeones y flotas de las Indias* in the same author's *Disquisiciones Náuticas*, 1877, *La Mar descrita*, p. 165.

it meant, and Hawkins was ready with an explanation. He was preparing the ships, he said, for the King of Spain's service, and produced a complete plan of campaign against the Turks which so entirely convinced the Spaniard that he began to urge the king to make Hawkins a definite offer. It was not till the expedition was ready for sea and on the very eve of sailing that his eyes were opened, and in no pleasant mood at having been so duped, he demanded an immediate audience with the queen. Once admitted to her presence he began to complain of her subjects being permitted to break the laws of her friend and ally, and to upbraid her with the complicity of her Council. This she admitted, but vowed they never meant Hawkins to go to prohibited places, and that on his last return home she herself had refused to see him until she was assured he had been driven to the Indies by stress of weather and had not traded without licence. And why, she argued, should not her subjects trade if the French did? De Silva replied the French were pirates.

It was unhappily a moment when the Catholic combination which was forming round the Queen of Scots for Elizabeth's overthrow was assuming proportions too alarming for Spain to be given a new cause of offence, and to pacify the indignant diplomatist she called in Cecil and told him to summon Hawkins and Fenner, who was also on the eve of sailing for Guinea with another expedition, and examine them as to their intentions. For the time this satisfied the ambassador. He knew too well, as he told the king, what Cecil's views on the matter were to doubt he would do his best. Still the prohibition he demanded was not issued; he suspected he was being played with and protested again. He was told that there was a difficulty in getting the required order through the Council, some of the members being opposed to forbidding Englishmen going to the Indies so long as Spaniards had full liberty of English ports. But it was no time to risk an argument on so abstract a question, and in the last days of October an order was issued compelling both Fenner and Hawkins to give a heavy security that they would not go to the Indies.[1] Hawkins at once resolved not to sail at all. What became of the expedition is a mystery. De Silva always said that it sailed without Hawkins and returned richer than ever, but the only trace we have of English authority for any such venture is a chance mention in the narrative of Drake's early voyages of an expedition in which for the first time he saw the Indies. In the years 1565–6, we are told, he received wrongs at Rio de la Hacha with Captain Lovell.[2] Who this Lovell was is not discoverable. He may have been one of Hawkins's captains, who took his place on this occasion. If so, the date 1565–6 must be a mistake for the following year, and some colour exists for the supposition: for Stowe states that Drake in 1566–7 was in a voyage to Guinea. No certainty, however, is attainable, and all we can say is that some time between Hawkins's second and third voyages an expedition in which Drake was serving did go out to the West Indies, and that at Rio de la Hacha it fell a victim to some such treachery as the Treasurer had attempted upon Hawkins.

Fenner having, as it seems, no intention of going beyond Guinea proceeded on his voyage, but only to find the Portuguese as hostile and determined as the Spaniards. Everywhere he was treated as a pirate. At Santiago in the Cape Verde Islands he only escaped a night surprise from galleys by cutting his cables ; and at the Azores, while, as the narrator innocently relates, he was following a Portuguese vessel to see if she could spare him a cable, he was caught by a royal squadron consisting of a galleon of 400 tons and two caravels.[3] Fenner was alone in the 'Castle of Comfort,' and his consort far away to leeward. Three times they engaged him and three

[1] *S. P. Dom. Eliz.* xl. 99. The whole of these transactions are detailed in De Silva's despatches printed in *Spanish Cal.* s. d.
[2] 'Sir Francis Drake Revived,' Arber's *English Garner*, v. 494.
[3] The account in Hakluyt has 'Galleasse,' but internal evidence shows she was not an oared vessel. She was without doubt a galleon of the low-freeboard class which English sailors called a 'gallcasse.'

times he beat them off. On the following day the Portuguese commander, being joined by four other caravels, renewed the action.[1] It was now seven to one; yet so roughly did Fenner handle them that with nightfall they drew off and allowed him to escape. The success of the 'Castle of Comfort' seems to have been due to her overmastering fire, and the action is memorable not only as being the first appearance of the Fenners of Chichester on the scene, but also as the earliest revelation to English seamen of the power their superiority in gunnery was to give them.[2]

Though thwarted for the time, Hawkins was far from abandoning his ideas of commercial expansion, but the precise line in which his mind was working at this time is almost impossible to unravel from the subtlety of his proceedings. During May 1567 it began to leak out that Ducket and Garrard had joined forces and were secretly fitting out an expedition at Rochester in which two of her Majesty's ships were to be engaged. All kinds of reports as to its strength and objects got about, till De Silva took alarm and mentioned it to the queen. She assured him it was meant to go no further than Guinea, and that the Adventurers were under oath to avoid forbidden places. Whatever Hawkins's ideas may have been, from Garrard's adherence and Cecil's approval it would seem the Adventurers did really intend to leave America alone. Everything indeed pointed to a different destination.

[1] The caravel was a small fast sailing vessel much used in the West Coast trade and generally for ocean navigation by the Portuguese. The normal type was about 100 tons and upwards, single decked, with half-deck, square poop, and forecastle, and of high freeboard. It was rigged usually with four masts and bowsprit. The foremast bore two square-sails, the rest each a lateen. Its lines and rig made it one of the most weatherly vessels of its time. The authorities concerning it are collected by Jal, *Glossaire nautique, sub voce.* Though it used sweeps at times, it was not regarded as an oared vessel.

[2] In the action fought on the Guinea Coast in 1557 between the combined forces of the English and French gold-dust traders and the Portuguese, the former were quite out-matched both in gunnery and seamanship. (See the *Second Voyage of Master William Towerson* in Hakluyt.)

Some Portuguese, who were said to be Jewish refugees from the Inquisition, had been introduced to Wynter and had brought to him some mysterious scheme for obtaining great treasure from a place they knew of upon the African coast beyond the Portuguese mines at Elmina. Some such adventure had been already undertaken by some Frenchmen under a son of the famous Marshal Montluc, which had led to a violent conflict with the Portuguese at Madeira, and it was said that Wynter's friends were the same men who had prompted it.[1] They had now come to try their fortune in England, and the tale they had to tell proved sufficiently attractive to induce the Garrard-Ducket syndicate to take up their idea. The exact object in view remains a secret to this day. A settlement was certainly contemplated, and immediately after Fenner's return with the news of his ill treatment an estimate was prepared of arms and material necessary to erect a fort on the Guinea coast and to garrison it with fifty men.[2]

The ambassador took new alarm, but the queen and Cecil pacified him with fresh assurances that the ships were not intended for America, and he was inclined to believe that the connection with the Portuguese fugitives meant a voyage to the East Indies. For a time indeed he was persuaded that the object of the expedition was reprisals for the rough handling the Guinea traders had been meeting with in Portuguese waters, and sent a friendly warning to Lisbon. Continuing his inquiries, however, he obtained information that Pedro de Ponte was at the bottom of the scheme, and that he and Hawkins had arranged with the West Indian governors for pretending they dared not refuse to trade. On the top of this he saw the 'Jesus' and the 'Minion' brought round from Chatham to the Tower to take in arms from the Royal Arsenal, and

---

[1] The *Dictionnaire de Biographie Universelle* places this in 1568; but the incident is mentioned in De Silva's despatch to the king dated July 1567. *Spanish Cal.* 431.

[2] 'Estimates for Establishing a Fort,' &c., June 24, 1567. *S. P. Dom. Eliz.* xliii. 24. Fenner put into Southampton on the 6th.

once more he went to the queen. In answer to his protests she vowed the arms were only meant for protection against ill usage from French pirates and the Portuguese, and Cecil swore a great oath they were only going to Guinea. This, combined with fresh information he had that Laras, a Portuguese fort beyond Elmina, was the actual objective, went far to convince him the Government at least were sincere. So the preparations went forward; Hawkins, before leaving London, came to take a friendly farewell of him and to desire his service to the King of Spain; the squadron assembled at Plymouth; and the Portuguese pilots were sent down to be ready to embark at any moment.

Hawkins, however, knew too much not to be on the look-out for a new move from De Silva, and was evidently still anxious and mistrustful. One day in August a strong squadron under Spanish colours appeared in Plymouth Sound, and with flags flying bore up for the Catwater, where his vessels were riding. It was the fleet which the Duchess of Parma, Regent of the Netherlands, had sent out under the Flemish admiral De Vachen to meet Philip on his intended visit to Flanders. Elizabeth had issued orders for its honourable reception at any place it might visit; but by the custom of the seas De Vachen, on entering a friendly foreign port, should have struck his topsails and national colours. There can be no doubt his intentions were not hostile, but Hawkins was clearly alarmed, and as soon as the strangers hove within range he ordered the Castle batteries and his own ship to open fire, nor did he cease till De Vachen lowered his flag. To the Flemish admiral Hawkins justified his violence on the score of the breach of international courtesy, and it is always as an assertion of his Sovereign's honour that his spirited conduct has been admired; but when called upon by the Government to explain his behaviour, he rather insisted on his suspicion of their purpose and protested he 'greatly feared their warlike intentions.'[1]

[1] 'Hawkins to Cecil.' *S. P. Dom. Eliz.* xliv. 13, Sept. 28, 1597. Cf. *Observations of Sir R. Hawkins* (Hakluyt Soc. lvii. 113), where a full

By the Spaniards the incident was not forgotten, but for the present it went no further. Hawkins's defence was accepted with no more than a caution from Cecil, and nothing seemed to stand in the way of his immediate departure. News of his sailing was daily expected; when suddenly it was announced that the Portuguese pilots had disappeared and taken ship for France. De Silva thought the Portuguese ambassador to the French Court had enticed them away; others seemed to suspect a deep design of Hawkins, and it is not impossible they were right. No sooner was the desertion discovered than he wrote direct to the queen with the news, and declared that although the proposed enterprise could not take effect (which he thought God had provided for the best) he was ready to proceed and bring home a profit (with God's help) of 40,000 marks without offence to her friends or allies. 'It shall be no dishonour,' he wrote, 'with your Highness that your own servant and subject shall in such an extremity convert such an enterprise and turn it both to your Highness' honour and the benefit of the whole realm;' and so after insisting on the danger of disbanding the crews, he coolly begs leave to load negroes in Guinea and sell them in the West Indies.

The permission to convert the voyage was not refused, but whether Cecil was admitted to the secret we cannot tell: the balance of evidence admits of a suspicion that he was not. On learning the desertion of the Portuguese he had written a letter to Lord Clynton, the Lord High Admiral, explaining that it was now impossible to carry out the original design and telling him of a new voyage

---

account of the incident is given. Sir Richard's memory, however, had seriously failed him, and is not to be trusted for the details. From his mention of the 'Jesus' it is clear he was thinking of this occasion, but says the Spanish admiral was on his way to Flanders to fetch the 'Queen Donna Anne of Austria, last wife of Philip,' an event which did not occur till three years later, when the 'Jesus' had ceased to exist. The Spanish admiral's report of the affair is dated Sept. 23, 1567, N.S. (*Spanish Cal.* 442, p. 676).

upon which it had been decided to use Hawkins's fleet. Clynton in his answer, after referring to Hawkins's negligence in letting the Portuguese slip, says he is glad 'that order is taken that he proceed on the other voyage that Cecil writes of whereof some good may come, though not so profitable as the other'—an expression it seems strange he should use if Cecil had told him the enterprise was to be converted into a slaving voyage, since the last undertaking of the kind had given unprecedented returns.[1] It is possible, therefore, that 'the other voyage' which Burghley had in mind was not the voyage on which Hawkins finally proceeded. The surmise gains additional colour from a letter which Cecil wrote to Hawkins on the eve of his sailing. It was brought by Fitzwilliam the Admiral's most confidential agent, by whom he had sent up his letter to the queen and who presumably was also taking back the queen's answer. Cecil's letter is not extant, but its contents may be gathered from Hawkins's reply. It would seem to have been chiefly in the nature of a mild reprimand for letting the Portuguese slip and for firing upon the Spanish flag, and to have contained no reference to a slaving venture. 'I am warned,' Hawkins concludes after defending his conduct, 'to avoid damages to Spaniards and Flemings, by your Honour's letter, wherefore I most heartily thank you, though I meant no less beforehand. I know they hate me and yet without cause; for they are the better for me by great sums, and I the worse for them by 40,000 ducats. . . . I have always enjoyed the name of an orderly person and have always hated folly.'[2]

That Fitzwilliam brought down with Cecil's good advice the secret consent of the queen is hardly doubtful;

---

[1] *Hatfield MSS.* (Hist. MSS. Comm.) vol. i. p. 347, Sept. 30, 1567.
[2] 'Hawkins to Cecil, Sept. 28, 1567.' *S. P. Dom. Eliz.* xliv. 13. It is worth noting that a Spanish copy of this letter found its way into the Simancas Archives (see Froude, *Hist.* viii. 69 n), and it is of course quite possible it was intended for Spanish eyes, so as to serve as evidence that Hawkins's venture was not authorised by the Government.

for on October 2, 1567, without more ado, Hawkins set sail; and with him went Francis Drake, now twenty-two years of age,[1] burning like his master to win compensation for the wrongs he had suffered with Captain Lovell at Rio de la Hacha.

[1] Stowe's *Chron.* It is this definite figure that fixes 1545 as the most probable date of his birth.

CHAPTER III

SAN JUAN DE ULUA [1]

THE third voyage of Hawkins marks in the Elizabethan epoch a step that could never be retraced. 'When its end was known,' says Camden, 'the military and seafaring men all over England fretted and demanded war against the Spaniards.' From this point Drake's and his master's attitude towards Spain became one of irreconcilable hostility. How far that attitude was justified and how far the Spaniards were to blame for the action they took is only to be judged from a careful study of the voyage.

The squadron [2] comprised two great-ships of the Royal

---

[1] The spelling this word occurs in every possible variety—Lua, Ulloa, Loo, Ullua, &c. The modern form adopted by Captain Duro is Ulua. For the authorities for the whole voyage see *post*, App. C.

[2] The details were as follows:

H.M.S. 'Jesus of Lubeck,' 700 tons, 180 men, 22 guns in battery, 42 of secondary armament pieces. *General and Captain*—John Hawkins. *Master*—Robert Barrett. *Captain of the soldiers*—Captain Dudley.

H.M.S. 'Minion,' 300–350 tons. *Captain*—John Hampton. *Master*—John Garrett.

'William and John,' 150 tons. *Captain*—Thomas Bolton. *Master*—James Ranse or Raunce.

'Swallow,' 100 tons.

'Judith,' 50 tons. *Captain and Master*—Francis Drake.

'Angel,' 32 tons.

Mr. Froude, in his *English Seamen* (p. 49), says: 'The "Judith" was brought in by his (Hawkins's) young cousin Francis Drake, who was now to make his first appearance on the stage. . . Enough now to say he was a relation of Hawkins, the owner of a small smart sloop or brigantine, ambitious of a share in a stirring business.' The passage conveniently shows the way all his work on maritime and naval history should be regarded—as a brilliant impressionist picture, true and convincing in its breadth, but making no attempt at correctness of detail. Almost every statement in the above passage contains some slight deviation from the existing evidence.

Navy, the 'Jesus of Lubeck,' Captain Hawkins, and the 'Minion,' Captain Hampton; a private ship belonging to the Hawkins Brothers, called after them the 'William and John,' and three smaller vessels, the 'Swallow,' the 'Angel,' and the 'Judith,' the last being commanded by Drake. With its Admiral, Vice-Admiral, and Captain of Soldiers, it was armed, equipped, and organised in all respects like a naval squadron, and the complement it carried can have been little less than five hundred men, among whom were several gentlemen of good houses.[1] A love of the picaresque has tempted our maritime literature to give the Elizabethan captains the air of lawless and irresponsible corsairs. Enough has been said to show that Hawkins was never such a man, and least of all on this occasion. The representative of the London merchant princes, he was something of a merchant prince himself. In this venture his firm had embarked a sum equal to sixteen thousand pounds of our money; his personal effects and furniture on board the 'Jesus' were valued at a fifth of that sum; and throughout the voyage he kept the state of one of her Majesty's Admirals-at-the-Seas. That he came home quite without stain of technical piracy is too much to say, but whatever he did cannot be viewed as the outcome of a lawless spirit. In the position he held the worst that can be laid to his charge is a too violent vindication of the legitimate aspirations of English commerce. To him had been committed the assertion of the doctrine that to forbid the Spanish Indies to the commerce of a friendly nation was a breach of

It was not Drake's first appearance, he had already appeared at Rio de la Hacha; the 'Judith' is always described as a bark, and not as either a sloop, a class of vessel which did not then exist, or a brigantine, which then meant a small galley; the only statement we have as to the ownership makes it the property of Hawkins, that Drake owned it there is no evidence at all; and lastly when he joined he must have believed with the rest he was going to the Portuguese gold coast.

[1] De Silva's final report, which rather understates the tonnage of the ships, gives 600 to 700 as the number of the men. *S. P. Spain, Cal.* 1567, No. 440. Herrera gives 500. *Historia general . . . del Señor Rey don Felipe II. el Prudente*, I. lib. xv. cap. 18.

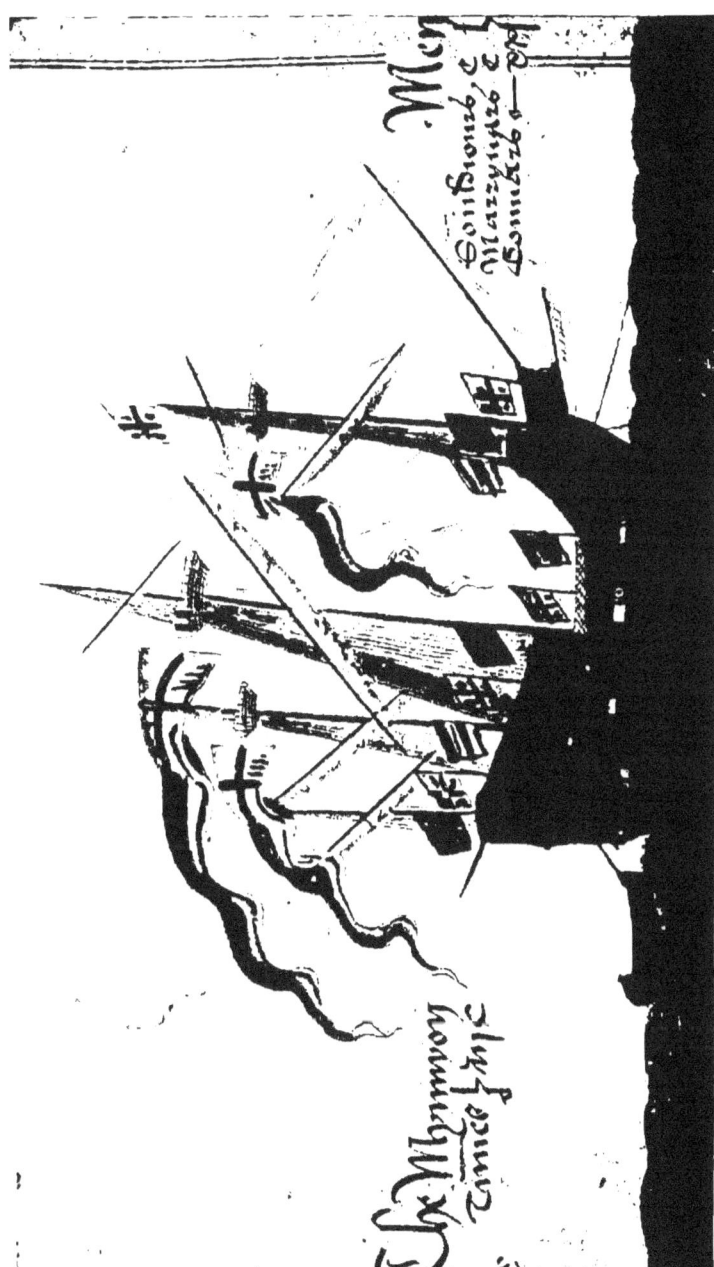

THE GREAT-SHIP 'MINION.'
Reduced from Anthony's First Roll (Magdalene College, Cambridge).

International Law, and that to forbid it to England was an actual breach of treaty. His method of preaching may have been too strenuous, but in his every act we see the deliberate and statesmanlike conduct of a man with a great policy to guide and a full sense of the dignity of his mission. Judge him by the standard of a time when all public affairs were conducted on rougher and more ruthless lines than those to which we are accustomed, and his methods will compare even favourably with much that in the competition for new markets is done to-day with little disapproval by all civilised nations.

From the first the 'Jesus' gave trouble. Five days out, off Finisterre, a gale was encountered, which lasted four days and dispersed the squadron, and so shattered was the flagship that Hawkins turned homeward resolved to give up the voyage. Next day, however, the weather cleared and he took heart to proceed. Touching, according to his practice, at Teneriffe with only Drake's vessel and the 'Angel' in company, he got news that the rest were at Gomera, the appointed rendez-vous. Thither he proceeded, and with the reunited squadron sailed for Guinea. Once in the waters of the Portuguese he began, with or without instructions, retaliation for their recent behaviour to his and his owners' vessels. His conduct is hard to defend. He had no commission of reprisal from the queen—at least we know of none—and his own omission of all mention of these transactions is evidence he did not himself consider them above suspicion.[1] It is from the narrative of Hartop, a gunner of the 'Jesus,' we learn that somewhere between the Canaries and Cape Blanco the 'Minion' chased and took a Portuguese caravel, which had been captured by 'a Frenchman of Rochelle called Captain Bland,' probably a Huguenot privateer

[1] The Huguenot commission which William Hawkins told Cecil he had 'from the Cardinal Chatillon for one ship to serve the Princes of Navarre and Condé' was probably not obtained till the Cardinal's mission to England in the autumn of 1568. (See 'William Hawkins to Cecil,' in Arber's *English Garner*, v. 210.)

or pirate. She was called the 'Grace of God,' and being a smart new vessel of 150 tons was added to the squadron and Drake placed in command. While searching the rivers along the coast for slaves from Rio Grande to Sierra Leone several more caravels were captured, and the negroes taken out of them. By January 12, 1568, however, they had collected no more than a hundred and fifty, and a good many men had been lost by sickness and poisoned arrows. The season, too, was getting late, and Hawkins was on the point of forcing a sale of his wares at Elmina and going no further when he received overtures from a native chief for assistance against other chiefs with whom he was at war. The offer was accepted, and a force of some two hundred men was landed, who captured a town and made up the tale of negroes to between four and five hundred. This was enough to warrant crossing the Atlantic, but their work on the African coast was not yet done. In the Rio Grande, where the ships which had been dispersed in the slave hunt were to rendez-vous for the western voyage, the first comers found seven more Portuguese caravels, all of which after a sharp action were driven ashore and captured. What they did with them is nowhere confessed: the 'Grace of God,' was the only one permanently attached to the squadron when it crossed the ocean.

After an unusually toilsome passage of fifty-five days, Dominica was made on March 27 and Hawkins began to trade. His own account of the proceedings is innocent enough. 'From thence,' says he, 'we coasted from place to place making our traffic with the Spaniards as we might; somewhat hardly because the king had straitly commanded all his governors in those parts by no means to suffer any trade to be made with us. Notwithstanding we had reasonable trade and entertainment, from the Isle of Margarita unto Cartagena without anything greatly worth the noting, saving at Cape de la Vela in a town called Rio de la Hacha.' Miles Phillips, who was serving in the 'Jesus,' says even less; but turning to Hartop's narrative, who in 1591, the date of his work, had nothing to conceal, we see that Hawkins told but half the truth. At Margarita, he says, 'our general, in despite the Spaniards anchored, landed, and took in fresh victuals.' At Borburata 'we came in, moored our ships and tarried two months trimming and dressing our ships;' for in those days, before copper and anti-fouling compositions, ships that had been six months in tropical seas became so badly clogged that careening was a necessity. From this place, Hartop goes on, 'our general sent us unto a town called Placentia, which stood on a high hill, to have intreated a Bishop that dwelt there for his favour and friendship in their laws; who hearing of our coming for fear forsook the town;' all of which would look as though things had not been quite so peaceable as Hawkins would have had them appear. What happened at Rio de la Hacha, however, was too serious for even Hawkins to pass over in silence. Still, here again, we have to go to Hartop to learn the whole truth.

While taking in fresh provisions at the Island of Curaçao, Hawkins sent forward the 'Angel' and 'Judith' to Rio de la Hacha. The occasion is a memorable one. The little advanced squadron must have been under the orders of Drake, as captain of the larger vessel. Bland, the Frenchman, having been admitted to the English fellowship, was again in command of his caravel, and Drake had returned to the 'Judith.'[1] Here, then, we have, as far as is known, his first separate command, and the way he conducted it was strangely characteristic of the man and of the ideas he was to develop. What his instructions were we do not know. It was probably a mere reconnaissance that was intended, for here at any rate a welcome must have been more than doubtful. His old enemy, the Treasurer, Drake found quite ready to

[1] The two vessels were certainly thus commanded two months later at San Juan de Ulua. The arrangement probably had taken place before leaving the African coast to fill the gaps which casualties and sickness had made in the ranks of Hawkins's officers.

receive him. The garrison had been reinforced with a hundred harquebusiers, and every possible approach to the town guarded by new works[1]; and directly Drake and his consort anchored before the town the batteries opened fire upon him. After replying with a shot through the Government house he withdrew his two vessels out of range, and there they rode five days 'in despite the Spaniards and their shot,' blockading the town. A 'caravel of advice,' or Government despatch-boat from the Viceroy at San Domingo, attempting to enter the port was chased, driven ashore, and brought off in triumph, as Hartop boasts, 'in spite of two hundred Spanish harquebusiers.' It was the act of a pirate, lawless, indefensible, and probably in excess of his instructions—the first of the long series of reckless exploits with which Drake was to display his scepticism of the Spanish power and to preach his new creed of the way in which their monopoly was to be broken down.

After so unpardonable an outrage, about which Hawkins preserves absolute silence, it was no wonder that when he came round with the rest of his fleet the Treasurer refused to trade or even to permit him to water. To stop to argue the point was either to lose his negroes from thirst, or else to land them for the Spaniards to seize. After a short negotiation, therefore, he landed two hundred men and carried the works by assault, with the loss of only two men, and drove the garrison some two leagues into the interior. In possession of the port he was upon a standpoint from which his arguments were more conclusive. 'Thus having the town,' says he, 'with some circumstance, as partly by the Spaniards' desire of negroes and partly by the friendship of the Treasurer, we obtained a secret trade: whereupon the Spaniards resorted to us by night and bought of us to the number of 200 negroes'—a curious passage which gives strange

---

[1] Hawkins uses the word 'bulwarks' (Italian, *baluardo*), which at this time meant technically an angular bastion. Here probably they were detached works of polygonal trace. See *Guglielmotti*, III. iii. cap. 95.

colour to De Silva's suspicion that his master was not too loyally served in the Indies, and that Hawkins and De Ponte, unknown even to Drake, had really some secret understanding with the colonial governors for a mere show of resistance.

Having completed his business, Hawkins continued westward along the coast, visiting Santa Marta and other small settlements, where, he says, 'the Spanish inhabitants were glad of us and traded willingly,' till they reached Cartagena, the capital of the Spanish Main. Here the Governor absolutely refused to have any dealings with them, and according to Hawkins's account, though he still had some fifty negroes left, besides a quantity of European goods, his trade was so nearly done and the hurricane season so close at hand that he decided not to hazard the danger and delay of another action and sailed away. Hartop, however, says the 'Minion' stood in and bombarded the castle and town while a landing was made; and that the welcome result was the discovery in a cave of a quantity of malmsey and sack, which they carried off, leaving as a protest of the genuineness of their principles woollen and linen cloth of equivalent value in its place.

So far the voyage had been a very fair success, and the only thing to fear was the weather. It was not till the end of July that they left Cartagena; August and September were the storm months. The right course homeward, as Hawkins had learned in his two previous voyages, lay northward through the Yucatan channel and along the path of the Gulf Stream. Hardly, however, were they past Cape Antonio at the west end of Cuba when a hurricane caught the fleet. For four days it blew, and when the weather cleared the 'William and John' had parted company, and the old 'Jesus,' with all her cageworks cut away, her rudder sprung, and leaking like a sieve, was little better than a wreck. To repair her was now absolutely necessary before the homeward voyage could be attempted. Working into the Bahia de Ponce de Leon (or the Mare Punjo, as it was then called) behind the Tortugas, for two weeks or more they searched the coast of Florida for a convenient place to repair damages. Everywhere the water was too shoal, and at last Hawkins resolved to make the best of a bad case and boldly enter the only port he knew, which was that of the city of Mexico itself.

The town of Vera Cruz at this time stood some fifteen miles to the northward of its haven, San Juan de Ulua, which then as now was nothing better than a roadstead protected from the fury of the prevalent northerly gales by a low island 'not above a bow-shot over.' The natural breakwater thus formed lay about half a mile from the mainland. On its landward side it was artificially scarped so as to make a kind of quay, and to this—so bad was the anchorage—every ship must be made fast by the permanent moorings that were provided before she could consider herself safe.[1] Here, say the English accounts, when Hawkins appeared a number of treasure ships were lying with over a million and a half of bullion on board according to present values, awaiting the annual *flota* of New Spain and its escort, which were daily expected from Spain.[2] For this fleet the officials mistook Hawkins's ships. He had taken the precaution to stay three small passenger vessels which he had fallen in with in Campeche Bay, in order to provide himself with hostages, and this probably confirmed the Spaniards' delusion. Their fright when they came on board and discovered their mistake must have been great. The whole year's produce of Mexico, as Hawkins believed, was at his mercy, and so relieved did they seem at being dismissed with the assurance that he merely wanted victuals and repairs that

[1] See the description in *The Voyage of Robert Tomson, marchant into Nova Hispania in the year* 1555, in Hakluyt, and cf. Cobb's chart of the port made in 1843, British Museum 77,905 (2) and Lopez's *Atlas*, Madrid 1786, B.M. S., 156 (7).

[2] The Spanish official *Relacion* (*post*, App.) says nothing of these treasure-ships, and from all we know of the system of the trade it is difficult to see how they could have been there, for we should expect the bullion to be in the treasure house of Vera Cruz awaiting the arrival of the *flota*. See *post*, vol. ii. cap. x.

without further demur he was suffered, seeing there was
no help for it, not only to moor at the quay but to mount
some guns which were found on the island in two batteries,
so as to cover his squadron and command the entrance
to the port.[1]

That he had any designs on the treasure-ships, even if
they were there at all, there is no ground for asserting.
He had always found trade a better business than piracy,
and had paid his way as honestly as might be. For him
piracy as then understood was folly he hated, and setting
aside his small reprisals for the acts of hostility committed
by the Portuguese slavers, to the last his hands were clean
of it. That he had intended to force a market for his unsold
negroes at Vera Cruz is very possible; but it is certain
that, often as he had used the pretence falsely before, in
this case stress of weather had really compelled him to seek
the port. Far from touching any treasure or seizing the
shipping, he released all his hostages but two, and procured the despatch of a message to the authorities at the
city of Mexico requesting permission to refit and purchase
what his necessities required, and further that order should
be taken to prevent any conflict between him and the
Mexico fleet when it arrived.

This of course was his great anxiety. It was on September 16 he had entered the port; the same night the
messenger left; and the very next morning they saw
open of the haven thirteen Spanish ships with a royal
galleon at their head. Hawkins was now in a great
perplexity. During the last few years the system of
Menendez had been gaining completeness. Driven from
their former haunts by his energy, the French Protestants
had combined to seize Saint-Augustine in Florida and
established there a permanent settlement. Menendez's

---

[1] Captain Duro says he seized all the vessels in the port, beginning with
that of Captain Maldonado (see *Armada Invencible*, i. App. B, and *Armada
Española*, ii. 824), but this seems to be a mistake. The *Relacion* says nothing
of it, and agrees with the English accounts that Maldonado's vessel was one
of those detained in Campeche Bay.

genius at once perceived the strategical danger of this new departure, and in a memorial to the king had pointed out how it imperilled the Spanish position in the Indies. At his urgent representation a powerful naval and military force had been entrusted to his command, and in 1565 he had succeeded in annihilating the colony with a severity that gravely embittered the struggle and left a dark stain upon his character.[1] The exploit and the danger had served to emphasise Menendez's position. Further measures were taken for the safety of the *flotas*. Orders were issued that the *capitana* and *almiranta* (that is, the flagship and vice-flagship) of the two fleets were always to be equipped as men-of-war, and to carry no cargo except treasure in order to leave them freer to fight. Besides this a squadron of twelve galleons was ordered to be built in the Biscay yards, to form a permanent squadron for the protection of the Indian trade. These were the famous galleons of the Indian guard, the first fruits of the Spanish oceanic Navy, and this very year for the first time Menendez was bringing them out to clear the Indies of all foreign intrusion.[2] This cannot have been unknown to Hawkins, and however innocent his intentions he could not doubt that for every Spanish admiral he was a pirate. For all he could tell the fleet he saw was Menendez's armada bent on his destruction. As a matter of fact it proved to be the Mexican *flota* under the command of Don Francisco de Luxan, with nothing but its armed 'capitana' and 'almiranta' to protect it. On board of it, however, was Don Martin Enriquez, the new Viceroy of Mexico, and he could not

[1] Ruidiaz endeavours to defend him from the grosser charges of cruelty and affirms that he did not do anything that was not excusable to a deeply religious man of his fanatical temperament (see *La Conquista de Florida*, Introd.).

[2] The galleons were not strictly part of the Royal Navy. They were built and maintained by a 'general average' assessment levied by the Contractacion House on merchants trading to the Indies. It was really a private 'Insurance' squadron belonging to the Contractacion House. No Royal Navy yet existed in the Atlantic.

doubt that these two men had orders, like Menendez, to treat him as an enemy wherever and whenever they found him. As things stood they were at his mercy. Being in possession of the island and the roadstead he was, as he said, very well able with God's help to keep the king's ships from entering; and if he chose to do it, the first northerly gale meant present shipwreck for the whole Spanish fleet. This, however, he considered 'he would not be able to answer, fearing the Queen's Majesty's indignation in so weighty a matter.' The only alternative was to make terms for himself, terms that he knew by experience the Spaniards would not keep if they had a chance of breaking them. For the more high-handed course Hawkins was too 'orderly,' nor was the time yet ripe.

The lesser evil, therefore, was chosen, and negotiations were opened with the Spanish Admiral, who since the discovery that the English were in possession of the haven had been lying off some three leagues to seaward. Meanwhile an answer had come to Hawkins's application to the authorities at Mexico referring him to the new Viceroy, who must have felt acutely the indignity of his position. If we may trust Hartop, the negotiations opened stormily. Hawkins seems first to have suggested that the Spaniards should supply him with necessities and that he should then leave by one mouth of the haven and they enter by the other. To these overtures Don Martin replied 'that he was a Viceroy and had a thousand men, and therefore he would come in.' 'If he be a Viceroy,' was Hawkins's answer, 'I represent my Queen's person and I am Viceroy as well as he: and if he have a thousand men my powder and shot will take the better place.' Although both Hawkins and the Spanish authorities give a smoother impression, it is certain there was a long struggle on the question of the possession of the island. On this Hawkins was bound to insist, and the negotiations were prolonged four days before either the fear of a gale or Hawkins's tact brought Don Martin to reason.

The terms eventually agreed upon were as follows:

the English were to be allowed to repair their ships and to buy victuals and have licence to sell goods for that purpose; by way of security for preservation of the peace and performance of the articles, they were to remain in possession of the island and keep in position the eleven brass guns they had mounted there; no Spaniard was to land with any kind of weapon, and finally ten hostages were to be exchanged. On Monday evening the Spaniards weighed and took up a fresh anchorage just outside the port for the night. Next morning they came in, the two fleets saluting each other. At first the Spanish vessels began to take up berths among the English, but this Hawkins insisted on altering, and all Tuesday and Wednesday the Spaniards and English laboured amicably together to get the two fleets snug at separate moorings. The ships of each nationality were thus eventually berthed apart, with stern-fasts out to anchors in the road and their bows so close ashore that their 'beak-noses' overhung the quay and the crews could land without boats. Outermost of the English vessels on the Spanish side lay the 'Minion' and next to her the 'Jesus.' So confined, however, was the space that an interval of less than twenty yards was all that could be allowed between the two fleets, and with this exception the ships all lay hard aboard one another.

While lying outside Don Martin had ordered up some six score soldiers from Vera Cruz,[1] and on Monday night, under cover of darkness, had managed secretly to get them aboard his fleet. Thus reinforced, he occupied himself, according to the Spanish official *Relacion*, all Tuesday and Wednesday in maturing a scheme for chastising the corsair.[2] Next the 'Minion' and outermost of the Spanish squadron had been placed a large 'hulk'[3] of some eight or nine hundred tons, and this during Wednesday night it was

[1] This is Herrera's figure. The English put them at 1,000 or 1,500, but there can hardly have been so many at such a place as Vera Cruz.

[2] Herrera says that he went up to the city of Mexico and left De Luxan in command. But the *Relacion* distinctly states he remained in the *capitana* all the time.

[3] *I.e.* an ordinary cargo vessel. Spanish, *urca*.

found had been connected by a hawser with the head cable of the 'Jesus' and filled with men. An unusual movement of troops and a new activity in planting guns and cutting ports to command the English ships and the batteries increased Hawkins's suspicion, and he sent to the Viceroy to protest. An answer was returned that the ordnance objected to should be removed. Still nothing was done, and Hawkins sent a new protest by Barrett, his master, who spoke Spanish. Ashore some of the Spaniards, it is said, were fraternising with the Englishmen and supplying them with drink,[1] and while awaiting the answer to his second protest Hawkins himself sat down to dinner, apparently, as was then the custom, in the forenoon.

If he had any doubt left that the Spaniards intended treachery it was now removed. Seated as a guest at his table was one of his original hostages, Don Agustin de Villa Nueva. From this gentleman's sleeve an attendant suddenly snatched a concealed dagger. Hawkins sprang to his feet and ordered the assassin into instant arrest, but before he could act further a white napkin fluttered in the Spanish Admiral's hand and then a loud trumpet call from the *capitana's* deck rang out to the Spaniards their signal. Ashore every man of them drew a concealed dagger upon his half-drunken English comrade: the soldiers from Vera Cruz leaped ashore over the bows of the vessels where they had lain concealed, rushed upon the batteries, slashing right and left among the unready guards, and sending them flying for refuge to the ships. At the same time the men in the hulk began hauling on the hawser they had made fast to the 'Minion.' But aboard the ships they were better prepared. Already, sudden as was the alarm, each of the Spanish flag-ships had been badly hit before they could fire a shot, and the *almiranta* was bursting into flames with a perrier-ball in her magazine. As the hulk fell aboard the English vice-admiral, some three hundred soldiers swarmed over her sides; 'whereat,' says Hartop,

[1] Cabrera de Córduba.

'our general with a loud and fierce voice called unto us saying "God and St. George! Upon those traitorous villains and rescue the 'Minion'! I trust in God the day shall be ours," and with that the mariners and soldiers leaped out of the "Jesus of Lubeck" into the "Minion" and beat out the Spaniards.' Not a moment was given them to recover their repulse. At the first suspicion of treachery Hawkins had warned Captain Hampton, of the 'Minion,' to be on the alert, and before the attack on his ship could be renewed he had slipped his shore moorings, hauled clear by his stern-fasts, and was soon pouring a heavy fire into the burning Spanish vice-admiral. Meanwhile every Englishman ashore had been massacred except three. Among them, it is said, was Drake, who only saved himself by swarming aboard his ship by her hawser.[1] As the 'Minion' drew clear the Spanish hulk swung aboard the 'Jesus;' two other vessels assaulted her at the same time, and a desperate attempt was made to capture her by boarding. But again the boarders were flung back, and kept at bay until with heavy loss Hawkins managed to cut his head-fasts and to haul off to a position beside the 'Minion,' some two ships' length from the Spanish fleet.

A furious action ensued, in which the English superiority in weight of metal soon told.[2] Hartop says the official return sent to Mexico put the loss of the Spaniards at five hundred and forty men. Hawkins claims that in the hour he had practically silenced the fire of the king's ships, the vice-admiral being in flames and the admiral and another vessel in a sinking condition. Philips confirms this, and Hartop the gunner, who had swum aboard the

---

[1] *Herrera*; but this is very doubtful. Hartop, who was one of the three, does not mention Drake.

[2] The 'Jesus' could throw over 250 lb. from her battery alone, besides her 42 secondary or quick firing armament. The details were: Cannons (50- or 60-pounders), 2; culverins (long 18-pounders), 2; demi-culverins (long 9-pounders), 8; sacres (long 5-pounders), 8; falcons (3-pounders), 2. Her breech-loading pieces were: slings, 2; fowlers, 10; bases, 30. The Spanish vessels certainly carried nothing like such an armament.

'Jesus,' says their admiral was also on fire for half-an-hour and had sixty shot through her, and that the vice-admiral blew up. This the *Relacion* confirms. The vice-admiral, it says, was entirely consumed with a score of her crew, and nothing was saved of all she contained but a boat-load of cloth. So terrible was the English fire, that for a time the Viceroy was almost alone on the *capitana* and was in great danger. The *Relacion* infers that but for the batteries all would have been lost. These De Luxan had seized, and he was now turning the guns on the English ships. Hawkins was still undismayed. Calling for a tankard of beer, he stood cheering on his men, and crying to the gunners 'to stand by their ordnance lustily like men.' As he set down his silver goblet a demi-culverin shot knocked it over. 'Fear not,' cried Hawkins, 'for God who hath delivered me from the shot will also deliver us from these traitors and villains.'

The fire of the batteries had sunk the 'Angel' and rendered the 'Swallow' untenable, and the Frenchman Bland, in the midst of a courageous attempt to get to windward of the Spaniards and send his ship in flames into the midst of them, was forced to fire her where she was and bring his crew aboard the admiral in his pinnace. As for the 'Jesus,' her rigging was soon so cut up that it was decided to bring her into a position to cover the 'Minion' till nightfall, and then to take out her victuals and treasure and abandon her. In the midst of their deliberations, however, it was suddenly seen that the Spaniards had loosed two fire-ships upon them.' It was a well-known manœuvre of the time and as dreaded as it was well known. Without waiting for orders or to see if the fire-ships would drift clear the 'Minion's' men in a panic made sail. Wounded, treasure, and many of the crew were left to their fate in the 'Jesus;' Hawkins himself had only just time to spring on board the 'Minion' as her sails began to draw; some few more managed to follow in a small boat, but these and the crew of the 'Judith' were all that escaped. At the outset it would seem Drake had warped his bark clear and got her out of the haven, and probably, owing to the lightness of his armament, had taken little part in the action. He was now ordered in alongside the 'Minion' to take in as many men as he could and to get outside again. For the rest of the day they lay-to a bow-shot from the Spanish fleet, and at nightfall as the land wind sprang up they set sail. The wind rapidly increased to one of the dreaded northerly gales, and for two days Hawkins lay under Sacrifice Island unmolested close to the port. When the weather abated he proceeded on his course, and so cut up were the Spanish vessels that no attempt was made to brave the gales and follow him.

Such was the famous affair of San Juan de Ulua, the first action of the long series that were to come, and in all our annals rarely surpassed as an heroic and successful defence against a treacherous surprise. As far as can now be judged, it would seem that had Hawkins been able to retain the shore batteries even long enough to spike the guns the whole Spanish fleet must have surrendered or been destroyed. That he could not do this was no fault or weakness of his. However doubtful the details, one thing is clear and certain, that the Spaniards acted with confessed and deliberate treachery in breach of a formal military convention. There was no attempt to deny it at the time. The only excuse the Viceroy offered was that he believed Hawkins meant to break his word and fire the Spanish fleet, but in justification of his distrust he had not a scrap of evidence to offer. As the highest modern authority in Spain has written with admirable impartiality, 'It was an affair of foxes and not of lions;' and he lays no blame on Hawkins or Drake for the implacable rancour with which they visited upon the whole Spanish nation the unexampled perfidy of Don Martin Enriquez and Francisco de Luxan.[1] Whatever the degree

[1] Captain Duro, *Armada Española*, ii. 226. Mr. Froude in his *English Seamen* (pp. 56 et seq.) gives 'Alvarez de Baçan' as the commander of the Spanish squadron, a man who, as he relates in his *History* (viii. 26),

of Hawkins's guilt, he had shown himself an honourable man and no pirate, and it is to his undying honour that when the Spaniards took possession of the derelict 'Jesus' they found there all the hostages. By every law of arms it was his right to have butchered them, but not a hair of their heads had been touched: they had nothing but praises of their gentle treatment.[1]

had previously attacked some English ships at Gibraltar. But all the Spanish authorities distinctly state it was Don Francisco de Luxan, and in this they are supported by the English narratives. Pedro de Santillana even wrote in 1570 a poem in De Luxan's honour on the subject of his victory over Hawkins, which is printed by Captain Duro (*Armada Invencible*, ii. 490). Alvaro de Bazan was the name of the famous Marquis of Santa Cruz who originated the idea of the Great Armada and was to have commanded it (*Ibid.* i. 15). There is yet a third admiral to whom the affair is attributed. In the Calendar of Spanish State Papers (p. 569) is a despatch of Mendoza's, dated March 31, 1578, in which he seems to imply the commander was Pero Menendez, and in Biggs's narrative of Drake's 'Indies Voyage' of 1585, the writer says the Governor of the Florida settlements was 'Pedro Melendez, marquis, nephew to that Melendez the Admiral who had overthrown Master John Hawkins in the Bay of Mexico some 17 or 18 years ago.' Mendoza, however, shows by the context that he had no clear recollection of the incident. As Menendez was commanding the armada on the station the mistake is natural, and it is possible also Mendoza had confused the San Juan de Ulua affair with Menendez's exploit against some defenceless English merchantmen at the Azores some years previously (see Froude, *History of England*, viii. 20). Biggs, of course, is an authority of no weight upon the point. It should also be noted that the English fleet was not under fire from Vera Cruz, as Mr. Froude seems to picture it; for the town was not then in its present position opposite the island of San Juan de Ulua, but, as has been explained (*ante*, p. 110), some fifteen miles to the northward.

[1] There seems some doubt whether Hawkins had succeeded in transferring his treasure to the 'Minion' before the 'Jesus' was abandoned. The *Relacion* says nothing of value was found on board, except some fifty slaves, some bales of cloth, and the Admiral's silver cabin service.

CHAPTER IV

DRAKE'S FIRST SERVICE IN THE NÁVY

THE feature of international relations which most sharply distinguishes the sixteenth century from our own time is the length to which hostilities could be pushed without leading to an open rupture. Continually we encounter the phenomenon of two powers standing with regard to each other in a position that was neither peace nor war. As by the municipal law an aggrieved person may still assert his rights by distraint, impounding, and other similar proceedings without resorting to the ultimate remedy of an action at law; so it was then in foreign affairs a recognised proceeding for a sovereign to seek redress in one of the various forms of hostility which by the consent of international lawyers were regarded as falling short of war. A succession of treaties between the Great Powers had fully established the conditions under which these minor remedies could be put in force; they had come to be an ordinary and definite part of the machinery of foreign politics, and it is only by keeping this fact in mind that it is possible to grasp the extraordinary phase into which our relations with Spain were to be precipitated by the affair of San Juan de Ulua.

While Hawkins was forcing his wares upon the Spanish Main, at home a great Catholic coalition, borne on the flowing tide of the Counter-reformation, seemed once more to be closing round England. So threatening was the outlook that nothing but the domestic troubles of the chief parties to the league appeared to stand in the way of a combined attack upon the heretic queen. The points from which there was present danger of assault were France and the Spanish Netherlands. But in France the Huguenots, with Rochelle for a base, were still holding the Government at bay and paralysing its action abroad. In the Netherlands, Alva, the Spanish governor, was equally afraid to move. The 'Beggars,' as his rebels called themselves, were in command of the sea; his army and treasury were exhausted by the effort of reducing his province to obedience, and it was all he could do to hold his own. So long as these conditions held, everyone felt that Elizabeth could rest in comparative security. So clear was the situation that Cecil himself had been converted to a policy of supporting the Protestants abroad, and, impatient of his mistress's finessing, was pushing her forward towards an open hegemony of the new religion For the Huguenots something was already being done. Under pretence of violence and extortion suffered at Bordeaux, the wine-fleet, convoyed by a squadron of four of the queen's ships under Sir William Wynter, was going to Rochelle with secret supplies for the rebels. Nothing but an opportunity was wanted for a similar service to be rendered to the Netherlands, and it was not long in coming.

About the end of November, as Wynter was leaving the Thames, some treasure ships bound from Spain to Antwerp were driven by Huguenot privateers to seek sanctuary in Southampton, Plymouth, and Falmouth. The money they carried was part of the proceeds of a loan which Philip had negotiated in Italy for the payment of Alva's troops, and Bernardino Spinola, the great Italian banker in London, who would seem to have been one of the contractors for the loan and was their agent in England, applied to Don Guerau de Spes, the new Spanish ambassador, to request from the Council a safe conduct for the treasure overland to Dover. Not only was this request favourably received, but the queen offered a naval squadron to escort the vessels to their destination by sea, if the ambassador preferred that way to the other. The matter was referred to Alva. He chose the overland route, and eventually, on December 2 the safe conduct was signed.

Whatever were the real intentions of the Government, up to this time there is no suggestion discoverable that they were not acting in perfect good faith. It happened, however, that Spinola, who had been a shareholder in Hawkins's second venture and was possibly also interested in the last, had received from his correspondents in Spain a rumour that some great disaster had happened to the expedition in the Indies. It was to the effect that having landed and gone into the interior to effect his trade Hawkins had been led into an ambush, and he and all his men massacred.[1] Spinola sent the news down by road to Wynter, to whom urgent orders had been despatched to delay his voyage to Rochelle, and to put into Plymouth in order to protect the Spanish treasure from the French privateers, who were still hovering off the port as though they meant to seize it where it lay.[2] Wynter at once communicated the ominous tidings to William Hawkins, who, with some strange foreboding of the truth, was deeply distressed. Without a moment's delay he wrote off to Cecil what Wynter had told him, begging that Spinola should be examined as to the truth of his news, and at the same time boldly suggesting that if it were true an embargo should be laid upon the King of Spain's treasure, which he and Wynter had been ordered to protect. This letter was written on December 3, the day after the safe-conduct for the passage of the treasure to Dover had been signed. Before it reached London the safe-conduct must have

[1] Though the affair of San Juan de Ulua had happened but two months before, it is possible that some report of it may already have reached Spinola. The Atlantic voyage was sometimes made in small fast vessels with extraordinary rapidity. Menendez in 1567 is said to have sailed from Florida about the middle of June, and reached Galicia on July 7, or say twenty-five days (Ruidiaz, *La Florida*, Introd.). Drake once made Dominica from Plymouth in twenty-five days (*post*, p. 157), and in 1573 he did the homeward voyage from Florida in twenty-three days.

[2] *Spanish Cal.* p. 115.

been in Don Guerau's hands, for on the 8th his messengers arrived with the document at Southampton, and having duly notified it to Horsey, the Governor of the Wight, proceeded with it next day on their way to Plymouth. Hardly, however, were their backs turned than, upon orders from London, Horsey suddenly seized the whole of the treasure and brought it ashore on pretence that it was not safe from the privateers so long as it remained on board. Close on the heels of Don Guerau's unsuspecting messengers went orders to Hawkins and Champernowne, Vice-Admiral of Devon, for the same precautions to be taken in the West.

In London during the week that this change of front took place two things had happened. One was the receipt of William Hawkins's letter to Cecil; the other, the discovery from Spinola, who was probably examined in accordance with Hawkins's suggestion, that by the terms of the loan the money was payable to Philip in Antwerp, and therefore still the property of the Italian bankers.[1] It must have been these two pieces of information that showed the Council the way clear to do what Don Guerau said some of them had urged from the first. On the 11th the news of Horsey's action reached the ambassador. A hot-headed, fire-eating Catalan soldier, with an overweening sense of his country's power and importance, he was the last man who at this juncture should have been opposed to Cecil's level head. Without waiting to consider the ingenuity of the diplomatist, whom he despised as a cunning and low-bred heretic, he wrote off in a fury to Alva urging him to lay an embargo on the property of English subjects in the Netherlands. Alva in a moment of exasperation acted on his advice, and on the 19th, the very day Don Guerau made his formal demand for the restitution of the treasure, the embargo was put in force.

[1] It was afterwards officially denied that Spinola gave this information; but both Alva and Don Guerau were sure he did, and official denials were of even less worth then than they are to-day. See *Spanish Cal.* 1568-79, pp. 90, 92, 131, 163, 171.

The Spanish Government thus found itself placed completely in the wrong. Subsisting treaties provided that before any reprisals could be enforced there must have been a distinct refusal or an unreasonable delay of justice. In the present case there had been neither, and with a light heart the queen ordered retaliation. Every vessel, every bale of Spanish property in the country was seized; the Spanish sailors and merchants were imprisoned; the treasure was ordered up to the Tower; and Don Guerau himself was placed under arrest in his own house. Elizabeth was mistress of the situation. Not only was Alva left at the critical moment with an unpaid army, not only was Philip's credit shattered and his prestige shaken, but the private property of his subjects seized exceeded by many times the value of English effects in Spanish hands. To declare war was out of the question, so crushing had been the blow to Spanish finance; to play a waiting game was to play into Elizabeth's hands, who was actively preparing her fleet and territorial forces for mobilisation at any moment; and every week was seeing fresh prizes brought in by English privateers and her own ships. There was nothing for it but for Spain to make the first advance, and Alva sent over Dr. d'Assonleville, a member of the Council of State, accredited by himself to treat. Not being able to show regular credentials from the king, he was at once arrested, and the disclosure of his mission demanded. Till he had seen the ambassador he refused to say a word, and things were again at a deadlock.

Such was the state of affairs when, on the evening of January 20, 1569, the 'Judith' was seen entering Plymouth Sound alone.

On the night after the action she had parted company with the 'Minion;' the following day a northerly gale had separated them still further, and Drake, overloaded with men, short of victuals, and with no rendez-vous but Plymouth, had resolved to make the best of his way home. For this he was much blamed at the time, as though he had wilfully deserted his leader, and the story was never forgotten against him. Why this was so is impossible for us now to understand. With the information we have we can only applaud the course he took as under the circumstances the most seamanlike, the most expedient, and thoroughly justified as much by the custom of the service as by the distress of his own condition.[1]

Late as it was when Drake landed he was suffered no rest. William Hawkins was no man to let the grass grow under his feet, and having heard the tale he had been so anxiously waiting for, he sat up writing to Cecil and to the Council begging for a commission of reprisal for his own and his brother's wrongs. With these letters the young captain was hurried off to London to tell the Council the long expected news. Five days later the 'Minion' struggled into Mount's Bay. One hundred of her crew Hawkins had been compelled to land in the Bay of Mexico, numbers more had died of hunger and disease on the voyage home, and it was not till assistance had been sent by William Hawkins that she could be brought round to Plymouth. The treasure that had been seized in the Spanish vessels that lay there was on the point of starting for London under a strong guard, and with it went John Hawkins, with all he had been able to save from the disaster upon four packhorses. On February 4 he reached London. By the next day at latest the Government must have been in full possession of the facts, but still not a word was said. With renewed insistence d'Assonleville was pressed to disclose the object of his mission, and when at last he gave way it was found to relate only to the seizure of the treasure and to have nothing to do with Hawkins's voyage. The cards were therefore still in Cecil's hands. In vain the envoy endeavoured to open negotiations for the release of the money; he was reminded of the limits of his authority. It was pointed out to him that he was a mere delegate of a delegate; that the embargo was no longer confined to Alva's province, that

[1] Appendix C.

it had spread to Spain, and numbers of injuries to the queen and her subjects in all parts of Philip's dominions remained unredressed; and that therefore she must refuse to listen to anyone but a plenipotentiary specially authorised to settle the whole question of the strained relations between the two countries. The position was unassailable. D'Assonleville had to return to the Duke of Alva empty; and while the next step from Spain was awaited, an inquiry into the affair of San Juan de Ulua was opened by the Lord Admiral.

Meanwhile Drake disappears. He was not examined at the inquiry. Herrera would have it believed that on Hawkins's accusation he was imprisoned for three months as a deserter until intercession was made on his behalf and he was released. The *English Hero* on the other hand, says he now served for some time upon one of the queen's ships to his great advantage. The authority is doubtful, but the fact more than probable. We were on the brink of war not only with Spain, but with France also. Wynter's relief of Rochelle had brought to a head a long series of mutual recriminations on the score of piracies and irregular reprisals, and in February the French ambassador presented an ultimatum. Already adepts at the art of playing off France and Spain against each other, in a moment the queen's Government was all compliance and the danger passed. Naval preparations, however, were in no way relaxed. In the Thames were lying two large fleets of merchantmen awaiting convoy. One was the wine-fleet again bound for Rochelle, the other the wool-fleet bound for Hamburg. Through that port the London merchants had resolved to push their way into the Central European markets and so turn Alva's closure of the Flemish ports. This Hamburg fleet Alva was said to be preparing to attack, and seven ships were brought forward for its protection. Besides these some thirty or forty privateers were at sea snapping up every Spanish or Portuguese ship that came in their way; the merchantmen, too, were all half armed according to the English custom, and strongly manned ; so that hands for the Navy were hard to come by. So experienced a master as Drake, if he did not volunteer, would certainly have been pressed ; and the probability is that he sought refuge from the accusation against him by serving as master of one of the queen's ships that were being fitted out to reinforce Wynter's guard for the wool-fleet. An action with Alva's ships was confidently expected, numbers of gentlemen volunteered on the prospect, and Drake would hardly have held back. Both fleets sailed in April; that for Rochelle under convoy of Sir John Basing with some privateers and four small queen's ships; that for Hamburg under Wynter with seven large ones. No action took place, and having escorted the wool-fleet safely to its destination, Wynter, leaving two ships behind him for its protection, returned with the rest early in June and was ordered up to Rochester to pay them off. The Rochelle fleet did not get back till July. If, therefore, Drake was serving at all it must have been under Wynter; for on July 4, after what must have been a real sailor's courtship for brevity, he had won the heart of a Devonshire girl called Mary Newman, and was married to her at St.-Budeaux.

His midsummer wooing on the banks of the Tavy was one of the few short intervals of peace his stormy life was to see, and even that was clouded with the threat of imminent war. Hardly had Wynter paid off than he was ordered to get crews together again. The embargo was still spreading. The Portuguese had adopted the Spanish measures of retaliation, had closed their ports, and were preparing to force a merchant fleet through the Channel to Flanders. Cecil and the Lord Admiral had been elaborating a scheme by which the whole Navy could be mobilised at the shortest notice, and by the end of the month twelve great-ships, besides the two at Hamburg and three at Rochelle, were ready for immediate commission. This formidable but by no means adequate force represented practically the whole strength of the Navy. The

Sea-Queen, as we are wont to think of her, had been ten years on the throne, and this was all she could show—a Navy sunk to almost the lowest ebb it ever reached since it began, the sorry result of an unsteady naval policy halting and hurrying as financial exigences or present alarm swayed its fortunes.

To regard her as the creator of England's maritime reputation is a mistake too often committed. England was a first rate naval Power before ever she came to the throne, and, after the scare which had followed the loss of Calais had worn itself out, the first part of her reign did little to increase the prestige she was heir to. Of her father's splendid Navy she had inherited little more than the ruins. Yet it must not be assumed that the naval policy which the first Tudors had inaugurated had been lost sight of by either of her predecessors. If the religious and political troubles of Edward's reign had for a while preoccupied the attention and resources of his Government, they had none the less emphasised the danger of neglecting the fleet. During the Scottish war and the French attempts upon the Channel Islands, the Navy had done all that for the moment was required of it; and it would seem at any rate that when Lord Lisle, as Duke of Northumberland, became Lord Protector he did not forget the service in which his reputation had been chiefly won, and that he made a real effort to maintain the efficiency of the Navy.

At Henry's death it had consisted, it will be remembered, of between fifty and sixty sail. Under Edward in 1552 a report was made to the Lord Protector upon the state of the royal ships, which shows very clearly how things had been progressing.[1] Henry's four classes are reduced to two. His 'ships' and 'galleasses' appear together as 'ships,' his 'pinnaces' and 'row-barges' as 'pinnaces.' Of his fourteen great-ships ten were reported as fit for service, though five required overhauling. Of his fifteen 'galleasses' nine were fit for immediate service and two only wanted overhauling. One great-ship and

[1] *Derrick*, p. 16.

two 'galleasses' required 'new-making.'[1] Besides these there appear one new ship and four of the pinnace class that were not on Henry's list. Of his ten pinnaces only three, and of his thirteen row-barges no more than two, were fit for service, making in all an effective Navy of twenty-two ships and nine pinnaces. The rest that remained, including two ships, three 'galleasses,' and six row-barges, were reported 'not worth keeping' or 'meet to be sold.' The last item of the report relates to the oared vessels. 'The two galleys,' it runs, 'and the brigantine must be yearly repaired, if your Lordships' pleasure be to have them kept;' from which we may gather that the opinion of the service members of the Navy department, though inclined to pronounce against the type, had not yet done so definitely enough to convince the Government. Notwithstanding the report of the experts that only thirty-nine sail were of any use, forty-five were ordered to be retained.

With the death of Edward Northumberland's short administration came to an end. Whatever may have been the sailor-minister's dream of making England the invincible maritime Power of his old master's ideal, they were brought to an end on Tower Green. But others recognised as well as he where the main-spring of Henry's power had lain, and Mary's reign was to prove one of unexpected naval activity. An undated list of her early years, it is true, shows mere neglect. The 'Great Harry' has disappeared, burnt accidentally in 1553. Twenty-three vessels are still classed as great-ships, but three of them at least were some of her father's pinnaces.[2] In the pin-

[1] The process of 'new-making' seems properly to have been an entire reconstruction of the vessel out of her old ironwork and so much of her old timbers as could be used after the decayed parts had been cut away. (See Sir W. Raleigh, 'Observations on the Navy. Of the Building of Ships.' *Works*, viii. 337), but sometimes a ship was said to have been 'new-made' when she had merely been thoroughly repaired.

[2] Derrick, p. 20. Its probable date is 1555, since the 'Mary of Hamburg,' which was sold that year (Oppenheim, p. 109), appears in it and the new 'Marie Rose' (1555-6) does not.

nace class appears nothing but four of the old row-barges, but besides these the two old galleys and the brigantine still existed. This was probably her whole force. It is not till the advent of Philip that there is any sign of renewed activity. It was that Mary's kingdom might be absorbed into the vast dominions of his house that his father had sacrificed him. For Charles V. England was but another province, and its special office was to supply the great want of the Spanish empire. As yet Spain had no semblance of an ocean-going navy. Even the galleons of the Indian Guard did not yet exist. Philip's arrival in England was coincident with the culminating exploits of the French corsairs in the Indies, and with the commencement of Menendez's system of trade defence. The weakness of Spain was still her weakness at sea, and it was here that England was strong. There is nothing that has done more to confuse the history of the rise of our sea power, than the persistent ignoring in modern times of this fact. Contemporary naval authorities thoroughly appreciated it. For them the opening of the Elizabethan war was the struggle of an enemy that had no organised maritime forces at all against the first naval Power in Europe. In their eyes the defeat of the Armada was rather the foundation than the eclipse of the Spanish sea power. 'The Kings of England,' wrote Raleigh early in the next century, 'have for many years been at the charge to build and furnish a navy of powerful ships for their own defence and for the wars only: whereas the French, the Spaniards, the Portugals and the Hollanders (till of late) have had no proper fleet belonging to their princes or States.'[1] His history may not be quite accurate, but the passage serves to show how a great sailor could regard the situation. Sir William Monson, the leading naval expert of the time, is equally emphatic. Writing of the opening years of the war, he says: 'The King of Spain in those days was altogether unfurnished with ships and mariners; for till we awaked him by the

[1] 'The Invention of Ships,' *Works*, viii. 324.

daily spoils we committed upon his subjects and coasts, he never sought to increase his forces by sea.' And again: 'To speak the truth, till the King of Spain had war with us, he never knew what war by sea meant, unless it were in galleys against the Turks in the Straits or in the islands of Terceras against the French, which fleet belonged to him by his new-gotten kingdom of Portugal.... The first time the king showed himself strong at sea was in the year 1591, when the " Revenge " was taken.'[1] How the English power was regarded even in Mary's time by the most capable foreign critics, we have the best possible evidence, that of the Venetian ambassador. In making his official report to the Doge about the year 1557, he wrote: 'England is the most powerful of all nations in the north in its number of warlike men and the strength of its fleet, in which respect this kingdom is superior to all its neighbours.'[2]

Of supplying the defect of the Spanish military position, the Netherland provinces were as yet incapable. 'When King Henry VIII.,' writes Raleigh, 'had wars with the Emperor Charles V., who was also lord of the Low Countries, the English received no prejudice from the main ships of the Netherlands ; it is true, and I myself remember, that within this thirty years two of her Majesty's ships would have commanded one hundred sail of theirs.' Further we know that at the time of the Habsburg and Tudor alliance against France, the Emperor insisted on stringent rules for the government of the allied fleet on the ground that the English admiral was so much superior in force that he had the Imperial captains completely in his power.

[1] *Naval Tracts*, Purchas, iii. 241 and 321 ; and cf. Jurien de la Gravière, *Chevaliers de Malte et la marine de Philippe II.* i. 77.
[2] As evidence of the sense the English had of their own power, of the mental activity and growth of national spirit that was going on, he adds that they are partial to novelty and hostile to foreigners, and that they attempt to do anything that comes into their heads just as if all that the imagination suggests could easily be accomplished.—*Venetian Calendar*, 1561, p. 274.

The value of the English province then to the Habsburg system was that it could put Spain on an equality with France as a naval Power, and here doubtless is the secret of the renewed activity in Mary's dockyards. Whether it was due directly to Philip's influence we cannot tell. All we know is that his wisest councillor charged him specially to look to the Navy; one of his few communications to an English Minister that are extant is a letter thanking the Lord Admiral for his activity and zeal, and certainly the laying down of Mary's two chief additions to the Navy coincide with the nuptial visit.[1]

When Philip departed in despair of overcoming the stubborn insularity of the English Government, a fresh impetus to the Navy was given by Sir Harry Dudley's attempt to repeat Wyatt's anti-Spanish design. Those of his hare-brained young associates who escaped took to the sea, and inspired with that fantastic devotion to their distressed Princess Elizabeth which she so strangely was able to arouse in men of action even after all her personal charms had faded, joined hands with the French in their ruthless war upon Spanish commerce. Squadrons were organised by Mary against them, and further demands upon the Navy were made by the action of the Scottish filibusters upon the coasts of Ulster,[2] yet no further additions to the Navy List appear till in 1557 Philip came back for one last effort to drag England into his quarrel with France. Before he left war was declared, and the dockyards were again busy. Still the Navy must have remained in a state of lamentable disorganisation; for in spite of the long warning, when Calais was in *extremis*, not a ship could be moved to drive off the weak French squadron that was blockading it, and it was found impossible to throw in reinforcements till too late.

[1] The new 'Mary Rose,' 500 tons, and the 'Philip and Mary,' 450 tons, assigned respectively to 1555 and 1556 and therefore probably ordered in 1554–5. Philip reached England in July 1554 and left in August 1555.

[2] See 'Acts of the Privy Council in Ireland.' Hist. MSS. Comm. xviii. 4 and 6.

It was on Jan. 6, 1558, that Calais fell. The shock to English feeling which the loss of our last continental possession caused, was unexampled in history, and its immediate result was an outburst of feverish energy in naval preparation. In the year 1558, it would seem that no less than nine great-ships and two pinnaces were ordered to be built or new-made, and at Mary's death, including pinnaces and the smaller class of ships (now for the first time called 'Barks'), her Navy numbered thirty-four sail ready or making ready for immediate service.[1]

How far this was a real effective force we are fortunately able to determine with exactitude. The ultimate effect of the Spanish match and Mary's uncompromising Catholic attitude was that Elizabeth came to the throne in the midst of what we now call a Navy scare: and, under present apprehension of war with France, one of the first acts of her reign was to call for a departmental inquiry into the state of the Navy. The report of the committee has come down to us, and under the title of 'The Book of Sea Causes' forms one of the most valuable Navy papers extant. From a note on the first page it would appear to have been chiefly the work of Edward Bashe, General-Surveyor of the Victuals, and William Wynter, who, though still retaining his post as Surveyor of the Ships, had recently been appointed to the office of Master of the Naval Ordnance. Both were veterans in the Royal Service, and Wynter, until the rise of Hawkins and Drake, continued to be the most trusted and conspicuous of the Queen's

[1] Eight are assigned to this year by a doubtful Hatfield Paper of 1562 (see Oppenheim, p. 110). The eight vessels it mentions were not completed, however, in 1558. 'The Book of Sea Causes' gives officially the state of affairs in Feb. 1558-9. Four of the Hatfield Paper vessels, viz., The great-ships 'New Bark' and 'Greyhound' and the pinnaces 'Phœnix' and 'Sacre' were ready for service, of the other four, one, the 'Jennet,' was 'new-making' at Portsmouth, and three, the 'Hart,' 'Antelope,' and 'Swallow,' were at Deptford 'to be repaired.' Besides those specified by the Hatfield Paper the 'Book of Sea Causes' states that Henry's old 'Peter Pomgranate' was being new built as an 800 ton ship at Woolwich (afterwards the 'Elizabeth Jonas'), and at Portsmouth was the 'Sweepstake' and at Deptford the 'George' waiting repair.

officers. Gonson, too, probably had a hand in it, as one of the 'Officers of the Queen's Majesty's Navy' by whom the report is expressed to be drawn up. Of Mary's thirty-four sail, eleven great-ships of 200 tons and upwards, ten barks and pinnaces and the brigantine, with an aggregate tonnage of 5,500 tons, are classed as 'meet to be kept.' The rest, including the two galleys, were condemned as much worn and 'of no continuance and not worth repair,' and therefore to be sold towards the cost of 'new ships of better service in their place,' and amongst these was the ill-fated 'Jesus of Lubeck.'

The effective force, then, which Philip was compelled to abandon to his sister-in-law, consisted of twenty-two sail of all classes. This, however, was far from representing the full naval power of the kingdom. It had become, as we have seen, something like a tradition to encourage ship-owners, by various exemptions from custom dues and otherwise, to build vessels which might form a reserve in case of war, and foreign ambassadors were constantly reminding their sovereigns that it was the peculiar custom of English merchantmen to sail half armed. All that was required to turn them into serviceable men-of-war was to fit them with gun-platforms fore and aft, and with proper 'close fights' or barriers to hold boarders at bay should they enter. The success of this policy showed itself in the vast fleets Henry had been able to put rapidly upon the sea, and now Elizabeth's naval committee was able to report that of 'merchant ships which may be put in fashion of war' there were no less than forty-five with a tonnage of 8,640, an average, that is, of nearly 200 tons. Besides these there were twenty vessels fit for victuallers, and the whole force, both royal and private, they consider could be mobilised in two months, provided ready money were forth-coming and that no ship of the realm were permitted 'to go forth of merchandise.' The number of men required they put at 10,600, to be about equally divided between the Queen's ships and the auxiliary merchantmen. If a larger fleet be required, they calmly report in accordance with a universal practice of the time, it is to be had 'by making a stay of the hulks (that is the foreign merchantmen) that pass through the Narrow Seas to France in the beginning of the year,' an operation which Drake was destined to carry out. As to the headquarters of the fleet, they are in favour of a return to Gillingham Reach below Rochester, which during Mary's reign had been in some degree supplanted by the old station at Portsmouth. The new anchorage they considered as the best place for the Queen's ships to lie in time of peace. In time of war they advise that after grounding and rigging in the Thames, they should be sent to Portsmouth ready victualled for the five summer months, that is from May to August. In September they were to be brought round to Gillingham again and laid up for the winter.

It is however when we come to their recommendations for the future that the report attains its highest interest. In response probably to a requisition from the Government a naval programme—the first it is believed that we have—was drawn up, whereby in five years the sea service could be brought up to what the experience of the Admiralty officers considered the requirements of the kingdom. It is as follows:—

Ships, 24 ..	of 800 tons .	1
	700 ,,	1
	600 ,,	2
	500 ,,	4
	400 ,,	4
	300 ,,	6
	200 ,,	6
Barks, 4 ..	80 ,,	2
	60 ,,	2
Pinnaces to row	40 ,,	2
Total	. 9,660 tons .	. 30 vessels.

The programme deserves the most careful consideration, as being the expression of the latest ideas of practical English seamen and an indication of the point to which their conceptions of naval warfare had reached. To appreciate this thoroughly it is first necessary to compare the proposed programme with the foundation on which it was intended to proceed. In this way we are able to form an estimate of how far it was ideal and how far influenced by existing conditions. From the list of ships 'fit to be kept' we get the following table :—

Ships, 14	of 800 tons	1
	600 ,,	2
	500 ,,	1
	400 ,,	1
	300 ,,	4
	200–160 tons	5
Other classes, 10	100 tons	2
	70 ,,	2
	60 ,,	6
Total	5,580 tons	24 vessels.

Taking first the great-ships we note there is no suggestion for providing any vessels of the largest size, those floating fortresses which throughout the middle ages had been regarded as a necessary element in a first class fleet. The chief additions proposed are in the middle class, of ships from 400 to 500 tons. Of Henry VIII.'s twenty-five great-ships no fewer than nine had been of this class, and Wynter's practical experience of their superior handiness and seaworthiness had probably shown him already, what Drake was finally to demonstrate, the superiority in fighting value of many small and handy vessels over fewer large and unwieldy ones. This is clearly the idea of a man of the new time, a man, that is, who was regarding the broadside sailing vessel as the battle-ship of the future, and who desired first of all a ship that was handy and weatherly. The truth is that by this time the English school had discovered the real function of the great-ship. For them it was no longer the floating fortress, impregnable to boarders, overbearing all ordinary craft, and capable of transporting a whole garrison of horse and foot. Wynter already must have seen it as a mobile gun-carriage, and here was the great secret. It has been well said that the real arm of a trooper is his horse. For the new school the arm of the sailor was his ship. Hitherto the offensive force of a war-vessel had been measured mainly by the number of boarders it could throw upon the deck of an enemy, and guns had been valued chiefly as a means of crippling his power of eluding this form of attack. But now the ship with its guns was itself the weapon, the captain the eye, the crew the muscles that played it. Already during Henry's last French war the power that lay in the broadside had begun to be seen by the English seamen. When in 1574 Philip, under colour of reinforcing his Low Country army, was about to make a naval demonstration in the Narrow Seas, a Spanish agent in England wrote to Requesens, Governor of the Netherlands, that he had better warn the Spanish admiral to be on his guard against the new English tactics. 'If the fleets come to hostilities,' he wrote, 'it would be well to give orders, when they (the Spaniards) approach them (the English) that the ordnance flush with the water should be at once discharged broadside on and so damage their hulls and confuse them with the smoke. This is their own way of fighting, and I have many times seen them do it to the French thirty years ago. I advise his Majesty's ships to be beforehand with them and they will send to the bottom all that are opposed to them. This is a most important piece of advice.'[1] Here we have foreshadowed with complete distinctness the principle of attack that was to become the cardinal article of faith in the English Navy—to crush resistance by weight of metal in broadsides aimed low ; to hull and not to waste powder on the rigging ; to board when the enemy's fire was silenced and not before. It was a creed that once born took a firm hold, and so soon as it was grasped in the

[1] Letter of Intelligence to the Grand Commander of Castile, &c., London May 10, 1574. *Spanish Calendar*, p. 480. This was directly contrary to the Spanish practice. De Chaves lays down the rule that ' the guns of the lower ports must not be fired except when the enemy's ship comes to lay herself broadside to broadside at close quarters.' ˙ See in Duro, *Armada Española*, i. 382.

fulness of its possibilities it was only a matter of time for all warships to be designed so as best to give it effect.

Passing to the smaller classes we see signs of reforms still more suggestive of what was in the mind of the Committee. To begin with, there is the new class of 'Barks.' Hitherto this term had been applied to vessels of all sizes, from the 'Great Bark' of 500 tons down to the 'Bark of Boulogne' of 60; the former being a great-ship, the latter classed with Henry's pinnaces. But now it is pretty clear the term was officially adopted to express the smaller kind of sailing vessels which Henry had classed by the name of 'Pinnaces,' and which may be taken as the technical equivalent of the eighteenth century 'Frigate.' The 'Pinnace' now resumes its old signification. It practically takes the place of Henry's row-barges and the term is definitely applied to the smaller kind of oared vessel which was not a ship's boat, and this meaning it retained in the English service throughout the century. This small class of 'Pinnaces to Row,' it will be observed, is the only oared type the report admits. It may therefore be taken that Wynter and his colleagues had carried the northern ideas to their logical conclusion and had come to condemn all oared vessels as an obsolete type of sea-going fighting ship. The two pinnaces can only have been intended as tenders to the two flag-ships and to be used primarily at least for despatch and intelligence purposes. No condemnation so emphatic of the time-honoured type of war-vessel had yet been heard, and the new programme, with its light great-ships and its elimination of oars, must be held memorable, as the first confession of faith of the modern school of naval warfare.

That a real effort to improve the Navy was intended is clear from the fact that in the same year the Admiralty was organised with a view to making it a thorough working body. 'The Office of the Admiralty and Marine Affairs' remained as it had been established by Henry VIII. in 1546. The Minister of Marine was the

Lord High Admiral. The officers of his department were the 'Vice-Admiral of England,' the 'Master of the Ordnance,' the 'Surveyor of the Marine Causes and Officers,' the 'Treasurer,' the 'Controller,' the 'General-Surveyor of the Victuals,' the 'Clerk of the Ships,' and the 'Clerk of the Stores.' No ordinance however had been issued since Henry's time defining the duties of the several officers or the way in which the business of the office was to be conducted. This defect was now remedied and a minute was drawn up, which, after reciting that 'in these days the Navy is one of the chiefest defences of the kingdom,' proceeds to lay down rules for its good administration.[1]

The officers, as already established, were to meet at least once a week at the Admiralty on Tower Hill to present a report to the Lord Admiral, or in his absence to the Vice-Admiral. Ships when laid up at Gillingham were to be kept in good condition as cheaply as possible; and the Captain of Upnor Castle, which protected the anchorage, and his gunners were placed under the orders of the Admiralty. The Master of the Ordnance was further to make a quarterly return of the state and requirements of his office, and it was to be inspected quarterly by a departmental committee appointed and presided over by the Vice-Admiral. The Treasurer besides his weekly report was to furnish a special return monthly to the Lord Admiral and to make up his accounts quarterly. No payment was to be made except by warrant signed by three or four of the other officers, of whom the Vice-Admiral must be one. The same order applied to the Surveyor of the Victuals. For the actual condition of the fleet the Surveyor of the Ships, the Controller and the Clerks of the Ships and of the Stores were directly responsible. Their duty was to see the ships careened or dry-docked from time to time and kept in such order, that a squadron of from twelve to sixteen sail could be mobilised

[1] *S.P. Dom.* 1560, xv. 4. The titles of the offices as recited in this minute differ slightly from those in the original patents (see Oppenheim, p. 85).

in a fortnight, and the rest in a short time after. To this end they were to deliver a special report every month. The particular duty of the Clerk of the Ships was to provide timber for building and repairs: that of the Clerk of the Stores to see a proper reserve was kept up 'for sudden service': and to insure elasticity in the whole system and the personal attention of each officer in his department it was specially enjoined that no assistant was to be considered a 'head officer' but was to work in any department where he was ordered.

The practical thoroughness of the organisation is remarkable for the time. In conception, if not in practice, every head of department, it will be seen, was directly responsible to the Lord Admiral but under the supervision of the Vice-Admiral of England, who was, as we should say now, a naval Chief-of-the-Staff and the real working head of the Navy. The office of Lord Admiral was still a civil and political rather than a military appointment. It was filled with regard to the power and position of the candidate's family, rather than to his personal qualifications and experience as a naval officer. His civil jurisdiction, as a kind of Minister of Commerce with control of Harbours and the Police of the Coasts, and all Admiralty cases probably consumed the greater part of his attention. Even on his naval side he corresponded in his functions more nearly to a modern First-Lord or Minister-of-Marine than to a Naval Commander-in-Chief, and although on great occasions he might go to sea, it was rather as President of the Naval Council-of-War than as an Admiral-of-the-Fleet. His usefulness was by his high station to carry authority over rival officers, who could hardly be brought to submit to one of their own number. Feudal traditions, too, still made it impossible for so high a charge as the command of the Navy to be trusted to a commoner, however great his reputation. The dignity of the gentleman still required a nobleman to be in chief command, nor in the eyes of the nation would it seem that the whole force of the realm was being put forth unless one of the great feudatories was in his place to give due solemnity to the unfurling of the royal banner. The disciplinary value, too, of the office, as an imposing screen to prevent too profane a contact with the fountain of honour, must not be forgotten. Behind it would be held, in a kind of sacred reserve, the power and majesty of the throne, which no man could approach to measure, and to which he must bow in almost religious veneration. Still it will be seen the Lord Admiral was not of essential necessity to the machinery of the Navy. It would work without him, and, indeed, sometimes did. In time of peace the Vice-Admiral, his Chief-of-the-Staff, for all practical purposes, could supply his place, and in a great measure Lord Burghley made himself his own Minister-of-Marine.

For all who regard civilian influence in the Admiralty and a haphazard naval policy as the peculiar defects of modern administrations, it will be a consolation to know that the service report was almost wholly disregarded. A Navy List for the year 1565 has come down to us,[1] and from this we are able to form a very just conclusion of how widely the programme of the 'Book of Sea Causes' had been departed from at the end of the five years stipulated for its completion. Through some influence that is not to be traced, the list shows a distinct reaction towards the early ideas of Henry VIII. The energies of the dockyards had been spent upon the construction of two more unwieldy vessels, the 'Triumph' of 1,200 tons and the 'White-bear' of 1,000, while another large vessel of 800 tons, renamed the 'Victory,' had been purchased of some English merchants. Of the proposed tale of twenty-four great-ships no more than seventeen existed. Of these, besides the three already named, only two, the 'Hope' of 600 tons and the 'Aid' of 250, were new, and to make up even the reduced number of seventeen the 'Jesus' had to be retained and two other old ships, the 'Minion' and the 'Primrose,' that had been disposed of, were bought back into the service.[2] Nor was

[1] Printed in Derrick, p. 23.
[2] See note in Cecil's hand at the end of the list of February 1558-9, S.P. Dom. Eliz. ii. 30.

this all. At the end of the list appear not only several new pinnaces, but three galleys called the 'Speedwell,' the 'Try-right,' and the 'Eleanor.' Two of these vessels were probably the 'Black and Red Galleys' which the 'Book of Sea Causes' had condemned and possibly identical with the 'Galley Subtil' and the French prize of Henry's time, and the third perhaps the 'Brigantine.' But in any case the fact remains, that however strong and well-founded may have been the reforming convictions of Wynter and his school, it is clear they had not been able to persuade the Government to break away from the old ideas. Both French and Spaniards were developing their galley power with an energy that showed no suspicion of the senility of the type, and galleys were still regarded as necessary to encounter galleys, and indispensable for coast defence. So strong was Italian influence still in all departments of the art of war—if we may judge at least by the numerous translations of technical military works that were taking possession of the English market—that it is easy to understand how hard it was for the radical sea reformers to get a hearing. The renaissance had taken fast hold of every corner of English thought; in every department of knowledge men were bowing the knee to classical origins; and a theorist who could quote an Italian book, and point to a classical precedent would be sure to gain an easy victory over the most practical and experienced opponent, whose opinions were not so fashionably armed. It is possible that the necessity of providing oared vessels to act as police against the pirates that infested the Narrow Seas and St. George's Channel may have had some influence on the preservation of the smaller oared types, but in any case Wynter and his friends had to stand by and see the Navy stagnating in the compromise where Henry had left it.

For five years more this stagnation continued. The naval energy which Mary had bequeathed to her sister as the result of the loss of Calais, wore itself out, and till the time Drake first joined the service the dockyards reveal nothing but idleness. The queen, it is clear, seeing herself in possession of a navy so far in advance of any other oceanic power, considered it strong enough. It was a period too during which, by her lawless encouragement of the 'Beggars of the Sea' and the Huguenot privateers, she was able to keep command of the Narrow Seas without incurring new expenditure for naval construction. Her fleet, instead of increasing, gradually diminished. Four of Henry's old great-ships, including the 'Minion' and the 'Jesus,' disappeared and were not replaced; so that the tale of great-ships was reduced from seventeen to thirteen. The old pinnaces and the old galleys still retained their places on the list, and it was with this reduced and decaying force that England found herself compelled to face the most formidable coalition that had ever threatened her national existence.

To this low ebb then was the Navy reduced after the first ten years of the Sea Queen's reign when Drake's first period of service under the royal banner came to an end, and he left it to complete his education in a younger and more vigorous school.

CHAPTER V

NOMBRE DE DIOS

THE new stream of tendency upon which Drake was about to embark was beginning at this time to flow with increasing force and volume into the development of Elizabeth's Navy. Of all the elements that went to make up her sea power it is the most fascinating: for it is the one that gave it the special touch of daring and contempt for effete traditions, which we have grown accustomed to associate particularly with Drake's name, and which lent to the ripening of our maritime supremacy that colouring of romance which has come to obscure almost entirely its scientific aspect. For this reason and not a little from the excellent narrative Drake left behind him, his famous raid on the Spanish Main, or as it was always known, his 'Voyage to Nombre de Dios,' has attained perhaps an undue prominence in the history of these times.[1] Although one of the most daring and successful it was as we have seen by no means the only expedition of its kind, nor was it even the first. While Hawkins and the English merchant princes were trying to force the gate of the Indies on the basis of existing treaties, and others were content to harass Spain into reason with equivocal reprisal in European seas, there were some more venturesome and less scrupulous, who saw a field for their ambition in the far West where laws did not reach and consciences went to sleep.

The Spanish Indies at this time cônsisted of four main governments: Peruana or Peru, lying inaccessibly on the

[1] See Appendix D, *Sir Francis Drake Revived*.

South Pacific Coast with its capital at Lima; New Spain, withdrawn from observation behind the unknown waters of the Bay of Mexico; Guatemala, comprising with the provinces of Verapaz, Honduras, Nicaragua, and Veragua, the greater part of Central America; and finally the government of Española, which included with all the Islands the provinces of Tierra Firme, or Golden Castille, up to the confines of Guatemala.[1] Though the oldest and once the most important the latter government was now quite eclipsed by her younger sisters. The City of San Domingo it is true still retained, as the rendez-vous of the outward-bound convoys and the point of distribution for European goods, its old position of the Queen City of the Indies, and but two or three cities in the whole Spanish dominions could rival it for strength, size, and importance. But already the reckless native policy of the earlier colonists had exhausted the islands; most of them were uninhabited and valuable chiefly for their timber and the hides of the cattle that had run wild upon them, and the rest, including Española, or, as we called it, Hispaniola, were given up to roving tribes of escaped negroes, who having taken Indian wives were rapidly forming a new and savage population known to their former Spanish masters as *Cimaroñes* or 'Hill-men.' Darien was in no better case, and owed its importance solely to the fact that through it lay the road to Peru, which was almost all the Spaniards really held. Tierra Firme or the Spanish Main had been arrested in its development by the superior attractions of Peru and Mexico, and still consisted of a few scattered settlements along the coast and the course of the principal rivers with but one town of any importance—which was its capital, Cartagena. With this exception, as Hawkins demonstrated, the whole coast was practically without defence, and the sugar, pearls, and precious metals upon which the struggling settlements mainly subsisted, were conveyed to the rendezvous of the homeward-bound

---

[1] Heylyn's *Cosmographie*, 1657.

convoys in small vessels, that offered an easy prey to adventurous and well-armed visitors.

Into this promising arena it was the Frenchmen who showed us the way, as into so many others where by some seemingly inevitable destiny their exploits have come to be overshadowed by our own. In this case it was but natural that they should be the pioneers. It was during the long-continued wars between the Valois and the Habsburgs that the weight of the western treasure was first felt. For long after Columbus's discovery America was not regarded as of peculiar richness in precious metals. Las Casas himself in setting forth the advantages of the Indies admitted that Hispaniola could not rival England for silver and pearls and based its value on its sugar mills. Indeed it was not till the discovery of the Potosi mines of Peru in 1545, the year assigned to Drake's birth, that the real value of the Spanish Colonies became fully apparent. The prizes that were brought into the ports of France during the wars revealed to French sailors the fabulous richness of the Spanish Indies, and it was only to be expected that when persecution drove the Huguenots to the sea, the most daring of them should seek across the ocean for the fountain head of Catholic wealth. Even as early as 1536 a single French ship had captured and held to ransom the town of Havana. Since then almost every settlement in the West Indies of any importance, except San Domingo itself, had been sacked at least once. Havana had suffered twice, and encouraged by the defenceless condition of Spain at sea the Huguenot depredations had gone on increasing in daring until we have seen them culminate in the ambitious colonial projects that heralded Hawkins's appearance on the scene. With English seamen serving aboard Huguenot privateers, and with Huguenot privateers using English ports for the disposal of their prizes it was impossible that Englishmen should not be fired to do better where Frenchmen had done well. For the lawless work to begin, it wanted but a smart sufficiently sharp to goad them out of the lines of the traditional commercial friendship with Spain, and this the affair of San Juan de Ulua most amply afforded.[1]

The conditions under which Drake embarked upon the new phase in the great struggle with Spain are difficult to fathom but important to a right judgment of both the man and his time. The new phase has been regarded simply as one of lawless and even piratical reprisals, which Drake in imitation of the Huguenot example inaugurated on his own responsibility in order to redress his own alleged injuries with a not too accurate eye to striking a correct balance. By the family narrative his early expeditions were given frankly this colour.[2] At San Juan de Ulua it says he had been grievously endamaged 'not only in loss of goods of some value but also of his kinsmen and friends . . . and finding no recompense could be recovered out of Spain by any of his means or by Her Majesty's letters, he used such help as he might by two several voyages to the West Indies.' The first was with two ships, the 'Dragon' and the 'Swan,' in 1570, and the other in the 'Swan' alone in 1571. The English Government too maintained the same view, and to the complaints of Spain replied that he was a mere private adventurer for whose actions they were in no way responsible.[3] The Spaniards however took a different view. They suspected there was some kind of official recognition behind him, and it is difficult to believe their suspicions were unfounded.

If we read the laconic statement of the family narrative in the light of concurrent events, it assumes a different aspect. It was a time when the Counter-Reformation seemed about to overwhelm Elizabeth. A Catholic rising was looked for at any time; invasions again threatened from France and the Spanish Netherlands; and every kind of precaution both by land and sea was being taken

---

[1] For a long list of official reports relating to French depredations in the Indies from the year 1537 till the truce of 1556, see Duro, *Armada Española*, i. app. 14.

[2] *Sir Francis Drake Revived*, Arber v.

[3] 'Draft answer to the complaints of Spain,' 1580 ? *S.P. Spain.* xxvi.

to grapple with the dangers. On November 12, 1569, De la Mothe Fénelon, the French ambassador, reported the activity that was going on: 'They tell me too,' he said after detailing the movements of the Royal Navy, 'that Hawkins is pushing forward the armament of seven other good men-of-war, but they want to make me believe that they are for a new voyage he is undertaking to the Indies.' He himself was convinced the real destination was to succour the Huguenots at Rochelle. In December Menendez believed Hawkins had actually sailed for the Indies with a large fleet.[1] This was untrue, but there can be no doubt, as afterwards plainly appeared, that he was preparing a naval force and that his intention was to attempt the rescue of the men he had been compelled to abandon in the Bay of Mexico and to exact reprisals for the breach of the convention at St. Juan de Ulua. For the time however its object was left uncertain. Before the end of the month the Catholic insurrection in the North broke out. Alva was assembling a force in the Netherlands to come across to the support of the insurgents. England's hour seemed to have come and all her strength was needed. The whole Navy was mobilised and Hawkins's private squadron was required for the defence of the realm.

As is well known the Catholic combination failed. The insurrection proved premature and was easily suppressed and Alva stayed where he was. Still, it remained to be seen what new dangers the ensuing spring would have in store. In February, Hawkins, apparently in despair of being allowed to put his design into execution, went to call on the Spanish ambassador and begged his intercession for the release of the English hostages and prisoners, whose fate, to do him justice, seemed always to trouble him much more than the fortune he had lost. In reporting this interview Don Guerau assures the King that no fleet had left for the Indies but only three moderate sized vessels, which sailed for the Guinea coast on their

---

[1] See his letter of December 4. Letters of Menendez, *ubi supra*.

way, as he supposed, to America.¹ In June he mentioned these same ships again, as belonging to Sir William Wynter. 'One of Wynter's ships,' he says, 'which went to Guinea has returned and the other two, if they can escape the Portuguese fleet, will go to the island of Hispaniola.'² Now we know that Drake went to the Indies early this year with the 'Dragon' and the 'Swan,' and as Don Guerau, who was watching the western ports like a lynx, was sure that no more than three vessels had sailed, it is extremely probable that the two ships, belonging to Wynter, which continued their voyage to Hispaniola were none other than the 'Dragon' and the 'Swan' and that Drake was sent out in advance for intelligence purposes by the same group of politicians, financiers, and naval officers for whom he had been acting before.³

This is all the more likely since directly the third vessel returned from Guinea, with intelligence possibly of the Portuguese movements, Hawkins was suddenly hurried off to Plymouth, to complete the equipment of three of his own ships and three of other owners which were supposed to be bound for the Indies.⁴ The summer was passing without sign of a campaign by the Catholic powers, and Hawkins could renew his hopes of vengeance. All July the preparations went busily forward, and the Earl of Bedford himself went to Plymouth to push on their completion.⁵ The service of a famous Portuguese pilot called Bayon, who knew every inch of the Indies and

¹ *Spanish Cal.* p. 236. ² *Ibid.* p. 254.
³ The only account we have of this voyage is in a paper entitled 'A summary relation of the harms and robberies done by Fr. Drake an Englishman, with the assistance and help of other Englishmen.' It runs: 'In the year 1570 he went to the Indies in a bark of 40 tons, with whom there went an English merchant of Exeter called Rich. Dennys and others, and upon the coast of Nombre de Dios they did rob divers barks in the river Chagres that were transporting merchandise of 40,000 ducats of velvets, and taffetas, beside other merchandise, besides gold and silver in other barks, and with the same came to Plymouth, where it was divided amongst his partners' (*Ashmole MSS.* 830). Being of Spanish origin, it probably exaggerated the damage.
⁴ *Spanish Cal.* p. 253. ⁵ *Ibid.* pp. 261, 263.

all the secrets of the treasure trade, had been secured, as well as those of some Spanish refugees. Don Guerau grew anxious and did his best to penetrate the secret of the fleet's destination. He reported that originally it had been intended to establish a settlement near the Strait of Magellan, but the present idea was to go to the Rio del Oro near New Spain. 'They take with them,' he writes, 'pinnaces to enter the river, at the mouth of which there is a good port, which they intend to colonise, after having stolen all the gold they can lay hands on in the interior, which they think will be a large amount.'[1] At another time he reports the colonisation scheme is to be prefaced on the voyage out by a dash at the treasure fleet in conjunction with Sores, the great Huguenot privateer captain, who in one year with a single ship had harried the whole Spanish Main and two of the most important ports in the Islands. He tampers with Bayon, and Bayon tells him they do not mean to settle at all, but to seize and hold the island of San Juan de Ulua and have the whole treasure trade at their mercy, and again in a few days he is sure Bayon is a liar.

Just when Hawkins's preparations were nearly complete, it would seem that Drake came home. 'The second ship that Wynter sent,' the ambassador wrote to the King on August 5, 'has returned hither and they have bartered their goods there at Capo de la Vela and Jamaica for hides and silver of which they bring large quantities.' If this vessel was indeed Drake's he came with his intelligence in the nick of time. Everything was ready for sea; sailing orders were hourly expected; but instead of them, there came a command that Hawkins must wait. In vain he pressed to be allowed to sail. The anxiety of the spring had been suddenly reawakened. A strong Spanish fleet was coming to the Netherlands, and its ostensible object of escorting Philip's new Queen to Spain was believed to mask some great design against Elizabeth. The Royal Navy was hastily prepared for mobilisation,

[1] *Spanish Cal.* p. 264.

and all that came of Hawkins's prayers to be let loose was a summons to London, where he received orders that he must employ his squadron in watching the movements of the coming fleet in the West.

The Spaniards came, were met by the Queen's ships, and attended ceremoniously till they were safe out of the Channel again. The acuteness of the crisis was over, but still Hawkins was held in. It would seem he began to despair of being permitted to seek redress by force. In September hints reached Don Guerau's ears that he might be tempted to abandon his object altogether, and here we have the first note of the masterly intrigue in which he eventually outwitted the acutest of Philip's diplomatists.[1]

Hawkins's era of aggressive commerce may now be said to be at an end; Drake's era of piracy was beginning. In this fateful year of 1570 the great struggle distinctly changed its character. The Counter-Reformation had shown its hand, the Pope's Bull of deposition had been nailed to the gates of Lambeth Palace, and England saw herself branded in Christendom as an outlaw. It was no longer a question of commerce: it was a question of national existence and religion; and the people, with the half-blind instinct for foreign policy which will sometimes feel further than the ripest wisdom of statesmen, began the war into which at last they were to force their unwilling sovereign.

At the end of November Don Guerau obtained an order of the Admiralty Court to stay the sailing of seven private vessels that were bound for the Indies, 'But I am afraid,' he laments, 'some of the ships will go.'[2] He was right. The movement was now beyond the power of the Council to control even if they wished it. Accordingly in January 1571 he had to report: 'Three vessels and a thirty-ton boat have left Plymouth for the Indies and another boat and frigate are ready to leave. All the efforts made and promised by the Judge of the Admiralty

[1] *Spanish Cal.* pp. 274 and 277.   [2] *Ibid.* p. 286.

are insufficient to prevent them going.'[1] Again in March some eight or nine more were being equipped for the same destination, some of them Wynter's and some of them Hawkins's which were on the point of sailing.[2] Amongst others as we know Drake sailed in the 'Swan.' This time it may have been on his own account. More impatient by his character even than his cousin of the constant disappointments he had experienced, it may be that he fitted out the little vessel with the proceeds of his last voyage, resolved to seek redress with his own hand.

Of this venture all we know is that it proved 'both rich and gainful' and was not confined to trade. From Cartagena harbour, the Spaniards complained, he cut out a ship of 180 tons. There were other prizes, too, and prisoners, whom he carried to a romantic natural harbour which he had discovered in the silent recesses of the Gulf of Darien. Here too he established a regular base for future operations. Close upon the track of the treasure frigates and yet completely hidden it was an ideal pirate's lair, where fish and game of all kinds abounded, and especially the *Guan*, in honour of whose delicate flesh he named the place 'Port Pheasant.' It was probably that *Puerto Escondido*, or 'Secret Harbour,' which lies some four leagues to the South-West of Caledonian Bay. The Narrative describes it as 'a fine round bay, of very safe harbour for all winds, lying between two high points, not past half a cable's length over at the mouth; but within eight or ten cables every way having ten or twelve fathoms of water more or less, full of good fish; the soil also very fruitful.' From this remote and secret haunt he continued his inquiries into the Peruvian treasure trade. Lope de Vega in his 'Dragontea' tells us that trusting to his mastery of the Spanish tongue he actually visited Nombre de Dios disguised as a Spaniard. Though this is probably an invention of the poet's, for it is more than doubtful whether at this time Drake could speak Spanish at all, he certainly displayed a strange familiarity

[1] *Spanish Cal.* p. 294. [2] *Ibid.* p. 294.

with the plan of the place when the time came to act. In any case he got to learn how the treasure was brought from Peru to Panama by sea, thence by mule trains across the Isthmus to the point where the Chagres River becomes navigable and so either by road or water to Nombre de Dios to be shipped for Spain. Having thus ascertained all he wished to know, he buried his surplus stores in his stronghold, released his Spanish prisoners, and returned home with the plunder he had secured, and his head full of the daring scheme upon which his reputation was founded.

In England during his absence events had marched in a direction entirely favourable for the furtherance of his project. Hawkins had paid the Spaniards in their own coin. Convinced of the futility of trying to stop the West Indian voyages by legitimate means Don Guerau had been tempted to listen to the cunning seaman while he played his old trick of pretending to be desirous of deserting to the Spanish Crown. During the late crisis part of the national system of defence had been an auxiliary squadron of merchantmen stationed off Scilly to see that no Spanish fleet entering the Channel detached vessels to operate against Ireland. This Western Squadron, which was placed under Hawkins's command, he persuaded the Spanish ambassador he was ready to carry over to Philip's flag at the critical moment. Though at first naturally suspicious the ambassador was soon entirely taken in. To convince Philip was a more difficult matter. At the moment however the offer was too tempting to be rejected. Not only was Philip engaged in concert with the Pope and the Venetians in preparing for a gigantic effort to crush the sea power of the Turks ; but the Ridolphi plot was also on foot for the assassination of Elizabeth to be followed by a combined invasion of England by Alva and the Guises to put Mary Stuart on the vacant throne. The cleverness of Hawkins's confidential agent Fitzwilliam did the rest. The price Hawkins asked was the release of his imprisoned comrades and some substantial compensation for his own losses. By the end of August every one of the prisoners had been sent home with ten dollars in his pocket and Hawkins with 40,000*l.* in his own was laughing in his sleeve at his royal dupe. Not only had he gained all he wanted, but to Cecil Fitzwilliam was able to hand the ends of the threads which made up the tangled skein of the Ridolphi plot. Don Guerau still believed Hawkins meant to fulfil his promise, so that Fitzwilliam was able to draw from him all he knew of the scheme. During the winter every knot of it was bit by bit unravelled till its whole extent was laid bare. The recently published Bull of the Pope dissolving Elizabeth's subjects from their allegiance stood out in its true colours and all the world could read in it the declaration of a Catholic crusade for the destruction of the heretic Queen and the setting up of Mary Stuart in her place. In January 1572, Don Guerau was summarily ordered to quit the kingdom and we seemed to be on the very brink of war with Spain.

No matter therefore how indefensible the piratical venture upon which Drake was bent, neither from official quarters nor from his own conscience was any hindrance likely to arise. As the danger which the country had passed through was realised a bitter change came over the national spirit. 'The case,' says Fuller, 'was clear in sea divinity,' and English seamen could no longer hesitate to share with the Huguenots and the 'Beggars of the Sea' the doctrine that to prey upon Catholics was pleasing in the sight of God. To men who went to their Bibles for their opinions, as we go to our newspapers, the 'Papists' easily became Egyptians to be spoiled, Amalekites to be destroyed. It was a creed that came comfortably to a pirate, and yet it would be to misread the times to doubt it was not also a real conviction. To the earnest, and particularly the uneducated Protestant, the Catholics were idolaters; for him the Mass was an abomination as honestly loathed, as by earnest Catholics it was devoutly loved. The two sentiments are correlative, and to ignore the force of the one is to underrate the depth of the other. Nor must we forget the large class that stood between the two extremes of religious opinion—a class of men ambitious of name and fortune, bent on achieving their career, and yet, by instinct or education, scrupulous enough to reject any means for which a religious sanction was not to be found. To this class both Drake and Hawkins probably belonged; nor can anyone who considers the horrors which the success of the Ridolphi plot would have meant for England, how the country must for years have been the scene of tragedies such as those which were filling France with lamentation, blame them if before such a prospect their own will seemed for them and their like the will of God. It would be almost incredible if Drake's early life had not left some mark of fanaticism upon his character, and from this time forward, if not before, there can be little doubt that he set out to seek his fortune in something of the spirit of a crusader who was doing Heaven a service. Fuller says that the chaplain of Drake's ship, meaning probably the Navy ship on which he had been serving, had solemnly told him that it was lawful to recover his losses upon the King of Spain; and Bishop Jewell, we are told, had given to Elizabeth his opinion that to exact reprisals from the Spaniards would be pleasing in the sight of God.

In Spain it was believed that the Queen actually subscribed to the cost of Drake's new expedition, but for this there is no shadow of real authority. Still, in any case, no difficulties, we may be sure, were put in his way, and on May 24, 1572, he was able to set sail from Plymouth upon his famous adventure. From various French and English ports a swarm of privateers had gone already in the same direction. Growing every year more adventurous, they had seen how Spain's preoccupation with the Turks in the Mediterranean rendered her powerless to protect her oceanic commerce and possessions; and now, as she lay panting from the exhausting effort of

Lepanto and strove inadequately to reap its fruits, their
daring redoubled. From Havre alone some twenty sail
had set out for Guinea, the Brazils, and the Indies, and so
helpless was Spain to interfere that they and others had
been boldly making use of such Spanish ports as Vigo
and Bayona as watering and victualling stations.[1] From
England Sir Edward Horsey, the Governor of the Wight,
had despatched a vessel under one Captain James Ranse,
the same man probably who had been master of the
'William and John' in Hawkins's last expedition.[2]
Another had gone from Plymouth under one John
Garrett, probably the same who had been master of the
'Minion' at San Juan de Ulua; but who was his patron,
or how many other officials in high station were also
repeating their previous ventures and seeking reprisals
for their loss we do not know; for on the dismissal of
the Spanish ambassador, his system of secret observation
became for a while disorganised and we have no more of
his spies' reports. There can be little doubt however
that Wynter, or some other of them, was at Drake's back;
otherwise in view of the extensive naval preparations that
were being made he hardly would have been allowed to
leave the kingdom.[3]

The force under his command consisted of the
'Pascha'[4] of 70 tons, which he calls his 'admiral'
or flagship, and the 'Swan' of 25 tons, his 'vice-
admiral,' in which his brother John Drake was Captain.
His crews numbered seventy-three men and boys, of
whom the eldest was fifty and all the rest under thirty,

---

[1] *Spanish Calendar*, Nov. 22, 1571.

[2] This man's name is variously spelt, Ranse, Rause, Raunce, and Rouse.
Sir William Davenant in his Masque of the *History of Sir Francis Drake*,
called him Rause. In *Sir F. Drake Revived* it is also spelt Rause, but in
the Nutwell Court copy is inserted an MS. page of errata, and amongst
them is this: 'For *Rause* reade *Ranse* and also in other pages,' so that
there can be little doubt the name should have the 'n' and not the 'u.'

[3] The *Ashmole MS.* says Wynter and Hawkins were his partners.

[4] This word is so variously spelt, that it is difficult to say whether it was
called from 'Pascha,' Easter, or from 'Pasha,' the Turkish title.

and it is specially recorded that they were all voluntarily enlisted, which would look as though he had had authority to impress men and was proud like captains of all times of not having had need to use it. Among them was his brother Joseph and Mr. John Oxenham of famous memory, whose romantic tragedy Kingsley has made common knowledge. Of the ships it is said: 'both were richly furnished with victuals and apparel for a whole year and no less heedfully provided of all manner of ammunition, artillery [which meant in those days all kinds of firearms], artificers' stuff and tools, that were requisite for such a man-of-war on such an attempt; but especially having three dainty pinnaces made in Plymouth, taken asunder all in pieces and stowed aboard to be set up as occasion served.' From subsequent hints it is clear that all the equipment was abreast with the latest ideas of English military science; the whole affair indeed bears very little the aspect of an irresponsible piratical adventure; and small as was its importance historically beside some of Drake's subsequent achievements of which we know less, it is impossible to resist the temptation of following it in some detail, not only for the intrinsic interest of the voyage, as being the first in which a raid into the interior was attempted,[1] but also for the picture it affords of the condition of the Spanish Colonies and the methods of the rovers, and for the insight it gives us into the character of the man who of all that strenuous time raised himself highest in the sight of Europe.

With his well-found but diminutive squadron in twenty-five days without striking sail he made the channel between Dominica and Martinique. There on the south-side of a rocky island three leagues from the Dominica coast he anchored and remained for three days to refresh his men ashore and water his ships. Thence proceeding westward he made his next land-fall at the Sierra Nevada, that lies behind Santa Marta on the Spanish Main, and keeping well out to sea, on July 21

[1] Lopez Vaz in Hakluyt.

he arrived unperceived off his secret harbour. Secure in the knowledge that there was no Spanish settlement within a hundred miles of the place, he was going ashore in his boat unarmed and with only a few companions, when to his astonishment he perceived smoke rising from his fastness. Returning at once for his other boat and arms, he boldly entered the harbour to turn out the intruders. Except the rising smoke not a sign of life was to be seen. Indeed the place looked as virgin as when he had first found it, and with wondering eyes his men saw that all the paths and alleys they had cleared the previous year were completely overgrown. Proceeding cautiously through the thick undergrowth, still with no sign of the intruders, they came suddenly upon a leaden plate fixed to a tree, and upon it was written this inscription: 'Captain Drake! If you fortune to come to this Port, make hast away! For the Spaniards which you had with you here, the last year, have bewrayed the place and taken away all that you left here. I depart hence, this present 7th of July, 1572. Your very loving friend John Garrett.' It was then Garrett's fire that was still smouldering and this friendly warning explained the mystery. With Garrett had sailed some of Drake's old crew and they had revealed the place to their new captain. To find that the Spaniards had discovered and plundered his lair was a bad beginning, but here he had resolved to set up his pinnaces and he was not to be alarmed out of his intention. The two vessels were brought in and a fort of pentagonal trace, according to the fashion of the time, marked out ashore. One side was upon the sea and open to it, and the others were closed with an impenetrable abattis of trees. But one narrow gate-way gave egress towards the land and around it was cleared a glacis fifty feet wide. Within the enclosed space the carpenters at once set to work on the pinnaces, but the very next day when they had hardly got to work and before the fort can have been completed, three strange sail, two of them Spanish built, appeared off the once unknown port. They proved to be nothing worse than Sir Edward Horsey's vessel in company with a Spanish caravel of advice and a shallop which Ranse had taken.[1] Such company was by no means welcome, but to make the best of it, Drake determined to take the strangers into his confidence. His design he told them was nothing less than to seize Nombre de Dios itself at a time when he knew the Treasure-houses would be full and to hold the town till they had emptied them. Having heard the project Ranse requested to be allowed to join it, and articles of partnership were then and there drawn up between the two captains.

In a week the pinnaces were set up and equipped, and the combined squadron stole out of its hiding place.[2] Proceeding north-westward along the Darien coast towards their goal, in three days they reached a cluster of fir-clad islands, which were known to them as the Islas de Pinos or Pine Islands. At this place they intended to conceal their vessels while the attempt was made in the pinnaces; but here too they found themselves forestalled, this time by negroes loading planks into two frigates from Nombre de Dios.[3]

---

[1] A 'caravel of advice' was a sailing despatch boat. A 'shallop' was the Spanish equivalent to the English 'pinnace,' and had oars.

[2] These pinnaces he named the 'Minion,' the 'Eion,' and the 'Lion.'

[3] This type of vessel, which was to play a conspicuous part in Drake's life, was something quite different from the frigate of the next centuries. The *fregata* was a Mediterranean type and would seem originally to have been the tender of a galley. About the middle of the sixteenth century it developed into a special kind of galley, with one mast and from eight to twelve oars a side, sometimes decked and sometimes not. Being of finer mould and having a less lofty and cumbrous poop than the Brigantines, they were found faster and more handy, and rapidly replaced them as the cruisers of a galley fleet. Jal, *Glossaire*, p. 718; Guglielmotti, 1. 186. When they became sailing ships is as usual difficult to determine. Generally it is considered this was not so until well into the seventeenth century, but in a Papal Inventory of 1590 (*ib*. vii. 76) they are already characterised as *Fregate a remo*, 'Rowing-frigates,' as though there were some that had only sails. In 1591 when we were making great efforts to intercept the Plate ships, an English spy in Spain sent home a drawing of the new treasure 'frigates' that had been specially designed to elude our cruisers, and this drawing represents a three-masted sailing ship, carrying guns on two decks, which was in fact a small galleon (*S.P. Spain*, xxix. 56). Whatever the

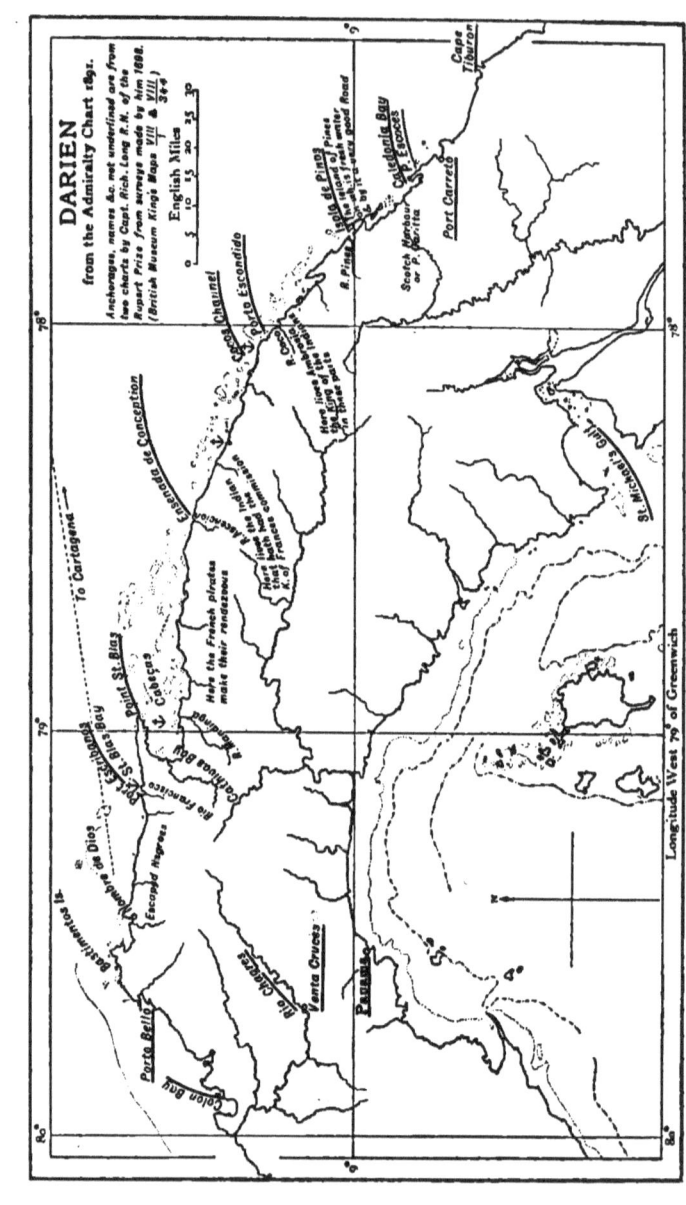

These were at once seized and questioned, and the information they had to give was far from pleasant. In the waste of hill and forest which lay on each side of the road from Panama to Nombre de Dios the *Cimarones* or 'Maroons,' as they came to be known in our marine, had become exceptionally bold and powerful. It was some eighty years before that a party of escaped negroes had taken to the mountains, and finding favour with the Indian women had grown into two strong tribes each under its own chief, with the Isthmus road dividing their respective territories. By nature savage and war-like, of splendid physique and alarmingly prolific, they were feared and treated by the Spaniards like wild beasts. This very year, to put an end to the reign of terror that prevailed, a chivalrous Spanish gentleman had offered to lead a force against one of their strongholds. It had been almost annihilated, and the Maroons taking the offensive had nearly succeeded in surprising Nombre de Dios itself. This was but six weeks past, and the negroes' news was that the alarmed citizens had sent off to Panama an urgent demand for reinforcements. As Drake was trusting for success to the weakness and apathy of the garrison no tidings could have been worse. Still, for him it was but another reason for immediate action.

The negroes were first set ashore and given their liberty to join the Maroons if they could, whereby Drake was able to follow his invariable policy of ingratiating himself with these people, and at the same time to insure their not getting to Nombre de Dios before him. These precautions completed, the three ships and the prize caravel were left in charge of Ranse, while Drake himself took command of the four pinnaces, the shallop making the fourth, with a draft of fifty-three of his own men and twenty of Ranse's. With this force he proceeded westward without loss of a day.

special character of the *fregata* in question, it was something that Drake highly approved, and there is reason to believe that it was he who introduced the type into England (see *post*, p. 194 n., and vol. ii. p. 340).

In five days they had reached an island some twenty-five leagues from the Pine Islands, and here in the early morning Drake landed his men and served out the arms.[1] The whole morning was spent in drill, and in the afternoon a fresh start was made under sail, in order that before sundown they might make the mouth of the Rio Francisco, a small river that falls into the sea a little to the eastward of Nombre de Dios Bay. Hence they kept close in along the shore out of sight of the watch-house on the point of the Bay, till six miles from it they anchored to wait for night. So soon as it was dark they stole on again in deep silence as far as the point of the Bay, and here under the high land came another anxious wait for dawn. As the dark hours dragged wearily on, Drake saw his young hands growing more and more nervous. Round the point lay a world renowned town, 'as big as Plymouth,' they murmured, and perhaps already full of the invincible Spanish infantry. An oppressive silence reigned, with nothing to break it but their own anxious whispers as they discussed the negroes'

[1] The curious in military lore will see in the nature and proportions of the arms served out, the action not of a mere pirate arming his desperadoes to the teeth, but of an officer conversant with the military practice of the time. They were as follows: targets, 6; fire-pikes, 6; pikes, 12; muskets and calivers, 24; bows, 16; partizans, 6; drums and trumpets, 2; showing the influence of a man acquainted with the complicated arrangement of a regular infantry *tertia*. The organisation, it will be seen, was according to rule approximately three-fold: staff-weapons (i.e., pikes, fire-pikes, and partizans), 24; small-shot (i.e., muskets and calivers), 24; archers and sword-and buckler-men, 22. The fire-pikes and the bowmen alone are irregular, the latter being a national and conservative modification of the received Italian organisation which is not unfrequently met with. For the English had not yet entirely lost faith in the weapon which had made their infantry once the first in Europe; nor in view of the superiority of the bow both in rapidity and accuracy of fire over the firearms of the time was their conservatism without some justification. The doubling of the drums and trumpets was to allow of the force acting in two different parties. The whole as detailed numbers seventy-four, so that it includes Drake himself. It will also be noticed that no defensive armour was served out. The English seamen's prejudice against its use was insuperable. Drake himself, in spite of the fashion of the time, was never painted in anything heavier than a gorget and a quilted doublet. (Cf. Sir Richard Hawkins's lament on the subject in his *Observations*, p. 302.)

news. Drake, watching the rapid demoralisation of his force, saw it was impossible to keep them in hand till daybreak. There was still a good hour to wait, but his ready wit seized a way to shorten it. The rising moon was just silvering the horizon. He boldly proclaimed it to be the dawn and ordered out the oars.

It was an hour before the time and still dark. Yet no sooner were they well into the bay than they knew they were detected. A newly arrived ship could be made out taking up her moorings and as they looked a boat sped from her side and hurried for the landing-place. Quick as thought, Drake dashed away for her and succeeded in heading her off to the opposite side of the bay, so that in the end they reached the shore unperceived. Springing aland they began tumbling the guns of the shore battery into the sand, but not before the sleepy sentry made off to give the alarm. Already on the alert in fear of a renewal of the Maroons' attack, the town was immediately aroused, and while the Englishmen were forming on the sands, the bell of the church rang out an alarm, and the streets were filled with the cries of the panic stricken townsfolk, and the roll of drums moving up and down.

Having rendered the shore battery useless Drake told off twelve men to guard the pinnaces and with the rest of his company hurried to a hill on the east side of the town. Part of the scheme of Colonial and Trade defence into which the depredations of the Corsairs had driven the reluctant Spaniards was the fortification of the principal ports of call; and the previous year Drake had learnt that they were about to erect a work upon the hill in question to command the town and its approaches. To ascertain how far the design had been carried out was necessarily his first care. The new battery was found completed, but still unarmed, and Drake at once determined to proceed to the Plaza. His company was divided into two parties, one under his brother John and John Oxenham with orders to skirt round the King's Treasure-house and enter the

Plaza from the eastward, the other he himself was to lead up the main street. So with fire-pikes blazing and drum and trumpet sounding they marched by their several routes yelling as they went to the complete confusion of the Spaniards. Not only did the division of the force enhance its apparent numbers, but having seen men mounting to the fort, the Spaniards believed that half the English had been left there; and the whole place was thrown into a helpless panic.[1] Drake's column was the first to reach the Plaza. Here a number of soldiers and townsfolk had had time to form beside the Governor's house barring the approach to the Panama gate with intent probably to cover the flight of the terrified inhabitants. As Drake debouched into the square he was received with a volley. His trumpeter fell, but stopping only to return the fire with shot and arrows, he rushed in and came at once to push of pike and clubbed muskets. At the same moment the fire-pikes of the eastern party were seen blazing in at the other corner of the square, and not knowing how weak were their assailants the Spaniards broke and fled, casting away their arms as they ran and were chased by the exultant sailors clear out of the Panama gate.

In complete possession of the Plaza they now reformed to hold it, while Drake forced two prisoners to show him the Governor's house, where he knew the *recuas* or mule trains from Panama were unloaded. In the cellars they found a pile of silver bars, as they guessed it, 70 feet in length, 10 feet in breadth, and 12 in height, each bar weighing about 35 to 40 lb.; in all there were some 360 tons of silver ready for the Fleet of Tierra Firme. But Drake would not suffer his amazed followers to touch a bar. It was pearls and gold he was seeking and these he ascertained had been removed to the King's Treasure-house down by the waterside. Still standing to his arms, for the town was yet full of people and soldiers running in confusion hither and thither and unable to escape, he

[1] Lopez Vaz in *Hakluyt*.

despatched a party to break open the Treasure-house. Meanwhile came an alarm that the pinnaces were being attacked, which was only allayed by sending Oxenham down to report; and then there burst upon them a tropical thunderstorm in all its terrors with a deluge of rain, from which for the protection of their powder and bowstrings they had to take refuge under the verandah of the Treasure-house. Thus compelled to abandon their post of vantage in the Plaza, they made a desperate attempt to get at the treasure from where they were; but in vain they wearied themselves trying to break in; the solid masonry resisted every effort; and with the revulsion from the excitement of the fight something like a panic began to take hold of the men. A negro who had deserted to the boatguard had told them that a week ago in response to the demand for reinforcements, a hundred and fifty soldiers had arrived to strengthen the garrison. As the news spread and the more faint-hearted began to realise how critical was their position, mutterings were heard in the ranks. It was one of those moments with which Drake had an unsurpassed genius for dealing. The rain was now ceasing: so crying to them that he had brought them to the mouth of the Treasure-house of the world and that if they went away empty they must blame nobody but themselves, he ordered his brother and Oxenham with their party to go round and break open the door of the King's Treasure-house while he returned to hold the Plaza. The panic was checked. Determined not to let it go further he stepped forward at once to put himself at the head of his party, and then rolled over in the sand.

At the first volley he had been hit in the leg, but fearing his men would make it an excuse for getting off with the plunder they had already managed to secure, he had resolutely concealed it, till he fainted from loss of blood. How much he had lost the sand revealed in the growing light and now nothing would hold them. Revived with a cordial he bound a scarf round his leg to stop the bleeding and called to them to go on, but in vain. Their Captain's life they vowed was worth all the treasure of the Indies, but it was not till they added force to their entreaties that they got him to the boats. Many men besides the Captain were wounded; and for the sake of these, as they said, in passing out of the bay they captured the newly arrived ship which happened to have a cargo of wine; and with this in company as the day broke they coolly established themselves outside the bay on the Isle of *Bastimentos* or Victualling Island, where were the gardens and poultry yards that supplied the town.

Such is the English account of this daring attempt, nor can it be seriously doubted that it is substantially true, and that but for Drake's untimely wound he would have accomplished his object. The account of Lopez Vaz and Herrera would suggest that the English were driven out of the town by force. This is of course the version the Governor would naturally have given out, and uncorroborated it is of no weight. Vaz's account we know to be coloured favourably to the Spaniards, for it makes no mention of the Spanish loss, which is put at eighteen killed in the official complaint which Philip made to the English Government.[1] The only foundation for this boast seems to be that the Spaniards succeeded in remounting a gun in the shore battery and firing on the pinnaces as they retired, but it was probably at long range and certainly did not prevent the capture of the wine-ship which the official complaint also mentions.[2]

In their luxurious retreat they remained two days while the surgeons attended the wounded, and here, under a flag of truce from the Governor, they were visited by one of the officers who had brought in the reinforcements from Panama. The real object probably was to ascertain

---

[1] *Memorias de los Cossarios Ingleses*, S.P. Spain, xviii. 1580–81. See *post*, Appendix D. Lopez Vaz says only one Spaniard was killed, who was looking out of a window to see what was the matter.

[2] For the authenticity and general credibility of the English Narrative, see Appendix D.

the pirate's strength; but the officer, whose profuse civility and elaborate manners greatly entertained the seamen, protested his only desire was to see whether their leader, as some of the townsfolk alleged, was the same Captain Drake who during the last two years had used his prisoners so kindly, and if so whether there was anything the Governor could have the pleasure of supplying him with. At first he said it was feared they were French, but that, when the arrows proclaimed their nationality, they knew that whatever happened to the treasure their persons were safe from cruelty. This was probably true; for the French had no long tradition of commercial friendship with Spain to soften their dealings with them, nor had the English as yet been goaded into the savage and the implacable hostility to which Menendez's extermination of the Florida Colony had driven the Huguenots.[1] Still, the officer ventured to inquire whether the arrows, which had wounded many of his men, were poisoned, and, if so, how the wounds should be treated. To this Drake answered that he was the man they meant; that it was never his manner to use poisoned arrows, and the wounds should be treated in the ordinary way. As to the Governor's offer of supplies, he found there was everything necessary where he was, except the special commodity of that country which alone would satisfy his company. So let the Governor, he ended, hold open his eyes, for before he departed, if God lent him life and leave, he meant to reap some of their harvest, which they got out of the earth and sent into Spain to trouble all the earth. Though knowing he had to deal with a spy Drake was not to be outdone in courtesy. The officer was entertained to dinner and finally dismissed

[1] The only act of cruelty alleged against Drake occurs in the *Memorias de los Cossarios*. The third article relates how he captured a caravel bound for Havana, 'Y llevo preso a un Francisco Ravano que yva por piloto, y le echo a la mar, porque no le quiso mostrar los puertas.' This probably means that he ducked the refractory pilot from the yard-arm, an ordinary sea punishment of the time and by no means the most severe Such an action would be quite justified by the usages of war, and would be a regular proceeding in the case of a prisoner who refused to act as guide. It is not said the man was killed.

with presents, pouring forth high flown compliments upon their valour and gentility, and protesting he had never been so much honoured of any in his life. The scene reads like a chapter of Dumas, and yet it bears the plain stamp of veracity. It could not have been invented, and we may see in it with certainty how the young Captain was already evincing that love of display and ceremonial, that desire to be the fine and chivalrous gentleman, which constantly display themselves in his conduct; no less than that scrupulous adherence to the gentler rules of civilised warfare with which he was always credited by friend and foe alike.

No sooner had the Spanish officer gone than Drake was forming a new plan to carry out his threat. Diego, the negro deserter, informed him that his name was already honoured among the Maroons, and that if he would only permit him to open up communication with them he was sure that gold and silver enough could be obtained. Another idea was to seize the treasure boats as they came down the Chagres River, and detaching his brother and Hixom, another of his officers, to reconnoitre it, he proceeded to rejoin his consort at the Pine Islands. To Ranse neither plan recommended itself. In view of the danger of remaining on the coast now that they were discovered and of the plunder already secured, he was for going home. Drake was no less willing to be rid of him. So the partnership was dissolved and on the return of the two pinnaces from the Chagres River, Ranse parted company.

CHAPTER VI

THE SPANISH MAIN

THE extraordinary ease with which Drake had made himself master of Nombre de Dios flushed him, now that he was left to himself, to take in hand an adventure yet more bold. This was nothing less than to attempt the Capital of the Spanish Main itself.

Setting sail with all his five vessels, in six days he made the islands of San Barnardo, some three leagues from Cartagena, and at nightfall entered the harbour with the pinnaces, and seized a frigate which her crew had temporarily deserted 'to fight about a mistress.' An old man left in charge informed them that but an hour ago a pinnace had arrived from Nombre de Dios to give the alarm, and that all the frigates and small craft were by this time snug under the guns of the Castle. Behind the next point, however, he confessed there was a large ship of Seville ready laden and on the point of sailing. This, amidst the alarm of bells and cannon from the town, was seized, not without some difficulty, and with the crew fast under hatches they towed her out in triumph in spite of the fire of the troops, both horse and foot, that were marched down to the channel to impeach them.[1] Lying off the

---

[1] The first article of the *Memorias de los Cossarios* is as follows: 'Nel puerto de Cartagena un Ingles vezino de Plemue (Plymouth) llamado Francisco Drake, Piloto, que fue con Juan Haquins (Hawkins) quando estuvo en St. Juan de Lua, entro de noche en el puerto de Cartagena, quebrantandole y saco un navio de Bartolome Farina de ciento y ochenta toneladas, y haviendo tomado lo que en el havia que era de valor, le quemo y llevo preso à Inglaterra al dicho Bartme. Farina.' According to the Narrative, the ship was of 240 tons, and it makes no mention of a prisoner carried into England,

port, he next morning intercepted two frigates that were attempting to enter. They proved to be from Nombre de Dios carrying two Government officials with despatches in duplicate to warn the authorities at Cartagena that 'Captain Drake had been at Nombre de Dios, had taken it, and had it not been that he was hurt with some blessed shot, by all likelihood he had sacked it; that he was yet still upon the coast; and that they should therefore carefully prepare for him.' It was clear from this that any further attempts at surprises would be in vain, and setting all his prisoners ashore he retired with his whole squadron, which with the prizes now numbered eight sail, to the islands of San Barnardo to consider his position.

The result of his deliberations was a new departure in the tactics of the rovers. Hitherto, as we have seen, their operations against the Spanish Colonies had been confined to the seas and coast-towns. It was Drake who first dared to carry his depredations into the interior. It was probably Diego, the negro deserter from Nombre de Dios, who henceforth followed Drake like a dog, that put the idea into his head; he can hardly have intended it from the first. But now his failures and the hornets' nest they had raised at sea, must have convinced him that his best chance was, as Diego had suggested, to get into communication with the Maroons and attempt a stroke by land. His first step was to reorganise his squadron, and this he did in a highly characteristic manner. For the amphibious project in view, the pinnaces would have to play the leading part, and they must be fully manned; but so long as he had two ships this was impossible. He therefore determined that the 'Swan,' although she was new and his own and a particularly good sailer, must be sacrificed. So proud, however, of their smart little craft were his brother and the crew, that the order to scuttle her was more than

nor is anything said about the burning. The *Ashmole MS.*, however, explains that Farina was taken in 1571, and says he was carried to England, where Drake gave him 300*l.* to hold his tongue.

he cared to give. Still, it had to be done. So, summoning to his cabin the 'Swan's' carpenter, one Tom Moone, he told him that in the dead of night he must bore three holes with a spike-gimlet through her bottom as near to her keel as possible, and cover them up so that there should be no noise or bubbling to indicate the position of the leak. In vain the carpenter pleaded for his beloved vessel, and vowed he would get his throat cut if he were caught; the Captain was inexorable and convinced him of the necessity.

Early next morning Drake rowed to his brother's vessel and hailed him to come out fishing, and as he rowed away, asked casually of the men on deck 'why their bark was so deep in the water.' Orders were at once sent down to the steward to see what was wrong, and before he knew where he was, he was wet up to his middle and shouting that the ship was full of water. In dismay the men flew to the pumps, while John Drake hurried after his brother to tell him the extraordinary thing that had befallen his ship, and to beg he might be excused fishing till he had got her dry and found the leak. Till three in the afternoon they slaved at the pumps, Drake himself and his pinnace's crew taking spells from time to time, till John Drake in despair threw himself on his brother's advice. Francis at once counselled him to give up attempting to save his bewitched vessel, and offered him the command of the 'Pasha,' saying that he himself would continue in his pinnace, till he had captured some handsome frigate to replace the doomed 'Swan.' To this John consented. and after everything of value had been taken out of her into the pinnaces, she was set on fire; and so, as the Narrative remarks, 'our Captain had his desire and men enough for his pinnaces.'

The object before him was now twofold; first, to persuade the Spaniards he had left the coast, and secondly to get in touch with the Maroons. To this end, having abandoned or burnt his prizes, he once more disappeared into the Gulf of Darien to some spot well out of the ordinary trade routes, where he could hide his ship and refit: and here in a clearing embosomed in the tropical forest he set up his forges, and under Diego's directions built a leafy village after the manner of the Maroons. To the hardworked seamen it must have been a paradise. The woods swarmed with game, the sea teemed with fish: archery butts, a bowling green, and other games were instituted, and day and day about, while one half of the company were on duty the other refreshed themselves with pastimes and sport. A fortnight was so spent, and then Drake, mindful of his second purpose, set out with two of the pinnaces for the Magdalena River with the double object, as it would seem, of getting certain necessary stores and of putting the Spaniards on a wrong scent by a demonstration to the eastward of Cartagena. Upon the Magdalena lay the Province of Nueva Reyna, which at this time was not only supplying the victualling yards at Cartagena, but was doing a considerable trade in sugar, precious metals and pearls; and in ten days he was able to return with his pinnaces and two prize frigates laden with beef which he had bought of the Indians, and breadstuffs and all kinds of stores and delicate preserves, which he plundered from the Spanish store-houses and coasters.

Meanwhile John Drake, who had been left in command at the hiding place with orders to endeavour through Diego to communicate with the Maroons, had succeeded in his object; and head-quarters were removed some five leagues apparently to the westward. For, at the mouth of a river they named the Diego after their faithful negro and behind a network of wooded islands and intricate channels, he had discovered a better and still more inaccessible port to conceal the 'Pasha,' where also they could be in closer touch with the Maroons. A new fort was built and armed with the ship's guns; and at this and various secret points along the coast were established a number of magazines so that in case some were discovered, others would always remain. Of supplies to fill them there was no lack. So rich was the plenty ashore and so numerous the victual frigates that were always passing between Cartagena and Nombre de Dios, that had they been four thousand men, they said, yet with their pinnaces they easily could have supplied themselves. The reason of this elaborate provision was that from the Maroons they had learnt that nothing could be done ashore for five months till the rains were over; for till the dry season came and the rivers fell no treasure was moved from Panama.

Drake's great anxiety was to keep his men employed during the prolonged period of inaction, and it must have been more with this idea than anything else that he with Oxenham and two of the pinnaces made another cruise on the Spanish Main, again leaving his brother in command 'as Governor of Fort Diego.' His avowed object was to gain intelligence of the state of the country and the movements of the fleets. On this plea, he called at Tolou and robbed its orchards and fruit gardens and visited Cartagena, where he picked up several small prizes. Here however being overtaken by bad weather he was compelled to take refuge in the harbour, and there and in the adjacent roads he defiantly remained for a fortnight in spite of every effort by force or stratagem which the Spaniards could make to capture or drive him off. During the whole time his men suffered severely from cold and wet, and provisions were running short; but the more miserable their condition the higher ran Drake's spirits and the more reckless his daring. On one occasion he actually leaped ashore alone in the face of a body of troops in ambush as though defying them to come and take him, and for no reason, it would seem, but to put new heart into his men.

The boldness of the rovers was only equalled by the helplessness of the colonial authorities. A day or two later Drake made an attempt to get to sea, but the weather forced him back into the harbour. Thereupon the Spaniards, in order to drive them out again into the storm, sent against them ' a great shallop, a fine gundaloe (or ship's boat) and a great canoe,' manned with musketeers and Indians with poisoned arrows, so at least the Englishmen believed. Instead of retreating, Drake advanced to attack them; but after an interchange of shot the Spaniards fell back to land and abandoned their boats. Pressing on to seize them, he soon saw it to be a stratagem; the musketeers had but retired to their ambush in the woods, which at that point came down close to the shore, and to leeward a frigate, accompanied by two pinnaces, manned like the other boats, was being warped up towards him in the teeth of the gale. 'They attempted us very boldly,' the Narrative relates, ' being assisted by those others, which from out the wood had gotten aboard the gundaloe and canoe, and seeing us bearing from there (which we did in respect of the *ambuscado*) they encouraged themselves and assured their fellows of the day.' But once out of gunshot of the shore Drake ordered his second pinnace into line immediately ahead of him and so anchored: and surrounding both pinnaces 'with bonnets as for a close fight,' that is with sails instead of boarding nettings, waved the enemy to come on.[1] The Spaniards, however, finding the English disposition too formidable to attack, lay on their oars a caliver shot away and opened an ineffective fire, which after some two or three hours wounded only one man. The Spanish pinnaces, the Narrative affirms, were shot through in several places and the magazine of one of them was blown up. Seizing the chance Drake weighed, intending in the confusion ' to bear room to overrun them,' that is, to get well aweather and then ram them with the wind fair astern. For this bold manœuvre the Spaniards did not wait; so violent was the wind that the frigate had not yet been able to get into action, and not caring to face the threatened attack without support they rowed away and once more sought refuge in their masked defences ashore, leaving the intruders to ride out the gale unmolested.

[1] 'A bonnet' was, and is, an additional piece of canvas that laced on the foot of a sail to increase its size.

The following day the weather moderated, but as it was still westerly so that he could not return to his depôt, Drake resolved to go in search of provisions to the Magdalena. But here too the alarm had spread. Besides himself several French rovers were at work on the coast, as we know from his having relieved two of them from his secret magazines. Every storehouse on the river he found empty and all the live stock driven off to the hills. In despair they proceeded to Santa Marta, and being caught in another gale attempted to repeat their exploit at Cartagena. As before they boldly entered the harbour, but here a heavy fire of musketry from the rocks to which they could make no effective reply forced them out to sea again. The violent westerly wind still held and Drake now saw there was nothing for it but a bold push still further to the eastward for Rio de la Hacha or Curaçoa. Oxenham's men, however, protested they had not provisions enough for the voyage. It was something like a mutiny, but Drake did not waver. Calling to them that they had as much as he, and that he did not doubt they would take such part as he did and willingly depend upon God's Almighty providence, which never failed them that trusted in Him, he hoisted sail, and the refractory pinnace dejectedly followed on his wake. In little more than an hour their captain's piety seemed to be rewarded by the sight of a sail. Like sharks they dogged it through the heavy sea. 'We spent not two hours in attendance,' says the Narrative, 'till it pleased God to send us a reasonable calm, so that we might use our pieces and approach her at pleasure in such sort that in short time we had taken her; finding her laden with victuals well powdered and dry; which at that present we received as sent of God's great mercy.'

Such expressions occur again and again in the various accounts of his exploits and in his own letters. Neither he nor his followers seem ever to have doubted that Heaven had some special interest in their depredations. And now was coming a time that would have been enough to shake any faith less stout than his own. Having obtained through his prisoners by promising them their liberty all he wanted ashore and the weather having become fair, he set sail with his prize for Fort Diego. The first news that greeted him was that his brother John, to whom he seems to have been deeply attached and of whose abilities he had a high opinion, was dead, killed in a rash attempt, contrary to Drake's orders, to capture a Spanish frigate. She was full of musketeers and pikemen; the English, being upon fatigue duty, had no weapons but a broken rapier and two old rusty firearms; yet so reckless and confident had Drake's men become that they succeeded in taunting their officer against his orders and better judgment to attack. At the first onset the promising young captain had fallen fighting with reckless bravery beside the man who had been foremost in goading him into the mad enterprise. On the top of this calamity it was found that the Spaniards had discovered and rifled some of their magazines. Drake therefore saw the necessity of lulling his enemies into security by keeping absolutely quiet till the Maroons brought news of the arrival of the fleet from Cartagena, which would be the signal for the mule trains to leave Panama.

For a month all went well. The undiscovered magazines and the skill of their allies kept them well supplied, but as the year 1573 opened the climate and inaction began to tell. Ten men were suddenly seized by an unknown sickness, and most of them died within two or three days. At one time thirty were down together; Joseph Drake was one of them, and he died in his brother's arms. Drake himself must have been as near to despair as his nature could come. His surgeon was worse than useless, and his own medical skill, for which he was famous, at fault. But with the intangible enemy he grappled in the same unflinching spirit that danger and difficulty always aroused in him; and with a fortitude we can hardly realise determined to get to the bottom of the terrible visitation. Though dissection of a human body was still regarded by the vulgar with horror as a kind of sacrilege, he ordered the surgeon to perform a *post-mortem* examination, and that no one might protest he chose the body of his own brother for a subject; and this, says the Narrative, with dry pathos, 'was the first and last experiment that our Captain made of anatomy in this voyage.'[1]

Whether it was from the knowledge thus acquired, or rather thanks to the death of the surgeon, who poisoned himself with a purge after the operation, things seem thenceforward to have mended; and to complete what medicine could not achieve the Maroon scouts brought word that part of the Plate fleet was at Nombre de Dios. A pinnace sent out to verify the news quickly returned with a frigate that was on its way with provision for the fleet, and the prisoners, among whom was a woman and an official from Tolou, confirmed the welcome intelligence.

All was now movement in preparation for their land venture. This had for its object nothing less bold than the seizure of one of the treasure trains as it left Panama, and for the daring project eighteen men were all of the original seventy-three that were available. Twenty-eight were dead, many more were sick, and a few sound men had to be left behind as a rear-guard under Hixom, to tend the sick and guard the prisoners as well as to protect them from the fury of the Maroons. Of the shore party Drake himself took command with Oxenham for his lieutenant, and on Shrove Tuesday, February 3, they began their march accompanied by a Maroon chief called Pedro, with thirty of his tribe, who insisted on bearing the whole of the stores, so that the Englishmen had nothing but their arms to carry. Thus they set forward up the forest clad spurs of the Cordilleras in ever increasing admiration at the wonders and the luxuriance of the

---

[1] The malady they described as a 'calenture,' and attributed to the sudden change from heat to cold or to drinking brackish water. The autopsy showed the 'liver swollen, the heart as it were sodden, and the guts all fair.' It was probably yellow fever.

tropical vegetation and at the marvellous woodcraft of their negro allies, who led them with unerring instinct through the forest where not a glimpse of sun or sky could penetrate to help them. On the third day they came to the stronghold, which the year before the Spaniards had attempted so disastrously to destroy. Such by this time was the Englishmen's delight with their allies, with their cleanliness and good order, with their skill, endurance, and devotion, that Drake was moved to save their souls and persuade them to lay aside their crosses and learn the Lord's Prayer; and as the Narrative innocently says, 'to be instructed in some measure concerning God's true worship.' In return for these blessings they begged him to remain a few days till they could double his force, but he protested he had enough and would not have a man more.

On the morrow, then, they continued their march, and in four days reached the highest ridge of the Cordilleras at a point where Pedro had promised them they should see both oceans at once. And here occurred the memorable scene where Drake first set eyes upon the fabled South Sea. In a glade the Maroons had cleared for one of their hamlets rose 'a goodly and great tree in which they had cut and made divers steps to ascend up near to the top, where they had also made a convenient bower, wherein ten or twelve men might easily sit,' and south and north of it they had felled trees to open out the view. Here Pedro 'took our Captain by the hand and prayed him to follow him, if he was desirous to see at once the two seas, which he had so longed for. . . . After our Captain had ascended to this bower with the Chief Cimaroon, and having, as it pleased God, at that time by reason of a breeze a very fair day, had seen that sea of which he had heard such golden reports, he besought Almighty God of his goodness to give him life and leave to sail once in an English ship in that sea. And then calling up all the rest of our men he acquainted John Oxnam especially with this his petition and purpose, if it would please

God to grant him that happiness; who understanding it presently protested that unless our Captain did beat him from his company he would follow him by God's grace. Thus all, thoroughly satisfied with the sight of the seas, descended and after our repast continued our ordinary march through the woods.' 'From that time forward,' says Camden, 'his mind was pricked on continually night and day to perform his vow.'

Two days' march brought them clear of the cool protection of the forest and the real danger of the attempt began. Between them and Panama lay an open stretch of pampas, where they must be exposed, not only to the pitiless sun, but also to the risk of being discovered by wandering hunters from the city. For two days more they stole across the rolling plain, getting continual peeps of the golden city, as they topped the rising ground; and on the third day they came in full view of the harbour crowded with the treasure ships of Peru. Here so greatly was the peril of detection increased that they left the trail and, creeping like cats through the tall grass, managed by way of a dry river bed to reach unperceived the shelter of a small wood, which lay beside the Isthmus road about a league from Panama. A Maroon who had served a master in the city was sent in disguise to get accurate information of the movements of the treasure, while in the outskirts of the wood the captain lay studying the plan of the city, as before he must have studied that of Nombre de Dios.

It was the custom, as soon as the fleet arrived, for the treasure to leave Panama in the evening, that the pampas might be crossed in the cool of the night; and it was partly for this reason that Drake probably chose this distant point of attack and partly because here he would be least expected. Of the royal *recuas* or mule trains employed in the transport service there were twenty-eight of from fifty to seventy mules in each, besides others that could be hired privately, and each was escorted by an advance and rear guard of soldiers to protect it from the Maroons, by whom they frequently had been plundered. In due course the spy returned with his report of their movements for that night. Two royal *recuas* were about to start, laden mostly with victuals, but partly with silver, and in front of them was to proceed on his way to Spain no less a person than the Treasurer of Lima himself accompanied by his daughter and a private train of fourteen mules, eight of which were laden with gold and one with jewels.

No better news could have been prayed for, and a move was at once made inland towards Venta Cruz, the depôt which had been established at the point where the Chagres River became navigable. On the way two negroes who were in advance brought in a Spanish sentry. They had smelt him out by his musket-match and caught him asleep. This man, grateful for being released by Drake from the violence of his captors, confirmed fully the spy's report, and the march was continued to a point some six miles from Venta Cruz. Here every man was ordered to put his shirt on outside his other clothes, according to the usual military practice for a *camisada* or night attack, in order that friend could be known from foe; and then, divided into two parties, they concealed themselves in the grass on each side of the highway, so disposed that the rear and the advance guard of the *recuas* could be attacked simultaneously.

So they lay listening in the silence of the night for about an hour, when the sound of mule bells told them that *recuas* were approaching both from Venta Cruz and Panama. The orders were that everything from Venta Cruz was to be allowed to pass unmolested, but as ill luck would have it a gentleman came riding thence along the road, and a drunken sailor, impatient to show his valour, sprang to his feet. In a moment his negro comrades had knocked him down and sat on him, but not before the gentleman had caught sight of his white shirt and was heard galloping off on the hard road towards Panama. To the rest the reason of his hurry was unknown, and they lay on listening to the mule bells coming nearer and nearer. At last with beating hearts they could tell two large *recuas* were abreast of them. Drake's shrill whistle broke the stillness. In a moment they were on their feet ; there was a rush through grass in front and rear : and almost without a blow the *recuas* were in their hands.

In high exultation at their success the hands fell to rifling the packs, but had hardly begun before they knew something was wrong. Of the Treasurer of Lima and his daughter and his gold not a sign was to be seen, and among all the hundred mules not more than two loads of silver were found. It was one of the chief muleteers who explained. The gentleman whom they had heard gallop down the road had reported something suspicious, and had persuaded the Treasurer, whom he met leading the way, to allow the royal victual-trains to pass him and spring the trap if there was one. The disappointment of Drake's men was profound, nor could they explain it except on the ground that the Treasurer had come by his gold honestly and that it was the will of God he should keep it. Still their loss of the plunder was not the whole disaster. It had rendered their situation in the last degree critical. Already the alarm might have been given in Panama, and troops would be hurrying out against them. They had already marched four leagues, and to regain the shelter of the woods by the way they came was four leagues back. By going forwards they could reach the forest in two leagues, but the only road lay through Venta Cruz and was known to be held every night for fear of Maroons by a regular guard of soldiers. This was the way Drake preferred, and when Pedro declared he would rather die at his feet than leave him to the Spaniards, it was the way he chose.

To within a mile of the town they rode the captured mules and there dismissed them and the muleteers. By this time they had re-entered the forest ; the way was but twelve feet broad ; and here it was on each hand the picket was accustomed to conceal itself ; nor was it long before the advanced Maroons reported they could smell burning matches. Still advancing they were soon challenged by the captain of the picket calling upon them to surrender. Crying boldly that for the honour of the Queen of England, his Mistress, he must have passage that way, Drake fired his pistol into the Spaniard's face. His truculent answer was followed by a hail of buck-shot, which killed one man and slightly wounded Drake and several others. As the Spanish fire slackened Drake blew his whistle, and the English with one discharge of muskets and arrows began an orderly advance. But no sooner did the Maroons hear the forward movement than, as the Narrative tells, ' they all rushed forward one after another, traversing the way with their arrows ready in their bows and with their manner of country dance or leap, singing "Yó pehó, yó pehó!" and so got before us where they continued their leap and song, after the manner of their own country wars.' Before the dreaded war-dance the Spaniards retired, and as they fell back the pace of the advance increased, growing quicker and quicker till at last the English front was mixed with the Spanish rear and the place was carried with a rush. At every approach guards were set and for an hour and a half Drake held the town, giving strict orders to his savage allies that no woman or unarmed man was to be touched, while his men refreshed themselves and searched for plunder. Little was found except what pleased the Maroons either in the storehouses, the monastery, or the fifty dwellings of which the town consisted. Besides being a trade depôt it was also a sanatorium where the ladies of Nombre de Dios came to be confined, and such of these who were there at the time were greatly alarmed at the presence of the Maroons, and though informed of the humane orders Drake had given would not be comforted, it is said, until at their earnest entreaty he himself came in person to assure them of their safety. A party of horse was then reported to have appeared before the Panama gate, and though it had retired before the fire of the picket which Drake had placed there, he thought it expedient to waste no more time, and when the pursuit arrived from Panama not a sign of him was found.[1]

By forced marches he was hurrying to the coast, not from fear of pursuit, since he knew no Spaniard would be mad enough to follow his trail through the forest, but rather in anxiety to rejoin his weak rear-guard. Day after day he urged his harassed men onward, till, depressed as they were with failure, they were ready to drop with hunger and fatigue. Hardly a man had a whole boot to protect his bruised and lacerated feet. The captain himself, it is said, complained as loudly as the rest, 'sometimes without cause but sometimes with cause indeed, which made the rest bear the burden the more easily,' and in this way he got them all in an incredibly short time back to the coast.

The rear-guard they found unmolested. The sick men were nearly whole, and the enthusiasm of their welcome and the reiterated determination of their captain not to leave the coast till the voyage was 'made' quickly restored their spirits, and all were eager for a fresh attempt.

The only question was what should be done to employ the time until the *recuas* should start again. The Maroons were urgent for a raid under their guidance upon the *hacienda* of an enormously rich mine-owner in Veragua; others were for seeking a supply of victuals for the homeward voyage; and others for a cruise against the treasure-frigates that would be mustering towards Nombre de Dios. Rejecting the first scheme as too arduous, Drake adopted both the others. Cruising himself to the westward in the 'Minion' pinnace, he captured a small frigate in which were some gold and a Genoese pilot. This man, who had just come from Veragua, persuaded Drake to attempt the cutting out of a frigate

---

[1] The account of this exploit in the *Memoria de los Cossarios* is as follows: 'Tambien robo el anno de setenta y uno (sic) en la Venta de las Cruzes, que es entre el Nombre de Dios y Panama, mucha hazienda de Lope Ruiz de Lezo, y Balthasar Diaz.'

which lay there with above a million of gold aboard. So feverishly alert, however, were the Spaniards, that at his first approach to the Bay the alarm flew along the coast by means of signal guns, and 'finding it was not God's will they should enter at that time' they abandoned the enterprise. Returning to head-quarters they found the other pinnace which had been cruising to the eastward had captured a fine new victual-frigate laden with everything they most required and herself so strong, taut, and well designed that Drake resolved to keep and equip her for a 'man-of-war,' since he had ascertained that at Nombre de Dios two small galleys had been armed against him.

With the new vessel and a pinnace Drake started on another cruise to the westward, where he fell in with a large Huguenot privateer in distress for water and victuals, whose commander, Captain Têtu, vowed he had been seeking him for five weeks past and asked to be taken into partnership for the next venture.[1] The French force was more than double that of Drake: he had but thirty-one men left and Têtu had seventy: it was therefore thought well, after some deliberation and not without misgiving, to put a good face on the matter and consent, but only on condition that in spite of the French preponderance both in men and tonnage the proceeds should be shared equally between them. Compassion for the Huguenots had not a little to do with Drake's complaisance, for from Captain Têtu he learnt the first news of the massacre of St. Bartholomew, an event which, coming as it did soon after the discovery of the Ridolphi plot, emphasised still more deeply the

[1] Captain Têtu, or probably more correctly Le Testu, seems to have been a Huguenot of distinction. He owned a 'scimitar' which had been presented to him by the Admiral Coligny, who had had it from the famous mercenary general Strozzi. Têtu afterwards gave it to Drake, who gave it as a parting gift to the Maroon Chief Pedro. It is possible he was identical with the Guillaume Le Testu, a famous western pilot of the town of Francoiyse de Grace, who in 1555 dedicated a MS. atlas to Coligny (see Marguy, *Navigations françaises*, p. 138).

religious character of the crisis through which England was passing, increasing the passion and bitterness of the growing antipathy to Spain and the Guises, and drawing still closer the bonds which united the English Reformation party with the Protestants abroad.

After a delay of five or six days to enable the Frenchmen to refresh themselves and revictual from the secret magazines, a new landing party was organised. It was composed of twenty of Têtu's men, fifteen of Drake's, and his band of Maroons; and with this force the two captains embarked in the new frigate and two pinnaces, leaving both ships in their places of concealment. The point from which the new raid was to start had been fixed at the Rio Francisco, the small river that falls into the sea some four leagues to the west of Nombre de Dios. The frigate, drawing too much water to enter the river, was left under a mixed guard of French and English at a place known to them as the Cabeças or Headlands. The remainder ascended the river in the pinnaces and there landed, leaving a boatguard with orders to retire into hiding and meet them in the river again in four days without fail.

For this time there was no long march before them. At the very gates of Nombre de Dios, where now he would be least expected, Drake had resolved to strike his blow; and after another stealthy march of about seven leagues through the trackless forest they were once more lying in ambush beside the Panama road. Below them was the town, and so close that all night long, as they lay silently listening for the mule-bells, they could hear the carpenters at work upon the treasure ships in the harbour. Towards morning the first welcome tinkle was heard, and as the sound grew to a fuller and yet fuller peal the Maroons came grinning to tell them they were in luck at last. Nor was their instinct at fault. Soon all could see winding up the slope towards them three royal *recuas*, one of fifty mules and two of seventy, each *recua* with a guard of fifteen men—that is, forty-five in all. So small a force was nothing to fear. As the head of the long train reached the ambush the leading mules were stopped, and all the rest, as their habit was, lay down. At the same moment a volley of shot and arrows threw the guards into confusion. Still they managed to rally, but after a sharp struggle, in which one Maroon was killed and the French captain severely wounded, the Spaniards broke and fled to the town to give the alarm. By the time assistance came the mules had been stripped, and the exuberant marauders were struggling back to the river with as much gold as they could stagger under, and in the land-crab holes and shallow brooks were buried some fifteen tons of silver.

With the same haste as before and with still greater fear for the safety of their boats they pushed on all that day and the next without rest, and when at last, fainting with exhaustion and drenched with a storm that had raged all night, they reached the river, nothing was there to receive them; and to complete their dismay, out to sea was the ominous sight of seven Spanish pinnaces rowing directly from the place where their own had been lying hid. Despair now took the place of their former exultation. To everyone it was clear their boats had been captured, their comrades taken prisoners, by torture the Spaniards would discover where the ships were hidden, and all hope of ever reaching home again was gone. But Drake was still undaunted. Reminding them, in answer to their murmurs against him, that they were in no worse case than he, and that even if all they dreaded were true it would still take time before their ships could be captured, he pointed to the trees the swollen river had brought down and vowed if they would make a raft of them, he himself would sail on it to the Cabeças and fetch the frigate to carry them off. Under this ray of hope they set to work with a will; the raft was soon made, a biscuit-bag rigged for a sail, and with one Englishman and two Frenchmen who insisted on sharing the perilous voyage, he set sail, crying as he bid them farewell: 'if it pleased God he should put his foot in safety aboard his frigate, he would, God willing, by one means or other get them all aboard in despite of all the Spaniards in the Indies.'

So frail was the craft that as they clung to it every surge wet them up to the armpits; the sun and salt blistered their skin; they were parched with thirst. For three leagues they sailed in this miserable plight, when 'God gave them sight of two pinnaces' trying to beat towards them in the teeth of the wind before which the raft was driving, and Drake knew them for his own. Still they were not safe. The pinnaces had not seen them, and unable to make head against the wind ran out of sight under the lee of a point ahead of them. Without hesitation, Drake ran his raft ashore, and landed on the weather side of the headland. Determined at once to punish his men for disobeying orders and to relieve his own elation by a practical joke, he called to his men to follow him round the point as though running for their lives. The astonished boat-guard were quite taken in, but to their anxious inquiries for the rest of the company Drake would give no reply. It was not till they had explained how the gale had made it impossible for them to reach the river at the time appointed that he had mercy, and then 'to relieve their misery he took from his bosom a quoit of gold, thanking God that their voyage was made.'

That same night in the teeth of the wind they succeeded in reaching the river with the pinnaces, and by dawn all but the wounded French captain, who early in the forest march had heroically insisted on being left behind for fear of hindering the escape, and two of his men who refused to leave him, were embarked with the booty; and so, picking up the frigate on the way, they reached the ships in safety.

Here the plunder was shared with the French and a fortnight spent in reorganising the squadron for the homeward voyage. The 'Pasha' was dismantled of all they required for the frigate and pinnaces, and then presented to the Spanish prisoners as some compensation for their long detention. Before, however, a final start was made one thing remained to be done, and that was to attempt the recovery of the buried silver and the French captain. A new shore party was formed, but Drake was not suffered by his devoted crew to run the risk of commanding it. Oxenham took his place, and succeeded in bringing off one of Têtu's companions, who reported that both the captain and his comrade had been taken prisoners. As for the buried treasure they discovered but little of it; for the captured Frenchmen had been compelled to reveal where it was hidden, and Oxenham's party found 'that the earth every way a mile distant had been digged and turned up,' and all but thirteen bars of silver and a few quoits of gold recovered.[1]

Still they were rich beyond their dreams. Besides this last great haul of gold their plunder must have been considerable. Both in Nombre de Dios and Venta Cruz they had obtained something, and 'there were,' says the Narrative, 'at that time belonging to Cartagena, Nombre de Dios, Rio Grande, Santa Marta, Rio de la Hacha, Venta Cruz, Veragua, Nicaragua, the Honduras, Jamaica, &c., above 200 frigates, some of 120 tons, others but 10 or 12 tons, but the most 30 or 40 tons, which all had intercourse between Cartagena and Nombre de Dios and the most of which during our abode in those parts we took, and some of them twice or thrice each': and in most, no doubt, something worth having was found. This boast may be an exaggeration, but the Spanish official complaint, after specifying several prizes they made, goes on to say: 'They took many other frigates with a great quantity of gold and silver and merchandise, that were engaged in the coasting trade of Tierra Firme and Veragua.' Not one of these, except when engaged in act of war against them, had they burnt, and not a single prisoner had been ill-treated or even detained longer than was absolutely necessary for their own safety.

[1] This incident is confirmed in the *Dragontea*.

Whatever the amount of their plunder their only idea
was to get home. For this purpose a ship large enough
to carry sufficient victuals for the voyage had to be captured, and with this object in view no less than to shake
off his unwieldy French consort that still clung to his
company, Drake resolved to brave the Seville ships and the
Galleons of the Guard that were still lying in Cartagena
and once more to beat up the Magdalena River. And this
he did, says the Narrative, 'passing hard by Cartagena, in
the sight of all the fleet, with a flag of St. George in the
main-top of our frigate, with silk streamers and ancients
down to the water, sailing forward with a large wind.'

What they sought was not to be found. Off the
mouth of the river, however, they fell in with another
frigate, which was captured after a sharp engagement. It
was but of 25 tons—a little larger, that is, than the one they
already had—but it was laden with fresh victuals, and with
it Drake resolved to be content. Returning to his station
at the Cabeças to careen and refit his frigates, he broke up
the pinnaces, that he might give the ironwork as a farewell gift to his trusty Maroons, and with his two little
vessels ballasted with gold and silver and his crew reduced
to thirty souls, laid his course for home.

What excellent vessels the frigates which Menendez
was turning out at Havana and other local yards must
have been is shown by the extraordinary speed of the run
across the Atlantic. 'Within twenty-three days,' the
Narrative concludes, ' we passed from the Cape of Florida
to the Isles of Scilly, and so arrived at Plymouth on
Sunday about sermon time August 9, 1573. At what time
the news of our Captain's return brought unto his [friends?]
did so speedily pass over all the church, and surpass their
minds with desire and delight to see him that very few or
none remained with the preacher, all hastening to see the
evidence of God's love and blessing towards our Gracious
Queen and country, by the fruit of our Captain's labour
and success. *Soli Deo Gloria.*'

CHAPTER VII

DRAKE AND THE WAR PARTY

FROM the hour Drake emptied Plymouth church till in the spring of 1575 he re-appears in Ireland he is lost to view, and what his movements were during the interval can only be a matter of conjecture.

During his absence the political atmosphere had changed entirely. He had left his country on the brink of war with Spain; he returned to find both sides eager for peace. The effects of the Ridolphi plot were seen only in a new diplomatic cordiality: the danger seemed to have completely passed away. A week ago the last adherent of Mary Stuart had been hanged in Edinburgh; her party in England were discredited by the failure of the Catholic rising: and Alva, turning his back upon them, was making overtures to Elizabeth for a settlement of all outstanding differences. Diplomatic relations, which the discovery of the plot had ruptured, were not yet resumed officially, but in London was a recognised Spanish agent through whom the English Government was paving the way for a peaceful understanding.

At such a moment Drake's return was in the highest degree inconvenient. Not only had he added a large item to the Spanish side of the account to be settled, but if his punishment as a pirate were demanded, it would be almost impossible to refuse without bringing the promising negotiations to a deadlock. True there is no definition of piracy accepted by modern publicists under which he was guilty —he had not acted as a *hostis humani generis*, but as an enemy of Spain and Portugal alone; he had not pillaged *animo furandi* but under colour of right; yet at that time international law did not distinguish so nicely between piracy and irregular reprisal. That under the old law of nations Drake was entitled to reprisal there is no possible doubt. He had been wronged, he had applied to his Government for redress, and redress had not been forthcoming. But it must be remembered that it was now a recognised doctrine, that before a subject of one country could put into force his remedy of special reprisal against the subjects of another he must obtain a commission from his own Prince or from some authorised official of his Government. Whether Drake or his employers had such a commission is at least doubtful. In any case a great part of his plunder would have to be disgorged, and there can be little doubt that he received a hint from his friends in authority to disappear.

In the recesses of Queenstown Harbour, a notable haunt of pirates in Tudor times, is a land-locked creek which still bears the name of 'Drake's Pool;' and here a persistent tradition says he used to lie hid, and pounce out upon Spanish ships. The details of the legend vary; the only feature that is constant is that at one time or other Drake was there in hiding, and so closely are we able to follow his steps for the rest of his life, that if he ever did make use of 'Drake's Pool,' it must certainly have been at this time. Nor is the tradition without documentary support. Amongst the Spanish State Papers is a curious draft memorandum of the answers that were to be given apparently to the Spanish 'Memoria de los Cossarios.'[1] Where Drake's case is dealt with the draft becomes a confusion of erasures, interlineations, and amendments, as though its authors were at their wits' end to know how to excuse his conduct or cover the Government's complicity. 'For the matter of Drake's spoils,' it runs, 'for that which was in '72, he that did it was a private man of mean quality, little thought at his going to have intended such a matter, *as might well appear by*

[1] *S. P. Spain,* xxvi.

his return, when he kept the seas till he had obtained his pardon.' The whole passage in italics is erased and over it a different excuse is inserted, to the effect that the matter was *res judicata*, 'ended by the treaty of Bristow.' Still the document remains as testimony that he did actually keep the seas till after his return. There is also evidence that it was to Ireland he retired. At the famous court-martial in Patagonia on Doughty, who was serving in Ireland at this time, it was sworn by several witnesses that the prisoner had said 'Our Captain was glad to come into Ireland for fear of my Lord Admiral and the rest of the Council because of his Indian Voyages.'[1]

There is little room, then, to doubt that he did disappear and probably to 'Drake's Pool,' until such time as his friends could smooth things over in his behalf. The circumstances under which this was eventually done are of the greatest interest. For they bring us for the first time in contact with a characteristic feature of Tudor government, which in our time has been revived and carried further than even Elizabeth ventured to push it, and which was to have a marked influence on our first great naval war. This was a system, as we should say now, of administration by chartered companies. With the decay of the feudal system and the elimination of the great vassals from the machinery of government, the modern system of 'concessions,' or 'patents' as they were then called, had grown up to fill the gap. Whenever the central authority was confronted with an ugly or difficult piece of work, which it had neither money nor inclination to undertake, it was contracting the habit of granting a patent to some powerful subject to get the thing done and make what he could out of it. Armed with this concession, which often contained a very large delegation of the executive power, such as the right to press men and ships, requisition victuals, and appoint

[1] Vaux, *World Encompassed*, p. 171. See also the Chaplain Fletcher's Deposition, art. 13 (*ibid.* p. 170): 'That our general fled into Ireland for that he durst not abide in England.'

officers in the area to be treated, the patentee went into the market and with the help of his city friends formed a syndicate or 'company of adventurers' to carry out his powers. It was the misfortune of Ireland to offer an ideal field for this slipshod and irresponsible system of administration. The central Government at this time falling into the common error of deducing principles of naval strategy from too close an analogy with those of the art of war by land, was disturbed with the now familiar but never realised idea, that in case of war a discontented Ireland offered an opening for some fatal operation on the part of a foreign enemy. The necessity of stiffening the queen's authority there was sharply felt, and the Earl of Essex, whose chivalrous nature was weary of court intrigues, had obtained and floated a concession for the pacification of Clandeboye in the rebellious province of Ulster.

Hitherto all we have known of Drake's connection with the venture is from Stowe's statement that immediately after his return from the Indies 'he furnished at his own expense three frigates with men and munition and served voluntary [that is, he was not pressed] in Ireland under Walter Earl of Essex, where he did excellent service both by land and sea at the winning of divers strong forts.' Essex sailed for Ireland a few days after Drake's return to Plymouth, and it may be that with the two frigates he had and another he at once joined the Earl and invested some of his plunder in the company of adventurers. Among the Irish State Papers, however, there are some official statements of account which hardly confirm Stowe's allegation. One of these is 'An account of wages accruing due under the Earl of Essex between April 30th and October 16th, 1575.' Together they show that the whole naval force under Essex was as follows:

The 'Falcon'	Captain Francis Drake
The 'Reindeer' } The 'Cork' }	Captain James Syday
The 'Limner'	Captain John Potter
The 'Fortunate'	Master George Allen

From details disclosed by the account there is reason to believe that two, if not three of these vessels were frigates, and none for doubting they belonged to Drake and were brought by him into the venture.[1] That he joined Essex immediately after his return, however, the accounts almost clearly disprove. He did not begin to draw pay until May 1, 1575.[2] This agrees with the assertion in the memorandum of answers to the Spanish complaints that he kept the seas till his pardon was obtained, or what is more likely until the treaty of Bristol had been signed. Thus by a piece of sharp practice that was quite in accordance with the diplomacy of the time the account with Spain could be settled up to

[1] The class of the 'Falcon' is not stated, but once Drake is described as the captain of a 'bark.' She can hardly have been Henry VIII.'s old bark, or pinnace, the 'Falcon' of 100 tons, though that vessel was still on the Navy List in 1570 and might have been lent to Essex, as the 'Jesus' and the 'Minion' were lent to Hawkins's company. There is evidence that she was otherwise employed at this time (*Spanish Calendar*, August 27, 1575). Her complement, too, was eighty men; and the crew for which Drake drew pay was much smaller. It consisted of a master, pilot, boatswain, steward, gunner, and eighteen mariners, which would be about the complement of a 25-ton frigate. The victuals he drew were for himself, his master, and thirty-three mariners, which still, whatever the explanation of the discrepancy, gives a total not too large for his Spanish prize. The 'Reindeer' is described variously as a 'frigate,' a 'brigandine,' and 'Her Majesty's pinnace.' The 'Limner' is not classed. The 'Fortunate' was a 'flyboat,' and the 'Cork' a 'hoy,' hired by the ton. It is possible, therefore, that three of these vessels were 'frigates,' which, as this was their first introduction to the English service, Essex's officials were uncertain how to class, and that they were Drake's property, contributed by him as capital in the company.

[2] In the 'Estimate of wages accruing due under the Earl of Essex between the last of April, 1575, and the 16th October following' (*S.P. Ireland*, lii. 49) Drake and his crew are entered for five months fourteen days beginning *primo Aprilis* 1575 and ending *ultimo Sept. eodem anno*. This, however, must be a mistake for May 1 to September 30, which is 153 days, or five lunar months and thirteen days. The audit of Fitton's accounts of his Treasurership of the Army, &c., from April 1573 to September 30, 1578 (*S.P. Ireland*, folios, vol. viii.), gives the total due to Drake the same as in the 'Estimate.' The items also are identical in the two accounts, showing pretty clearly that Drake was not serving before May 1, 1575, or after September 30. In the list of captains discharged by Sir William Fitzwilliam, dated September 19, 1575 (*S.P. Ireland*, liii. f. 126), all the captains mentioned in the accounts appear with the exception of Drake, whose services must have been retained for the time.

date without her being able to set-off Drake's recent delinquencies in reduction of the English claim. It was certainly about the time of Drake's appearing in the Irish accounts that the settlement was arrived at, and what is still more significant is that shortly afterwards, on July 25, De Guaras, the Spanish agent, reported that a ship had arrived at Plymouth laden with rich plunder which had been taken with the assistance of the Cimaroons between Panama and Nombre de Dios. For a long time he had known of Drake's depredations, and was watching the port of Plymouth keenly, yet this was the first occasion he was able to report the arrival of any vessel with the plunder.[1] It is therefore difficult not to suspect that Drake and his booty were at least semi-officially kept out of sight during the progress of the negotiations with Spain.

There is another aspect of Drake's disappearance of still higher interest, which more than excuses any sharp practice there may have been in connection with it, and furnishes a possible explanation of how he earned his pardon as well as a confirmation of the suspicion that his whereabouts was not unknown to the Government. It is now long ago forgotten that the year 1574 came within an ace of seeing what was reserved for 1588. Shortly after Alva's convention was concluded he was superseded in the Netherlands by Don Luis de Requesens, and the new Governor soon found his action paralysed by the amphibious exploits of the redoubtable admiral Boisot and his flotilla of oared vessels. To his urgent requests for a similar force Philip had listened, and early in 1574 he ordered a large flotilla of frigates, shallops, and zabras to be concentrated at Santander. It was to consist of a hundred of these light vessels and twenty great-ships to escort them. Pero Menendez, now at the zenith of his reputation as well for his conquest of Florida as for his successful handling of the Indian Guard,

[1] *Spanish Calendar*, De Guaras, October 1574 and July 25. 1575, pp. 485, 500.

had just brought home the West Indian fleets, and was called on to take the command. No choice could have been wiser. It was with small handy vessels such as composed the bulk of the Flanders fleet that he had made his name, and he had pinned his faith to them as the best instruments for dealing with the corsairs. To carry out his ideas he had invented and built in the Havana dockyard two new types of frigates, one called a *ballandra*, probably from its resemblance to the old balynger, the other a *gallizabra*, as being hybrid between a galleon or galley and a *zabra*, the Spanish pinnace. The latter especially earned themselves at once a great reputation, and when in 1569 three of the galleons of the Indian Guard were wrecked he obtained leave to replace them with some of his new frigates.[1]

Owing to constant diversions from corsairs and the Turks the work of organising the fleet proved very slow, and before Menendez was ready to sail Boisot, having increased his force with the wildest of the 'Beggars of the Sea,' had carried out the operations which the Spanish flotilla was intended to prevent. But still the force grew, till in the summer it reached 176 light craft with 24 great-ships and 12 barks (*pataches*), the whole carrying a force of 12,000 men. On all hands grave suspicions of its object were aroused, at Rochelle, in the Netherlands, and above all in England. There, to act in concert with the Dutch, a fleet of sixty or seventy sail, including twenty-seven of the Royal Navy, was prepared for mobilisation. In the West and down far into the Bay private vessels were on the watch, and not without cause. The fact was that Menendez's presence had given the scheme a wider and more ambitious scope. The report he had to bring home from the Indies was of the increasing activity of the English rovers with Drake's exploits at their head, and he had persuaded Philip that the existing system of trying to keep the station clear with local squadrons was useless by itself. With the instinct of a great naval genius, which

[1] See his letter of November 12, 1569, Ruidiaz, *op. cit.*

goes far to warrant the high position now claimed for him, he saw that the evil must be dealt with at its base, and submitted to the king a minute embodying a complete scheme for carrying out his ideas. The key of the situation, he pointed out, was the mouth of the English Channel. Hence issued to their various stations the English, Norman, and Low-Country pirates, who were the most formidable and difficult to intercept. In Scilly and the ports of Cornwall and the South of Ireland they could always find a ready refuge from bad weather and Spanish cruisers, as well as lurking places for sudden attacks on the Spanish Flanders trade.[1] His proposal, then, was first to seize Scilly and establish there a naval base whence on the one hand Requesens might easily be relieved in Flanders and possibly Falmouth occupied : and on the other communications might be opened with the Irish malcontents for securing other ports in Ireland and giving the English trouble in their already restless province. To complete the scheme a squadron of fifteen or twenty ' galliots ' was to be built of a special type, which he commends as being weatherly and good sea boats.[2] These were to be kept permanently on the station, so that every spring they might take up a cruising ground at the mouth of the Channel, where in conjunction with a contingent of pinnaces he considers they would be able to stop any force of corsairs getting into the Atlantic. It is probable the scheme must have failed, for it reckoned without the English naval power. Without first crushing the English Navy it was certainly impracticable. Still so plausible was it that Philip approved. In vain Requesens, like his predecessor in the government of the Netherlands, warned his master against the danger of provoking the English at sea.

[1] It is noteworthy as showing how wide and sagacious was Menendez's grasp of the situation that the points he proposed to occupy are just those which this year (1897) it has been decided to fortify, as necessary for the refuge of our trade from hostile cruisers.

[2] He undoubtedly means a sailing vessel or small galleon, like those which our shipwrights called 'galliots,' such as the 'Greyhound' (Oppenheim, p. 51, n.).

Philip would not listen, and in spite of the subsistence of Alva's convention he ordered Menendez to carry out his scheme.[1]

The Admiral's first step was to send an experienced officer to the coast of Ireland to reconnoitre and open communications with the rebels. There the officer says he encountered a number of English pirates, who had been ordered thither by the queen. Of this there is no trace in any English record, but such a device was quite in accord with Tudor methods. We know that Hawkins and others had been employed for some time past in watching for Spanish action in that quarter, and nothing would be more natural than that at such a national crisis Drake and the other rovers, who had raised the new storm and consequently had returned in disgrace, should be given to understand their offence was only to be purged by guarding the Irish coast against the danger they had brought about. That the danger would have been a serious one if Menendez could have reached Scilly while the main fleet was lying in wait to fight him in the narrows of the Channel is certain. But it was destined not to be. Early in September, in the midst of Menendez's last preparations, an appalling epidemic broke out in the fleet. Still he hoped to get to sea and shake it off, but before it was possible to sail he himself was seized and died. The loss of the great sailor completely demoralised the force. In panic it broke up, and in a week it was in fragments along the coast.[2]

So passed away the most promising naval officer Spain had yet produced, the only man who by his training and temperament was fit to do for Philip what Drake did for Elizabeth. It was the king's great misfortune that as the one passed from the scene the other reappeared in official employ a purged man, with whom the Government never again lost touch.

This view of the real significance of Drake's Irish ser-

---

[1] 'Minutes of Menendez' in Ruidiaz, *op. cit.*
[2] Duro, *Armada Española*, ii. cap. xvii.

vice receives no small corroboration from the experience
of another famous western captain at this time. In the
winter following Drake's return Mr. Richard Grenville,
'a great pirate,' in concert with Sir Arthur Champernowne,
Vice-Admiral of Devon, began to fit out a strong expedition
of seven sail. Its real destination was unknown. The
Spanish agent heard it was to attempt the Magellan
Straits: the French ambassador feared a Huguenot scheme,
but was told it was intended for a discovery of the North-
west Passage. There can be little doubt that it was not
entirely unconnected with Drake's recent experiences and
his intentions on Panama. For long the friends of Spain
and Portugal succeeded in delaying the necessary permission to sail for which Grenville was pleading, but at
last in the summer of 1574 leave was obtained to prosecute
'the discovery he had in hand,' but only on condition
that he first performed some service, which he was instructed to carry out for the assistance of Essex in Ireland.[1]
Whether this service was ever performed by Grenville is
unknown. It is possible that Drake's employment the
following summer may have been in discharge of the condition, but it is more likely that it was entered upon
independently, although upon a similar understanding.

To follow in detail Drake's service in Ulster need not be
attempted. It has no bearing on the growth of the Navy,
and little or nothing is known of it except by deduction
from Essex's movements. In supporting the flying
columns that raided the wretched Irish and in actions
with the Scottish filibusters who infested the coast his
time must have been principally occupied, and it is almost
certain that he was in command of the three frigates
which escorted the Rathlin expedition on its heartless
mission. This last exploit of Essex's administration will
give light enough on Drake's occupation. To the isle of
Rathlin off the coast of Antrim the Irish chiefs and the
Scottish filibusters, with whom they were acting, had

[1] 'Fénelon au Roi,' June 4, 1574; *Corr. Diplomatiques,* vi. 127. See
also *Spanish Calendar,* May 17, 1574, p. 481.

sent their women and children for safety during the progress of Essex's raids in the summer of 1575. For Englishmen at this time the remoter parts of Ireland were what Central Africa is to-day—a region where their human kindness was in danger of becoming changed and brutalised by the savageness of their surroundings, and yet it is almost impossible to conceive how Essex, the pattern of Elizabethan chivalry, could harbour the inhuman idea of destroying without mercy these defenceless refugees. Yet so it was. As exhausted with his devastations he retired to the Pale, John Norreys, who was to become one of the most famous captains of his time, was left behind at Carrickfergus with his company, under orders to concert with the sea-captains the surprise of the sanctuary. One day in July a flotilla escorted by three frigates suddenly left the harbour. Two days later, in spite of every difficulty, a landing was effected at Rathlin. The only guard the refugees had was a small garrison of Scots in Bruce's Castle, and this was at once attacked. The first assault was repulsed, but upon the seamen getting two guns ashore into position the Scots captain surrendered. The inmates were given over by Norreys to the vengeance of his men; two hundred souls were massacred as they marched out of the castle, and then day after day a hunt went on through the cliffs and caves of the island, till not a soul—man, woman, or child—was left alive. With the massacre itself Drake can have had little to do, for during its progress the frigates were busy capturing and burning eleven Scottish galleys; and even if he had been as much to blame as Norreys we yet should have to judge him by the standard of his time, and to remember it was an exploit which the paragon of Elizabethan knighthood could describe to his mistress in an exultant despatch.

It says much for Drake's character that this horrible apprenticeship to civilised warfare seems to have left unchanged the natural humanity with which the victims of his piracies always credited him. The chief result of his service was the formation of a friendship, which serves to show that his surroundings rather emphasised than dulled the gentleness of his instincts. It was the only one as far as we know that he ever permitted himself, and it was that which ended in one of the most dramatic tragedies in history. The man to whom he gave his confidence was by no means, as might have been expected, one of the hot-headed fire-breathing soldiers or ruthless adventurers by whom Essex was surrounded, but a man rather of the new 'Italianate' type, that the influence of the Renaissance was breeding about Elizabeth's court, a type which from our habit of regarding the Elizabethan age as one of burly English manhood is much lost sight of, though its influence was felt in every fibre of the time and not always for good. It was the type that in its more pronounced shapes was deplored and satirised by writers of every complexion, and which gave birth to the Italian proverb, 'Inglese italianato è diavolo incarnato.' This gentleman was Mr. Thomas Doughty, and we have a picture of him left by a sea-chaplain of Drake's, of whom it had been Doughty's interest to make a partisan. 'He feared God,' says he, 'he loved His word, and was always desirous to edify others and confirm himself in the faith of Christ. For his qualities in a man of this time they were rare and his gift very excellent for his age, a sweet orator, a pregnant philosopher, a good gift for the Greek tongue and a reasonable taste of Hebrew; a sufficient secretary to a noble personage of great place and in Ireland an approved soldier, and not behind many in the study of the law for his time.' The portrait ends with a further expatiation on his godliness, insisted on in terms so ardent that we are driven to suspect his piety must have been a little forced for the good chaplain's benefit. Still it was thus he probably appeared to Drake and thus also at first to the Earl his master, but the Earl had found him out.

When Essex's troubles in Ireland began he seems to have conceived an idea that there was some influence working at court to prevent his success and to have despatched Doughty on a confidential mission to discover what it was. Doughty returned with a report that it was the Earl of Leicester who was his enemy, and Essex, entirely trusting his servant and quick to believe his great rival was anxious to see him bury his reputation in Ireland, used some hasty expressions on the matter in his correspondence home. The result was an open rupture between the two noblemen, which Cecil now Lord Burghley succeeded in making up. Leicester was induced to write a letter of explanation, and Essex thereupon, in writing to thank Burghley for his good offices, enclosed a letter of apology to Leicester. It is from this letter we get our knowledge of the affair and an unpleasant side-light on Doughty's character. 'My good lord,' it begins, 'I have received your lordship's letters and have heard Flood's speech concerning the former report made to me by Doughty. Your lordship's letter and Flood's words do indeed concur and are both so different from the former information made to me, as I see how perilous it is to believe any servant's speech. And yet I was rather induced to give him credit because he had before that time spoken as much as any other of his devotion to me and my cause. . . . And as I mean not to use the man any more in that trust or any way in soliciting my causes, so if I have been over-earnest in my late letters, I pray you impute it to my plain and open nature.' Later on Essex explains that Doughty had brought back from England a tale that Leicester had been charging him with ambition and ingratitude. This letter is dated : 'At Dublin, this 7th October 1574.'[1]

[1] See Devereux's *Lives of the Earls of Essex*, 1. 76. That this Doughty was no other than Thomas Doughty is clear from a document in the Dublin Record Office, a transcript from which was kindly sent me by Mr. Barry. It is the 'account of George Viege, servant to Walter Earl of Essex, Governor-General of the Province of Ulster in the north parts of Ireland from 1st Aug. 1573.' The first relevant entry is one by which Viege charges himself with the receipt of 44*l*. 15*s*. 'by the hands of Yo. L. Servant Thomas Doughtye' for certain commissariat purposes. Then under date August 18, 1574, is the following : 'Payed for the chardges of Mr. Broughton,

Doughty would thus seem to have fallen into disgrace
before Drake joined. He used to boast, however, that it
was he who had introduced Drake to Essex, but this
Drake denied, affirming that it was upon a letter of
recommendation from Hawkins that Essex employed him,
and as for Doughty, he said : ' I think he never came about
him : for I that was daily with my lord never saw him
there above once and that was long after my entertainment
with my lord.'[1] This is additional evidence that Drake
did not join till the campaign of 1575, for had he been
there in the previous year he would have known that
Doughty had once been in favour and would hardly have
trusted him so implicitly. Yet so he did, confiding in him
the manner in which he meant to carry out his great
project for an attack by sea upon Panama, while Doughty
in return would seem to have persuaded Drake he had
influence to find favour for the scheme at court. And
so the two friends, probably on the termination of Essex's
mission in the autumn of 1575, went home together to
push their fortunes.

It was high time Drake was stirring if he did not wish
to be forestalled. A secret known to thirty sailors could
hardly be kept quiet, and rumours of projected attempts
to reach the South Sea were in the air. Besides the
expedition which Champernowne and Grenville had
contemplated, and with which he may or may not have
been connected, we know that in the autumn of 1574 two
vessels were being fitted out to repeat his operation;[2]
and John Oxenham, unable to wait longer, was already
sailing on his ill-fated voyage which ended on the gallows
at Lima. Eager as Drake was to start, it would seem he

Mr. Doughtie and their servants at Mr. Pulteneys by the space of   days
uppon their comeinge from Englande &c. VIIIs.' In November 1574 Thomas
Doughtie receives 100*l*. ' for his Lordship's use,' and after that there is no
further trace of his being about Essex's person. The only other entries in
which he appears are two relating to gifts of clothing which Essex made to
his followers ' for winter Lyvereys.'

[1] See Cooke's narrative, *Vaux*, pp. 203 and 205.
[2] *Spanish Calendar*, October 1574, p. 485.

had no mind to make his attempt except on an adequate scale, and for this, as we have seen, official sanction was necessary. To obtain it was a delicate matter, in which no doubt he trusted to his new friend's experience and parts for assistance. As far as Drake's ambition was concerned the court may be said at this time to have been divided into a war party and a peace party. In the war party the leading spirits were Leicester and Walsingham, the new Secretary of State—Leicester from his soldierly ambition, Walsingham from his desire to force on a war, which his sagacity in sympathy with the national spirit told him to be inevitable, before the queen's bewildering foreign policy had driven the Dutch, her natural allies, into the arms of Spain. To the peace party belonged the friends of Spain—men, that is, who like Crofts, the Controller of the Household, were in Spanish pay, and others who, like Bacon and Burghley and the bulk of the merchant princes, had finally accepted the same views in the belief that England's prosperity depended on her trade with Spain and that in any case war without perfected alliances was suicidal. Any such provocation to Spain, therefore, as Drake had in contemplation was as pleasing to the one party as it was distasteful to the other.

It was not, however, entirely to his friend that Drake had to trust. Sir William Wynter was still at the Admiralty[1] and Hawkins had high influence in the same quarter, and from Essex Drake, according to his own account,

[1] His position at that time is not quite clear. Mr. Oppenheim is of opinion that he held the offices of Surveyor of the Ships and Master of the Naval ordnance from the date of his appointment under Mary till his death in 1589. (*Administration of the Navy*, p. iii.) But an ordnance report of 1582 (*S.P. Dom.* clxxxvi. 23) speaks of the 'Surrender of his Charge' anno xi^{mo}, *i.e.* in 1569, and in this very year De la Motte Fénélon, who was carefully studying the English naval mobilisation, gives him the rank of Vice-Admiral. No patent, however, appointing him Vice-Admiral of England appears to exist. Mr. Oppenheim says the Naval Ordnance Department ceased to exist after Wynter's death. Possibly it was absorbed earlier, in 1569, and that this is the meaning of Wynter's surrender. In 1585 Drake certainly drew his stores from the Master of the Ordnance and not from the Naval ordnance. (*Queen's Remembrancer Excheq. Accounts*, 64, 9.)

brought a glowing letter of introduction to Walsingham. 'My lord of Essex,' he is reported by an enemy to have said, 'wrote in my commendations unto Secretary Walsingham more than I was worthy, but belike I had deserved somewhat at his hands, and he thought me in his letters to be a fit man to serve against the Spaniards for my practise and experience that I had in that trade.'[1] That Drake was armed with such a letter is more than likely. In the autumn of 1575, when he left Essex's service, Walsingham's ideas were gaining ground. The term of Alva's convention was running out, and as yet there seemed little prospect of its ratification as a permanent treaty by Philip, and a special ambassador was in Madrid endeavouring to come to terms with him. Elizabeth's chief complaints against him were the harbouring of adherents of Mary Stuart and her own Catholic refugees in the Spanish Netherlands, the claims of the Inquisition to religious jurisdiction over English ships in Spanish ports, and his refusal to grant reasonable terms to his Protestant subjects in the Low Countries. The mission proved a failure; and when in November the envoy returned Elizabeth began seriously to think of accepting the sovereignty of the Netherlands, which Philip's rebel provinces were offering her. In the Spanish ports the outrages on English ships continued, the Council was daily debating war with Spain and the acceptance of the Dutch offer, and in March 1576 Parliament was summoned to provide for the defence of the realm. Everything now looked fair for Drake's venture. But by the end of the month the queen's mind had changed. She had quarrelled with her Parliament and the Dutch envoys, and was once more turning to Spain. Dutch ships in English ports were embargoed; in retaliation English ships were seized in Holland, and things went so far as mobilising a squadron under Sir William Wynter for their release. By August Elizabeth was actually contemplating hostilities in concert with Philip against his rebellious provinces,

[1] Cooke's narrative, *Vaux*, p. 215.

and Walsingham was in despair. Don John of Austria arrived in the Netherlands, and although it was suspected he had in his head some wild project in connection with the Scottish Queen, Elizabeth procured his acceptance as Governor, convinced that Philip really desired her friendship and would never countenance Don John's scheme unless she provoked him too far. In vain Walsingham brought on his head one of her fiery outbreaks for urging that no lasting peace could be where there was no community of religion. A new envoy extraordinary was despatched to Madrid to settle the question of the religious exterritoriality of merchantmen and all other outstanding differences, and to negotiate the resumption of diplomatic relations.

Drake's prospects were now at their lowest ebb, and yet in six months he was hard at work organising his expedition. Although it had been arranged that Philip should send a resident ambassador to London, during the spring of 1577 suspicions of Don John's intentions began to grow. In spite of the Convention, the Marian refugees were gathering round him, he was known to be in communication with the Scottish Queen, and in the early summer letters were intercepted revealing the whole of his romantic idea of conquering England for the love of his distressed princess.

It was probably at this time that Elizabeth was persuaded to let Drake loose in order to show Philip she had not forgotten how to play her old game. Still how the affair was managed is naturally uncertain. Doughty used to boast, if we may believe the deposition taken at his trial, that it was done through him. Though still apparently unbroken of his love of scandalous intrigue, he had fallen on his feet and had obtained the position of private secretary to Mr. Christopher Hatton, at this time Captain of the Guard, and Gentleman-of the Privy Chamber, and the queen's new favourite, and by this means, as he asserted, Drake's suit was preferred. His account, as sworn to by one of the witnesses against him, was as follows: 'When the Earl of Essex was dead that he the said T. Doughty preferred our captain to his master Mr. Hatton, and that the said T. Doughty and our captain conferred about this voyage in Ireland to do it by themselves, so that T. Doughty should have ventured a thousand pounds for his part; and that afterwards our captain came to London and sought him the said T. Doughty at the Temple, and challenged him for his promise as touching this voyage.[1] And then the said T. Doughty considering with himself that the voyage was more meet for a prince than a subject, continently went to Mr. Secretary Walsingham and to Mr. Hatton, and like a true subject broke the matter to them and they took it to the Queen's Majesty, who had great good liking of it and caused our captain to be sent for and commanded this voyage to go forward.'[2]

In this story there is a false ring which is certainly absent from the account of the affair which Drake is reported by a hostile witness to have given. No doubt Hatton did his best to further the voyage, for already he was ambitious of being regarded as a patron of adventurous navigators. The famous Dr. Dee had just dedicated to him his 'General and rare memorial pertaining to the perfect art of Navigation,' addressing him as 'a singular favourer of all good arts and sciences,' and making him sponsor of his ambitious scheme for forming a standing auxiliary fleet. But that the promotion of the enterprise was entirely due to Hatton is very unlikely. Drake's account, according to Cooke, differed materially from Doughty's. It was after presenting his letter of introduction from Essex, Drake said, that 'secretary Walsingham did come to confer with him and declared unto him, that Her Majesty had received divers injuries of the

[1] On another occasion he seems to have said this interview took place in Hawkins's house. (Fletcher's Dep. art. 14, *Vaux*, p. 170.)
[2] *Vaux*, p. 171. That Doughty did say what this deposition alleged is corroborated by Sarocold's, art. 2 (*ibid.* p. 166); also dep. 2, 4, 6, and 14, *ibid.* pp. 169, 170,

King of Spain, for the which she desired to have some revenge.' 'And withal,' he continued, 'he showed me a plot [i.e. a map] willing me to set my hand and to note down where I thought he might be most annoyed; but I told him some part of my mind, but refused to set my hand to anything, affirming that Her Majesty was mortal, and that if it should please God to take Her Majesty away it might be that some prince might reign that might be in league with the King of Spain, and then will my own hand be a witness against myself.' This is so exactly in accordance with the fears that were the common topic of the hour, ever since Parliament had been dissolved without being allowed to touch the question of the succession, that it seems likely that Drake was giving a true picture of what passed. The matter, however, did not end here. 'Then,' he goes on, 'was I very shortly after and in an evening sent for unto Her Majesty by Secretary Walsingham, but came not to Her Majesty that night, for that it was late; but the next day coming to her presence, these or the like words she said: "Drake! So it is that I would gladly be revenged on the King of Spain for divers injuries that I have received." And said further that I was the only man that might do this exploit and withal craved my advice therein; who told Her Majesty of the small good that was to be done in Spain, but the only way was to annoy him by the Indies.'[1] With that he disclosed the whole of the daring project that was in his mind, of a raid into the South Sea and an attack on Panama by way of the Straits of Magellan. It was one that seems to have hit the queen's fancy immediately, and she promised to subscribe a thousand crowns to the venture. But it was a dangerous game for her to play, and secrecy was of the last importance. 'Her Majesty did swear by her Crown,' so Drake said, "that if any within her realm did give the King of Spain to understand hereof (as she suspected too well) they should lose their heads therefor.'

[1] Cooke's narrative, *Vaux*, p. 215. In the text a few grammatical corrections have been made to render the crabbed passage clear.

And further he said on another occasion when labouring under great provocation and excitement, 'Her Majesty gave me special commandment that of all men my lord Treasurer should not know it.'[1]

In view of what followed, the last prohibition is of the highest importance. It is of course possible to discard the fact as an invention of Cooke's or of Drake's, but there is no real reason for doing so. It was Burghley's upright and statesmanlike policy at this time, in hope of arriving at a lasting peace with Spain, to abide by the understanding that had been come to and to avoid giving any further provocation by piracy or otherwise. From the first he had set his face against the whole piratical system as a disgrace to the country. He was still as much as ever of the same honourable opinion, and to the last he remained a steadfast advocate for restoring Drake's plunder to Spain.[2] In the prohibition itself there is nothing incredible. At this time Burghley had not the unassailable position he afterwards held. We know that about the time of Drake's return from Ireland the queen carried her suspicion of him so far as to be induced to doubt the loyalty of his relations with Mary Stuart[3]; and Mendoza's first report on the political situation in England at the time of his arrival lends additional probability to the truth of Drake's statement. 'During the few days I have been here,' he wrote to the king a few months after Drake sailed, 'and in my conversations with the queen I have found her much opposed to your Majesty's interests, and most of her ministers are alienated from us, particularly those who are most important, as although there are seventeen councillors the bulk of the business really depends upon the Queen, Leicester, Walsingham and Cecil, the latter of whom, although he takes part in the resolution of them by virtue of his office, absents himself

[1] Cooke's narrative, *Vaux*, p. 216.
[2] *Spanish Calendar*, p. 569, and *ibid.* 'Mendoza to the King,' December 25, 1581.
[3] 'Burghley to the Earl of Shrewsbury,' December 25, 1575, printed in Aitkin's *Court of Queen Elizabeth*, ii. 36.

on many occasions as he is opposed to the Queen's helping the rebels so effectively and thus weakening her own position. He does not wish to break with Leicester and Walsingham. They urge the business under cloak of preserving their religion, which Cecil cannot well oppose, nor can he afford to make enemies of them, as they are well supported. Some of the councillors are well disposed towards your Majesty, but Leicester, whose spirit is Walsingham, is so highly favoured by the Queen that he centres in his hands and those of his friends most of the business of the country, and his creatures hold most of the ports on the coast, so that your Majesty's friends have had to sail with the stream.'[1] From this it is abundantly clear, as far as Mendoza could penetrate the situation, that Burghley at this time was holding aloof from a policy of filibustering warfare against Spain, which he regarded as disastrous and which he was powerless to oppose openly. Unless Mendoza was deceived in his view, it is evident Burghley would have done all he dared to prevent the new provocation to Spain upon which Walsingham was bent. Nor must it be forgotten that Elizabeth was never above instructing one of her ministers behind the back of another, and if she did subscribe to Drake's piratical venture, and this has never been doubtful, it is perfectly credible that she tried to keep it secret from the high-minded minister of whom she always stood in awe, and who she knew was in despair at the dangerous course she was pursuing.

Another point in this connection, though by no means so clear as the other, must not be overlooked. During the preparations for the voyage Drake found that his friend was paying visits to Lord Burghley, and the explanation Doughty gave of their object was that the Lord Treasurer was trying to persuade him to become his private secretary, but that he was resolved to sail with Drake. This was one of Doughty's boasts which was sworn to at the court martial by Fletcher, the chaplain of the expedition and Doughty's warmest admirer, in these

[1] 'Mendoza to the King,' March 31, 1578, *Spanish Calendar*, p. 572.

terms 'That our General (i.e. Drake) did know and was witness that my Lord Treasurer of England sent for the said Thomas Doughty two or three times to be his private secretary and he refused it to come to him.' He was partly corroborated by another witness, who, however, did not remember Doughty's saying that Drake knew it.[1]

Here again the whole affair may be set aside as an invention of Doughty's, but on the other hand it must be noted Drake never contradicted this statement as he did Doughty's boast about Essex. In the fact of the alleged visits there is nothing incredible. The important part which the secret service played in Burghley's administration is well known. He cannot have been ignorant that something was in the wind, when Walsingham was bringing Drake to secret interviews with the queen, and when at the same time he was being patronised by Leicester, Walsingham's most dangerous ally, by Hawkins, the arch-enemy of Spain, and by Hatton and Wynter, both of whom at this very time Burghley was suspecting of being 'comforters of pirates.'[2] Under the circumstances there is nothing more likely than that he should endeavour to get to the bottom of the mystery through Doughty. The man and his character, it must not be forgotten, were well known to him in connection with the great quarrel between Essex and Leicester, and since that time there is reason to believe Doughty had incurred fresh notoriety in the same sphere. It will be remembered that after Essex's sudden death on the termination of his Irish mission an unfounded scandal got abroad that he had been poisoned by Leicester's order. In November 1575, by order of the Council and for no alleged reason, Doughty's younger brother John had been thrown into prison, and about a year after he was given to understand that his release might be procured by a petition to the Council, and it was from Leicester the intimation had come.[3]

[1] *Vaux*, p. 168.   [2] *Hatfield Papers*, ii. 156, 162.
[3] 'The petition of John Doughtye to the Earl of Leicester. Most humbly besecheth your Honour, Your lordship's poor suppliant John Doughtye,

The nature of his offence and the reason of his release are both hinted by Camden. Confusing the two brothers, he tells us that there were some 'who pretending to understand things better than others gave out that Drake had in charge from Leicester to take off Doughty upon any pretence whatever, because he had reported abroad that the Earl of Essex was made away by the cunning practices of Leicester.' That Thomas had not held his tongue about it either, would appear from a passage in Cooke's narrative. On one occasion, as he relates, Drake in an outburst of anger ' gave divers furious words unto Thomas Doughty as charging him to be the man that poisoned my Lord of Essex, as he thought.' The point, however, is of no great importance except as showing the atmosphere of intrigue in which the Doughtys were moving the year previous to Drake's sailing, and that they were known to Burghley as corruptible men who would not be unwilling to do an ill turn to a project that was supported by Leicester. It shows, too, that the alleged invitation to become the Lord Treasurer's private secretary must have been a mere pretext; Burghley, knowing what he did, could not have offered the post to such a man as Thomas Doughty, and if he had, Doughty, being what he was, would certainly not have refused so brilliant a position.

The result of the evidence then is, that while Drake was organising the expedition, which he had been specially charged by the queen to keep secret from Lord Burghley, Doughty, who was his closest friend and entirely in his confidence, was in communication with Lord Burghley and that he explained the matter to Drake with a lie. Long afterwards, in a moment of intense excitement, he blurted out an entirely different explanation, and this was

that whereas it is your lordship's pleasure that your suppliant should write his petition to the Lords of the Council for his liberty, his petition is that it would please your honour to stand his good lord with your good word toward the procuring of his liberty, who hath been in captivity these eleven months, six months whereof your suppliant hath lien in the common jail, a very noisome place and apt for infection, replenished with misery, &c.' (*S.P. Dom.* cix. 24. Dated in a more modern hand, ' October 1576.')

nothing less than that his business was to betray to Lord Burghley the whole secret of the undertaking.[1]

Meanwhile Drake without suspicion of treachery, or at least disclosing none, was pushing forward his preparations. Support he found in plenty; for it so happened that public opinion was just then freshly stirred towards distant enterprise. Since Cabot's 'Company of the New Trades,' which was to penetrate to Cathay by the North-East, had failed in its purpose and degenerated into a company trading to Muscovy, little or nothing had been done to turn the barriers by which Spain and Portugal stopped the way into the Pacific. The disastrous end of Hawkins's attempt to share the benefits of the New World as a matter of right had only deepened the lethargy, and he himself, abandoning the struggle, had settled down as a Government servant. But now a new star had arisen in the maritime world to take his place. This was Martin Frobisher, the third great name in the Elizabethan roll, whom even before his famous venture De Guaras described as 'the best seaman and the bravest in the country.' That the Spanish agent should so regard him was natural; for he seems to have belonged rather to the peaceful school of Cabot than to the militant school of Hawkins and Wynter. Nowhere does his name occur in connection with the provocations of which Spain complained; his dream was to find in the northern parts of America what Spain and Portugal had found in the South, and above all to reach Cathay through the still unclaimed and undiscovered passage by the North-West. A large school of cosmographers, of whom Gilbert was the exponent in England, had persuaded themselves by arguments drawn from every source between heaven and earth that America was but a huge island, which lay between the 'horns of the old world,' tapering to the north as it did to the south. Tierra del Fuego was still believed to be part of Asia and continuous with New Guinea, and to the north of the great American island it was supposed

[1] See *post*, p. 241.

there must exist a strait giving access to Cathay similar to that which Magellan was believed to have discovered in the South. Of exploring this route and occupying with an English colony the shores that commanded it Frobisher had been dreaming for fifteen years. About the time that Drake came home from Ireland the patronage of the Earl of Warwick had enabled him to put his great idea into practice, and he was now returned in the firm belief that he had discovered the passage. Moreover, by chance he had brought back a specimen of a certain black rock which an Italian expert pronounced to contain gold in paying quantities, and he was soon busy preparing a new expedition on a larger scale with the 'Aid' of 200 tons, one of the best ships in the queen's Navy, for his flag-ship.[1]

Drake's new venture was therefore in a way the complement of Frobisher's, at least for those who, like the queen, were privy to his design. His real destination was kept a profound secret. The men were enlisted for a voyage to Alexandria, and De Guaras, who of course had his eye on the preparations, could make nothing of them. Hatton he regarded as his friend. In reporting a strong expedition that was being fitted out in 1575, as he believed for the Indies and promoted by Hawkins and Hatton, he comforted himself with the reflection 'that Hatton was such a good gentleman that they would certainly do no harm with his consent.' In May 1576 he was still of the same opinion.[2] On September 20, 1577, when the expedition was on the eve of sailing, he reported that Drake the pirate was to go to Scotland with some little vessels for the purpose of kidnapping the Prince of Scotland. 'They have ordered Bingham,' he wrote, 'and other important people to embark, as if for the Indies under the command of this sailor Drake, whereupon they are greatly surprised.' That Bingham, who

---

[1] She was built in 1561, and was therefore by no means a worn-out ship like the 'Jesus' and 'Minion.' She is classed in the list of 1570 as 250 tons.

[2] *Spanish Calendar*, May 29, 1575, and May 28, 1576.

already had won himself a considerable reputation as a soldier, should be ordered to serve under a sailor at all and especially under one so obscure as Drake, would naturally surprise him, and the report may have been merely some tavern gossip which De Guaras had got from one of his spies. It may, too, have been a trick of Walsingham's to deceive him. One thing is certain—and this is a most important point, which must not be forgotten—De Guaras never penetrated the secret, nor until long after Drake had sailed did the Spanish Government get so much as an inkling of his real design.

Don Bernardino de Mendoza, the new Spanish ambassador, who had been accredited to St. James's to reopen diplomatic relations, still lingered on his way and had no chance of finding out anything. Before he arrived Walsingham and Leicester had succeeded in persuading Elizabeth she was being betrayed, and De Guaras, caught in the act of corresponding with Mary and accused of treachery by the representatives of the Netherlands, was thrown into prison. This was on October 19. Once more the country was tossing in a fever of war. Leicester began to prepare to lead a force to the assistance of the Prince of Orange, Norreys went over to command the companies of English volunteers who were flocking to the Netherlands flag, and in the height of the war fever on November 15, 1577, Drake slipped away to sea almost unnoticed.

CHAPTER VIII

THE VOYAGE OF CIRCUMNAVIGATION[1]

ALTHOUGH it is abundantly clear, as well from what we have already seen as from what was to follow, that Drake's exalted promoters had succeeded up to the time of his sailing in keeping their aims a profound secret, yet the Spaniards naturally had their suspicions. But though they could not believe, as was given out, that his venture was an innocent voyage to Alexandria in search of currants, they could make nothing of what was really in his mind. When Mendoza arrived in March 1578 as resident ambassador, he could only make a confused report that Captain Drake, as he had heard, had sailed with four or five ships for Nombre de Dios and the land of the Cimaroñes, 'which voyage he made before with Captain Hawkins very successfully and fought with Pero Menendez.'[2] If Doughty had been in Spanish pay, as has been suggested, Mendoza must have been informed more accurately. Nothing indeed can show more clearly than this despatch that if as Doughty boasted, he had betrayed the secret to Burghley, he had certainly not betrayed it to Spain.[3]

That they did not suspect how daring his project was is not surprising. For thirty years they had given up the route by Magellan's Strait as impracticable, and the whole South Sea trade, as we have seen, was carried on overland by the way of Nombre de Dios and Panama. Since Magellan's successful passage in 1520, though the

---

[1] For authorities see Appendix E. [2] See *ante*, p. 119 n.
[3] *Cf.* also Mendoza's later despatches, *post*, pp. 306 *et seq.*

THE VOYAGE OF CIRCUMNAVIGATION 217

greatest explorers had sought to repeat his exploit, almost every attempt had ended in failure and disaster. He was first followed by two Genoese ships, which reached the Straits, but did not enter them. In 1525 a knight of Malta called Garcia de Loyasa, who sailed with seven ships, got through and reached the Moluccas with only one and was there killed. Some fifteen or twenty years later, Vargas, Bishop of Placentia, passed with one of his ships, leaving another a wreck in the Straits. In 1528 Cortez sent an expedition; Sebastian Cabot tried and failed; Amerigo Vespucci did not even succeed in finding the Strait at all. Attempts from the West had met with no better success. Sailors began to have a horror of the place; mutinous conspiracies to force commanders to turn back became a common feature of the voyage, and Simon de Alcozova, the last who had made the attempt, had been murdered by his men on the way. 'The Straits,' says a contemporary, 'were counted so terrible in those days that the very thoughts of attempting it were accounted dreadful,' and he considers it the conspicuous merit of Drake's famous achievement that he was able to get his men there at all.[1]

The force with which Drake undertook this hazardous enterprise was by no means small for the times, and was considerably larger than that with which Frobisher had already sailed for the North-West. It was composed as follows:

'The Pelican,' Admiral, 100 tons, 18 guns. Captain-general—Francis Drake. Master—Thomas Cuttill.

'The Elizabeth,' Vice-Admiral, 80 tons, 16 guns. Captain—John Winter or Wynter. Master—William Markham.

'The Marigold,' bark of 30 tons, 16 guns. Captain—John Thomas. Master—Nicholas Anthony.

'The Swan,' a fly-boat or store-ship, 50 tons, 5 small guns. In charge of Mr. John Chester. Master—John Sarocold.

[1] See Monson's *Naval Tracts*, book iv.; Burney's *South Sea*, vol. i.

'The Benedict,' pinnace of 15 tons, 1 gun. In charge of Thomas Moone.[1]

The strength of the crews was about 150, and in addition there were a number of gentlemen, including the two Doughtys.[2] That either of them held any regular command there is no independent evidence, and though Doughty alleged he was in equal authority with Drake he probably had no commission and was nothing more than a gentleman volunteer representing Hatton's interests. Besides the mariners and gentlemen, skilled artisans and experts were engaged, including two cartographers. The equipment, indeed, was on the most elaborate scale. Beyond the ordinary furniture of regular ships of war, four pinnaces were carried in pieces, and San Juan de Anton, one of Drake's Spanish prisoners, says he was shown great store of wild-fire, chain-shot, harquebusses, pistols, corslets, bows and other like weapons of all sorts in great

[1] *Authorised Narrative, Vaux*, p. 6. The guns are taken from John Drake's deposition. San Juan de Anton says the 'Pelican' had 'seven cast iron pieces a side under hatches, two at the nose, and six above hatches whereof two of brass,' some of which were probably breech-loading pieces of her secondary armament and so not counted by John Drake (see *post*, vol. ii. 181). John Drake says only the three men-of-war had captains, and that the victual-ship was commanded by John Gista (Chester), the principal person on board. Pretty's narrative makes it clear that the 'Christopher,' as the Authorised Narrative states, was not part of the original squadron.

[2] *Sloane MS.*, '150 men and some boys.' *John Drake's Deposition*, '140 people of war and mariners.' The *Authorised, Pretty's* and *Cooke's Narratives*, '164 able and sufficient men.' The names of the other gentlemen appear from various sources to have been: Thomas Drake, the admiral's youngest brother; John Drake, his page, whose relationship is disputed; a Mr. Robert Winter or Winterhey; Mr. Leonard Vicary, a friend of Doughty's, probably from the Temple, for Drake called him a 'crafty lawyer;' Mr. Charles; Mr. Caube; Mr. Gregory, who was in command of the vessel on which Doughty was last confined; Mr. Francis Pretty, one of Drake's 'gentlemen-at-arms' and author of the narrative printed by Hakluyt; Mr. Elliot; Mr. George Fortescue, who wrote a narrative of the voyage which was quoted by Fuller; and William Hawkins, nephew of John Hawkins (cf. Professor Laughton's note in the *Western Antiquary*, July 1889, vol. ix. p. 16). Who John Winter was is not certain, but there is reason to believe he was a relation and nominee of Sir William's, who had a nephew of that name. John Thomas was Hatton's man. Mr. John Chester may have been connected with Sir William Chester. Thomas Moone, we may suppose, was the trusty carpenter who had scuttled the 'Swan' off Cartagena in 1572.

abundance. 'Neither had he omitted,' says the Authorised Narrative, 'to make provision also for ornament and delight, carrying to this purpose with him expert musicians, rich furniture (all the vessels for his table, yea many belonging even to the cook-room, being of pure silver), and divers shows of all sorts of curious workmanship whereby the civility and magnificence of his native country might amongst all nations whithersoever he should come, be the more admired.'[1]

To follow the outward voyage in detail is needless. The marvels which amazed the Elizabethan sailors are commonplaces to-day. Until the entrance of the Straits the living interest of the voyage is Drake's relations with Doughty. For it is on these that the political significance of the expedition, as well as his own personal character, must be judged. The tragedy of St. Julian's Bay has always been a blot upon his reputation, and on this charge as far as is possible with the scanty and contradictory evidence that remains, it is time he were finally condemned or acquitted.

From the first it would seem that Drake had been warned that something was wrong. The Authorised Narrative declares that 'the very model' of his friend's mutinous intentions had been 'showed and declared to him in his garden at Plymouth before his setting sail,' but that either he would not believe it or thought he could win him over.[2] This is extremely doubtful; but the statement must not be rejected, as it has been, on the ground that if Drake had been warned he would have dismissed Doughty on the spot. It must be remembered Doughty was his close friend, and was also in Hatton's confidence, and therefore a man not to be lightly cashiered. Where two reasons are given for a doubtful piece of conduct there is usually a third suppressed which is the true one. In this case a third irresistibly suggests itself. Drake may have suspected an intrigue against him, but it was impossible to tell how far it reached. All that he

[1] *Vaux*, p. 7.   [2] *Ibid.* p. 62.

can have known was that Doughty was the instrument. For Doughty, once at sea, he no doubt felt himself a match; and he may well have preferred to affect ignorance, rather than take any steps which might lead his opponents to adopt stronger or more dangerous measures.

However this may be, signs of trouble were not long in showing themselves. Off the Lizard a south-west wind forced the squadron back into Falmouth, and here it was struck by a gale of extraordinary violence. To save the 'Pelican' Drake had to sacrifice her main-mast, the 'Marygold' did the same and yet drove ashore, and the whole fleet was so badly shattered that it had to return to Plymouth to refit. Here Drake found occasion to cashier James Syday, probably the same man who, in command of the 'Reindeer,' had served with him in Ireland. He had been engaged, it is alleged, at Doughty's earnest recommendation, and having been entrusted with the superintendence of the victualling, presumably had neglected his duty.[1]

It was not till December 13 that a fresh start could be made, but this time the weather was fair. On Christmas Day they made Cape Cantin on the west coast of Morocco, a distance of some 1,500 miles, and two days later they put into the road behind the island of Mogadore to set up one of the pinnaces. The intention was to provide themselves with necessaries out of the fishing boats and coasters from the Canaries that frequented those seas, and half-a-dozen smacks and caravels were soon picked up. With these they put into the inlet behind Cape Blanco, seizing a Portuguese ship they found riding there. Here the men were landed and drilled by Doughty, and before they reimbarked all the prizes were dismissed with the exception of one Portuguese caravel and a *cantera* or smack of forty tons, which was exchanged for the 'Benedict,' and under the name of the 'Christopher' permanently attached to the squadron. Thus reorganised, after a stay of four

[1] Bright's deposition, *Vaux*, p. 171. Cooke's narrative, *ibid.* 87. Vaux transcribes the name variously as 'Lydye' and 'Stydye.'

days the fleet sailed for the Cape Verde Islands. At Maio, which was a regular victualling depôt, they intended to complete their provisions for the ocean voyage; but though under Wynter and Doughty a force was marched some distance into the interior it returned empty handed. Evidence was afterwards given that Doughty used this opportunity to tamper with the men, but there was no suggestion that the failure of the expedition was due to him, or that he did anything more than resent the subordinate position in which he was placed.[1]

Seeing no hope of success at Maio Drake crossed over to Santiago, and coasting along its shores fell in with two large Portuguese vessels on the point of sailing for the Brazils. These were chased, and before they could get back under cover of the shore-batteries one of them was captured. It was a most welcome prize, laden with costly dry goods and wine, of which they were in great need; and yet it proved a source of serious trouble. Up to this time Doughty had been sailing with Drake in the 'Pelican,' and so far from being unfairly treated he had caused some jealousy by the favour and friendship which the Admiral had shown him.[2] As a fresh mark of goodwill he was now given command of the prize, with orders that bulk was not to be broken until the Island of Brava was reached, where Drake intended to complete his revictualling and discharge his prisoners. Arrived at the rendez-vous he received information through one of Hatton's men, who was now the Admiral's trumpeter, and others on board the prize, that Doughty had been pilfering the cargo.[3] Drake at once went on board to inquire into the matter and was received by Doughty with an accusation of the same kind against his own brother, Thomas Drake, who was one of the prize crew. Unfortunately for Doughty's credit, however, he was

[1] Bright's deposition, *Vaux*, p. 172, where 'Isle of Man' is clearly a mistake for 'Isle of Maio.'
[2] Cooke's narrative, *Vaux*, p. 192.
[3] Fletcher's narrative, *Vaux*, p. 61, n.

found in possession of some articles belonging to the prisoners. In vain he protested they were presents; where prize goods were concerned such a defence was inadmissible, and Drake seems to have flown into a passion and shown for the first time how his suspicions lay. He told his friend, 'not without some great oaths,' that he doubted it was not Thomas but Francis Drake he meant covertly to disparage; he accused him of seeking to sap his credit with the fleet, and swore by God's life he would not suffer it; and ordering Doughty back into the 'Pelican' he gave his brother charge of the prize.[1] It would seem that Drake had in his mind to take immediate steps to prevent Doughty's doing further harm, but Mr. Leonard Vicary, the 'crafty lawyer' and 'Master Doughty's very friend, gave greatly to persuade him for and in the behalf of Mr. Doughty and praying him to be good with him, which in the end he yielded unto and to the outward show (so Cooke puts it) forgave and seemed to forget all that had passed.'

So for the time the matter ended and preparations were pushed on for the ocean voyage. For this a fresh change was made in the squadron. The Brazil ship so nicely suited Drake's needs for an extra victualler that he resolved to retain it. As usual the prisoners were first dismissed—to the astonishment of some of his new hands, who all along had wondered at the mildness of Drake's behaviour. Some of the Portuguese passengers in this case were men of wealth and position; yet not only were they liberated without ransom, but the newly set-up pinnace well furnished with wine and food was presented to them

[1] See Cooke's narrative (*Vaux*, p. 191), which account is here mainly followed, as the one most unfavourable to Drake, and probably the most correct, if allowance be made for the adverse construction the author puts on all Drake's actions. It has not suffered like the Authorised Narrative from editing, and it gives us at least a vivid and lifelike picture of the events as they appeared passing before the eyes of a violent partisan of Doughty's. In his heat, too, there is a certain honesty which betrays him into constant admissions that tell in Drake's favour, though he himself was unable to see the construction an impartial mind would put upon them. (Cf. Appendix, p. 405.)

in order that they might get back comfortably to Santiago. Only one prisoner was retained, and this was the 'pilot' or navigating officer of the ship, one Nuño da Silva. He was thoroughly familiar with the South American voyage, and no sooner did Drake inform him of his project and offer to take him into his service than he accepted and became a most valuable addition to the squadron. The only other change was that Drake, leaving Doughty on board the 'Pelican,' transferred himself to the 'Mary,' as the prize was called, and in this order the course was laid for Brazil.

It was not long before Drake began to find the clemency into which he had been persuaded was a mistake. What he intended Doughty's position to be on board the 'Pelican' is not quite clear. All Cooke says is that he was 'thought by the company to have the authority of Captain from Drake.' Fletcher asserts 'the General in discretion deposed him from his place (i.e. as commander of the prize crew) and yet sent him in his own stead to the admiral, as commander of that company for the time of his absence,' but he admits he was thought to have 'exceeded his authority, taking upon him too great a command.' The speech which Doughty is reported to have made to the crew when he came aboard probably represents very fairly the attitude he assumed. It was as follows :

'My masters, the cause why I call you together is for that I have somewhat to say unto you from the General. The matter is this, that whereas there hath been great travails, fallings out, and quarrels among you and that every one of you have been uncertain whom to obey, because there were many who took upon them to be masters, one commanding to such, another one forbidden, another commanded, therefore hath the General by his wisdom and discretion, set down order that all things might be the better done with peace and quietness. And for that he hath a special care of this place, being his admiral and chief ship and indeed his treasury for the whole fleet, as he the said General had appointed sufficient men to rule and govern the other ships, that order might be kept, so because our said General could not be in two places at once and must needs look to the prize which must do us all good, he hath sent me as his friend whom he trusteth to take charge in his place, giving unto me special commandment to signify unto you that all matters by-past are forgiven and forgotten; upon this condition, that we have no more of your evil dealing hereafter. And for the safer accomplishing hereof I am to tell you, that you are to obey one master in the absence of your General, who is to direct you in your business, as touching navigation, which is Mr. Cuttill, whom you know in this case to be a sufficient man. And for other matters, as the General hath his authority from her highness the Queen's majesty and her Council such as hath not been committed almost to any subject afore this time :—to punish at his discretion with death or other ways offenders; so he hath committed the same authority to me in his absence to execute upon those which are malefactors. Wherein I will not disappoint his expectation and credit which he hath and doth look for at my hands, for the respect of any person : but whosoever offendeth (by God's body) shall feel the smart. Be honest men : by God's body and by the faith of an honest gentleman I love you and mean to do you good. And I hope that a great company conceive of me that I will be rather your friend than your enemy, wherefore I wish as an honest gentleman that you will so use yourselves that I may not have cause to lay that upon you which I have power to do, and therefore desire you will give me cause to think well of you. I make an end.'[1]

The speech is of great interest as pointing to the

---

[1] See *Harleian MSS.* 6221, f. 7. 'The sense of Thomas Doughty his oration upon the "Pelican," when he came from the prize to the "Pelican" to remain, the company being called by the boatswain together.' This paper was overlooked by Vaux and is not printed by him.

existence of that feeling of jealousy between the sea-officers and the gentlemen volunteers which was then the great difficulty of naval commanders. At a time when the idea of a fleet as an integral factor in the Art of War distinct from and co-ordinate with the army was as yet not fully developed, the soldier was still the only recognised fighting man; the sailor but an instrument to carry him to the scene of action: nor was it till the splendid achievements of Drake and his contemporaries raised their profession to an independent status that soldiers could come to regard themselves as the secondary element of a naval expedition.[1] It is possible that Doughty as the principal soldier on board considered himself entitled to command over the head of the master, but it is incredible, even if Drake had power of life and death, which Doughty afterwards denied, that it would have been delegated to so dangerous an instrument. If therefore the speech is correctly reported, we are forced to see in Doughty's attempt to circumscribe the master's authority an intention to usurp the control of the ship, and for his own ends to play upon the old-standing jealousies; and this probably is what Fletcher refers to when he says he was thought to be taking upon himself too great a command.

Much as the great Elizabethan seamen did to settle which way the conflict of authority must end, it was long before the question was definitely settled, and had this been Doughty's only offence much excuse might be found for him. But his action did not end here. There is evidence that some one was tampering with the crew of the 'Pelican' to induce them to mutiny and carry her off. Fletcher got wind of it, and being still loyal was for informing Drake, but Doughty, fearing, as he said, that suspicion would fall on him, dissuaded the chaplain from doing his duty. Further, after winning the confidence of Cuttill the master, he seems, if we may believe the

[1] Cf. Bingham's disgust at the idea of serving under Drake, *ante*, p. 214, and *post*, vol. ii. p. 280.

evidence on this head, to have tempted him to desert and take to piracy, promising to keep him safe in the Temple out of reach of the Admiralty officers after the manner which Scott has made familiar to us in the 'Fortunes of Nigel.'[1] In mid-ocean, it would seem, Drake was informed of Doughty's behaviour, again through his trumpeter Brewer. The man had been sent on board the 'Pelican' in the course of his duty, and while there had been made the subject of a rough practical joke in which Doughty himself took part, and to this Cooke attributes Brewer's report to Drake. Cooke, however, was sailing in the prize, and knew or tells nothing of what was going on aboard the 'Pelican.' Drake evidently thought the case serious enough for severe measures, and when the trumpeter returned with his report the boat was sent off again for Doughty. She came back with the culprit in the midst of divine service, but Drake, hearing her alongside, 'stood up and Master Doughty offering to take hold of the ship to have entered, quoth the General " Stay there, Thomas Doughty, for I must send you to another place." And with that commanded the mariners to row him aboard the fly-boat, saying unto him it was a place more fit for him than that from whence he came. But Master Doughty, although he craved to speak with the General, could not be permitted, neither would he hear him.' And so, as Fletcher says, he was removed out of the flagship into the victualler a prisoner in utter disgrace.[2]

The most extraordinary feature in Drake's changed attitude to his old friend has yet to be told. On coming aboard the ' Swan ' Doughty informed the Master, Sarocold, that he had been sent there as a prisoner suspected of being a traitor to the general and a conjuror, or in other words of practising the Black Art. How far Drake's strange suspicion was real and how far affected it is of course impossible to tell, but the reality of witchcraft was

[1] 'Proceedings against Thomas Doughty,' *Vaux*, p. 165.
[2] *Vaux*, pp. 62 and 193,

then almost a canon of faith with the Protestant party, and from Saga times the belief that sorcery was at the bottom of much foul weather was rife amongst northern seamen. The idea seems to have grown up in Drake's mind, if not from the first disaster in Falmouth at least during the passage across the Doldrums. 'The truth is,' says the Authorised Narrative, 'we often met with adverse winds, unwelcome storms and to us at that time less welcome calms, and being as it were in the bosom of the burning zone, we felt the effects of sultring heat, not without the affrights of flashing lightnings and terrifyings of often claps of thunder.' Nor were their experiences during the whole of the voyage down the American coast calculated to remove the impression Drake had formed.

It was on April 6, after over two months without sight of land, that with their ships clogged and foul and themselves depressed with sickness they made their landfall in $31°\ 40'$ 'towards the Pole Antartick'—that is, about Rio Grande do Sul. Rejoicing at the prospect of being able to purify and clean the ships and refresh ashore, they were standing in for what seemed a convenient place to careen and land, when in the midst of the serenest weather they were suddenly enveloped in impenetrable fog, and while lost 'in a palpable darkness of Egypt' were scattered in a storm of unprecedented suddenness and fury. When the weather cleared, as suddenly as it had grown foul, and the dispersed ships came together again, it was found that the 'Christopher' had disappeared.

If Drake believed he was the victim of magic it is not to be wondered at. The coast they had now reached was imagined by the Portuguese seamen to be enchanted and was called by them the *Terra Demonum* or Demonland. The pilot could only explain the unprecedented weather by telling how the land was occupied by natives who had fled from their homes before the cruelty of the white men, and for protection had sold themselves to devils as the gentler masters. 'And now,' said he, 'when they see any ships upon their coasts, the shore being sandy, they cast the sand up into the air, whereof ariseth suddenly such a haziness, as a most gross and thick fog, that there followeth a palpable darkness, that the land cannot be seen, no, nor the Heavens; besides this they hurled the sands into the Heavens, which as they increased, so the shoals increased in the way of the ships in the seas to ground them; and withal such horrible, fearful, and intolerable winds, rains and storms, that there is no certainty of life one moment of time.' 'Whereof,' adds the chaplain, 'we had present experience and had perished, if God had not by His mercy and power prevented the same. By these means,' the pilot assured him, 'did they continually overthrow the Portugals, when they came with their armies of men and huge *armathos*, whereof many had been cast away and none that ever came in the dance did ever escape.'[1]

As they left this *Terra Demonum* behind them, better luck began for awhile to attend them. After searching the coast for a week to find the missing vessel but still without any trace of her, they entered the River Plate. This was the rendez-vous, appointed before leaving Brava, and here two days later, as they rode under a headland, which they named Cape Joy, the trusty Tom Moone managed to rejoin with his ship.[1] It was but a

[1] *Vaux*, p. 36. Pretty who, as far as possible, avoids the subject of Doughty, does not refer to Drake's suspicion; but it is significant that at this point, immediately before relating the loss of the 'Christopher,' he has the following passage. 'Being discovered at sea by the inhabitants of the country, they made upon the coast great fires for a sacrifice (as we learned) to the devils; about which they use conjurations, making heaps of sand and other ceremonies, that when any ship shall go about to stay on the coast, not only sands may be gathered together in shoals in every place, but also that storms and tempests may arise to the casting away of ships and men; whereof, as it is reported, there have been divers experiments [i.e. experiences].' The Authorised Narrative has an almost identical passage (*Vaux*, p. 34). It is these superstitions which, being reproduced by Eden, are supposed to have given Shakespeare the magic of Prospero's Island in the *Tempest*. The Authorised Narrative speaks even of 'ministering spirits' who, like Ariel, 'made wreck of vessels.'

[2] So inaccurate were the charts of the River Plate, even up to the end of the eighteenth century, that it is impossible to determine their movements

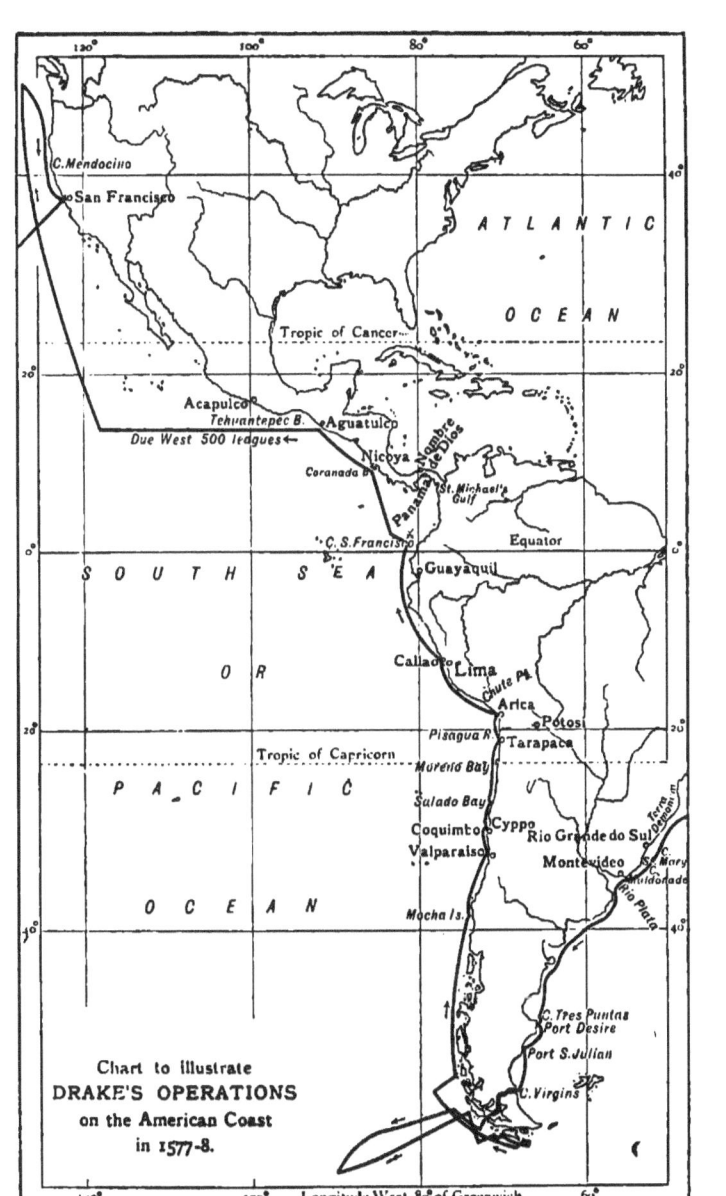

short respite from their evil star. Failing to find a harbour suitable for overhauling his re-united squadron Drake, after a fortnight's refreshing in the river, was compelled to continue his southward voyage, he himself once more taking command of the 'Pelican.'[1] But it was only to fall into new trouble. In bearing out to sea they unaccountably lost sight of the 'Swan,' in which Doughty was still in disgrace, and all search for her proved vain. Drake's suspicions of witchcraft grew stronger than before. 'During the whole time of her absence,' writes Cooke, 'our General never ceased to inveigh against him (Doughty) terming him a conjuror and a witch, and at any time when we had any foul weather he would say that Thomas Doughty was the occasioner thereof and would say that it came out of Tom Doughty's cap case and would avouch the same with great oaths, which he at no time scanted, they cost him so little.' That Drake had some excuse for his belief appears from the fact that John Doughty was said to have boasted to some of the men 'that he and his brother could conjure as well as any men and that they could raise the devil and make him to meet any man in the likeness of a bear, a lion, or a man in harness.' In vain he

in this place. On April 14 'we passed by Cape St. Mary,' the Authorised Narrative says, ' which lies in 35° near the mouth of the River Plate, and running within about six or seven leagues along the main we came to anchor in a bay under another cape, which our General afterwards called Cape Joy.' On the 16th they ' removed some twelve leagues furthe.· up into another (bay ?) where we found a long rock, or rather Island of rocks, not far from the main, making a commodious harbour, especially against a southerly wind.' Here they killed and salted seals or sea-wolves by way of provision, and then sailed still further up till they had only three fathoms and were in fresh water. Pretty says they watered at the ships' side on first entering the river in 54 and 53¼ fathoms. Fletcher says the river at the mouth of it from northerly to southerly cape was about ten leagues wide, and on his chart he marks Cape Joy on the east coast of *Terra Demonum* well outside the river. Cooke says they entered the river at the island harbour, that is, about eighteen or nineteen leagues from Cape St. Mary. It is thus very difficult to decide what they regarded as the mouth of the river or whether Cape Joy was at Maldonado or Montevideo. Possibly they mistook Cape Maldonado for Cape St. Mary, and their resting-place was near Montevideo, where the river may have seemed ten leagues broad (*Vaux*, pp. 173, 195).

[1] J. Drake, p. 59.

sought to recover the missing vessel; the futility of his search, combined as it was with the ill luck that kept him company even after he had left the *Terra Demonum* behind, seems only to have deepened his conviction that it was Doughty's work. But characteristically he would leave no practical means untried to baffle his difficulties, and in order to lessen the risk of dispersion and to render the squadron more compact and better manned he resolved to reduce its number by one sail, and for this purpose, in a constant struggle with contrary winds and foul weather, he continued southward exploring the coast for a convenient harbour.

On May 12, in latitude 47°, under a cape that was probably Tres Puntas, they found a bay which seemed to promise well. The bay however proved rocky, and Drake, unwilling to trust anyone with so important a duty, went in person in the 'Elizabeth's' boat to survey it. No sooner was he well inshore than once more the fleet was caught in fog and storm, and had it not been for the devotion of Captain Thomas, who stood in with the 'Marygold' to the rescue of the surveying party and in spite of every danger anchored under the lee of the headland, Drake must have perished. As it was he managed to reach the 'Marygold' in safety, while the rest of the ships lying further out were driven to sea, and when on the morrow a beacon which Drake lit ashore enabled them to re-assemble, his brother in the 'Mary' was missing. Two vessels were now lost; but the harbour proving impracticable he was obliged to proceed, trusting to find the missing ships at the next rendez-vous in Port Saint Julian where Magellan had wintered. Still searching the coast, in two days they hit upon Port Desire and there came to anchor. Finding the place all he wanted Drake resolved to stay, but first, in order to find the missing ships, he sent Wynter in the 'Elizabeth' to the south, while he himself made a cast northward, and almost directly fell in with the 'Swan,' which had been missing ever since they left the River Plate.

It was this vessel Drake meant to abandon. She was accordingly brought alongside the 'Pelican' to discharge her cargo and was then broken up for her iron-work and firewood. Doughty was transferred to the flagship in greater disgrace than ever, as appears from the graphic picture Cooke gives of what had been going on aboard the 'Swan' in her absence and of the action Drake took on her Master's report. 'But here may not be forgotten,' he says, 'how hardly Master Thomas Doughty, and some other gentlemen were dealt withal in this their absence by a sort of bad and envious people as sailors and such like, but specially Master Doughty. . . . For there [that is, on board the 'Swan' while she was separated from the fleet] the Master put himself from the mess of Master Doughty and the other gentlemen and did sit himself amongst the sailors, nothing at all sparing but rather augmenting his own diet; but how simply these gentlemen did fare there is some come home that (except they will deny their own words) can make relation thereof. Master Doughty seeing himself and one Master Chester, whom Drake had made captain of the fly-boat, so ill-used, told him, "I marvel Master Chester that you will take it at his hands to be thus used considering you were here authorised by the General." And with the same intent he came to the Master and told him that he did use too much partiality considering the extremity for want of victuals they were like to fall into, and it was against reason that he and his mates should be so plenti-fully fed and others to be at the point to starve. The Master hereat beginning to storm swore that such rascals as he was should be glad to eat the tholes when he would have it.' The wrangle continued till, as Cooke was told, it came to blows, and 'then Master Doughty turning to Master Chester, said unto him, "Master Chester, let us not be thus used at these knaves' hands. Lose nothing of that authority that the General hath committed unto you. If you will, we will put the sword again into your hands and you shall have the government."' This, he concludes, he can well avouch to be true, for there were two or three who swore to the charge as the gravest of Doughty's offences. Comparing this with the sworn

CHART FROM FLETCHER'S 'NOTES' TO ILLUSTRATE THE VOYAGE TO THE STRAITS OF MAGELLAN AND THE DISCOVERY OF AN OPEN SEA SOUTH OF THEM
(*Sloane MSS.* 61)

testimony to which Cooke refers, we get a fair idea of his credibility and of what really occurred. Most of the articles relating to what passed on board the 'Swan' refer to speeches made by Doughty to the effect that Drake owed everything to him; that he had a hold upon Drake through certain secrets he knew about his life; and that they were sent out in equal authority. One which was sworn to by Fletcher, Sarocold the Master, John Chester and another distinctly alleges that Doughty endeavoured to persuade Chester to assert his authority over the Master by force, saying that if Chester would be ruled by him he would put the sword into his hands to rule as he thought good and make the company be ready to cut one another's throats. Another set of depositions corroborates this and leaves no room to doubt that he did actually try to tamper with the crew and to induce Chester to seize the vessel.[1] The lamentable condition of affairs which Doughty's presence had brought about on board is further shown by another suggestive piece of evidence. John Sarocold deposed that 'there was certain talk one day after dinner concerning such as should be in any respect enemies or traitors unto either the General or the voyage. Unto the which it was my fortune to answer, that our General might do well to deal with them as Magellan did, which was to hang them up to be a sample to the rest. To the which Mr. Doughty answered, "Nay, softly, his authority is none such as Magellan's was, for," saith he, "I know his authority as well as he does himself. And as for hanging it is for dogs and not for men."'

Upon the report of these matters Drake must have seen that something had to be done to restore harmony and discipline in the fleet if it was to accomplish anything. His idea of winning over his old friend by forbearance had proved worse than a failure. It is clear it had only led Doughty to underestimate the unflinching resolution of the man he had set himself to thwart, and that he did not appreciate the risk he was running. Though to exalt his own position he had told the crew of the 'Pelican' that Drake had power of life and death, he probably knew that he had not and felt sure that

[1] *Vaux*, p. 166–71.

however far he went, Drake dared not lay hands on him.[1] But already the harassed admiral must have been contemplating the ultimate necessity of taking his friend's life. Sarocold's discussion with Doughty shows us that the well-known story of Magellan's mutiny and its drastic suppression was a subject of common talk in the fleet, and must have been in Drake's mind. Still, he seems to have shrunk from extreme action. At first during the stay in Port Desire, Doughty was kept under a loose arrest upon the 'Pelican,' until one day, while the ships yet lay together, as Cooke reports, 'upon some unkind speeches . . . the General did not only strike him, but commanded him to be bound to the mast,' a common sea-punishment of the time. The nature of the unkind speeches which so violently provoked Drake Cooke does not relate. Don Francisco de Zarate, however, whom Drake subsequently took prisoner, tells us that in talking the matter over with him Drake gave as the reason for his severity that Doughty had urged him with indecent persistence to give up attempting to enter the South Sea and to confine his operations to the Atlantic, on the ground that in seeking new discoveries in the face of the bad weather that prevailed he was wantonly risking the lives of his men; and that thereupon he had ordered him to be taken below and placed in irons.[2] There can be little doubt, then, that this was what finally exhausted Drake's forbearance. Nor can it be wondered at; for if he really believed that Doughty was brewing the bad weather, there must have been a sting of peculiar im-

---

[1] It is almost certain that Drake had no express authority to inflict capital punishment. He never distinctly said he had, and whenever the subject was raised he seems to have turned the matter off with some ambiguous answer. The editor of the Authorised Narrative seems to have had before him no definite evidence of a power of life and death, and all he can produce in justifying Drake's assumption of it, is a parenthetical statement that before he set sail the Queen committed to him 'her sword to use for his safety with this word, "We do account that he which striketh at thee, Drake, striketh at us."'
[2] Zarate to Don Martin Enriquez in Peralta's *Costa Rica*, p. 584.

pudence in the insubordinate energy with which he urged the abandoning of the main idea of the voyage.

His punishment over, Doughty was ordered into the 'Christopher,' and now for the first time he seems to have become seriously alarmed, 'for,' says Cooke, 'he knew them to be there that sought his life, as namely, the Master of the fly-boat (that is Sarocold) and some other desperate and unhonest persons.' Drake's only reply to his protests was to order a tackle to be rigged to sling him on board. 'Thus,' says Cooke, 'aboard the canter he went and his brother John Doughty with him.'

Still Drake could not bring himself to believe in his friend's guilt or else was dissatisfied with the evidence he had of it, if at least we may credit a curious story Cooke tells. They were on the point of sailing, the last men were leaving the Island where they had been encamped to refresh, when Cuttill, who for some unexplained reason had been deprived of his place as Master of the 'Pelican,' was seen to leave Drake, with whom he had been talking, in a fury and to begin wading over to the mainland. When up to his armpits, he stopped and cried out that he was going to stay behind with the cannibals rather than accuse Doughty falsely. But when everyone was embarked Cuttill was heard to fire his piece. Drake took it to be a signal for a boat and sent one to his rescue, the crew of which induced him to return. From this Cooke naturally deduces that Doughty had never tempted Cuttill to desert, but it may equally well be taken as evidence that Cuttill was afraid of admitting what he ought to have reported long ago.

So soon as Cuttill was received on board, the fleet set sail; but it was only to encounter another spell of foul weather and once more to lose immediately the vessel on which the Doughtys were confined. Three days were spent in searching for her, and when at last she was found Drake put in again into a little bay further to the southward, determined to cast her off like the 'Swan' and to place the prisoners in charge of Wynter. 'Our General,' Cooke here repeats, 'always thought, or at least would so give it out, when he saw any foul weather that Thomas Doughty was occasion thereof,' and indeed now he seems to have been convinced that the two brothers were practising sorcery. 'Upon giving up the canter,' says Cooke, 'Master Drake himself came aboard the "Elizabeth," and calling all the company together told them he was going to send thither a very bad couple of men, the which he did not know how to carry along with him this voyage and go through therewithal, "as namely," quoth he, "Thomas Doughty who is," quoth he, "a conjuror, a seditious fellow, and a very bad and lewd fellow . . . and his brother the younger Doughty a witch, a poisoner, and such a one as the world can judge of. I cannot tell you from whence he came, but from the devil I think." And so warning the company that none should speak to them or use any conference with them, for if they did he would hold them as his enemies, aye and enemies to the voyage, he willed that great care should be taken, that they should neither write nor read.' So promising he would fill the ships with gold and make the meanest boy in the fleet a gentleman, he departed. 'Shortly after he sent the said Thomas Doughty and his brother aboard the "Elizabeth," commanding them as they would answer it with their lives not to set pen to paper nor yet to read but what every man might understand and see,' from which it is clear that he meant to take every possible precaution against their weaving spells.

With now no more than his three original men-of-war, the 'Pelican,' the 'Elizabeth,' and the 'Marygold,' Drake stood on to the southward until on June 17th he reached 'another bay in 50° 20', lacking a little more than one degree from the mouth of the Straits,' and there he anchored. Magellan had fixed the latitude of his strait at 52°, so that this bay was probably Port Santa Cruz, where Magellan himself lay two months and which with less accuracy than Drake's improved instruments enabled him to do he had fixed at 50°. Still John Drake in the prize was missing and, resolved not to enter the strait without one more attempt to find him, Drake turned northward to search the whole coast as far as the latitude where they had parted company. On the 18th the search commenced and 'with hearty and often prayers,' the Narrative quaintly says, 'we joined watchful industry to serve God's good providence, and that with such happy reward that the very next evening a few leagues from Port St. Julian, the long lost vessel hove in sight, and giving God thanks with most joyful minds' they all together came to anchor in Magellan's old harbour.

It was here that Magellan's captains had mutinied, and it was here he had assassinated one, hanged another, and marooned two more, and here as soon as they landed Drake's men found still standing the stump of a fir-post, which they believed to be the remains of the gallows on which the execution had taken place.

The tragic associations of the ill-omened haven were soon still further deepened by an incident in which Drake came near to losing his life. He had gone off with his brother, Captain Thomas, a gentleman called Mr. Robert Winter (or Winterhey) and his Master-gunner in a boat to reconnoitre the mainland. At every spot where they had touched along the Patagonian coast he had entered into friendly relations with the natives. Here he did the same, but as the party were returning to the boat they were attacked with a shower of arrows from a number of Indians who had crept down amongst the rocks. Mr. Winterhey was shot through the lungs, but though mortally wounded managed to reach the boat. The Master-gunner attempted a shot from his caliver, but the piece missed fire and he immediately fell dead, pierced with an arrow. The situation was now critical. Calling to his men to keep shifting their ground and edging towards the enemy, and to think of nothing but covering themselves with their targets and breaking the arrows as they fell, Drake himself seized the gunner's caliver, reprimed it and shot the leader of the natives. Lacerated with hail-shot the wounded chief roared so terribly with pain that the rest ran away and the survivors of Drake's party were able to reach the boat unmolested. Next day the gunner's body was recovered and both Winterhey and he were buried in one grave.

Much as Drake seems to have felt the loss of his men, and especially Winterhey's, 'whom for many good parts he loved dearly,' a still deeper tragedy had here to be enacted. Harassed beyond bearing by the anxieties of his long struggle southward, and having before him the perilous passage where so many had found disaster, he resolved to clear himself of one great difficulty by bringing Doughty to trial. What it was that determined him at this point to act as he did we cannot tell. The Authorised Narrative would have it believed that it was the discovery of a plot to murder him and his most faithful supporters and to abandon the voyage, a plot, it says, which had been revealed to him before he left Plymouth and which at the time he had ignored. The statement has the hollow ring of a piece of discreet editing, nor is it supported by the articles in which, though afterwards Drake spoke of being in danger of his life, not a word appears about assassination. Pretty tells us that Drake here made inquiry into Doughty's conduct and found it tended to 'contention, or mutiny or some other disorder, which hazarded the success of the voyage.' The mariner Cliffe simply says he was accused on several articles. What is in all probability a copy of them exists amongst the 'Proceedings against Mr. Doughty' in the Harleian Manuscripts, but even from these the exact nature of the charge is difficult to ascertain. As was always the case at that time and for long afterwards, they display great confusion between pleading and evidence. Nearly all of them, indeed, consist of what we should now call evidence rather than the allegation of any offence, and not one lays a specific charge of any kind. From the mass of words and actions that the accusers swore to we have to gather what the crimes were which they wished to prove. Were an indictment to be drawn upon them to-day it would probably charge several different offences; such as incitement to mutiny, conspiracy to mutiny, witchcraft, defamation of Drake, insubordination. There is also a charge of using words treasonable to the queen and Council, but this at the outset of the proceedings was not much insisted on, and generally it may be said that the prisoner was put on his trial for conspiring by several means to prevent the voyage going forward.

The tribunal before which he was arraigned partook rather of the nature of a Lynch court than a court-martial, and whether or not Drake had by his commission the power of life and death, it seems certain that no definite procedure for its exercise can have been provided. Pretty simply says the trial was conducted as near as might be to the course of the laws of England. From the other narratives we gather that this was certainly the case. One of the rocky islands of which the desolate harbour was full was chosen for the place of trial, and here on the last day of June Drake mustered his whole company and took his seat as Judge, with Hatton's man, Captain Thomas, beside him as assessor. On Doughty being brought before him he charged him in these words. 'You have here sought by divers means, inasmuch as you may, to discredit me to the great hindrance and overthrow of this voyage, besides other great matters where I have to charge you withal;' and then, according to the time-honoured formula, he asked him how he would be tried. 'Why, good General,' Doughty answered, 'let me live to come to my country. I will there be tried by Her Majesty's laws.' 'Nay, Thomas Doughty,' said Drake, 'I will here impanel a jury.' 'Why General,' objected Doughty, 'I hope you will see your commission be good.' 'I warrant you,' Drake answered, 'my commission is good enough.' Doughty then called upon him to produce it, whereupon Drake's patience for legal technicalities seems to have been exhausted, and he ordered the prisoner to be bound. 'My masters,' cried he, 'this fellow is full of prating. Bind me his arms, for I will be safe of my life.' The provocation was probably greater than Cooke represents it in his report, for Drake, he says, now gave furious words unto Thomas Doughty, saying he believed it was he who had poisoned Essex and using other invectives to the prisoner's prejudice after the manner of English judges of that time and some continental ones of to-day.

A jury composed of over forty of the leading men in the fleet was then impanelled,[1] including some at least of Doughty's warmest partisans, and with Wynter, the Vice-Admiral, as foreman. To them Captain Thomas read over the articles, 'all which,' says Cooke, 'Doughty did not greatly deny,' until one Edward Bright, who seems to have been a most devoted follower of Drake's and a personal enemy of the prisoner's, accused him of having said in Drake's garden at Plymouth, before the expedition sailed, 'that the Queen's Majesty and Council would be corrupted.' In an unsigned deposition, which from internal evidence is almost certainly Bright's, the accusation appears thus: 'And the said T. D. said that the whole Council would be corrupted with money. Yea, the Queen's Majesty herself, which grieved my conscience to hear it.'[2] The gravamen of this charge is clearly that Doughty had hinted that the voyage was not officially sanctioned by the Government, but that Drake had bribed the queen and the Council to wink at the piracies he meant to commit. Doughty gave no categorical denial to Bright's evidence, and it is clear it was this that was considered fatal to him. What followed exactly Cooke does not report; he gives us only the culmination of the wrangle that ensued. 'Then it fell out,' he says, 'upon further talk that Master Doughty said that my Lord Treasurer [that is Lord Burghley] had a plot of the voyage. "No, that hath he not," quoth Master Drake. The other replied that he had. "How?" quoth Master Drake. "He had it from me," quoth Master Doughty.'

This startling admission that he had betrayed the

---

[1] *Authorised Narrative.* Camden says twelve, 'after the English manner.'
[2] *Vaux*, p. 172.

secret of the voyage, which it must be noted was against his
interest to make and which is reported by his violent
partisan, seems finally to have opened Drake's eyes.
'"Lo, my masters," quoth he. "What this fellow hath
done! God will have all his treacheries known. For her
Majesty gave me special commandment that of all men my
lord Treasurer should not know it; but to see how his own
mouth hath betrayed him." So this,' continues Cooke,
'was a special article against him to cut his throat, and
greatly he [Drake] seemed to rejoice at this advantage.' A
fairer way probably to put it would be that Drake was
immensely relieved to find that his harsh treatment of his
friend was really justified. Doughty himself seemed to
regard his hasty admission as fatal, and said he would sign
anything they liked to draw up if only he were permitted
to live till he came to England. But the anxiety, which
on all occasions he had evinced to be allowed to get home,
can only have deepened the conviction, which seems now
to have possessed Drake's mind—that the culprit had
some great personage behind him on whose protection he
was relying. He replied that the case must now abide
the verdict of his comrades, and with that he ordered
Captain Thomas to swear in the Jury and delivered the
articles of indictment to Wynter the foreman.

Doughty's friend Vicary, who was on the jury, here
made a formal protest against the proceedings as illegal,
but Drake's answer was short and sharp. 'I have not to
do,' he said, 'with you crafty lawyers, neither care I for
the law, but I know what I will do.' Vicary still protested. 'He knew not,' he said, 'how they should answer
for taking the prisoner's life;' but Drake silenced him by
saying, 'You shall not have to do with his life. Let me
alone for that. You are but to see whether he be guilty
in these articles.' The jury then retired, and presently
returned with a unanimous verdict of 'guilty' on all
counts, but adding a rider that they had some doubts as
to whether Bright was a credible witness. 'Why,' said

Drake on receiving it, 'I dare swear that what Ned Bright hath said is very true.'[1]

The fact is that it was not on Bright's evidence that the question turned, at least in Drake's eyes. It is clear, as we have seen, that what suddenly persuaded him of Doughty's guilt was his admission that he had betrayed the secret of the voyage to Burghley. Not a word was said after this about witchcraft. For Drake the obscurity which he had been unable to penetrate was dispelled as it were in a flash. In a subsequent speech to his crews he justifies the proceeding on this ground alone, and speaks of the prisoner's admission again as an interposition of Providence. 'His own mouth,' he said, ' did betray his treacherous dealing: and see how trusting in the singularity of his own wit he overreached himself unawares. But see what God would have done; for Her Majesty commanded that of all men my lord Treasurer should have no knowledge of this voyage, and to see that his own mouth hath declared that he hath given him a plot thereof.'[2] It is equally clear that this admission in itself was not enough to produce the impression it did. There must have been something at the back of it, and few reading Cooke's narrative as supported by the Articles can doubt that Drake believed Doughty to have had some one at home behind him, and that that man was Lord Burghley. Nothing else will explain why he grasped so eagerly at a vague charge of treason, instead of relying chiefly on the much more clearly proved accusation of conspiracy to mutiny.[3]

[1] The reason for doubting Bright's 'honesty' was not apparently from the nature of his evidence but from the fact that he had concealed it so long and that he bore a grudge against Doughty for having said his wife 'had an ill name in Cambridge' (*Vaux*, p. 210). The Authorised Narrative purports to give the terms of the written verdict and says nothing of the rider, but the whole passage bears so clearly the marks of editing in Drake's favour, that no reliance can be placed on it, nor is the version it gives of the whole proceedings even credible. It is only valuable as evidence that there was something to conceal.
[2] Cooke in *Vaux*, p. 214.
[3] In this connection may be noted also a very curious and apparently

That Doughty was in fact what is now called an *agent provocateur* of Burghley's there is no direct evidence. It is indeed almost impossible that there should be in a matter necessarily so secret. Drake's belief may have been unfounded. Doughty may have left Burghley with the impression that if he could prevent Drake giving fresh provocation to Spain he would curry favour with the Lord Treasurer, and he may have been acting on his own initiative; but Drake's belief, if without foundation, was certainly not without excuse. He believed, as afterwards appears, that he had been sent out to set Elizabeth and Philip by the ears; he knew he had been sent out behind the Lord Treasurer's back; he could not be ignorant that the Lord Treasurer was doing all he could to prevent fresh provocations disturbing the new relations he had succeeding in establishing with Spain; and it was small blame to him and no disparagement to the great minister if the overwrought sailor was convinced that one of the ordinary devices of contemporary statecraft had been used against him. It was what every man who became involved in the tortuous politics of the sixteenth century had to expect, and to Drake, knowing that he was being used as an instrument to upset Burghley's policy of peace, it must have been the obvious explanation of his fellow-adventurer's suicidal opposition. Whether his belief was correct is another matter. It was whispered at the time, as we have seen, that behind Doughty's execution was some grave state secret. So generally, indeed, was it believed that we can hardly venture to doubt it now. Drake's idea may have been the solution, but on this point it is only from the sequel that we can get so much as a hint upon which to form an opinion.

irrelevant piece of evidence given by Drake himself. '*Item*—the said T. D. making comparisons aboard the Fly-boat, said that he was as honest as any in the company, or as my Lord Burghley' (*Vaux*, p. 173). Why Drake attached importance to this apparently innocent remark, I confess myself unable to understand, unless it were that he had been trying to remember if Doughty had ever spoken of his connection with Burghley, and could recall nothing but this.

So soon as the verdict was received Drake retired down to the sea, and calling about him all the company with the exception of the two Doughtys he opened before them a bundle of letters and papers, and 'looking on them said, " God's will! I have left in my cabin that I should especially have had," as if,' Cooke continues, ' he had there forgotten his commission ; ' and it certainly looks, as Cooke hints, as though he had never had one. Passing on, however, he read out letters from Hatton, Essex and others to prove that he did not owe his advancement to Doughty, and that the prisoner had only made the allegation to discredit him ; and then, after dwelling on the man's infamous schemes, and the danger their enterprise had run, he concluded with an appeal to their love of gain and the honour of their country, the two ruling passions which were so markedly the note of the Elizabethan seamen. 'And now, my masters,' he cried, ' consider what a great voyage we are like to make. The like was never made out of England, for by the same the worst in this fleet shall become a gentleman. And if this voyage go not forward, which I cannot see how possibly it should if this man live, what a reproach it will be not only unto our country, but especially unto us,' and finally he called upon them to declare by a show of hands if the man were worthy to die. Whether the vote was unanimous we do not know, but no one is recorded to have held up a hand to save the prisoner, and Drake, returning to his judgment seat to pass sentence, ' pronounced him the child of death and persuaded him withal that he would by these means make him the servant of God.'

Still there seems to have been a desire to save the unhappy man's life, and Drake gave out that if he or anyone could devise a method by which his life might be spared without prejudice to the voyage it should be done. Doughty, Cooke says, begged to be carried to Peru and there set ashore, and Wynter offered to be responsible for his safe custody, but Drake felt himself unable to accept either proposition and Doughty prepared for death.[1]

[1] The version of this in the Authorised Narrative is hardly credible.

The second day after the trial was fixed for the execution, and Doughty being ordered to make himself ready to die, begged he might be allowed to receive the Sacrament. Drake himself offered to accompany him to the Lord's table, 'for the which Master Doughty gave him hearty thanks, never otherwise terming him than "My good Captain."' His behaviour indeed seems to have been exemplary, either because he really felt remorse, or because, like the heroic gambler he must have been, he meant, now that the game was lost, to lose like a gentleman. 'By the worthy manner of his death,' says the Authorised Narrative, 'he fully blotted out whatever stain his fault might seem to bring upon him.' 'It was not seen,' says Cooke, 'that of all this day before his death that ever he altered one jot his countenance, but kept it as staid and firm as if he had had some message to deliver to some nobleman.' The Communion having been duly administered by the Chaplain Fletcher, the two friends rose from where they had knelt together and sat down to a banquet such as the place might yield, and there 'they dined also at the same table together as cheerfully in sobriety as ever in their lives they had done aforetime, each cheering up the other and taking their leave by drinking to each other, as if some journey only had been in hand.' Dinner over Doughty begged a few minutes' private speech with the General, the purport of which was never known, and then with bills and staves the Provost Marshal escorted him to the place of execution. 'Here,' says Cooke,

professes that Drake gave the prisoner the choice between death, marooning, and being sent a prisoner to England, and that Doughty begged for death, because marooning amongst heathens would imperil his soul, and the detachment of a ship to take him home would endanger the prospects of the voyage, while to return in disgrace was worse than death, and that from this attitude he could not be persuaded. Cooke's story is probably nearer the truth—that Drake was actually contemplating the acceptance of Wynter's proposal, but was dissuaded by 'a company of desperate bankrupts that could not live in their country without the spoil of that which others had gotten by the sweat of their brows,' a phrase which is interesting as showing that Cooke's bias may have been due to a real distaste for the piracy that was in prospect.

'kneeling on his knees he first prayed for the Queen's majesty of England his sovereign lady and mistress, he then prayed to God for the happy success of the voyage and to turn it to the profit of his country. He remembered also there divers of his friends and especially Sir William Wynter, praying Master John Wynter to commend him to that good knight; all which he did with so cheerful a countenance, as if he had gone to some great prepared banquet.'

With Sir Thomas More's grim jest upon his lips he then declared himself ready, and after begging Drake to forgive those who were suspected of being his accomplices he embraced him, ' naming him his good captain and bidding him farewell, and so bidding the whole company farewell laid his head on the block.' The axe fell; and Drake, ordering the head to be held aloft, cried out 'Lo! this is the end of traitors.'[1]

---

[1] This romantic scene, in which the fantastic chivalry of the age seems to touch its highest elevation, was rejected by Southey in his *Life of Drake* as apocryphal. He was of opinion that the person who invented it could have no expectation of obtaining belief from anyone 'except by a reflex supposition in the reader's mind that a circumstance so incredible never would have been invented.' Unfortunately he did not know of Cooke's narrative, and so was ignorant that the story told in the Authorised Narrative is corroborated and even amplified in every detail and in entirely different words by an actual eye-witness hostile to Drake. Amongst the many marks of Cooke's genuineness is his version of Doughty's last words. Had he been inventing he certainly would have got the jest right. This he did not do. He gives Doughty's words thus: 'Now truly I may say, as did Sir Thomas More, that he that cuts off my head shall have little honesty, my neck is so short.' What More said was, 'My neck is very short. Take heed, therefore, that thou strike not awry, for saving of thine honesty.'

CHAPTER IX

THE VOYAGE OF CIRCUMNAVIGATION—(*continued*)

THE tragedy in St. Julian's Bay was a crisis in Drake's life. Hereafter we seem to lose the spirit of boisterous confidence in which his earlier exploits were performed. He begins to appear more as the matured leader of men, sobered by a clearer sense of the difficulties that surrounded him, more inclined to harsh judgment and sterner in his method of command. We can see, too, how great a shock the experience had been to him, and feel the tension of spirit under which he set about the completion of his arrested enterprise.

The way was still far from smooth before him. The work of clinching his ascendency had yet to be completed; the lesson had still to be forced home. Doughty's execution, it would seem, had only served to heighten the discord between the sailors and the landsmen. Like Magellan, Drake had resolved to winter in the port, and as the time dragged wearily away the ill-feeling which the cold and misery accentuated grew every day more dangerous. Before a month had passed away it became evident that something must be done to check the demoralisation of the force, and the harassed commander resolved in a thoroughly characteristic way to take the matter seriously in hand. First every man in the fleet was ordered to confess and to receive the Sacrament the next Sunday, and then on August 11 the whole company was ordered ashore. In an open tent Drake took up his position, and calling on each side of him his captains, Wynter and Thomas, unfolded before him a great paper book. Fletcher offered himself to make a sermon, but Drake cut him short. 'Nay, soft, Master Fletcher,' said he, 'I must preach this day myself.' With that he ordered the men to be marshalled by ship's companies, and addressed a few words by way of preface to the speech he meant to read. 'My masters,' he began, 'I am a very bad orator, for my bringing up hath not been in learning, but what so I shall here speak let every man take good notice of and let him write it down; for I will speak nothing but I will answer it in England, yea and before Her Majesty, and I have it here already set down.' Then followed the famous speech in which he laid down the splendid tradition that was thenceforth to govern the English sea-service and to save it from the disease that did most to enfeeble that of Spain. After reminding them of the desperate nature of the service to which they were committed, he told them that their mutinies and discords must cease. 'For by the life of God,' he cried, 'it doth even take my wits from me to think on it. Here is such controversy between the sailors and the gentlemen and such stomaching between the gentlemen and sailors, that it doth even make me mad to hear it. But, my masters, I must have it left. For I must have the gentleman to haul and draw with the mariner and the mariner with the gentleman. What! let us show ourselves all to be of a company and let us not give occasion to the enemy to rejoice at our decay and overthrow. I would know him, that would refuse to set his hand to a rope, but I know there is not any such here. And as gentlemen are very necessary for government's sake in the voyage, so have I shipped them to that, and to some further intent;[1] and yet though I know sailors to be the most envious people of the world and so unruly without government, yet may I not be without them.' Thus placing clearly before them

[1] His intention in bringing so many gentlemen seems to have been to train officers for further and larger operations against the Spanish colonies. It was the presence of these Cadets that made thinking Spaniards take so serious a view of the voyage. See 'Zarate to the Viceroy of Mexico,' *Peralta*, p. 580.

the conditions on which he meant to insist so long as they were under his command, he offered the 'Marigold' to any who did not like the prospect and desired to return home, 'but let them take heed,' said he, 'that they go homeward; for if I find them in my way I will surely sink them. Therefore you shall have time to consider hereof until to-morrow; for, by my troth, I must needs be plain with you. I have taken that in hand that I know not in the world how to go through withal; it passeth my capacity; it hath even bereaved me of my wits to think of it.'

He paused and not a voice was raised for going home. He challenged their willing obedience and every man agreed to follow him, and because they knew not what wages to ask to leave them to the General's generosity. With the crews thus in his hand he startled the officers by formally discharging everyone of them from his post. Wynter and Thomas protested, asking what his reason was for cashiering them. Was there any reason, he sharply returned, why he should not; and they had no answer. Then with the officers as subservient as the men, he stringently forbade all talk upon what had passed, and once more justified Doughty's execution by his confession that he had betrayed the voyage to Lord Burghley. 'More there are,' he said, 'who deserve no other fate, but as I am a gentleman,' he added, 'there shall no more die.' One or two of the worst offenders he picked out for special reprimand and they humbled themselves on their knees before him. Continuing, so as finally to refute Doughty's tales to his discredit, he gave them minutely the whole story of how the enterprise was set on foot, proving his assertions as he went by letters and documents. Finally he produced the bill of the queen's share in the adventure, and showed them upon how high an affair of state they were embarked. 'And now, my masters,' he concluded, 'let us consider what we have done. We have now set by the ears three mighty princes, as first Her Majesty [and then] the Kings of Spain and

Portugal; and if this voyage should not have good success, we should not only be a scorning or a reproachful scoffing stock unto our enemies, but also a great blot to our whole country for ever. And what triumph would it be to Spain and Portugal! And again the like would never be attempted.' With this appeal to their patriotism, in which he seems to have clearly faced his position, to have understood the enterprise would be held a glory or a disgrace to his country according to its success or failure, and to have even grasped by some sagacious intuition that it was the turning point at which the future-position of England would be decided, he made an end; and then restoring every man to the place of which he had just been deprived and once more impressing on them that it was not himself but their queen whom they were serving, he dismissed them to their duty.[1]

A week later, after a solemn religious service, they finally sailed from the ill-omened port, and in three days, on August 20, they made Cape Virgins at the mouth of the Straits. Here before entering, as though desirous of keeping up the impression he had made, Drake ordered the ships to strike their topsails upon the bunt in homage to the queen and acknowledgment of her full right to his discoveries; and not content with this he took the significant step of changing the name of the 'Pelican' to 'The Golden Hind.' We are told it was done in honour of Hatton, whose crest was a 'hind trippant or.' We may therefore safely infer that his motive in taking the step at this juncture was to allay the resentment which Hatton might naturally feel at the execution of his servant, and by thus emphasising his patronage of the voyage and attaching conspicuously to his name whatever glory was

[1] For this incident we are indebted to Cooke (*Vaux*, p. 212), who says his report is 'the effect of and very near the words,' and I have therefore followed him except for one or two alterations where the grammatical construction is obviously wrong. The highly favourable picture he gives of Drake's behaviour on this occasion leaves little room to doubt his blundering honesty throughout. Fletcher and Pretty refer to the episode but quite shortly (*ibid.* p. 69, n.).

in store for the enterprise, to secure the support of the rising favourite at Court. For what it is worth it is one more indication of the nature and power of the opposition, which Drake now expected to encounter on his return.

Having thus secured his position as far as possible, on the morrow he entered the Straits, and on the fourth day reached the group of three islands which lie close by the mainland where the passage turns to the southward. On the largest of these he landed, and with his gentlemen about him solemnly took possession of it in the queen's name and called it after her 'Elizabeth Island.' Here too they reprovisioned with some three thousand penguins, which they found 'a very good and wholesome victual' and salted down. Continuing their way down the Broad Reach they soon were involved in a maze of tortuous channels, where, buffeted hither and thither by constantly changing winds that without warning swept down upon them in icy squalls from every direction, they were in continual danger of wreck. Above them frowned tiers of glaciers and peaks higher and more fantastic than they had ever seen: below them were depths no cable could fathom; all the terrors of the abandoned passage were about them, and they seemed at the mercy of God. Still they struggled on, and by the seventeenth day had the South Sea open before them. On Cape Pillar, then called Deseado or 'Desired,' it had been Drake's intention, 'after a sermon,' to have left a monument of her Majesty's title engraven in metal for a perpetual remembrance. He had all the materials in readiness; but the wind proving foul for landing and the anchorage bad, without further delay he stood out to realise the fulfilment of the prayer and vow he had made on the summit of the Darien Cordilleras.

For two days they stood north-west—for on the Spanish charts of the time the trend of the coast was thus marked[1]—and the worst of their dangers seemed past,

[1] This error was corrected by Ortelius in the 1587 edition of his *Atlas*, probably in consequence of the survey which Sarmiento was ordered to make

when they were struck by a gale from the north-east which proved to be of a severity far beyond anything they had ever heard of. 'God,' says the Narrative, 'by a contrary wind and intolerable tempest seemed to set Himself against us.' Day after day they drove in snow and darkness to west-south-west before a storm that continually increased in fury. To add to their terrors, at the end of a week there was an eclipse of the moon, and a fortnight later in the night-time the 'Marigold' disappeared and was never heard of again. Bright the chief witness against Doughty was in charge of her, and Fletcher, whose watch it was at the time, says he heard the fearful cries of the crew as she was overwhelmed in the 'mountains of the sea,' and knew it was a judgment.[1] By the end of the month they had been driven, as they calculated, beyond the 57th parallel and some two hundred leagues to the westward. With October the weather slightly mended, and they managed to work back to the northeast, so that by the 7th they were able to anchor among some islands a little to the north of the point where they had emerged from the Straits. It was the first land they had seen since a month before they had met the gale. Exhausted with their toil they were enjoying the prospect of riding out the storm in peace, when a few hours after anchoring a squall caught them. The 'Golden Hind' parted her cable, the 'Elizabeth' had to slip hers, and though both vessels managed to regain the open sea, they almost immediately lost sight of each other and never met again. The 'Elizabeth' recovered the mouth of the Straits, and after waiting there till the end of the month, making fires as a signal to his consort, Wynter lost heart, and though Drake had given him a rendez-vous on the

with a view of fortifying the Straits against a repetition of Drake's exploit (see *post*, pp. 258, 336).

[1] He says Bright had been made captain of her before the departure from Port St. Julian. No other authority mentions this, and the Authorised Narrative distinctly states that Thomas was still in command. Bright, however, may have been made master in recognition of his fidelity (*Vaux*, p. 79, n.).

coast of Peru he induced his men to abandon the voyage and return home.¹

Meanwhile the Admiral was once more driving to the southward, nor was it until he had been carried as low as the 55th parallel that the terrific weather moderated.² At this height he was able to run in among some islands, which seem to have convinced him that he had made a great geographical discovery. It was a discovery which if known to the Spaniards had been jealously concealed by them, and if not was a secret of the last importance to his country. We have already noticed that by all cosmographers of the time the passage which Magellan had discovered was represented as a strait between America and a vast antarctic continent, which they called *Terra Australis Incognita* and believed to stretch east and west about the world and to be continuous with New Guinea. Already, however, if we may believe the Authorised Narrative and Fletcher's notes, in passing the supposed strait Drake's observations had raised in his mind a suspicion that Tierra del Fuego was no part of the fabulous continent, but only a group of islands, and that Magellan was far from having discovered the only way into the Pacific. While passing the Straits they had

¹ The Authorised Narrative hints that the desertion was not entirely without premeditation. Neither Cooke nor Cliffe, who were both aboard the 'Elizabeth,' attempts any defence of Wynter. The latter says the desertion was on compulsion and against the mariners' wishes. Wynter's defence was that he thought Drake must be lost, and that he despaired of ever getting a fair wind for Peru. If we may judge from his deposition before the Admiralty Court on his return, he seems to have had no stomach for the continuance of the voyage under Drake. In speaking of the capture of the 'Mary,' at the Cape Verde Islands, he says: 'The taking of which ship I protest was contrary to my good will, which I could not let or gainsay, for that I had no authority there, but such as pleased the said Drake to give and take away from me at his will and pleasure; and being in great fear of my life, if I should have contraried him or gone about to practise to withstand him in any part of his doing, he would have punished me with death; for that his words and threatenings many times tended thereunto by open speeches and by example of a gentleman whom he executed afterwards, and for that I was there with the said Drake where no justice would be heard was enforced to content myself with silence.' *S.P. Dom.* 1580, cxxxix. 41.

² *Vaux*, p. 84; *John Drake* (p. 60), who says, however, 'he took port in 54° behind an island.'

had, as they believed, on the north and west of them the continent of America, 'and on the south and east nothing but islands, among which lie innumerable fretes or passages into the South Sea.'[1] The group they had now reached in 55° they identified as part of the same archipelago through which they had already passed. On coming to an anchor they found the waters 'to have their indraught and free passage, and that through no small guts or narrow channels, but indeed through as large "frets" or straits, as it hath at the supposed Straits of Magellan.' They were probably therefore somewhere off Stewart-land, or else about the western approaches to the Beagle Channel, which are in about the described latitude.[2]

But even here they had but little rest. In two days a renewal of the gale drove them from their anchors and increased to such violence that they regarded their escape from the lee shore and the unprecedented seas as no less than a miracle. When it abated a little they ran in again amongst some islands, probably in Darwin Sound, 'not many leagues to the south of their former anchorage.' But again the foul weather increased. The 'Golden Hind' lost another anchor and cable, and once more Drake's consummate seamanship was like an interposition of Providence to save them. A storm of such fury and persistence was beyond all experience. The like of it, says the Narrative, 'no traveller hath felt, neither hath there ever been such a tempest, that any records make mention of, so violent and of such continuance since Noah's flood, for it lasted from September 7th to October 28th full fifty-two days.' These, however, were its last efforts and Drake interpreted it 'as though God had sent them of purpose to the end which ensued,' and this was, as the prolonged tempest died away to bring them to 'the uttermost part of the land towards the South Pole.'

[1] *Vaux*, p. 76.
[2] Unless, indeed, from Sir R. Hawkins's report of what Drake told him we may infer they had really been driven round the Horn and had made the eastern mouth of the Beagle Channel (see *post*, p. 257).

That Drake discovered Cape Horn and the existence of an open sea to the southward of Magellan's Straits has often been and is still denied; but a careful examination of the evidence, taken in connection with the testimony of contemporary geographers to his claim and the general accuracy of his recorded observations at the time, permits no serious doubt that he did; and if such honour as is due to the accident, for it was an accident, has been withheld from him it is only because at his first coming home he kept it as secret as he could that the Spaniards might not know the revolutionary strategical result of his voyage.[1]

The Authorised Narrative is particularly accurate and explicit. 'The uttermost cape or headland of all these islands,' it says, 'stands near in 56° without [i.e. outside of] which there is no main nor island to be seen to the Southwards, but that the Atlantic Ocean and the South Sea meet in a most large and free scope.'[2] Fletcher says

[1] A very weighty denial of Drake's claim has been given recently by Professor Laughton in the *Dictionary of National Biography*, mainly on the ground that after passing the Straits he was never again so far easterly as the Horn. This would be a difficulty had Drake claimed to have made the discovery the *first* time he was driven south to 57°; for there we know they placed their position by dead reckoning 200 leagues W. of the Straits, and calculating by the eclipse after their return home, in Long. 90° W. of England (Cliffe in *Vaux*, p. 280). The discovery, however, is not alleged to have been made until after they had regained the Straits, and the 'Elizabeth,' in which Cliffe sailed, had parted company. Drake was then driven south the *second* time on a lee shore, and therefore by a wind about N.W., which, blowing as long as it did, could hardly fail to bring him near to Cape Horn. Drake, too, told Sir Richard Hawkins that the gale veered from N.W. to S.W. (see next page). Captain Burney, R.N. (*South Sea*, i. 328), after a minute examination of the evidence, had no doubt of the reality of the discovery, and was of opinion that it was 'the uncouth and unconnected manner' in which Pretty drew up his narrative which led to the belief that the islands to which Drake was driven were not the group which terminates in Cape Horn. The explanation which the old geographers, going on Pretty's account, adopted to get over Professor Laughton's difficulty was to mark Drake's 'Elizabethides' as a group W. of Tierra del Fuego, in a position where it is known no land exists.

[2] John Drake also gives 56°. The actual latitude of Cape Horn is 55° 58′ 40″ S. It has been objected that this accuracy proves nothing, as Drake's latitudes were often wrong. This is true of observations taken at sea, but where he had time to make a careful observation ashore he is nearly always approximately right. His observations at sea were usually

they found that the land stretched southward 'from the main of America but three degrees at the utmost' and that 'both the seas in 55° and under are one.'[1] His observations were made independently. 'Myself being landed,' he relates 'did with my bag travel to the southernmost part of the island to the sea on that side, where I found that island to be more southerly three parts of a degree than any of the rest of the islands,' and there he set up a stone engraved with the queen's name and the date. According to Sir Richard Hawkins, Drake told him that he was sure that during the long storm he must have been beaten round about the Straits, and that 'standing about when the wind changed, he was not well able to double the southernmost island and so anchored under the lee of it, and going ashore, carried a compass with him, and seeking out the most southernmost part of the island cast himself down upon the uttermost point, grovelling and so reached out his body over it.' When he came on board again he told his people 'that he had been upon the southernmost known land in the world, and even further to the southward upon it than any of them, yea, or any man as yet known.' As the result of this information Sir Richard Hawkins lays it down as certain 'that if a man be furnished with wood and water and the wind good, he may keep the main and go round about the Straits to the southwards,' and this he considered the shorter way

given to half a degree only, those ashore to ten and even five minutes. Their position, as given by the Authorised Narrative, is confirmed by J. Drake, who says (p. 60) that after their cables parted 'they were driven to 56°, where they found an island very fertile'—that is, they found wood, water, and a kind of edible vetch (*yerva*). But he of course does not betray to his Spanish examiners the secret of the open sea.

[1] This would also look as if he were speaking of the east coast; it would not appear to be so on the west coast in lat. 55°. It is quite possible the current that sets from the west had carried them back to the east of Cape Horn, and this seems certainly to have been what Mendoza believed had happened, after diligent inquiry. He told Philip that Drake had run back, when the wind changed, in the direction from which he had been driven, in order to reconnoitre and then sailed northwards, outside the islands into the South Sea. *Spanish Calendar*, 1582, p. 341.

of the two.[1] Amongst Fletcher's notes are charts showing the continent terminating in islands which it was his

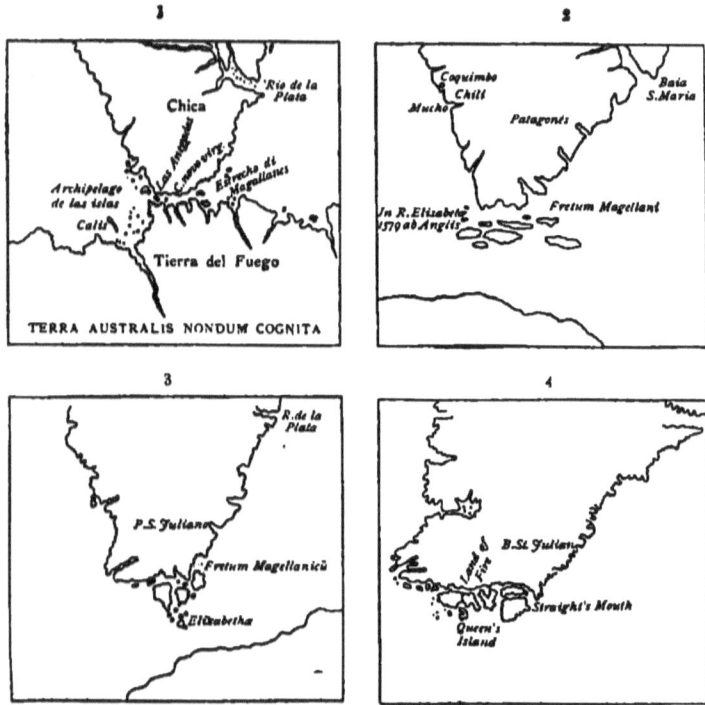

THE SOUTHERN EXTREMITY OF AMERICA, AS DELINEATED BEFORE AND AFTER DRAKE'S CIRCUMNAVIGATION

1. From Ortelius's Atlas 1587 and subsequent editions, ignoring Drake's discovery.
2. From a contemporary Dutch silver plaque in the British Museum, showing Tierra del Fuego as a group of islands in an open sea.
3. From Hondius's map prefixed to the Dutch account of Drake's voyage, apparently founded upon Fletcher's chart (*ante*, p. 233).
4. From the English 'New Map' of 1600.

[1] *Observations* in *The Hawkins Voyages*, *Hakl. Soc.* 1878, p. 224. The passage is unfortunately obscure from an obvious misprint in recording the latitude of their anchorage as 50°.

humour to call *Terra Australis nunc bene Cognita* as being no longer *Incognita*. Drake in honour of his mistress called them 'Elizabethides,' but Fletcher gives this name to the southernmost island only, of which he furnishes an enlarged plan, showing a pool of fresh water in the south part of it.[1]

Apart from this direct evidence it is certain that the existence of an open sea to the south of America, although not generally credited till Le Maire doubled the Cape in 1616, was regarded by contemporary cosmographers as a discovery claimed by Drake. In Hondius's famous map of the world, upon which he delineated both this voyage and that of Cavendish in 1587-8, America is shown as terminating in a group of islands and separated from the *Terra Australis* by a channel some two hundred miles broad. Upon the shrunken Antarctic continent is written in Latin the following note: 'Those islands at Magellan's Strait Francis Drake charted; but Thomas Cavendish and all the Spaniards contradict him, insisting there is nothing but a Strait, and it is credible that Drake, driven from his course by storms may not have made regular observations of these places; for he lost here two ships,' or in other words, Drake, though not necessarily romancing, had probably made a mistake.[2]

[1] *Sloane MSS.* 61.
[2] *Vera totius expeditionis F. Draci*, &c., B.M., S. T. W. (1): 'Insulas illas ad fretum Magell. Fr. Dracus posuit: verum Thos. Cavendish et Hispani omnes ei reclamant, fretum solum-modo affirmantes, et credibile est, Dracum tempestatibus fluctuantem vix loca illa serio observasse; duas enim naves hic amisit.' A copy of this rare map is in Vaux's volume. A probably still earlier representation of Drake's discovery is to be found on a Dutch silver plaque in the British Museum, which appears to have been executed in his honour, possibly on the occasion of his official visit to Holland in 1586. The great cartographer Ortelius adhered to the old ideas, at least in his published maps. In his edition of 1587 Tierra del Fuego is still part of the *Terra Australis*: but it must be remembered that he was at the time in the King of Spain's service, and for strategical reasons was bound at least officially to discredit the existence of a practicable open passage into the South Sea. That the Spanish Government had some hint of the discovery appears from a despatch of the Venetian Ambassador in June 1582. Drake, he writes, 'has discovered that the land hitherto supposed to be mainland is divided therefrom by a navigable channel like the Straits of Magellan,

Monson, in dealing with the 'two worlds undiscovered,' refers to Drake's theory that the Antarctic continent lay altogether to the southward of Magellan's Strait.[1] Hakluyt certainly believed him and attached to his 'Voyages' a map, where, on Drake's authority, the *Terra Australis* entirely disappears, giving place to an open sea, and the American continent ends in a group of islands.[2]

So deeply impressed was Drake with the importance of his achievement, that the fine weather which now set in was regarded as a sign from Heaven, that the terrible tempest had been sent by Him to lead them to their great discovery; 'which being made,' the Narrative reverently says, 'according to His will, He stayed His hand, as pleased His Majesty therein and refreshed us as His servants.' So after but two days' rest, so keen was their

---

where the King has recently sent to build a fort. But as the Governors have not been yet informed of this new channel dividing New Spain from Peru [sic] a ship has been sent to those parts to warn them of it (*Venetian Cal.* 1582, p. 37). See also *Spanish Cal.* 1582, p. 340, where Mendoza warns Philip about the Straits of Magellan, 'which Drake discovered not to be a strait at all, and that the land which in the maps is called Tierra del Fuego is not a part of the continent, but only very large islands with channels between them.'

[1] *Naval Tracts* in Churchill, iii. 388.

[2] Hakluyt in his first edition of 1589 certainly seems to ignore the discovery. But the reason of this is known. The only two narratives to which he could get access were those of Pretty and the Portuguese pilot Da Silva and on the point in question the pilot seems as studiously confused as Pretty. With curious unanimity they both speak vaguely of having entered a haven among some islands they came to in lat. 57°, where no land exists, and pass on hurriedly to the northerly voyage (*Vaux*, pp. 237, 253). Probably, however, Hakluyt never doubted it. In the first edition, it is true, he used Ortelius's map, but expressly states it was because Molyneux's globe was not finished. In his second edition, however, he rejected Molyneux, who it is clear from internal evidence can have had no direct information from Drake. The globe, which is still preserved in the Middle Temple Library, shows an antarctic continent on the old lines. To Hakluyt this was not satisfactory, for in the 'New Map' he adopted the *Terra Australis* entirely disappears. No land is shown south of Africa or America, and this is expressly stated to be on Drake's authority. The map is clearly not taken from Fletcher's diagrammatic charts. Curiously enough, it appears to ignore the existence of Magellan's Straits, and to make America end at the Beagle Channel. Below it are four large islands and several smaller ones bearing a rough resemblance to those which really exist.

THE VOYAGE OF CIRCUMNAVIGATION

anxiety to reach the appointed rendez-vous in the height of 30° south latitude, where they hoped to meet their lost consorts, with thanksgiving and renewed hope they stood to the north-west. But now a new difficulty was in store. On the second day they fell in 'with two islands lying like stragglers from the rest of the broken land,' which were possibly the Ildefonso Group.[1] Here they reprovisioned with birds' eggs, and proceeded on their course north-north-west, as their Spanish charts showed the Chile coast to trend. For twelve days they continued thus until they reached the height of 44°, but still there was no sign of the expected land. Chile seemed to have disappeared. Drake, sure he had made no mistake, at length decided the Spanish cartographers must be wrong, and boldly altered his course to the north-east. He was rewarded in a few days by making the Valdivia river, and all was well again. The river, however, afforded no fit harbouring for his purposes, and he resolved now that he had got in touch with the land again, to coast along it in search of what he wanted. In this way they reached the height of about 37° south, but seeing the coast still promised no good harbour for refreshing, and desiring now to keep out of sight of the mainland, he ran for the island of Mucho, which had been already sighted, and there came to anchor.[2]

Drake with a picked crew at once went ashore, where he was received by the natives with every demonstration of friendship, and returned laden with a feast of fresh mutton, poultry, and maize. At daybreak on the morrow he returned to water at a place the natives had promised to show him. Fearing no danger he had armed his crew with nothing but their swords and targets, and so came ashore in a reedy creek to which the natives signalled him. Two men landed with barrels, but no sooner had they set

[1] John Drake (p. 60), however, says the islands where they provisioned were in 55°; also that not finding land where the charts showed it, they feared that in threading about the islands they had got back into the Atlantic.
[2] San Juan de Anton.

foot ashore than they were seized and dragged off.[1] At the same moment some of the Indians hauled the boat in by the painter, others made a dash at the oars, while out of the rocks and reeds sprang some hundred and more who poured upon the boat a shower of darts and arrows. Crowded as the English were in the boat they could do nothing to protect themselves; their targets were almost useless, and at such close quarters the native fire was deadly. The surf was running high, the creek was full of rocks, they had but two oars left, and had it not been that 'one of the simplest of the company' cut the painter they must all have perished. As it was they reached the ship covered with blood. Every man was hit several times. Drake himself was wounded severely with an arrow under the eye as well as in the head and arm, and his gunner, a Dane called Great Niel, dangerously. Diego, his faithful negro, who seems to have become like his shadow, had twenty wounds, and John Brewer his trumpeter seventeen.[2] Another boat was quickly manned with a fresh crew armed to the teeth to rescue the prisoners, but so vast was the concourse of Indians that they had to abandon their comrades to their fate. In revenge they begged to be allowed to give a broadside into the dense throng, but Drake would not permit it, on the ground that the Indians must have taken them for Spaniards and were therefore justified in what they had done, a most humane piece of casuistry considering how severe was the blow. For the chief surgeon was dead, his assistant was in the 'Elizabeth,' and the 'Golden Hind' had no one but a boy, 'whose good will was more than any skill he had.' In the end, however, Drake's own knowledge of surgery proved enough, and thanks perhaps to the fresh food they had obtained, most of the wounded rapidly recovered; but

---

Legge says they were Thomas Flood and Tom Brewer (*Vaux*, p. 179). Both these men signed articles 9, 10 and 11 in the 'Proceedings' against Doughty (*ibid.* p. 169), showing they are the proceedings at the court-martial and do not relate to the subsequent inquiry.

[2] *Vaux*, p. 99. 'Observations of Sir R. Hawkins,' *Hakl. Soc.* p. 227.

he had to deplore the loss of his negro and his gunner, who both died of their wounds.¹

The same afternoon they sailed in search of a more hospitable port, still pushing northwards, till a little beyond Valparaiso at a place they called Philip's Bay they fell in with an Indian in a canoe. With him they soon made friends, and so kindly was he treated that he brought them to his people ashore, who supplied them with what provisions they could, and something better. For their chief offered to pilot them to a harbour a little to the southward, where they could have all they wanted for the taking, and where a large vessel richly laden had lately put in. It had been their intention to hunt the buffaloes they had seen in herds ashore, but now the Indian's offer was eagerly accepted and they stood back for Valparaiso.

The famous raid was about to begin; Drake's prayer had been granted; and he was on the eve of reaping the first fruits of what he had earned with so much danger and difficulty. For an Englishman, whether the voyage be regarded as piracy or as a calculated affair of state, there must be always something irresistibly attractive in the personality of the man who thus first dared to challenge the Spanish dominion of the Pacific. By a rare piece of fortune we have a picture of him and his company as they appeared at this time, drawn by a Spanish officer whom they took a few weeks later. 'The general of the Englishmen,' wrote Don Francisco de Zarate to Don Martin Enriquez, who had been Viceroy of New Spain ever since the affair of San Juan de Ulua, 'is a cousin of Juan Aquines. He is the same who five years ago took Nombre de Dios. He must be a man of about thirty-five years, short, with a ruddy beard, one of the greatest mariners there are on the sea alike from his skill and his power of command.² His ship is a galleon

¹ *Vaux*, p. 99. Legge (*ibid.* p. 179) is the only authority that mentions the deaths.
² Another prisoner describes him as of middle size and thickset or 'sturdy' (*mediano de cuerpo, membrudo*), Sarmiento's Report in *Documentos Inéditos*, vol. xcix. pp. 432-438.

of about four hundred tons, a very fast sailer, and
there are aboard her a hundred men, all skilled hands
and of warlike age, and all so well trained that they
might be old soldiers of the Italian tertias. Every one is
specially careful to keep his harquebuss clean. He treats
them with affection and they him with respect. He
carries with him nine or ten gentlemen, cadets of high
families in England. These are members of his council
and he calls them together upon all occasions however
simple, and although he takes counsel from no one, he is
pleased to hear their opinions before issuing his orders. He
has no favourite (*privado*). These of whom I speak are
admitted to his table as well as a Portuguese pilot whom
he brought from England. This man never spoke a word
the whole time I was there. He is served with much
plate with gilt borders and tops and engraved with his
arms, and has all possible kinds of delicacies and scents,
many of which he says the Queen gave him. None of
the gentlemen sit or cover in his presence, without first
being ordered once and even several times. The galleon
carries about thirty pieces of heavy ordnance and a large
quantity of fireworks,[1] and a great deal of ammunition
and other necessaries. They dine and sup to the music
of violins; and he carries all the appliances of carpenters
and caulkers, so as to careen his ship when there is
occasion. His ship is not only of the latest type but
sheathed.[2] I understand that all the men he carries
are paid, because when they plundered our ship, nobody
dared take anything without his orders. He keeps very
strict discipline and punishes the slightest fault. He has
painters, too, who sketch all the coast in its proper colours.
This troubled me to see most of all, because it was so

---

[1] *Artificios de fuego.* 'Fireworks' was the technical military equivalent in England (see *post*, p. 378). John Drake told the Spaniards they were chiefly 'balls to throw with the hand with a key or handle' to set fire to ships. 'There were other kinds as well, but he knew not whether they were compounded of gunpowder. Some were brought from England and some made on the voyage.' *J. Drake*, p. 59.

[2] See *post*, p. 358.

true to nature, that whosoever follows him can by no means lose his way. I heard that he started from his country with five ships and four sea-going shallops and that the half of the squadron was the Queen's; and I understand this is so, for the reasons I shall give your Excellency.'[1] San Juan de Anton, the captain and owner of Drake's largest prize, confirms the picture, saying that he had observed how the English captain was greatly feared and reverenced among his men, that he had a guard about his person, and was served at his meals to the sound of trumpets and other instruments. He also dwells on the elaborate armament of the 'Golden Hind,' but says she was greatly decayed.[2]

It is clear then we must think of him, as he broke with so much daring and so entirely beyond expectation the tranquillity of the Pacific, not as pirate or buccaneer of Kidd's or Morgan's stamp, but as a man like Hawkins surrounded by all the state and discipline of a queen's officer, insisting on the reverence due to a captain at sea by all on board his ship no matter what their station ashore, with the bodyguard due to his dignity as general of the fleet, with his gentleman standing hat in hand before him, and his music and his perfumes after the best fashion of the time. It was so at least he impressed the astonished Spaniards who were best able to observe and least inclined to think well of the heretic corsair, who had fallen on them, as Lopez Vaz wrote, 'like a visitation from Heaven.'

The surprise was complete. Though it was now more than a year since Drake had sailed, not a word of warning had yet reached any station upon the South Sea. On December 5, 1578, in Valparaiso, then a small settlement of some nine households[3] which served as the port of Santiago, there was lying a ship called the 'Captain of

[1] Peralta, *Costa Rica*, &c., p. 582.
[2] *S. P. Spain*, 18. 'Exam. of San Juan de Anton by order of the High Court of Panama, March 17, 1879.'
[3] Pretty.

Morial' or the 'Grand Captain of the South,' Admiral to the Islands of Solomon, the identical vessel which the famous navigator Sarmiento de Gamboa had commanded in Mendana's late expedition to discover the 'Isles of Ophir.'[1] Seeing a vessel entering the harbour from the sea where none but friends had been known before, the crew got up a *botija* of wine to entertain the strangers and beat them a welcome with their drums: nor did they discover their mistake till Tom Moone with a boarding party was over their side laying about him, shouting *Abaxo, perro!* ('Below, dog!')[2] Trusting to the prevalent fair weather, the crews of the South Sea ships were very small. In this case there were but half a dozen Spaniards on board, who were quickly driven below and secured, with the exception of one man who leaped overboard and swam ashore with the alarm. Thus ominously did Drake's epoch-making raid open with the capture of the first vessel in which the Spaniards attempted to spread their empire over the South Sea. The terrified inhabitants fled to the mountains, and Drake, manning his own boat and that of the prize, took possession of the town. Nothing of value was obtained except the altar cloth and plate of the chapel, firstfruits which Drake appropriately presented to his chaplain. The warehouses were stored with Chili wine and provisions of bread and bacon, to which they helped themselves according to their desire, and so, setting all the prisoners ashore except the master of the prize, a man of Greek birth whom they kept to pilot them to Lima, they put to sea again with their prize.[3] On ransacking her they

[1] Duro, *Armada Española*, ii. cap. 15; *Vaux*, p. 102. There was no trade with the Solomon Islands at this time. Her real name was *Los Reyes* (see Sarmiento's *Report*, pp. 437 and 450). She had her title from having been the *capitana* or chief of the two ships with which Mendana had discovered what are now called the Solomon Islands, and perhaps Australia as well, eleven years before (cf. Burney, *South Sea*, vol. i. cap. xvi.). The name of the other vessel, Duro says, was ' Todos Santos.'

[2] *Abaxo*, the modern *abajo* 'below, underneath,' was the common word for calling an enemy's crew to surrender by going below.

[3] Da Silva in *Vaux*, p. 260; Sarmiento, p. 437.

found that besides more Chili wine she contained some 25,000 *pesos* of fine Valdivia gold to the value of above 37,000 ducats, or over 80,000*l.* of our money, and ' a great cross of gold set with emeralds on which was nailed a god of the same metal.'[1]

Drake's chief care now was to rejoin his lost consorts at the appointed rendez-vous in 30° south latitude, and with this intent he began to look out for a convenient place to clean his foul ship and set up one of the pinnaces he had on board, since without a light vessel it was impossible to search the coast thoroughly for his friends, whom he expected to find in some snug creek occupied on the same business. While thus engaged in the mouth of the Coquimbo river a shore party were attacked by a strong troop of Spanish horse and some Indians from the neighbouring settlement, but were able to regain their boat without loss, except for one man who obstinately refused to run and so got himself shot.[2] The following day, however, a suitable place was found in Salado Bay, lying in 27° 55'. Here the remaining pinnace was put together on the deck of the prize, the 'Golden Hind' was thoroughly overhauled, and her heavy guns were got up out of the hold and mounted.[3] So soon as the pinnace was ready Drake himself started in her to the southward in hopes of finding his missing companions in some inlet he had overlooked, nor was it till he had waited a whole month in Salado Bay that, still hoping they might be gone on to Panama, he resolved to proceed alone. Yet unknown to himself his sojourn on the coast had not been without those effects he desired to produce. When, as a Spanish contemporary wrote, through God's inscrutable providence the heretics were permitted to penetrate the Straits, 'a navigation deemed impossible, a thing never before heard of or

[1] Southey says, apparently on some Spanish authority, they got 1,770 jars of wine, 60,000 *pesos*, some pearls and merchandise (p. 253, Hannay's edition) Sarmiento says 1,770 jars of wine and 24,000 *pesos de oro*.
[2] This place they knew as Cyppo. The man's name was Richard Minivy.
[3] *J. Drake; Sarmiento.*

imagined,' the Governor of Chile, Don Rodrigo de Quiroga, after a prolonged war, was on the point of bringing the hostile Indians to subjection. Drake's appearance upset the whole of his work. So long as the corsair remained on the coast the whole of the scanty forces of the new colony had to be diverted to watch him, and so harassed was the old Governor by the disappointment and the work thrown upon him that he fell sick and died a few months after.[1]

It was on January 19, 1579, that having thus thrown the whole of Chile into confusion, Drake again started northward. Every bay and inlet as he went was examined, and not without reward. Near a place called Tarapaca on the Pisagua river a watering party found a Spaniard asleep on his way from Potosi with thirteen bars of silver at his side 'weighing 4,000 Spanish ducats which they removed without waking him.' Further on, still in search of water, they met with another Spaniard driving a train of eight llamas each carrying a hundred pounds of silver.[2] 'We could not endure,' says the Narrative, 'to see a gentleman Spaniard turned carrier so, and therefore without entreaty we offered our services and became drovers: only his directions were not so perfect that we could keep the way he intended; for almost as soon as he had parted from us we were come to our boats.' In the same bantering tone the tale is told, as their successes multiplied. Everywhere the Indians came off to trade, and before Marmorena or Morro Morena, a large native town, Drake anchored and found the two Spanish officers who governed it willing more from fear than love to permit the people to sell him all kinds of necessaries.

The first Spanish town they came to was Arica, the port of the renowned Potosi mines, and here, in hopes perhaps of sacking its warehouses, they boldly entered.

[1] *Vida de Don Antonio de Quiroga*, *Doc. Ined.* xciv. 39 *et seq.*
[2] Da Silva (*Vaux*, p. 261) says 3,000 *pesos*. A *peso* = a real of eight. Sarmiento confuses the two incidents and says they took 3,000 *pesos* in silver bars.

Two small vessels were in the harbour, but so complete was the security of the coast that only one negro was on board to watch them though about a hundredweight of silver was found in one of them.[1] The appearance of a party of horse and some other troops at once convinced Drake of the risk of any attempt upon the town, and after keeping the place in alarm all night with his drums and trumpets, the following morning he sailed. Contrary to his usual practice, one of the barks had been wantonly burnt, but both Legge and John Drake concur in saying it was done by two seamen without orders. The other, which contained the treasure, he carried with him.

The stir on the coast seems to have hastened their movements for fear that news of their presence should reach Lima before them; and moreover they had got intelligence, apparently from the negro whom they had carried off, that a richly laden treasure ship was ahead of them. After a chase of over a hundred miles they came up with her at anchor in a haven called 'Chule,' but only to find that, two hours before, warning had reached her through two Spanish prisoners they had let go, and that she had discharged and buried all her silver.[2] A strong guard of Spaniards and Indians ashore diverted them from attempting to recover it, and Drake had to be content with carrying off the empty vessel. About a league from shore he made sail upon her, and doing the same for the other two prizes which he still had with him he left them to drive out to sea and went on his way to Callao de Lima.

A few leagues from the port they were lucky enough to pick up a prize which had just come out, and thus were able not only to learn that a treasure ship had recently arrived, but also to secure a pilot to take them in. Here, too, the same security prevailed. The harbour was full

---

[1] Thirty-three bars, *Sarmiento*.

[2] 'Chule' is probably a mistake for 'Chute.' Chuté Point is a little over a hundred miles beyond Arica, and here is Islay, the port of Arequipa. Anton calls the place Aryguma.

of shipping : besides smaller vessels, some twelve or fifteen of the finest ships in the South Sea trade were riding at one mooring with no watch kept, and as night fell Drake stood in and anchored quietly in the midst of them. Though told by some stray hands, whom they found amongst the deserted ships, that the silver had all gone ashore, Drake ordered a thorough search, and while it was going on a vessel from Panama came in and anchored close by him. At the same time a boat put off from the shore and came alongside the 'Golden Hind' to inquire what she was. By Drake's orders one of the Spanish prisoners was made to reply that she was Michael Angelo's ship from Chile, which was one of the vessels he had been overhauling. Thereupon a man from the boat began climbing up the side, but suddenly finding himself confronted by the mouth of a great gun hurriedly jumped back and the boat dashed away. In vain with a noiseless shower of arrows the Englishmen tried to stop her escape.[1] The Panama ship took alarm, and, cutting her cable, stood out again to sea, with Drake's pinnace at her heels. She was quickly overhauled and summoned to surrender. Her answer was a harquebuss shot that killed one of the English crew and sent the pinnace back discomfited. Drake at once gave the word to weigh, and in order to prevent pursuit quietly cut the cables of every ship in the harbour and the masts of the larger ones, and leaving them to the mercy of the wind gave chase with both his vessels to the offending Spaniard. This time she did not wait to be summoned. One shot through her sufficed to make the crew lower away their boat and leave the ship to her fate.[2]

She was laden with Spanish goods, but these things were of little importance. Though twice baulked of his expected treasure prizes, Drake had learned news of one that

[1] Lopez Vaz in *Vaux*, p. 289.
[2] *John Drake*, p. 61. De Anton says he was told that Drake killed all the crew, but no other account bears this out. Sarmiento only says her owner, Alonso Rodriguez, was wounded by an arrow.

threw all the rest into insignificance. A fortnight before, there had sailed from Lima the 'Nuestra Señora de la Concepcion,' 'the great glory of the South Sea,' laden with bullion on its way to the King of Spain's treasury. It was a long start, but knowing she was to touch at Paita they had still hope of catching her before she reached Panama. Whether Drake really intended to carry out his projected attempt on the Golden City single-handed we cannot tell, but before him was a prize that he was determined to have wherever he might find her. As ill luck would have it, before he was out of sight of Callao, it fell dead calm, and while he drifted with his prize on a glassy sea close to the island of San Lorenzo that lies in the mouth of the bay, the bells of the town rang out an alarm; loud cries of 'the French!' added to the confusion, and it was clear he was not even out of danger.[1] The morrow brought no change in the weather and he was still becalmed, when the Viceroy of Peru, hearing that enemies had appeared in the port and fearing a revolutionary outbreak, hurried down from Lima in alarm with horse and foot. Finding from the arrows that had been shot at the custom house boat who the enemy really were, he manned two vessels which had been saved from the general wreck with two hundred troops each, and as soon as a breeze sprang up sent them in pursuit of the corsairs. By this time, however, Drake by towing with his pinnace and boat had got an offing, and seeing two large vessels bearing down on him with the coming breeze he had time to act. His suspicion had been aroused already by the movements of a small boat that seemed to be watching him and he at once ordered away the pinnace to take his Greek pilot and the other prisoners on board the prize, and bring off the prize crew. There was some delay, and every moment was precious. Drake sprang into his gig, and rowing to the prize, rated his men soundly, and quickly had them all aboard the pinnace. Then he cast off the Spanish vessel and let her drive, while the 'Golden

[1] *John Drake*, p. 51; *Sarmiento*, p. 432.

Hind' spread every stitch she had north-west to get the breeze.[1] The decoy proved a complete success. The soldiers huddled in the two unarmed vessels were excusably unwilling to approach the English guns, and were only too glad it seems to make the recapture of the prize an excuse for leaving Drake to get away on the freshening breeze. All day, however, they laboured after him, but the Spanish vessels were without ballast and so crank they could bear no sail, and by evening, says Sarmiento, there was very little to be seen of the 'Golden Hind.' At nightfall they resolved to return, seeing they had no provisions and could do nothing if they caught the enemy; but what had most to do with the decision, says Sarmiento contemptuously, 'was that many *caballeros* were so sea-sick they could not stand and had no power to fight.' On their return to port, it is said, the exasperated Viceroy hanged some of them for cowardice, but nevertheless saw wisdom enough in their discretion to order guns to be cast to arm ships for a new pursuit.

Meanwhile the breeze had increased to a gale and Drake was flying northward after his prey. Every eye could now look forward without fear and every nerve was strained in the pursuit. As they drew near the line the wind failed, but in spite of the increasing heat they took to their oars and rowed. On the second day they met and captured a frigate and were told by the pilot that the chase was only three days ahead of them. Two days more brought them to Paita, where from another prize, which the pinnace cut out, they learned they had gained another day. The scent was now hot, and to add to the excitement, as they pressed on again, it was known that a fight was probable; for the 'Nuestra Señora de la Concepcion,' as though unusually well armed for a South Sea ship, was nicknamed *Cacafuego*, a word that may be decently translated 'Spitfire.' For fear of missing her the two vessels sailed in extended line, Drake in the pinnace close

---

[1] *Sarmiento*, p. 434. *Velejó la navio a popa y echó los juanetes, que son sobregabias*, which seems to mean she had top-gallant-sails.

in-shore and the ship a league and a half to sea, and to the first man who should view the chase the general promised a chain of gold. The next day a third prize was taken, and Drake's behaviour on this occasion gives us an insight into the hurry and excitement that prevailed. She carried as passengers two friars and, as her papers shewed, was bound from Guayaquil to Panama with a quantity of silver. All this was found, but the negro sailors said there was more unentered, as was frequently done to cheat the customs. The supercargo stoutly denied it, but Drake could not wait to inquire into the truth. The friars and the crew were set ashore, but the skipper and the supercargo carried on. As the latter persisted in saying the negroes lied, Drake in his impatience ordered him to be hung up by the neck till he confessed. Still he maintained his papers were correct, and no more silver being found by the searchers Drake was at last convinced and ordered him to be released before any harm was done. This is the one serious charge we have of Drake's having used cruelty to his prisoners, and if it be true the excitement under which he must have been labouring at the time is the only excuse to be found for it.[1]

Having obtained from his prisoners news of the chase that made him still hotter for the pursuit, he kept the prize in company only long enough to tranship the treasure to the 'Golden Hind' and then let her drive like the rest. Pressing on under every rag that could be carried, in three days they had passed Guayaquil without so much as looking into it; four more carried them across the line; and still there was not a glimpse of what every eye was straining to see. Five leagues from Cape San Francisco they gained fresh hope. Here a fourth prize,

---

[1] The story comes from John Drake's deposition. Sarmiento does not mention it. Nuno da Silva (*Vaux*, p. 265) gives a different account of it, saying the man was hanged 'because he would not confess two plates of gold which he had taken, which after they found on him.' Drake may therefore have had more ground for suspecting the man's honesty than the officer of the Inquisition records.

bound from Guayaquil to Panama with 15,000 *pesos* in gold, was stopped, and, better than the treasure, one of the prisoners told them the chase must be almost in sight.[1] Hopes beat high, as once more the long chase was renewed and not without cause. For a few hours later just as Cape San Francisco rose into sight, John Drake, the general's page, who had gone to the masthead, came to claim the golden chain.

To seaward of them he had seen the 'Cacafuego' quietly proceeding on her course. It was only midday, and Drake did not wish to attack before dark. To take in sail would be to arouse the suspicions of the chase. He therefore hit on the ingenious device of trailing at his stern some empty wine-jars, whereby his speed was reduced and the chase deceived as to his power of sailing; and as the two vessels thus held on he cleared for action.[2]

By eight o'clock, when the 'Cacafuego' had reached as far as Punta Galera, it became obvious to all on board that the strange vessel was making for them, and San Juan de Anton, her owner and captain, thinking that the Viceroy must be sending some message after him, went about and made towards the 'Golden Hind.' Drake at once cut away his drags, and running under the Spaniard's stern brought to alongside about nine o'clock. As they came up Anton hailed them, but there was no

---

[1] *Sarmiento.* He says Bravo, the owner, attempted after surrendering to make sail and escape. Whereupon Drake ordered all his sails to be wrapped round his anchor and thrown overboard, but afterwards he gave him some canvas to get to port.

[2] The narrative of Da Silva as given in Hakluyt (*Vaux*, p. 265) says that the 'Golden Hind' was 'by the head,' and the jars were a device to *increase* her speed. Professor Laughton, however, says it is a mistranslation (*Dict. Nat. Biogr.*), and this view is borne out by John Drake's Deposition, which implies the motive was as given in the text above. Henry Maynwaring, the famous corsair, in the *Treatise on Piracy and its Suppression* which he inscribed to James I. as a thank-offering for his own pardon, says it was a common device of pirates. 'If any ships stand in after them,' he writes, 'they have out all the sail they can make, and hang out drags to hinder their going, that so the other that stand with them might imagine they were afraid, and yet they shall fetch them up,' *MS., Brit. Mus., Bib. Reg.*, 17a, lxvii.

answer. He demanded what they were, and the answer came 'A ship of Chile.' With that he came to the side, but only to find out his mistake. As the stranger laid him aboard there arose from her decks a shout of 'English! Strike sail!' and then a solitary voice cried: 'Strike sail, Señor Juan de Anton, unless you wish to be sent to the bottom!' 'Strike!' cried the indignant Anton. 'What kind of a cruet-stand do you think this is to strike! Come a-board and do it yourselves!' Instantly there was a whistle, followed by a trumpet call and a volley of shot and arrows. In vain Anton tried to bear away. A chain shot from a big gun sent his mizen overboard, and a rain of shot and arrows frustrated every attempt to repair the damage. His men fled below, and in another minute he found himself laid aboard to port by a pinnace which he now saw for the first time. Some forty Englishmen were clambering into his chains and pouring tumultuously over his sides. Resistance was hopeless. He was alone on deck, and they carried him at once to the 'Golden Hind.' There he saw Drake in helmet and coat of mail already disarming. 'Accept with patience,' said he, laying his hand on Anton's shoulder, 'what is the usage of war,' and with that he ordered him below into confinement. So the thing was done. In spite of her name the 'Cacafuego' was practically unarmed; and almost without a blow Drake found himself in possession of the richest vessel in all the South Sea.[1]

All that night and the next day and night the three ships sailed out direct from land, till Drake felt himself well out of the trade routes and secure from disturbance while he gutted his prize. Its value is variously stated, and was never perhaps quite accurately known. There were found in her, the Narrative says, thirteen chests of pieces of eight, eighty pounds of gold, and twenty-six tons of silver, besides jewels and plate. The registered treasure alone was valued at 360,000 *pesos*; and Sarmiento says

[1] The details of the capture are mainly from Sarmiento, who had them from Anton.

there were over 400,000 *pesos* unregistered. As the Spanish pilot's boy watched it all going over the side he hit the Englishmen's humour with a joke, of which they never tired, by saying his master's ship must now be called, not 'Spitfire' but 'Spit-silver.' Besides this they were able to reprovision from the prize in the most luxurious way, and supply themselves with all the sails, cordage, and ship's stores they required. As for the prisoners, they were surprised at the treatment they received. Beyond the open contempt the 'Lutherans' expressed for the venerated symbols of their faith, they had nothing to complain of. Anton was entertained at the Captain's table, and before dismissing them Drake took him all over his ship, and after showing him his armament entrusted him with a message to Don Martin Enriquez. Having heard apparently of the execution of his old lieutenant Oxenham, he warned the Viceroy that he must hang no more Englishmen, and that if he did not spare those he had in his hands he should receive a present of two thousand Spanish heads. It was, he said, because Don Martin had broken faith with John Hawkins that the queen had in a manner constrained him to undertake the voyage much against his will. To Anton he gave among other things a present of a gilt corselet and a valuable German firelock. The Spanish officers all received gifts according to their station, every one of the crew had thirty or forty *pesos* and presents of clothing, and thus as contented as might be all the prisoners from the various prizes were given their liberty, and the gutted 'Cacafuego' allowed to continue her voyage to Panama. Nor was this the end of the corsair's clemency. For Drake, who constantly shows a lurking admiration for the personality of the Spanish gentleman, for his admirable demeanour in adversity, his pride, and his fine manners, as well as a paradoxical sympathy for the victims of his raids, furnished the captain with a letter of protection in case he should fall in with either of the missing consorts, the captain of one of which he said was a cruel man. 'Master Wynter,' it ran, 'if it pleaseth God that you should chance to meet with this ship of Saint John de Anton, I pray you use him well; according to my word and promise given unto them; and if you want anything that is in this ship of Saint John de Anton I pray you pay them double the value for it, which I will satisfy again, and command your men not to do any hurt. And what composition or agreement we have made at my return by God's help I will perform, although I am in doubt that this letter will ever come into your hands; beseeching God, the Saviour of all the world to have us in His keeping, to whom only I give all honour, praise and glory. What I have written, is not only to you Mr. Wynter, but also Mr. Thomas, Mr. Charles, Mr. Caube and Mr. Anthony with all our other good friends, whom I commit to the tuition of Him that with His blood redeemed us, and am in good hope, that we shall be in no more trouble, but that He will keep us in adversity, desiring you for the Passion of Christ, if you fall into any danger, that you will not despair of God's mercy; for He will defend you from all danger, and bring us to our desired haven, to whom be honour glory and praise for ever and ever, Amen. Your sorrowful captain whose heart is heavy for you, Francis Drake.'

The style is perhaps the Chaplain's, but the matter Drake's own; and with the penning of this strange letter, so full of piety and good nature, ends his triumphant raid on the virgin coast.

CHAPTER X

THE VOYAGE OF CIRCUMNAVIGATION—(*continued*)

THE voyage was now 'made.' Besides more precious plunder, the 'Golden Hind,' so John Drake confessed, was literally ballasted with silver, and the only thought was how to carry the vast booty home. When Anton had asked how they meant to return, Drake had produced a large chart which he said he had obtained in Lisbon for eight hundred ducats, and told him there were four ways home, one by the Moluccas and the Cape of Good Hope, one by the Straits of Magellan, the third by Norway, and the fourth he would not name.[1] Though Drake had asked many questions about the Cimaroons in Vallana, Anton believed this to be merely a blind, and that the nameless way was really through Nicaragua. Sarmiento took a deeper view. By the Norway route he apparently took Drake to mean what we call the north-east passage, which the Muscovy company had been formed to explore. By the unnamed fourth way, Drake probably meant the new route he had discovered round the Horn, but for Sarmiento it was the unknown 'north-west' passage, the Eastern outlet of which Frobisher supposed he had already found. The Spaniards believed that somewhere north of Cape Mendocino in California there was a passage through to Labrador, and Sarmiento felt sure the English cosmographers had the secret of it. The Narrative implies that this piece of exploration was an integral part of the original scheme

---

[1] *Sarmiento*, p. 450. Other accounts, including Anton's deposition, say only three, but Sarmiento as a great cosmographer and navigator himself is most likely to be correct on a point of so much interest to him.

of the voyage; in other words, that Drake had set forth not to follow the track of Magellan, but to perform the equally brilliant feat of circumnavigating the New World by way of what was then known as the 'Straits of Anian.' If from the west he could solve the problem which had baffled the most skilful navigators from the east, he hoped not only to do 'his country a great and notable service,' but also to have 'a nearer cut and passage home.' It is possible, therefore, that this was really 'the third way by Norway' at which Drake hinted; or, again, it may be that this and not the Horn route was 'the fourth way' which he would not name. He told Anton he would be home in six months. Anton said he would not do it in a year, because he was only going into a *cul-de-sac*, by which the skipper meant that the Straits of Anian did not exist. But Drake protested he was quite satisfied with his course and meant to go through with it.[1] For the courageous attempt the season was fast growing ripe; his consorts he had practically given up, believing, if still afloat, they must have been misled by the error of the Spanish charts into taking too westerly a course, and would go direct to the Moluccas; and he therefore resolved to seek to the northward without further delay a place where he could careen for the homeward voyage.

Meanwhile from Panama and Lima armed ships were scouring the sea to find him. Three weeks after the capture of the 'Cacafuego' the Peruvian squadron, reorganised under Don Luis de Toledo, reached Cape San Francisco in pursuit. Here they were at a loss how to proceed. Don Luis, who was bound for Spain, obstinately inclined to the view that they must make sure Drake had not gone for Panama or for the Gulf of St. Michael, to the southeast of it, where Oxenham's attempt to recross the isthmus had just been defeated. But Pedro Sarmiento de Gamboa, one of the boldest and most capable officers in the Spanish service, had been made Sergeant-major of the squadron, and he, on the contrary, was for boldly striking northward

[1] *Vaux*, p. 111; *Sarmiento*, p. 419.

across the open sea for Nicaragua. His instinct told him that this would be Drake's course; that there he would be able to water and refit in secret, and prey on the China ships. He argued that the corsair knew that the troops that had been sent after Oxenham were still posted at St. Michael's Gulf, and that in any case he would never abandon his fine galleon and seek to return overland. His real route, he was sure, would be by Cape Mendocino and the Straits of Anian. For that passage, he argued, although not known to the Pacific pilots, was familiar to cosmographers, and especially to the English, for whom navigation in high latitudes had no terrors. There was no doubt that a man so skilled in all kinds of navigation as the corsair they were pursuing would know the route and take it. In vain he exhausted every argument. In vain he staked his head on being able to guide the squadron across the unknown waters. From day to day as they loitered up the coast examining every port and haven, the general put off a decision, and at last having fallen in with Bravo, captain of one of the released prizes, and heard his report of Drake's strength, and how he went boasting he feared neither God nor man, he issued orders without further consultation to keep the ordinary course along the coast for Panama.[1]

So it was that on March 16, unperceived and unmolested, Drake quietly made the coast of Costa Rica, some hundred leagues to the west of Panama. In Coronada Bay is a lonely island called Caño. At the back of this he found a creek secret and sheltered enough for his purpose, and something better too; for the day after his arrival the pinnace captured a passing frigate, on board of which amongst other passengers were found two China pilots with all their charts and sailing directions, whom the Viceroy was sending to Panama to conduct a high official across the Pacific to the Philippines. The richest prize of bullion could not have been more welcome; for now, whether he succeeded in discovering a northern

[1] *Sarmiento*, pp. 440 *et seq.*

passage or not, he could not fail to find his way home. By this time the North Pacific voyage had become well known; at Nicoya in Nicaragua had been established a royal dockyard for building vessels for the China trade, and for some years past there seems to have been a regular annual service between Acapulco and other ports of New Spain and the Philippines. Twenty years before, the problem of the navigation of the North Pacific had been solved by the famous Padre Urdaneta, whom, from the cloister where he had hoped to pass the remainder of his days in devotion, Philip had summoned to resume his old profession. With extraordinary skill and labour he had penetrated the secret of the prevailing winds and calm belts, and had laid down the proper course outwards and homewards in charts which continued in use for more than half a century.[1] They must have been copies of these charts that Drake captured, so that his way was plain before him, and though he was the first commander that ever circumnavigated the globe, this part of his feat can in no way compare with Magellan's heroic venture across what was then an absolutely trackless waste.

The pilot whom he chose to honour with his preference stoutly denied his trade—but in vain. The ship's register was there to contradict him and he had to confess. Disliking, as he said, to carry any man against his will, Drake offered him a thousand ducats to navigate the 'Golden Hind' across the Pacific. More loyal than Nuño da Silva, he refused. The bribe was increased by an offer of fifty for his wife: still he refused; and then he was told he must go whether he would or not.[2] In Drake's persistence we may read how small was his faith in the existence of a practicable northern passage. It is clear he was determined to solve the problem, if he might; but that already, with the instinct of the great navigator he was, he divined what the result would be. The pilot,

[1] Burney, *South Sea*, vol. i. c. xiv. Cf. John Chilton and Henry Hawkes in *Hakluyt*.
[2] *Declaracion de Jusepe de Parraces*, Peralta, p. 586.

then, was detained as well as the frigate, which was found useful for receiving the heavy guns and cargo during the operation of careening, and in the pinnace the rest of the prisoners were dismissed.

The trimming of the vessel complete, the voyage was continued towards Guatulco or Aguatulco, a small but rising port of Guatemala in the eastern arm of Tehuantepec Bay, where they hoped to obtain provisions. On the way they fell in with a vessel, which was surprised and captured. This was the ship of Don Francisco de Zarate, from whose report to the Viceroy Don Martin Enriquez we have already obtained so graphic a picture of Drake and his ship: and now by the light he has left we are able, as it were, to walk in his company the deck of the 'Golden Hind' and see its captain live and move. Zarate was ten days out, we learn, from Acapulco, bound for Peru with a cargo of silks, porcelain, and other China goods, when on the night of Saturday, April 4, the steersman saw in the moonlight a large vessel apparently about to run them down. Thinking the crew were all asleep he hailed them to haul clear. There was no answer and he hailed again. This time a Spaniard replied they were the vessel of Michael Angelo. The stranger was now seen to be towing a smaller vessel at her stern, and as the two ships passed it swung close to the Spaniard's quarter. The next moment there was a volley of small shot fired over them and a number of men swarming over the rail were calling on them to surrender. So secure were these seas that Zarate thought it was a joke, and the surprise was too complete for any resistance to be attempted. No violence was offered to the prisoners—the passengers were merely deprived of their rapiers and keys, and Zarate at once ordered on board the strange ship into the presence of the commander. He found it a very fine galleon, as well armed and equipped as ever he had seen in his life. Drake was pacing the deck, and he went up to him and 'kissed his hands.' 'He received me,' writes Zarate, 'with a good countenance and took me to his cabin, where telling me to be seated he said : " I am a very good friend to those who deal with me truly, but to those who do not——. And so you shall tell me, for this is the best way to stand well with me, what silver or gold that ship carries." I replied " None." He repeated the question. " None," I answered, ' only one or two plates on which I am served and one or two cups and that is all." He remained silent awhile and then turned and asked me if I knew your Excellency. I said I did; and he asked if any relation of yours or anything belonging to you was with me.' Zarate answered no, and Drake, still rankling under his old injury, went on : ' Because I would rather meet with him than with all the gold and silver in the Indies, that I might show him how to keep the word of a gentleman.' Zarate discreetly made no reply, and Drake rose and led the way down to a lower steerage cabin which was used as a prison and called, the Spaniard says, the Ballast.[1] In the far end of it was an old man whom, in answer to Drake's inquiry, Zarate said he did not know. ' Then learn,' said Drake, ' that it is a pilot whom the Viceroy was sending to Panama to take Don Gonzalo to China and he is called Colchero,' and with that he ordered the prisoner to be let out and they all went on deck together. Here they talked till dinner was ready. At table Drake had Zarate to sit next to him and helped him from his own cover, and assured him he had no cause for alarm, for his life and property were safe. Water, he said, was all he wanted and so soon as he found it the prize should be released.

Amongst other matters discussed during Zarate's short stay on the ' Golden Hind ' was the question of Doughty's death. As we have seen above, Drake explained the reason of his execution to have been insubordination. ' He told me this,' Zarate writes, ' speaking much good

[1] The surface of the Ballast was always used as the lower deck, and upon it was built the cook-room. It became the receptacle of all the foulness of the ship, and hence the necessity for frequently changing it to keep a vessel in a sanitary condition.

of the dead man, but that he could do no less as it touched the service of the Queen and he showed me the injunctions [*provisiones*] which he had from her.' In answer to Zarate's inquiries some of the crew told him that the only relation the dead man had on board was a youth he had dined with at the General's table ; and he had noticed that during all the three days he was on board this youth, who must have been John Doughty, never left the ship as all the others did in their turn. That Zarate should have been thus careful to learn what private enemies Drake had was characteristic of the time. In the eyes of the authorities his report without information on the point would have been wanting in thoroughness; but though he inquired diligently no other trace of Drake's unpopularity could he discover. Everyone he questioned agreed that the General was adored.

The day following the capture being Sunday, Drake, he relates, ' dressed himself and made himself very smart and ordered out all the flags and streamers the galleon had,' and having thus marked his reverence for the day he spent the rest of it overhauling the cargo of the prize. 'What he took from me,' says Zarate, ' was not much, though he played the courtier ; for finding certain toys of mine he ordered them to be passed on board his own ship, and gave me in exchange a curved dagger and a silver chafing-dish and I promise your Excellency he lost nothing by the bargain. When he came back he begged I would excuse him, because he had taken them as presents for his wife, and he said I should go on the morrow when the sea-breeze came.'

The next day Drake returned to all the passengers their effects, and manning his shallop with two dozen harquebusiers and six small guns, went in person with Zarate to hand over the prize. To all the sailors and to some of the poorer passengers he gave a handful of silver coins.[1] Nevertheless when he asked for one of them to remain with him for a while to point out a watering place

---

[1] *Testones* = pieces of four reals, i.e. half ' pieces of eight,' value 3s. 4d.

they all fell to excusing themselves; whereupon in some exasperation he ordered the first that came to hand to be seized and removed by force into the shallop, vowing he would hang him if he said a word in protest. In taking leave of Zarate his last words were to beg him very earnestly to tell certain Englishmen who were in Lima of their meeting and that all was well with him.[1] His last act, either in distrust or pity for the old China pilot, was to give him up to Zarate, and with that he proceeded on his course to Guatulco, leaving Zarate to continue his voyage, deeply impressed with his chivalrous treatment and convinced that Drake was the greatest sailor that ever lived.[2]

So well had Drake ordered his movements that he was able to reach Guatulco before his dismissed prisoners could spread the alarm. When on April 15 he quietly entered the port, the authorities were engrossed in the trial of three negroes on a charge of conspiring to burn the town, and before they had any suspicion of danger they found the court-house surrounded and the tables turned, and without the possibility of resistance both prisoners and judges were carried off to the ship. From there the Chief Justice was made to write an order enjoining the inhabitants to quit the town, and this done the watering parties were landed to do their work in peace. Tom Moone again distinguished himself by giving chase to a Spanish gentleman, whom he caught running out of the town, and relieving him of his gold chain and jewels, but beyond this nothing of value was found in plundering the place except a bushel of reals of plate. A plentiful supply of bread and other provisions, however, which

[1] He was probably thinking of the men who had been taken with Oxenham.
[2] 'Don Francisco de Zarate to Don Martin Enriquez,' in *Peralta*, p. 578. A curious touch in Zarate's report which adds to the impression of its genuineness is that he makes Drake always use the second person plural in conversation, which is still the mark of a foreign tongue in Spain, and would also go to show that Lope de Vega was right in saying that Drake could speak Spanish. Zarate never once mentions an interpreter. (See *ante*, p. 152.)

they needed more than treasure, was obtained, and the following day, after releasing the judges, the homeward voyage was begun. On the point of sailing the pilot Nuño da Silva, who had served them so well, was left behind. For this Drake has been severely blamed. It is true no reason is given for the proceeding, but to have abandoned the man against his will or without serious cause to the mercies of the Spaniards is a piece of heartlessness so entirely contrary to Drake's usual behaviour that it is difficult to believe such a charge against him. Da Silva himself makes no complaint. All he says is that 'an hour or two before [sailing] they let Nuño da Silva go, putting him into another ship, that lay in the haven of Guatulco.' The probability is, that it was done at his own request, and that he preferred to take his chance of selling his knowledge like Magellan to the Spanish Government to either the dangers of Arctic exploration or the risk of capture in the Portuguese Indies.

Thus with nothing to guide him but his own brains and the Spanish charts Drake went forward in search of new discoveries, and as he left the last settlements behind him the alarm spread far and wide through Mexico and Central America. The whole country was thrown into a panic. It was generally believed that his other ships were somewhere on the coast. Hasty and even puerile steps were taken to defend the exposed ports, in which the pirates were hourly expected to appear. Helpless local authorities clamoured for troops and money; wild projects of pursuit were discussed; the Bishop of Guatemala offered the President of the Province the bells of his cathedral to be melted down into guns. In the city of Mexico itself Don Martin Enriquez, when he received Drake's message, was in fear for his capital and mustered all the inhabitants capable of bearing arms. Every available soldier was hurried off to the coasts, and such of Hawkins's men as had not perished at the hands of the Inquisition were questioned and denied all knowledge of the daring intruder. One of them was sent to the

Pacific coast as interpreter with a body of troops, whose commander, with more zeal than judgment, embarked them in three weak vessels. Fortunately for himself he took the opposite direction to that in which Drake had sailed, but none the less valiantly pursued him till all were so sea-sick that he had to return—to the interpreter's deep disappointment, for he said: 'If we had met with Captain Drake he might easily have taken us all.'

Those like Zarate whose heads were cooler saw even greater danger in the future. The South Sea was no longer their own preserve. Zarate implored the Viceroy to consider, if the daring captain he so much admired were allowed to get back to his country, what a spirit would there be awakened. 'If this time they send their cadets,' said he, 'the next they will come themselves': he feared that when they saw how sure Drake had made the way and how richly he had fulfilled his promises, they would be eager to follow in his track, and from his one ship alone twenty pilots would be found fit to conduct similar exploits. High officials thought no precautions too great for the occasion. Some were for fortifying Magellan's Straits without a moment's delay; others for the immediate despatch of orders to the Governor of the Philippines to intercept the corsair there; but when it was known he had released his pilot the general opinion was that even he would not be bold enough to return by the western route. Don Martin himself, having garrisoned his ports, had less anxiety, being sure that sooner or later the pirate would be forced by his necessities into one of the Spanish harbours, where infallibly he would be captured.

No one but Sarmiento and the few seamen who listened to him believed upon how bold an adventure Drake was bent. That after accomplishing so much he would attempt so difficult a discovery as the Straits of Anian was in itself incredible enough. Yet that he did attempt it there can be little doubt, though there are difficulties in the story of his adventures in the search, as we have it, that have caused some doubt to be felt as to how far he really persevered.[1] The story of the Authorised Narrative is that after sailing due west some five hundred leagues for a wind, they turned north, till on June 3 they observed themselves to be in 42° N.[2] So far all had gone well, but that night the temperature, which had been normally high, suddenly fell, with extreme and nipping cold. To their profound astonishment daybreak brought no relief; on the contrary rain came and froze as it fell, ropes grew stiff, and so pinched and numb were the crew that they could hardly work the ship. Still the General encouraged them to persevere, believing the phenomenon must be something unusual and passing. Yet the further they laboured the more bitter and intolerable grew the cold; the meat froze as they took it off the fire; six men could barely do the work of three. Another day passed and the wind, more cruel than ever, shifted to the north-west, forcing them eastwards, till suddenly and beyond all expectation they found themselves close to land. Still the weather did not mend. Compelled to anchor in the best road they could find, they were exposed to a succession of violent squalls that threatened to tear them from their anchors, and in the intervals 'there followed most vile, thick and stinking fogs, till the gusts of wind again removed them.' This was the first week in June and they were, as they reckoned, in 48°. Already they were far to the north of Cape Mendocino, and still there was no sign

[1] The only authorities for this part of the voyage are John Drake, Pretty, and the Authorised Narrative, which evidently borrowed from Pretty. He, however, says nothing about attempting the northern passage, and thought Drake sailed north to find an easterly wind for the Moluccas. This he certainly would not have done with Urdaneta's sailing directions in his possession. On almost every question of navigation throughout the voyage Pretty is either purposely or from ignorance unintelligible.

[2] John Drake says after leaving Guatulco they shaped their course N.E. and N.N.E. and proceeded as far as latitude 44°, 'always on the bowling.' Unless this be a mistake for N.W. and N.N.W. it is unintelligible. The passage is clearly corrupt, for he goes on to say that after 44° 'they tacked about and went to California and discovered land in 48° and there took up their quarters.' Here is an evident confusion between their first and second anchorages (see *post*, p. 289).

of the Straits or even of any trend of the coast to the Eastward.[1]

Drake himself began to doubt the use of proceeding. The question, however, was settled for him. To remain where he was was impossible, and no sooner had he got to sea again than a renewal of the north-westerly gale carried him back along the coast. In latitude 38° 30' they at last fell in with a convenient harbour and there came to anchor. Though for a whole fortnight they had been running south, the same cold and thick weather continued and the hills were covered with snow: yet practically unknown as is

[1] The Authorised Narrative, Molyneux, and John Drake all give 48° as the highest latitude reached. Molyneux, however, is not a high authority. Though he professes to mark Drake's course on his globe, it is very inaccurately done and he did not even know how to spell Drake's name. He writes it Draek in the Dutch fashion, although it was after his knighthood. Pretty gives 43°. As we have seen, he also is a bad authority, but Professor Davidson, of the United States Coast and Geodetic Survey and author of the *Coast Pilot for California*, &c., the most learned authority on the point, inclines to believe he is right. (See *Report*, 1886, *app.* No. 7, and his *Identification of Sir Francis Drake's Anchorage*, &c.) He grounds his opinion, as he kindly informs me, on the fact that Drake on June 3 reached 42°, and that 'when he struck the cold nor'wester he could not have beaten up against it to 48° in two days from June 3 to 5.' But here there seems a misapprehension. The cold did not come on till the 'night following' their reaching 42°, and was not unendurable till they had sailed two degrees higher (Authorised Narrative). Drake after this encouraged them to proceed, and it was not till the 5th that the wind came N.W. and they gave it up. As they had sailed on an average thirty leagues a day since leaving Guatulco (i.e. 1,400 leagues from April 16 to June 3), there is no reason why they should not sail with a fair wind six degrees, i.e. 120 leagues, from June 3 to 5 inclusive. Professor Davidson also relies on Hondius's map. Off California Hondius places an asterisk with this note: 'Hic præ ingenti frigore in Austrum reverti coactus. Lat. 42, die 5 Junii.' The asterisk, writes the Professor, is marked 'at the N.W. terminus of a reef in 43°, which I take to be the Cape Orford Reef, the " Dragon Rocks " of Vancouver in lat 42° 49'.' This, again, seems to be a mistake. The asterisk is placed not at the end of a reef (the map is much too small to show one), but well out to sea at the end of a row of dots that represent Drake's course. 'This,' the Professor continues, 'confirms the several assertions that he reached 43° and that he found his anchorage in 42°.' But Hondius expressly says he was turned back in 42°, not in 43°. The only original authority for the 43° is Pretty. Dudley, who professes to have had it from Drake, in his *Arcano del Mare*, 1647, places the anchorage in 43° 30'. There seems then to be no authority whatever, not even Hondius, for the Professor's identification of the anchorage, as at Chetko Bay under Cape Ferrelo in 42° 01'.

such weather at the place and season now, the port in which they had found shelter has been finally determined to be a bay a little above San Francisco harbour, which is now called after Drake.[1]

The description given of the Californian climate is almost incredible. The natives, it is said, went shivering in furs, the hills were covered with snow, the trees were leafless, the birds dared not leave their nests till the eggs were hatched. Some of the hands who had made the Muscovy voyage said they had experienced nothing like it even at Vadhus in 72° at the end of summer. It was no wonder then that Drake, having been so far north without finding any indication of a strait and seeing the trend of the land inclined more and more westerly, came to the conclusion that if a passage existed it must be unnavigable. Still it seems he did not abandon his project at once, but resolved to remain where he was to see if the cessation of the north-westerly winds would bring about a change of weather.[2] The ship too, had sprung a leak, so that it became necessary for her repair to land the bulk of the cargo and to build a fort for its protection. The result was a stay of over a month, the story of which would be hardly credible were not its most romantic incidents borne out by what is known of the customs of the Californian Indians.

Only once if ever before—and that more than a generation earlier, when in 1542 Cabrillo had explored the coast —had Europeans been seen in Northern California ; and it

[1] By Professor Davidson, who has very kindly furnished me with the results of his patient researches. (See his *Survey Report, ubi supra*, where all the learning on the point will be found.)

[2] It is this extraordinarily severe weather beyond all modern experience at the given season and latitude that has cast doubt on the whole story, and no explanation of the alleged phenomenon has been arrived at. Yet it is difficult to believe that Drake deliberately invented it, or to imagine what his motive can have been in belittling the advantages of his discovery of New Albion. It is conceivable that he may have been anxious finally to divert English enterprise from the north, where Frobisher was wasting it, into the more direct and drastic operations which he himself favoured, but this is pure conjecture. It may be noted that John Drake merely says ' the temperature of the country was rather cold than hot.'

was clear from the first day that the appearance of the English filled the Indians with superstitious wonder. As the seamen were busied pitching their tents and marking out the lines of the fort, they gathered excitedly together in warlike array, but halted a little way off to watch, as 'men ravished in their minds with the sight of such things, their errand being rather with submission and fear to worship us as gods, than to have any war with us as with mortal men.' Though timid at first, their confidence was soon gained by the tact Drake invariably displayed in dealing with natives, but the effect was only to increase the uneasiness of the pious Protestants with further demonstrations of a desire to worship them. For that night, however, the Indians retired to their huts, and the English as they laboured hard at their entrenchment could hear that some ceremony was in progress, which continued for hours and sounded to them like 'a kind of most lamentable weeping and crying out,' the doleful shrieks of the women rising shrilly above the rest of the lamentation.

After this night of weeping the Indians kept aloof and the English were careful to complete their defences. Two days later the whole tribe were seen assembling upon the summit of the hill at the foot of which lay the entrenched camp. Presently they advanced, preceded by a man who, at the extreme force of his lungs and with violent gestures, made a long and tedious oration till exhaustion stopped him. At the close of it the rest bowed themselves in a long drawn chorus and the men came forward with offerings for the gods, while the women, crying and shrieking piteously, tore their breasts and cheeks till the blood ran, and cast themselves down on stones and rocks time after time till they lay exhausted. Horrified by these bloody rites and unable to stop them, the General ordered the whole company to prayers, and all lifted their eyes and hands to Heaven to show where God was. To increase the impression, some chapters of the Bible were read and Psalms sung, and with excellent effect. The Indians sat round attentively, and 'observing the end of every pause, with one voice still cried "Oh!" greatly rejoicing in our exercises.' At the conclusion of the service, by some strange impulse they reverently restored all the presents they had received and departed. But in three days they were back again in greater numbers than ever, and at their head a great chief in the midst of a body-guard of a hundred braves and a mace-bearer before him, all of them clothed in furs, and behind him came the naked and painted tribesmen, and the women carrying baskets of feathers and tobacco as offerings. As they approached Drake retired within his entrenchment and drew up his pikes and muskets in 'a very warlike show.' Again the long oration was made and again concluded with their strange 'Amen' and prostrations. Then the mace-bearer, who was probably the medicine man of the tribe, began with a stately countenance a song accompanied by the measures of a dance. Both song and dance were gradually taken up by the whole multitude, and so they advanced in order down the hill and were allowed to enter within the defences of the camp. Singing and dancing still they gathered round the spot where they had signed to the General to be seated, and there invested him with a crown of feathers and chains of bone-work and greeted him with shouts of '*Hjoh*,' which the English took to mean 'king.' The visions of a great English empire in the West, which these savage ceremonies raised in Drake's mind, made him unwilling, though they smacked of treason and idolatry, to refuse the royal and divine honours so solemnly paid him; and considering 'to what good end God had brought this to pass, or what honour and profit it might bring to our country in time to come, in the name and to the use of her most excellent Majesty he took the sceptre crown and dignity of the said country into his hand.'

The ceremony ended with a song and dance of triumph, and in the enthusiasm that prevailed the commoner people crowded in after the braves, and seeking from seaman to seaman till they found a god whose face pleased them, 'which commonly were the youngest of us,' they fell into such a frenzy of shrieks and mutilations that the objects of their adorations were glad to escape into the tents, grieving in spirit to see the power of Satan so far prevail. Scarcely a day passed after this without the sick and maimed flocking in to be cured by the breath of the heavenly visitors, and every third day some ceremony of sacrifice was attempted until Drake was able to convince them how such proceedings offended him.

Before he departed he marched some way into his kingdom and found it a goodly country. The hill-sides swarmed with vast herds of fat deer; the natives were willing and strong to labour; the soil was fruitful, and nowhere could they take up a handful of earth without some probable show of gold or silver. This promising country he called New Albion, a name which some white cliffs near his anchorage suggested, and a monument was set up to record his having taken it into possession in the name of his sovereign.

The 'Golden Hind' had now been a month or more in 'Drake's Bay.' The north-west trades still continued to blow with undiminished force, and Drake, seeing how the advancing summer rendered it useless to hope for the success of a new attempt to find the Straits of Anian, determined to seek his way home by the Portuguese route round the Cape. His Indian subjects were in despair. 'As the time of our departure,' says the Narrative, 'was perceived by them to draw nigh, so did the sorrows and miseries of the people seem to themselves to increase upon them. For they did not only lose in a sudden all mirth, joy, glad countenance, pleasant speeches, agility of body, familiar rejoicings with one another and all pleasure whatever flesh and blood may be delighted in, but with sighs and sorrowings, with heavy hearts and grieved minds they poured out woeful complaints and moans with bitter tears and wringing of their hands tormenting themselves.' On the eve of the departure 'they stole upon us a sacrifice and set it on fire ere we were aware, burning therein a chain and a bunch of feathers. We laboured by all means to withhold or withdraw them, but could not prevail, till at last we fell to prayers and singing of psalms, whereby they were allured immediately to forget their folly and leave their sacrifice unconsumed, suffering the fire to go out; and imitating us in all our actions they fell a lifting of their eyes and hands to Heaven as they saw us do.' On July 23 the English finally put to sea, and the last sight they had of their worshippers was crowding the hill-tops and making fires, as though by a parting sacrifice to implore their divine guests not to leave them for ever.

So was sought to be established the first of those protectorates upon which so large a part of the British Empire has been built. Though it was destined to go no further, there can be small doubt that Drake believed he had laid the foundations in America of a New England which was to rival New Spain. To a man so deeply impressed as he was with the cruelty of the Spaniards' native policy, it was perfectly natural that the Californians should wish to become the vassals of a monarch who could protect them. It was but the feudal process of commendation, and there is no reason to doubt he really took the native overtures to be what he represented them. Were this the only episode of its kind that occurred during the voyage it would be enough to raise him out of the ranks of the pirates and buccaneers in which too often he has been made to stand. The space that is devoted to it in the Authorised Narrative is evidence of the importance he attached to his treaty. This alone should have been enough to suggest that however much he desired wealth, however much he sought to be revenged on Don Martin Enriquez, it was the real ambition of the man, as sincerely as it was Frobisher's, to be the leader of English colonial expansion, and to stand in the eyes of his country as Cortez and the Conquistadores stood in the eyes of Spain. His gospel was to teach that what Spain had done England could do and do better. In his own

time he was not understood except by few, and so was
looked upon askance as a pirate or little better, as he
is to this day. The 'spacious times' of Elizabeth is a
phrase that with cloying reiteration is used whenever
Drake's name is mentioned. The truth is, it was still
a narrow time that cramped the men of broad ideas.
The spacious times were not till Elizabeth was dead and
the peace gave England time to grasp the ideas of Drake
and Frobisher, to realise their vision of a New England
in the West, and to dream of a vast empire in the East
with Madagascar for its seat and centre.

On July 26, after they had victualled as usual on seals
and sea-birds at the Farellones Islands off San Francisco
harbour, the long voyage across the Pacific began. The
exact course Drake took is not quite clear. It would seem,
however, that not content with following the Spanish
route to the Philippines, he struck out a bold and more
direct line for himself. John Drake says they made a
straight course for the Moluccas, but by reason of the
current which was against them they turned their course
towards China (that is, the Philippines) a degree and a half
before coming to the line. This would seem to indicate
that they ran before the north-east trades between the
Caroline and the Gilbert Islands, until they felt the south
equatorial drift current where it sweeps northward and
eastward to the south of the Carolines, and that then they
turned north-west. This course would account for their
being without sight of land for sixty-eight days. For it
was not till the last day of September they fell in ken of
certain islands lying about eight degrees to the northward
of the line. Here, like Magellan, they were at once
surrounded by a number of finely decorated canoes, and
a throng of natives who displayed so thievish a character
that violence had to be used to keep them in order. So
unruly and shameless, indeed, were they that Drake sailed
again the next day, christening the place the Island of
Thieves. John Drake calls the islands Ladrones, and
says they lay in 9°, so that Captain Burney is probably

correct in identifying them with the Pelew group.[1] It was not till October 3 that they were able to shake off their unpleasant consorts. 'Thence,' the Narrative proceeds, 'we continued our course without[2] sight of land till the 16th of the same month, when we fell in with four islands standing in 7 deg. 5 min. to the northward of the line. We coasted them till the 21st day and then anchored and watered upon the biggest of them called Mindanao.' Clearly these four islands were part of the Philippines. If they made them, as they naturally would steering the Spanish course between Samoa and Leyté, they would see four of them in coasting south. The latitude given is probably that of the place where they watered. Caroga Bay (which was also known as Resurrection and Disappointment Bay) lies in 7°, and is marked on old charts as an anchorage with water.[3] The Narrative becomes no easier to follow as it proceeds. 'The 22nd of October,' it says, 'we passed between two islands six or eight leagues south of Mindanao,' which may well have been the East and West Savanganis. On the 25th, the Narrative continues, 'we passed the island called Talao in 3 deg. 40 min. We saw to the northward of it three or four other islands, Teda, Selan, Saran (three islands so named to us by an Indian), the middle whereof stands in 3 deg.' From this it is clear there is a clerical error in the latitudes, for an island in 3° N. latitude cannot be north of one in 3° 40′. Talao, then, may have been the Tulur Islands, which lie in about 4°, or the Talautse group, which lie in about 3° 50′.[4] Having sailed by 'the last save

[1] This group had not been named by the Spaniards. It is marked on the contemporary charts as 'Isola de Arrecifes' or 'Island of Reefs.' Magellan's Ladrones were the Marianne Islands, which still bear alternatively the old name.

[2] The Narrative has *within*, but, as Burney assumes, this must be a typographical error.

[3] Captain Burney thinks they made the Philippines in 7° 5′, but they could not have seen four islands if they had. John Drake gives no help. 'After leaving Ladrone Island,' he says, 'they came to a large island called Bosney, and there took in wood and water.' Why he should call Mindanao Bosney is inexplicable.

[4] In the sixteenth-century maps the 'Talao' or 'Terrao Islands' are

one of these,' on November 1 they passed 'the Isle of Suaro in 1° 30′ and the 3rd had sight of the Moluccas.' As the latitude of Ternate in the Moluccas is 1° 30′, we may safely conclude that there is here also a mistake, and that Suaro is Siaro or Siao, that stands in about 2° 45′, especially as Pretty says they also passed by Tagulanda, which lies immediately south-east of it.[1]

Some reason for the difficulty in following this part of the course is supplied by John Drake, who shows they were otherwise occupied than in making accurate observations. For on their way they met a European ship and spoke with her, demanding a trade for provisions, and threatening to take them if their request were not complied with. The stranger, however, stoutly refused to have any dealings with Lutherans and made off. All day and night Drake chased her, and that so hotly that the following day in order to escape she ran herself upon some shoals where it was impossible to follow her, nor did they ever ascertain what her nationality was. According to the Portuguese she was one of the King's own galleons.[2] From John Drake too we learn how it was they were able to find their way and to learn the names of the islands they passed. Shortly after their disappointment they managed from an island where they landed to carry off two or three natives, whom they induced to pilot them to the Moluccas, and under their guidance in due course the well-defined

---

marked midway between 'Sanguin' (the modern Sangir) and Doij, the northernmost point of Gillolo, which corresponds more to the true position of the Tulur Islands.

[1] Pretty, as usual, is entirely vague. 'Leaving the island' (that is, the Isle of Thieves) he says 'the 18th of October we lighted on divers others, some whereof made a great show of inhabitants. We continued our course by the islands of Tagulanda, Telon and Tewarra, being friends to the Portugals,' and that is all. He does not even mention having seen the Philippines. Telon and Tewarra I cannot identify, but it may be Pretty's bungling way of writing 'Talao' and 'Terrao.'

[2] See the letter of the merchant John Newberry, 'Goa, January 10, 1584,' who says he had been imprisoned in Ormus because Drake came to the Moluccas and fired two pieces of great ordnance on a galleon of the King of Portugal. (Arber, *English Garner*, iii. 181, and see Hakluyt.)

cones of the famous Spice Islands at length hove in sight.[1]

For the development of Drake's projects of colonial and commercial expansion his arrival could hardly have been better timed. 'The history of the Portuguese in the Moluccas,' says Southey, who was careful to draw from their own accounts, 'far unlike that of the mother country and its other conquests or colonies, may be described as a series of crimes with little to mitigate them and nothing to redeem the perpetrators from abhorrence and execration.' Some ten years before Drake's appearance there had been performed at Ternate, which was then the headquarters of the Portuguese, one of their most atrocious outrages. Hairun, who was then Sultan of the islands, with a number of his Rajahs, had been treacherously murdered whilst the guests of Lopez de Mosquito, Governor of the Moluccas. The crime, however, missed its aim; for the Malays fled into the mountains and placed themselves under the leadership of Baber, the murdered Sultan's son. His first act was to demand his father's body. The Portuguese answer was to cut it in pieces and cast it into the sea. The feud was thus rendered irreconcilable, and Baber in revenge began energetic operations against the Portuguese which ended in their being driven ignominiously from Ternate, to seek refuge in the rival island of Tidore. Even here Baber, now proclaimed Sultan, followed them; but though he inflicted severe losses on them they had hitherto been able to retain their hold.[2] Baber's power, however, continued to grow, until at the time of Drake's arrival he was said to be Sultan of a hundred islands, and with his brother was preparing for a fresh campaign against Tidore to avenge their father's death.

It was to Tidore that Drake was directing his course, intending apparently to force a trade in spices and victuals after the manner of his master Hawkins; but in passing

[1] *John Drake*, p. 84.
[2] Southey, *Drake and Hawkins*, p. 276 (Hannay's edition); Crawford, *Hist. of the Indian Archipelago*, ii. 504-6.

by a small island belonging to Ternate[1] he was boarded by a Portuguese half-cast, who apparently explained the state of affairs and told him he could take him to a place where he could get everything he wanted. On Drake's entertaining the idea, the man went ashore again, and presently returned with a 'Moorish Gentleman' of high rank, who proved to be the Rajah or Governor of the island under the Sultan Baber. This official, though at first naturally suspicious, was soon convinced that Drake shared the Sultan's feud with the Portuguese, and began to insist on the danger that awaited them at Tidore and to assure them of a warm welcome from his master at Ternate, who, he said, would never forgive them if they first visited his enemies. Drake without hesitation embraced the proposal, and next day under conduct of his new friends anchored before the port of Ternate and sent presents to the Sultan.[2]

His reception was all that had been promised. Three or four splendid war-canoes, rowed to the sound of music, armed with brass guns and musketeers, hung with costly mats, and carrying the most exalted officers of the court came out to receive him. The Sultan followed in state to assure Drake how greatly he should value an alliance with his Sovereign, and that he was ready in return for it to grant her the monopoly of the spice trade in his dominions. The 'Golden Hind' saluted with her ordnance and musketry, the trumpets sounded, and amidst a scene of the greatest enthusiasm she was towed into the harbour by the war-canoes, while the Sultan trailed at her stern listening in rapture to the strains of the ship's band, which by his special request had been placed in the cock-boat alongside him. At this hospitable island four days were passed which were occupied in a brilliant reception of Drake's officers ashore. The General himself his men, mindful of Magellan's fate, persuaded not to land.

[1] Pretty and the Narrative both say it was called 'Mutyr,' but this is probably another mistake, for Motir is south of Tidore.
[2] *Vaux*, p. 137 ; *J. Drake*, p. 84.

With their new friends they were well pleased, admiring especially their wealth and civilisation and the rigidness of their fast, for it was the month of Ramadan. The rest of their time was fully occupied in discussing the projected treaty, and in loading provisions of all kinds, and as much spice as they could safely stow away. Whether any treaty was actually concluded is not stated, but this visit was afterwards regarded as the great result of Drake's voyage. It was a picture of his reception at Ternate that the queen had engraved on the cup she gave him in honour of his achievement and the alleged treaty became a sheet anchor of our Eastern diplomacy for nearly a century afterwards.[1]

Having thus secured all he wanted Drake sailed, not caring probably to be drawn, like Magellan, into a native quarrel, and perhaps not entirely trusting so aggressive a potentate as Baber. So, although it was still a month before the bursting of the north-east monsoon would enable him to continue his journey, and although his ship was foul and required overhauling, he chose to seek some quieter spot for the work. What he wanted he found in an uninhabited island to the southward of Celebes, where once more he formed a fortified camp, and proceeded to refit his worn vessel. The place, which they called 'Crab Island,' proved for them an earthly Paradise, where after their toilsome voyage they lived for nearly a month without disturbance in the tropic luxury of a perfect climate and an abundance of wholesome and delicious food always in their reach. So that at the end of the time not only was the 'Golden Hind' clean and taut again, but the fifty-six men who were left were all as sound and hearty as the day they left England.[2]

[1] See *Colonial Calendar, passim*. The cup still exists in the possession of the family at Nutwell Court.

[2] Both Legge (*Vaux*, p. 184) and J. Drake relate that Drake left behind him at this place a negress who was with child and two negroes, all of whom he had carried from America across the Pacific. Legge seems to imply there was something in this discreditable to Drake, but it must be remembered that he rescued these people from slavery and one of them from death, and was leaving them to a life which to them was perfect bliss. See *post*, p. 407

It was well both ship and crew were staunch again, for the dangers Drake had to encounter as soon as he sailed equalled those of any part of his voyage. He was face to face, indeed, with dangers which the Spaniards considered must be fatal to his attempt to return the way he had chosen. His desire seems to have been to get back to the northward of Celebes, and so to have cleared the Archipelago by the Portuguese track through the Macassar and Sunda Straits; but this the north-easterly winds prevented, and after having mistaken the blind gulf of Gorontalo or Gunung Tella, which is not shewn on contemporary maps, for the Celebes Sea and taken three days to beat out of it again, he gave up the struggle and stood to the southward to find a way out for himself through one of the most difficult and intricate passages known. For some three weeks he was forced to beat up and down amongst the endless shoals, unable to get clear, nor was it till January 9 that he emerged through what seems to have been the Greyhound Strait, and, seeing the land trend to the westward, thought himself, as the chart showed, clear out in an open sea. The monsoon had settled down to a fine roaring trade, and they were running free before it under all sail, when without a note of warning about eight o'clock in the evening they were brought up hard on a desperate shoal, and in a moment gold, spice, and company were at the mercy of God.[1]

The situation was hopeless. Every moment they looked to see the old ship split, and Drake summoned them all to prayers. This done, 'that we might not seem,' says the Narrative in a curious apology, 'to tempt God by leaving any second means unattempted which he afforded,' the Captain cheerily called to them to hearten up, and having done the best they could for their souls to have an eye for their bodies. The ship was quickly freed from

---

[1] This shoal is described (*Vaux*, p. 156) as 'at least three or four leagues long,' and lying in 2° lacking 3 or 4 minutes S. Lat., which corresponds to the Mulapatia Reef, south of the Peling Island and just beyond the mouth of the Greyhound Strait.

water and was found, as it seemed miraculously, to have suffered but little from the extraordinary violence of the shock. The next thing was to seek for good ground to get an anchor out to warp her off. All day they searched and sounded, but to their dismay they could not so much as find a bottom with any line they had. Everyone was now in despair. It could not be long before the ship broke up, and they saw nothing before them but a forlorn refuge on some of the wild islands they had passed, where death or prolonged privation must await them and where they must be continually 'grieved by the devilish idolatries of the heathen.' Even this sorry expedient was hardly feasible. Though the company had by this time dwindled, we know not how, from the eighty-six they were on the Guatemala coast to but fifty-six souls, their boat would at best hold a score, and the nearest land was twenty miles dead to windward. The night was spent in prayer that the vessel would hold together till daylight, and then a fresh search was made for an anchor hold. There was still no better success, and in despair it was unanimously resolved that they must leave themselves to God alone 'to spill or save' them; and to that end Fletcher preached a sermon and administered the Sacrament to the whole company. Then, 'lest we should seem guilty,' the Narrative again apologises, 'in any respect for not using all lawful means we could invent,' Drake ordered the cargo to be jettisoned. Eight pieces of ordnance, three tons of cloves, and a quantity of provisions were discharged upon the reef, 'as much wealth,' says Fuller, 'as would break the heart of a miser to think on't.' It was nearly low tide, and to larboard was but six feet, the vessel drawing thirteen. A short distance to starboard they had no bottom at all. Fortunately the reef was to leeward, so that hitherto, in spite of her perilous position, as the tide left her the wind had been keeping her erect. About four o'clock in the afternoon, however, it suddenly slackened and she began to heel over. The end was now upon them; the last shred of hope was gone; when suddenly to everyone's amazement she freed her keel, and, as it seemed by a miracle, quietly slid off into deep water.[1]

So after being twenty hours at the mercy of God they were saved, and devout as had been their prayers and solemn their preparations for death, in a moment it was all forgotten in a scene that approaches a not too reverent comedy. How Fletcher the chaplain had incurred Drake's displeasure during those terrible hours is not stated, nor can we guess the cause unless it be that once more he had been improving the occasion by making of their misfortune a judgment on Drake for Doughty's execution. All we know is that shortly after getting off the reef he ordered the chaplain to be fastened by the leg with a staple and padlock to the fore-hatch, and then calling the company together he sat in judgment cross-legged on a chest with a pair of pantoufles in his hand, and passed judgment on the offending minister. 'Francis Fletcher,' said he, 'I do here excommunicate thee out of the church of God and from all the benefits and graces thereof, and I denounce thee to the devil and all his angels.' And then, presumably because the culprit had been tampering with the men, he charged him upon pain of death not once to come before the mast, and swore he would hang him if he did. He ordered a 'posy,' too, to be bound about his arm, and said he would hang him if he took it off, and the words of the posy were these : 'Francis Fletcher, the falsest knave that liveth.'[2]

Their dangers were still far from over, and finding them increase rather than diminish Drake resolved to give up his attempt to work to the westward and to 'bear with Timor'—that is, probably, to try to gain the open sea by what is now called the Ombay Passage. How he was so familiar with the navigation is not clear. It may have

[1] Pretty says the wind changed suddenly to starboard, and that Drake hoisted the sails to force her off. If he did do this, it was probably rather with a view of holding her up. If Pretty could blunder about seamanship he always did.

[2] *Vaux*, pp. 175-6. Pretty says they grounded on January 9 'of all days,' as though it were some anniversary. Could it be found out what it was, some light might be thrown on Fletcher's offence and punishment.

been that he had charts, which Hawkins had obtained from some of his Portuguese friends, or possibly he had got them at Ternate ; but charts or sailing directions of some kind he certainly must have had, unless indeed he was working again with native pilots of whom no mention is made. However this may be, the task of getting clear of Celebes was harder than he had thought, and for a month, with baffling winds, he beat about the Flores and Banda Seas in constant danger of repeating his late desperate experience, nor was it till some natives he fell in with conducted him to an island called Baratíva, and there refreshed him and set him on his way, that he was able finally, on February 16, to run out clear of the islands and to steer an open course for Java.[1]

On March 11 at some port on the south coast they put in, and were received by the Rajah with a cordiality that almost outdid that of Ternate. So entirely friendly indeed was the behaviour of the natives that Drake thought it safe to careen his vessel where she was, to clean her bottom for the last stage of his long voyage. So much time, however, was taken up with hospitalities and receptions both ashore and on board, that the work of refitting and victualling was barely accomplished when his native friends gave him intelligence that several ships as large as his own were upon the coast. With a cargo of precious spices that must have been a very substantial addition to his ballast of gold and silver, it would not do to risk an encounter with the Portuguese. Staying therefore but to take farewell of his genial hosts and to complete his stores, on March 26 he sailed and laid off his course

[1] The island of Baratíva is usually identified with Batjan, but he cannot well have been so far north again. The editor of John Drake's deposition says it is now called Bouton, which seems hardly more probable, since the deposition says it lay in 5° S. and the Narrative in 7° 13′. It may have been Damme, which is in 7° 13′ ; and here is marked in the old charts, an island called Bartubor. Molyneux seemed to think it was part of Celebes, for on the southern part of the island he writes 'Batachina,' but he did not even know Drake had been to the Philippines, and the course he marks must

THE VOYAGE OF CIRCUMNAVIGATION

for the Cape of Good Hope and home, with all plain sailing before him.

be rejected here as elsewhere as of small authority. The actual course taken after getting off the reef is very difficult to trace with certainty. The log, in so far as it can be reconstructed, would run approximately thus :

January 12.—Gale. Anchored on a shoal in 3° 30'.
,, 14.—Anchored and watered at an island in 4° 6' (possibly Manica or Weywongay Island).
,, 15–19.—Westerly winds. Many shoals. Sighted Southernmost Cape of Celebes in about 5°.
,, 20.—Small island close to this cape. Ship and boat nearly lost in a squall.
,, 20–26.—Continuing course towards Timur, i.e. about S.S.E.
,, 26–31.—Drifting under bare poles before W. and W.S.W. gales.
February 1.—Sighted very high land—inhabited.
,, 3.—Sighted a little island.
,, 6.—One island E. of them and four to W., at largest of which anchored and watered.
,, 7.—At Anchor.
,, 8.—Conducted by natives to 'Barativa' in 7° 13'.
,, 10.—Sailed from 'Barativa.'
,, 12.—Saw a green island to southward, while in 8° 4'. Not long after two others to S. and one great one to N.
,, 14.—Saw other biggish islands.
,, 16.—Passed between four or five big islands in 9° 40'.
,, 18.—Anchored under small island for wood.
,, 22.—Lost sight of three islands to starboard which lay in 10° some odd minutes.
,, 23 to March 9.—Westward, till in 8° 20' sighted Java.

CHAPTER XI

KNIGHTHOOD

IN England for more than a year, Drake had been anxiously looked for. Wynter had reached home in June 1578, and in spite of his desertion had been well received. For he brought news of the successful passage of Magellan's Straits and was able to justify his decision to return by the extraordinary fury of the weather in which his commander had disappeared. Doughty's execution was also reported, but for the present the matter was hushed up and orders were given that it was not to be spoken about till Drake came home.[1] Then for a whole year there was silence, broken only by a vague report, arising perhaps out of Oxenham's execution, that Drake had been captured and hanged.[2] And those who, like Burghley, feared the fatal consequences of the pirate's success could grow easy in their minds. At the end of the year a rumour was in the air that the Court had news of him and Mendoza was on the alert, but again the months went by and nothing was heard. In August 1579, however, while Drake was in mid-Pacific, the vigilant ambassador received from the King of Spain copies of despatches from

---

[1] 'Mendoza to the King,' 1579, June 20; *Spanish Calendar*, No. 516.
[2] See 'draft answer to the complaints of Spain' (*S.P. Spain*, xxvi.). The passage is amusing as showing the extreme difficulty the Government had in dealing with Drake's case. As evidence that the queen knew nothing about him, the draft here runs 'when the Queen heard it from the King of Spain that he was taken and hanged, the Queen was glad of it.' The last four words are struck out and 'not sorry' substituted. These are again erased and replaced by 'took no exception to it;' and so on through the whole paper.

the Viceroys of Peru and Mexico, as well as from the Government of the Spanish Main giving the first authentic news of what had happened. To the Spanish Government, so well had the secret been kept, it came as a complete surprise, and Mendoza was instructed to learn everything he could about the venture and to keep his eyes open for the return of the pirate, in case he eluded the measures that had been taken to capture him in America.[1] It was not till three weeks later the news became common property. On August 3 an express from the English merchants in Seville arrived with tidings that Drake had been in the South Sea and had captured 200,000 ducats of the king's property and 400,000 belonging to private owners. 'The adventurers,' wrote Mendoza, 'are beside themselves with joy,' and at the same time he was able to report, as the first fruits of his inquiries, that he had reason to believe some of the Privy Council were among the persons interested. In the City, so far from the great exploit being hailed with pride and delight, it was received with consternation. The merchant fleet for Spain was on the point of sailing. In dread of retaliation and trembling for their commerce, a deputation waited on the Council for information and advice. They were reassured by being told that Drake was nothing but a private adventurer who had gone on a voyage of discovery; that if he had done wrong the King of Spain would certainly not visit it on their heads, and they might let their ships proceed on their voyage without fear.

Drake's return was now more anxiously expected than ever. Rumours of his coming were once more in the air, and Mendoza, redoubling his vigilance, obtained information which confirmed his suspicions, that some of the Privy Council were implicated. Orders, so he heard, had been issued to all the Justices along the coast and to all port officers to assist Drake to land and conceal his plunder the moment he arrived. Later on he reported that men had been actually appointed in every port for this purpose,

[1] 'The King to Mendoza,' 1578, August 10; *Spanish Calendar*, No. 585.

and the matter grew every day more serious and the alarm of the City graver. Philip was collecting a vast armament by sea and land the destination of which was unknown. It was given out to be for the purpose of completing the work of the battle of Lepanto by the destruction of the pirates' nest at Algiers, but so often had Spain done this with disastrous results to her neighbours that an expedition against the pirates had become as much a diplomatic commonplace as is a scientific expedition to Central Asia or the interior of Africa to-day. The general impression in England was that it was meant to seize the kingdom of the dying King of Portugal, as a preliminary to some great design against Elizabeth and Philip's Dutch rebels. So threatening indeed was the outlook that even the queen began to be nervous about the possible consequences of her escapade, and although Mendoza was too proud and too diplomatic to admit the possibility of Drake's escaping the vengeance of his master's officers in America, he was not unwilling to play on her alarm and hint at the terrible reckoning there must be, if such an escape were possible.[1]

The gravity of the situation was that the patience of Spain was already stretched to breaking strain. Ever since the Treaty of Bristol had cleared the air, the English rovers had been growing more and more active. So entirely were they in command of the Narrow Seas, so powerless was Philip to protect his commerce even on his own coasts, that the dangers of the northern navigation had come to be regarded in the counting-houses of Seville and Cadiz as an ordinary trade-risk, and the practice had grown up amongst merchants and underwriters of concealing their losses from their ambassador in London in order to make terms behind his back with the pirate's agents. This impunity only increased their daring and their profits. Men in the highest position were known, or at least vehemently suspected, to be using their offices to share in the business. Foremost in the

[1] *Froude*, xi. 142.

work, and watched with hardly less anxiety than Drake and Frobisher, was Sir Humphrey Gilbert. Already a marked man in Spanish eyes for the assistance he had carried to Flushing in the early days of the Dutch rebellion and for his ruthless severity to his prisoners, he was now known to be acting in partnership with young Knollys, son of the Controller of the Household, and, although engaged in piracy, their squadron was always at the beck and call of the Government. Gilbert was in Government employ at this very time, having been ordered to assist some operations against the Irish rebels, and yet in the midst of the excitement which the news of Drake had caused, came tidings that he had pushed his contempt for the Spanish power so far as to land and sack a place on the coast of Galicia.[1]

As the year went on the outlook grew still more alarming. The King of Portugal died; the great Spanish armaments were set in motion; at a stroke Don Antonio, who claimed the crown, was flying for his life, and Philip was master of all the resources of the maritime kingdom and its vast colonial possessions. Before men had had time to realise the full meaning of the portentous change in the political situation came news that the Irish rebels, against whom, like Drake and Grenville under similar circumstances, Gilbert had been ordered to act, had received reinforcements from Spain. At such a crisis it was impossible even for the coolest heads not to see in this an operation preliminary to the coming of Philip's unused armada. The queen refused to give Mendoza an audience and war seemed inevitable. Ireland to many was as good as lost. Nothing but the most skilful diplomacy backed by some great concession to Philip's reiterated complaints, as every one thought, could avert the danger. And as fate would have it, the very week the alarming intelligence was received from Ireland, while the peace party were at their wits' end, came a fresh

[1] *Spanish Calendar*, 1579, pp. 695-6.

whisper that Drake had come home with untold plunder; and this time it was true.[1]

One day towards the end of September, after an absence of nearly three years without a word of news from England, the 'Golden Hind' was taking the last bearings of her immortal voyage as she opened Plymouth Sound. The position which Elizabeth had won in the eyes of the nation has no more suggestive testimony than that Drake's first question to some fishermen whom he passed as he sailed cautiously in was whether the queen were alive and well. To him at least it was of the last importance. They told him she was well and further that a pestilence was raging in the town. He therefore anchored in the harbour without landing, glad no doubt to make the sickness an excuse for feeling his ground. Here his wife came off to see him, and also the Mayor, who was probably the person under orders to warn him. The result of the visit in any case, so John Drake tells, was that without setting foot ashore, he sent a courier to the queen to report his return and also wrote to other personages of the Court.[2] Then in the company of his long widowed wife he quietly waited to hear his fate. The answer came at last from his great friends 'that the queen was displeased with him, for that by way of Peru and Spain she had heard of the robberies he had committed and the Spanish ambassador was there who said he would demand restoration of what he had taken.' On the receipt of these tidings Drake at once warped out of the harbour and anchored behind an island in the Sound (probably St. Nicholas or Drake's Island), prepared no doubt, if need were, to disappear as he had done before amongst his old haunts on the coast of Ireland. Thus he awaited the queen's answer. It came in the form of a summons

[1] The secrecy which surrounded Drake's return is probably the reason why almost every authority gives a different date for it. They vary from September 16 to November 3. The probability is that he arrived on September 26 and landed October 3 or 4.

[2] The man he chose for the mission was Brewer, Hatton's old trumpeter and Doughty's chief accuser. (*Spanish Calendar*, 1580, p. 55.)

to Court, with a meaning desire that he should bring with him some of the curiosities he had collected on his travels and an assurance that he had nothing to fear. At the same time came down a secret order to Mr. Edmund Tremayne, a neighbouring magistrate in the confidence of Walsingham and the queen, to see the treasure bestowed in safety.

Drake lost no time in obeying the queen's summons, and sagaciously interpreted her request by taking with him to London several horse-loads of gold and silver and all his most precious jewels. So soon as he arrived he was admitted to an audience, and remained some six hours closeted with the queen. Meanwhile the Council had been summoned to consider what was to be done. It was attended only by Burghley, Sussex, the Admiral, Crofts, and the Secretary Wilson. None of Drake's supporters were present, and a rapid decision was made to follow an old precedent and order the whole of the treasure to be registered and sent up to the Tower as a preliminary to restitution. The five councillors present signed, and the order was taken on to Leicester, Hatton, and Walsingham. Being members of Drake's syndicate, all three refused their signatures, saying they would first speak to the queen about it, and the result of their interview was that she, their royal partner, directed the order to be suspended.[1] How far the dazzling profits of the voyage and the splendid presents Drake made her braced the queen's purpose it is impossible to say, but there can be no doubt that from the first she intended to stand by him, and all credit must be given her for the courage with which she faced the situation. Still the matter had to be treated with caution. No sooner did Drake appear at Court than Mendoza sent to protest against his reception, and reminding the queen of her promise to punish him if he ever came home, demanded an audience. This was politely refused, but an answer was sent explaining that

[1] 'Mendoza to the King,' October 16, 1580; *Spanish Calendar*, p. 54 The precedent followed was that of Ronyger, Henry VIII.'s famous captain

she had been compelled to send for Drake to inquire into the allegations against him. At present she said there was no reason to believe that he had injured any of the King of Spain's subjects, or violated any part of his territory, but she had ordered all the treasure to be secured and registered that restitution might be made if justice demanded it. Drake, too, was sent back to Plymouth to assist at the registration, but with a private letter from the queen to Tremayne again commending to his best offices her beloved subject Francis Drake, and saying that the registration of the treasure was not to begin until Drake had been left alone with it, or in other words that he was to be permitted secretly to abstract a quantity of it, and no questions were to be asked. This was quietly done, and out of the portion so abstracted Drake as a first fruits of favour was authorised to keep 10,000*l.* for himself and more for his crew.

Meanwhile in London Drake's position was far from secure, and it looked by no means clear that the queen would be able to go through with the part she had taken up. Mendoza was furious. 'The Spanish ambassador,' wrote one at this time, 'doth burn with passion against Drake.'[1] In his soldierlike way he refused even to listen to the queen's subterfuges. Pointing to Drake's long career as a corsair, he loudly accused him of piracy, and as near as diplomacy permitted threatened immediate war.[2] His friends in the City he alarmed with the prospect of the disaster it would mean for them if the ancient commercial league with the House of Burgundy were broken, and the City, which was already beginning to be the real mainspring of English foreign policy, turned against Drake. 'The Company of Merchants trading to Spain and Portugal' was probably the richest and most powerful corporation of the time, and not only did they fear for their ships, but the shock Drake had given to Spanish commerce

---

[1] *S.P. Dom. Eliz.* cxliii. 46.
[2] 'The answer of the Spanish Ambassador to the speech delivered him by Mr. Beale.' *S.P. Spain,* xviii. 40. November 1580.

threatened them with serious bad debts.[1] A strong feeling began to show itself that he ought to be disavowed. 'Many misliked it,' says Stowe, and reproached him. Besides all this there were others that 'devised and divulged all possible disgraces against Drake and his followers deeming him the master thief of the unknown world.' He was charged with having mutilated his prisoners and committed all kinds of excesses, and Doughty's death, as we have seen, became a focus of sinister talk.

But a reaction seems soon to have set in. Drake had been sent down to Plymouth once more to bring up the treasure from Saltash Castle, where it had been first bestowed. The people were dazzled with the sight of the rich train of pack-horses with which he rode back to deposit his plunder in Sion House, whence it was conveyed to the Tower.[2] Tremayne, in explaining that it was only what Drake had let him see, wrote up in the highest terms of his conduct; he had come to regard him almost as a son; he praised his generosity, and fair dealing; he testified to the extraordinary devotion with which his crew were inspired. 'His whole course of the voyage,' he concluded, 'hath shewed him to be of great valour, but my hap has been to see some particularities, and namely in this discharge of his company, as doth assure me that he is a man of great government and that by the rules of God and his Book. So as proceeding upon such a foundation his doings cannot but prosper.' Before the crew was paid off the 'Golden Hind' was brought round into the Thames and anchored off Deptford for all the world to see. An inquiry was held into the obnoxious charges, and the whole company denied them on oath.[3]

[1] See their petition in 1582 to Lord Burghley (*Hist. MSS. Com., Hatfield Papers*, ii. 515), and *passim* in Mendoza's correspondence at this time. (*Spanish Calendar*, 1580, &c.)   [2] *Spanish Calendar*, p. 74.
[3] There are forty-nine names to the deposition. Drake, John Doughty, who was probably not examined, and William Hawkins, who most likely had remained at Plymouth with his father, make three more, so that probably all who came to town signed.

The reaction in the 'master-thief's' favour now grew apace. 'Drake has returned to Court,' wrote Mendoza to the king, 'where he passes much time with the queen, by whom he is highly favoured and told how great is the service he has rendered her.' The town followed suit. 'The people generally,' says Stowe, 'applauded his wonderful long adventures and rich prizes. His name and fame became admirable in all places, the people swarming daily in the streets to behold him, vowing hatred to all that misliked him.'

The chief of these mislikers, besides Mendoza and the Spanish Company, seem to have been Burghley and Sussex. It was at any rate thought necessary, if we may believe the ambassador, to attempt to bribe them, but some of them refused to touch what they called stolen property. It is probably true : for Camden says on Drake's return that 'nothing troubled him more than that some of the principal men at Court rejected the gold which he offered them, as being gotten by piracy.'[1] The ambassador himself took an equally high line. Drake's friends, so he says, offered him for himself or his nominees a sum of 50,000 ducats if he would lower his tone; but this he haughtily refused, protesting he would himself give much more for the pleasure of chastising such a rascal and thief as Drake. Others, however, were more complacent, and the queen firmly kept her ground in demanding proof of the Spanish allegations and in refusing to see the Spanish ambassador while a single Spanish soldier remained in Ireland.

Still things were far from comfortable for Drake at

---

[1] In this connection it is worth noticing a curious expression, which Burghley made use of in a memorandum drawn up on January 28, 1580, for the queen's guidance on the political situation, and the measures advisable in view of it. 'That you do abridge,' one article runs, 'all your extraordinary excessive charges, and seek honourably to increase your revenues.' The use of the word 'honourably' to the queen so shortly after the news of Drake's depredations had arrived is very significant of Burghley's attitude, and must have had for his mistress a sting of rebuke. Murdin, *Burghley Papers*, p. 340.

Court. 'During the space of one year,' says John Drake,
'while this deponent remained in England, one part said
the queen ought to return the treasure to the King of
Spain and others that they should send the person of
Captain Francis.' With one exception all his great
friends were more or less under a cloud and his opponents
in the ascendant. As a counter-move against the danger
which threatened from Spain, the queen was once more
coquetting with France and displaying a serious intention
of marrying the Duke of Alençon. The match was
intensely unpopular. Sussex, Crofts and Burghley were
almost all who had a word to say for it. At the outset of
the negotiations Walsingham had been ordered out of the
queen's presence for insisting too strongly on the Protestant and popular view. Leicester was sulking, and Lord
Bedford's daughter had been placed under arrest for
chattering unwisely on the subject. Sir William Wynter,
too, was in disgrace for having let the Spaniards get to
Ireland, and had been ordered peremptorily to resume
the station on the Kerry coast which at the approach of
winter he had left without orders. There only remained
Sir Christopher Hatton at Elizabeth's ear, and thus did
Drake reap the fruit of his policy in connecting him so
conspicuously with his immortal ship.

In November, Smerwick, the place on the Irish coast
where the Spaniards had entrenched themselves, fell, and
the invaders were annihilated. Although it was found that
the King of Spain had nothing officially to do with them,
the loss of the argument for Drake's protection made no
difference to the queen. It is clear she was resolved to
stand by him at any cost. 'The queen,' wrote Mendoza
after the new year's festivities, 'shows extraordinary
favour to Drake and never fails to speak to him when she
goes out in public, conversing with him a long time. She
says that she will knight him on the day she goes to see
his ship,' and a week later: 'The queen often has him
in her cabinet; often, indeed, walking with him in the
garden.' Rumours were afloat that he was to be speedily

employed again; two hundred thousand ducats of his plunder, it is said, were offered to Alençon to assist him in acquiring the sovereignty of the Netherlands; ten thousand pounds of it were laid out in the magnificent preparations that were being made to receive the embassy that was coming from France to negotiate the marriage treaty. The Sieur de Marchaumont, Alençon's special agent, had already arrived to feel the ground, and for some weeks past had been dividing with Drake the queen's most intimate attentions. At last in the midst of the preparations for the festivities, and on the eve of the arrival of the embassy, she threw off all disguise, and on April 4 went in state to pay her visit to the 'Golden Hind' at Deptford, and with her she took Marchaumont. A banquet was served on board, 'finer,' says Mendoza, 'than has ever been seen in England since the time of King Henry;' and it was only fitting that this should be so. For here in the presence of a vast concourse of her subjects, she gave open defiance to the King of Spain. He had demanded Drake's head. She made the culprit kneel before her, for now, she said, she had a gilded sword to strike it off. With the jest on her lips she handed the weapon to none other than Marchaumont himself, to give the accolade; and so, in the face of Europe, was knighted 'the master thief of the unknown world.' No scene in all our history is more fraught with the gravest political significance. Since Philip's conquest of Portugal the fate of Europe seemed to hang on the Alençon marriage. By the Valois prince's acceptance of the sovereignty of the Netherlands he was Philip's declared enemy, and in the eyes of diplomatists the scene on board the 'Golden Hind' could only be regarded as a final defiance to Spain and a declaration that at last Elizabeth was in earnest for an alliance with France against the 'overgreatness' of Philip's empire.

In vain Mendoza, like the high spirited soldier he was, fumed and fretted at the loss of his master's prestige. In his cabinet he had instructions that it was not just then convenient to press for satisfaction, and that he must try semi-officially to recover as much of the plunder as he could.[1] He was powerless to resent the indignity of the situation, and Drake's position was assured. In vain Burghley continued to urge a frank alliance with Spain, and as a first step to it the restitution of the plunder.[2] The die was cast. The arch-pirate had become the popular hero, the centre, as it were, of the growing feeling in England, to which Mendoza had drawn attention, of confidence in the national strength and contempt for the power of Spain. As though to emphasise her attitude he was kept constantly in the queen's company: she was seen to talk to him, says John Drake, ' as often as nine times a day.' 'Books, pictures, and ballads,' says Stowe, 'were published in his praise; his opinion and judgment concerning marine affairs stood current.' William Borough, hitherto the great authority in all maritime affairs, considered that in fame he had far surpassed all his contemporaries. There was no one, indeed, to stand beside him in popular estimation. Hawkins had never recovered the blow which the affair of San Juan de Ulua had been both to his credit and fortune, and for some years had been absorbed in the routine of his office. Frobisher, who up till the return of his grand expedition to the north-west had held the first place, had been compelled to see his great design degenerate into a greedy search for a refractory gold ore that proved almost worthless. Many of his promoters had been ruined, his men were unpaid, and he himself was suffering in purse and reputation from a splendid failure for which he was in no way to blame. Sir William Wynter, the first of the purely naval men, had grown old and cautious, as his last com-

---

[1] 'The King to Mendoza,' January 12, 1581. *Spanish Calendar*, p. 78.

[2] 'Mendoza to the King,' *ibid.* December 25, 1581, in which he describes a sitting of the council to discuss the rival policies of the Alençon marriage and of peace with Spain. At the same sitting, he says, on Crofts's information, 'the Treasurer raised the question of the restitution of Drake's plunder,' &c.

mand had shown, and there was no one else in the front rank.

Drake, on the other hand, had been entirely successful. His shareholders were enjoying untold profits; his men were rolling in riches; he himself must have been something like a millionaire; and besides the glamour of a feat which still for the people was half fabulous, there would seem to have been in his personality something that carried men away. Stowe at this time completes the portrait we have from the pen of Zarate, describing him as 'low of stature, of strong limbs, broad-breasted, round-headed, with brown hair, full-bearded, his eyes round, large, and clear, well-favoured, fair, and of a cheerful countenance.' Amongst his imperfections he remarks that he was 'ambitious for honour, and greatly affected to popularity.' His detractors, Monson tells us, charged him with ostentation and vain-glorious boasting, and with 'his high, haughty, and insolent carriage,' and these charges his friends could not entirely deny. But of his vainglory and ostentation they claimed it was not 'inherent to him alone, but to most men of his profession and rank.' And indeed we know against how many of our great admirals, from Nelson downwards, similar accusations have been made. Monson, though seldom a gentle critic of other naval officers, is inclined to palliate the charges and even to treat them rather as merits than defects. 'True,' says he, 'he would speak much and arrogantly, but eloquently, which was a wonder to many that his education could yield him those helps of nature. Indeed he had four properties to further his gift of speaking, viz. his boldness of speech, his understanding in what he spoke, his inclination to speak, and his use in speaking; and though vain-glory is a vice not to be excused, yet he obtained that fame by his actions, that facility in speaking and that wisdom by his experience, that I can say no more, but that we are all the children of Adam. His friends further say, that his haughty and high carriage is somewhat excusable, when it appears not but in his command; for a general ought to be stern to his soldiers, courageous in his person, valiant in fight, generous in giving, patient in suffering, and merciful in pardoning: and if Sir Francis Drake was to be praised for most of these virtues, let him not be blamed or condemned for one vice only.'[1]

The most intimate picture we have of the effect of his exploit upon his character and bearing comes from the pen of Mendoza himself. 'Not a day passes,' wrote the fuming ambassador to the king on March 1, 1582, 'that he does not say a thousand shameless things, amongst others that he will give the Queen 80,000 ducats, if she will grant him leave to arm ships to attack your Majesty's convoys, although of course he has not the slightest idea of doing such a thing.' The ambassador, it is clear, mistook his man, and regarded his exuberant confidence as mere boasting. 'The other night,' he adds, 'while supping with the Earl of Sussex, Arundel, and other gentlemen, he was boasting of what he had done, when Sussex remarked that it was no great thing for an armed ship to capture another vessel loaded with money, but with only eight unarmed men on board of her. Drake replied he was quite capable of making war on your Majesty; whereupon Arundel told him that he wondered how a man like him should have the impudence to imagine such a thing of the greatest monarch on earth, who was strong enough to wage war on all the world united.'[2] Drake's retort is not recorded, but it was enough if he pointed to the spirit he had aroused. The 'Golden Hind' became one of the sights of London, for it was agreed she must be preserved as a perpetual memorial of what Englishmen could do. The tall spire of St. Paul's, around which the luck of London was supposed to cling, had fallen recently in a storm, and one enthusiast was found to propose that the omen could not be averted better than by setting up the renowned ship on the stump of the tower. Eventually she was hauled ashore at Deptford, and there at a cost of nearly 3,000*l.* of

---

[1] *Naval Tracts*, p. 367.
[2] *Spanish Calendar*, 1580, &c., p. 307.

our money, she was laid up in a shed for a perpetual memorial of Drake's great achievement.¹

But although the arch-corsair was thus thoroughly established as a symbol of defiance to Spain and a benefactor to his country, his enemies had not abandoned their efforts. John Doughty prosecuted him in the Earl Marshal's court for the murder of his brother. Drake moved the Queen's Bench to stay the proceedings for want of jurisdiction. The case was heard before the Lord Chief Justice and a full court, and in the face of the popular sentiment in his favour they held that Doughty was entitled to proceed.² But there the matter ended. By some influence, which we do not know, the case must have been hushed up, and this no doubt, and with reason, increased the impression that some great secret of state which could not be disturbed lay hidden beneath the episode.

It cannot have been that young Doughty was not willing to proceed. He was burning to avenge his brother's death, and when fair means were denied him, he took to foul. Knowing from experience how vain it was to seek redress from the Government, the Spanish merchants had employed an agent, one Pedro de Zubiaur, to endeavour in the usual way to make terms with Drake for the restitution of part of his plunder.³ John Doughty, who was

---

¹ The account for this is in *S.P. Dom. Eliz.* The actual cost was 370*l*. An excavation was made to receive her, and over it was built a shed 180 feet long by 24 feet wide. The walls were 15 feet high, and the roof high pitched. Her lower masts must have been left standing, for on the mainmast the scholars of Winchester inscribed a copy of Latin verses in Drake's honour, which Camden, carried away by the spirit of the time, records with an apology, ' lest they should be thought to proceed from an idle brain and not beseeming the gravity of an historian.'

² In the great debate of 1628 on Martial Law, Sir Edward Coke thus quoted the case from his place in the House of Commons. ' Drake slew Doughty beyond sea. Doughty's brother desired an appeal (i.e. a prosecution for murder to be tried by battle) in the Constable's and Marshal's Court. Resolved by Wray and the other judges he may sue there.' (Rushworth, Ed. 1706, ii. 4.) By this curious chance we know that the assertion, which has always been made, that the execution of Doughty was never called in question, is not true.

³ The particulars of Zubiaur's claims are in *Lansdowne MSS.* xxx. 10.

probably being watched, was found to be in communication with him, and from an uncle of his whom Drake had apparently sent for to talk over the way the unhappy youth was behaving, he obtained sight of a slanderous letter from Doughty's pen. 'When the Queen,' he wrote, ' did knight Drake she did then knight the arrantest knave, the vilest villain, the falsest thief and the cruelest murderer that ever was born,' and he vowed he was ready to repeat his words before the whole Council. A servant of Hatton's had heard him using similar unguarded expressions, as though he were determined to have the whole affair made public. More than this, information had been obtained, through a Catholic, that Doughty meant to assassinate Drake. It would seem that he had been discovered in communication under suspicious circumstances with a man called Mason, who was an agent of Zubiaur's. Upon this both Doughty and Mason were arrested. Mason was examined, and his answers being thought unsatisfactory he was put to the torture. He then confessed that Zubiaur had shown him a letter out of Spain stating that the king had offered a reward of 20,000 ducats to anyone who would kidnap Drake or bring him his head; and that thereupon he had been ordered to approach Doughty with a view of getting him to undertake the exploit.[1] What happened to Mason we do not know, but Doughty's mouth was again effectually shut by his not being brought to trial. After lying sixteen months in the Marshalsea he petitioned that under Magna Charta he might be tried or released, and all we can learn of his fate is that his clerkly petition bears the laconic endorsement ' Not to be released.' [2]

In the face of this second hushing up by the extreme measure of what was in fact a *lettre de cachet*, it is not to be doubted that the rumour of a state secret was well

[1] *S.P. Dom. Eliz.* 1582, cliii. 50. The spelling of Zubiaur's name gave so much difficulty to Englishmen. that it is often hardly recognisable. In this document it appears as ' Sebure.'
[2] *S.P. Dom. Eliz.* clxiii. 19, October 27, 1583.

founded, and that there was indeed some real reason why young Doughty could not be brought to trial. The only evidence we have of what the mystery was is that Burghley was in some way connected with the elder Doughty. A solution that meets all the known facts (but not therefore necessarily the right one) is that Burghley gave Doughty to understand that if when it came to the point he could persuade Drake's men, who it must be remembered were only engaged for a voyage to Alexandria, to refuse to go into the South Sea, he would be doing a service to his country that would not be forgotten. Doughty very likely went beyond his instructions, but this, if true, it would have been impossible for Burghley to prove. If any connection at all had been shown to have existed between him and the mutineer the worst would have been presumed against him, and his enemies would have been given a vantage ground that it would have been hard to recover. That Elizabeth's great minister did in fact take any steps to frustrate the most brilliant exploit of her reign is far from being proved. It can be placed little higher than a reasonable conjecture that explains the puzzle, while at the same time it is at variance with none of the known facts and entirely consistent with Burghley's life-long attitude to the corsairs. And if the explanation offered be indeed the true one, it in no way shows to his discredit. Events subsequently justified Drake's exploit; but, at the time it was undertaken, it was in direct antagonism to all that was held most wise and enlightened in England. Burghley can only have seen in it a wanton sacrifice of the highest interests of the country to private avarice. It was for him a public duty to prevent it. Had he been less highminded or less patriotic he might easily have become a party to the piratical venture, and if he did indeed avail himself of one of the ordinary political weapons of the time, an *agent provocateur*, to save his mistress from the consequences of the temptation into which she had fallen, if for the sake of averting from his unready country war with the most powerful empire in the world, he thus risked his whole position as a minister, it is no more than we should expect from the most cautious and devoted of the queen's servants.

With the refusal of John Doughty's petition for a trial the incident closes. Zubiaur did eventually succeed, in spite of Mendoza's efforts to prevent any compromise being made, in getting restitution of part of the plunder, but chiefly it would seem to the benefit of the English creditors of the injured Spaniards.[1] All that did not find its way into English pockets fell into Philip's hands.

But these negotiations were but a minor detail in the fulness of Drake's life. From this point his action moves upon a higher plane. His career as a private adventurer is at an end, and the vehement stream of his life begins to swell the flood of history. In the growing turbulence of its movement he must henceforth be followed. He is no longer the daring rover, but has taken his place as a great military leader and statesman, upon whom the eyes of his country and those of all Europe are fixed.

'Much of the misconception which has prevailed with regard to the true character and position of Drake is due to a neglect to appreciate his periods of apparent inaction. The popular histories hurried from one exploit to another careless of how the master-mind was working in the silent intervals. But the significance of a great man, like that of a great age, lies as much in what he attempted as in what he achieved. The one can only be read in the light of the other. Viewed separately, Drake's actions appear but the triumphs or the failures of a daring seaman; it is only when we find the links that united them that we see him rise to his true proportions, as the man who first conceived the lines and possibilities of a great and statesmanlike naval policy.

Between Drake's return from the South Sea and the outbreak of the war in 1585 there is such a gap of apparent inaction—a gap which was in reality filled by

[1] Petition of the Spanish Company,' *Hatfield MSS.* ii. 515.

strenuous endeavours to complete what against all expectation the voyage about the world had failed to accomplish. The truth is that so far from lying idle after his return he was hardly allowed breathing time. Before his plunder was safe in the Tower, he was at work again on a scheme of still greater import, which explains at once Elizabeth's unswerving determination to recognise him and Philip's anxiety to get hold of him alive or dead.

To understand what this was, it must be remembered that during Drake's absence the situation in Europe had changed entirely. When he sailed European politics were still shaped and dominated by the Counter-reformation, by the attempt of the Pope in league with the great Catholic powers to carry out the conclusions of the Council of Trent and to force the erring States back into the fold of the Roman Church. But early in 1580 an event happened, the consequences of which we have seen engrossing public attention when Drake came home. Sebastian, the last of the Avis, the royal line of Portugal, had died without a legitimate male heir. Don Antonio, Prior of Crato, a natural son of a younger brother of John III., Sebastian's grandfather, claimed the throne ; Philip II. in right of his wife, the daughter of John III., asserted a prior title,[1] and had in readiness an overwhelming argument to back it. In one short campaign Don Antonio was driven into exile by the Duke of Alva, and the whole of Portugal and its vast oceanic trade and possessions fell into the hands of Spain. If Philip had been formidable before, he was doubly formidable now. Besides the whole of the East Indies, America, and the African settlements he could claim all the Peninsula ; of the Italian States Sicily, Naples, Sardinia, and the Duchy of Milan ; and in the north, all of what is now Holland and Belgium. As in the days of Charles V., Europe saw itself once more

[1] The only other surviving members of the House of Avis were the two daughters of Edward, John III.'s younger brother, viz. Mary, who married Alexander Farnese, the great duke of Parma, and had no issue ; and Catherine, who married John Duke of Braganza, from whom came the present line. Don Antonio had nothing to do with the modern House of Braganza.

threatened by a new and living Roman Empire, and the combination of the Counter-reformation began to exhibit a tendency to dissolve into combinations to resist the menace of a universal Spanish dominion.

To appreciate the prominence into which the new situation ultimately forced Drake, the position of the other Powers must be borne in mind. The Pope, between fear of the old rivalry of a real Empire and hatred of the heretic Powers, must be practically neutral. France was equally incapable of action. She was at this time divided between the Valois King at Paris, representing the national Gallican Church, the Bourbon Henry of Navarre head of the Huguenots and champion of Reformation, and lastly the Ultramontane Guises leaning on Rome and Spain. Germany was as much divided, and the Netherlands as yet were but an open wound in Philip's side. Such was the situation when Drake came home; and to meet it he was plunged at once with his old friend Walsingham into the elaboration of what was to become one of the great leading motives of English policy.

Terceira, and most of the Azores, were still holding to their old allegiance. Don Antonio had escaped with his life, and eager to establish himself in the important stategical position that was still open to him had appeared as a suppliant for assistance before the chief anti-Spanish courts, and not entirely without success. While Drake was still at sea proposals were already on foot for a joint French and English expedition against Spain under Don Antonio's flag.[1] When at the same time came news that the expedition of Papal filibusters, which had been organised in Spain, had landed in Ireland, the necessity for action was sharply accentuated; and Drake's triumphant arrival at the very moment must have seemed to Walsingham like a gift from heaven. Early in 1581 he was busy with schemes of which Drake was the centre for inaugu-

[1] Minute to Sir H. Cobham, September 18, 1580, *Murdin*, p. 345. Ralph Lane's proposals, *Lansd. MSS.* xxxi. 43. Robert Hitchcocke's 'Politic and warlike ways,' &c. *Ibid.* cxix. 17.

rating a Portuguese policy, and on April 3, the day before the queen was to proclaim her recognition of Drake by knighting him on board his ship, these projects were finally drafted for official consideration. One which appears in several alternative shapes was called the 'First Enterprise.' It was for sending him out with eight ships and six pinnaces and a thousand men to establish himself under Don Antonio's flag at Terceira and thence to operate against Spanish oceanic commerce by intercepting the homeward bound Plate Fleet, and so bring about a financial crisis such as had paralysed Philip's action when Elizabeth had seized his treasure ships after the affair of San Juan de Ulua. Another, called the 'Second Enterprise,' contemplated a more peaceful expedition to Calicut to secure the Portuguese possessions in the East and to take up their trading rights in Don Antonio's name. The 'First Enterprise' found the most favour; and it seems that the queen by the advice of Walsingham was ready not only to allow it but even to subscribe the greater part of the cost. The other chief promoters were Drake, Hawkins, and Walsingham, and apparently Leicester— much the same adventurous group, in fact, that had promoted Drake's last voyage. This time there was little attempt at disguise. The only stipulation the queen made, and this it is said was explained to Don Antonio's agent, was that nothing could be done unless France joined hands; for war with Spain would be the almost inevitable result, and Elizabeth had no mind to enter it single-handed.

On this understanding the preparations went forward, and Drake despatched a bark to the scene of action to obtain intelligence.[1] As matters progressed the ideas of the promoters expanded. Don Antonio through his agent in England pressed for a larger force, assuring the adventurers he had money coming from Terceira and the Low Countries, whither he had sent jewels as security for a loan. As none of the promoters cared to risk more, fresh

[1] *Colonial Calendar*, p. 166.

adventurers had to be brought in, and an attempt was made to combine the rival schools of Drake and Frobisher. Edward Fenton and Gilbert York, both Frobisher's men, and Luke Ward of Muscovy fame, were to have ships, and Captain Richard Bingham, the Irish officer who, as we have seen, was already jealous of Drake and had been increasing his reputation in the Desmond rebellion, was to be second in command.[1] So eager was Walsingham to see his scheme carried through, that poor as he was he seems to have underwritten the extra amount of capital required, receiving from Don Antonio a very valuable diamond ring as security for his guarantee. A definite promise of co-operation from France seemed as far off as ever, and he was naturally anxious to protect himself from loss in case after all the expedition was not allowed to sail.

To Drake and Hawkins the whole of the organisation was committed; all was to be ready in June, and at the end of the month Don Antonio came over from France. The 'Strange Guest,' as he was called, was lodged near the Court at Stepney, and on July 1 he had an audience with the queen. Still he pressed for more ships, but already Elizabeth was fretting at the increased expense, fretting too in her love of peace as the risk grew nearer, and fretting that though she had deeply entangled herself in the project of marriage with Alençon she could get no explicit promise of co-operation from France. Resolved not to commit herself alone, she determined to send over Walsingham in person on the hopeless mission of at once extricating her from her entanglement with Alençon and securing the co-operation of France against Spain.

For the expedition nothing could have been more unfortunate. The management of the affair passed into Leicester's hands, and with Walsingham's vigorous influence withdrawn everything went wrong. More money was required, but the season for action was fast

[1] *S.P. Dom. Eliz.* cxlviii. 46, April 3.

slipping away and Drake and Hawkins, anxious about the amount they had invested already, refused to advance another penny. The others too, 'upon some scruples,' says Burghley, began to hold back.[1] Drake, upon whose judgment of men the tragedy of Doughty had left an indelible mark, was always smelling treachery on the smallest provocation. The queen was given to believe that York was not to be trusted: Bingham was showing an inclination to act without orders: and Drake, it is only fair to believe, was exhibiting too much of that masterful spirit, that rough impatience of opposition, which was a growing feature of his character and which has been at once the vice and the virtue of all our greatest admirals. On August 15 Fenton's brother wrote to Walsingham that Drake had 'put Bingham, York, Ward and Fenton from the Portugal voyage.'[2] Burghley told him 'that upon some jealousy conceived and upon some articles presented to my Lord of Leicester by Bingham, Fenton and York, they with their own good wills are discharged, but Mr. Bingham and Fenton are promised all their charges.'[3] This was probably but a diplomatic view of the affair. George Fenton's letter makes it clear it was Drake's work, and from the way his men afterwards spoke of Fenton it is extremely probable that Drake believed he had an understanding with the Spanish ambassador, though that it was so there is no evidence whatever.[4]

Application was now made to the queen to provide another 2,000*l.*, but the only effect was to bring Drake and Hawkins into disgrace for the increased expenditure that had been run into, and in the end they had to provide it themselves. She grew cold in the 'Strange Guest's' cause, and vowed she had been persuaded into it against her will. Reports came, too, that the Plate fleet

[1] Digges, *Compleat Ambassador*, p. 379. [2] *Irish Calendar*.
[3] Digges, p. 389.
[4] William Hawkins's journal in the *Hawkins Voyages*, Hakluyt Soc. p. 353.

had already arrived home and Terceira had surrendered, and still there was no certain promise from France. 'All these things,' wrote Burghley to Walsingham in Paris '(though these advertisements are not very certain), do marvellously stay her Majesty from assenting to their departure, and yet she loseth all the charges spent in vain, the poor King utterly lost; and therefore her answer yesterday was that the voyage should continue in readiness, but not depart until the evening, before which time she looked to hear from you.'[1]

But Walsingham was quite unable to send the written assurance of French co-operation which the queen required, and unwilling to go on without it and unwillingly to entirely abandon her suppliant, she fell back on a compromise. Her idea was to keep the opportunity open by sending two or three of the ships under young William Hawkins and some troops under Norreys, Drake's old Irish companion-in-arms, with whom he seems to have replaced Bingham, to support the loyal islanders and encourage them to hold out till a force large enough to reconquer the whole archipelago could be organised. In an age when naval operations were never conducted in the winter, the project was by no means despicable. The season in which Spain could act with a fleet so far from her shores was nearly done, and with small assistance Terceira might well hold her own till the following spring; and before that time it was hoped Walsingham would have been able to negotiate a general offensive and defensive alliance with France 'for abating the overgreatness of Spain.'[2] Drake and Hawkins carried the new offer to the 'Strange Guest,' promising the reduced

---

[1] August 18, Digges, p. 389.
[2] Digges, 393. See also a long paper in Burghley's hand endorsed ' Consideration of the Enterprise for the Azores Islands, August 21, 1581 ' (*Lansd. MSS.* cii. 104). It appears to be Burghley's own minutes of the Council at which the resolution was taken, and which is referred to in the letter which Digges prints. Cf. a scheme dated August 20 for relieving Terceira, or in case it has fallen proceeding against El Mina and the Portuguese Indies; and copy of Burghley's notes dated August 23 (*ibid.* xxxi. 81, 82).

squadron should sail on the morrow. But Don Antonio would not listen. Persuaded the queen was playing with him or tempted with more plausible offers from France, he chose to consider the new suggestion as a breach of agreement by the adventurers, and demanded the return of his diamond. What happened is of considerable interest, especially as the queen has been represented at this point as behaving in a most heartless way to the unfortunate exile, and has been freely accused in concert with her fellow adventurers not only of breaking faith with him, but of swindling him out of his securities like the most unconscionable of money-lenders.

The story may be read in a correspondence between Burghley and Walsingham. On August 24, 1581, Burghley writes: 'This day Don or King Antonio hath pressed the Queen's Majesty to have restitution of his diamond, and by Mr. Weldmore he would have sent to my lady [Lady Walsingham] for it: but I mean my lady's answer shall be that it was left with her by you, and that without your commandment she may not deliver it except such money be paid as she knoweth you have borrowed on it. Her Majesty will not have it detained for her 5,000*l.*, which I see she could be content to lose, so he were satisfied.'[1] And again on the 27th he writes: 'I have such crooked dealing here with Lopez [i.e. Don Antonio's agent], for that the king urgeth the speedy delivery of the jewel without satisfaction of your charge. The Queen's Majesty for her part is content to stand to courtesy or to loss for the 5,000*l.*'[2]

To the letter of the 24th Walsingham replies from France on August 28, 'My very good Lord, I most humbly thank your lordship for the advice given my wife to stay the ring in her hand until I may receive some satisfaction for such money as I have disbursed and am become surety for, &c.,' and he goes on to explain that all the extra cost was due to Don Antonio's

[1] Digges, p. 394.   [2] *Ibid.* p. 412.

pressing for a larger force than that agreed for by his agent.'[1]

Next day the order for the final discharge of the expedition was drawn up, and in answer to Walsingham Burghley writes on September 2, 'At this present Don Antonio hath come to take his leave of Her Majesty; he will press (i.e. he continues to press) to have his jewel, and so that you may be satisfied, I agreed to it; and so sometimes doth Her Majesty; but in conclusion he would have the jewel answer for all the losses, which of the 13,000*l*. I think will be about 3,600*l*., whereof 170*l*. is desperate imprest and wages and victuals spent; the rest falleth out in the sale of the victuals.'[2]

From these letters it would appear that both Elizabeth and Drake, as well as his partners, behaved very handsomely. The money with which the expedition was fitted out was money lent to Don Antonio by the queen and her fellow adventurers, and lent without security, except in the case of Walsingham. On condition of France joining hands the queen had agreed to sanction an expedition of a certain size. The limit was exceeded by Antonio's own motion and the condition was not fulfilled. Nevertheless the queen was still willing to help him on a smaller scale, and when this was refused, instead of demanding back the money she had lost, she agreed to write it off as a bad debt out of pity for the exile's misfortunes. It was only Burghley's influence which prevented her ordering Lady Walsingham to give up the security to which the impoverished Foreign Secretary was fairly entitled; and finally the whole account was settled by the adventurers agreeing to accept the one diamond ring in satisfaction of all claims upon Don Antonio, amounting to more than 25,000*l*. of our money.[3]

[1] *Hist. MSS. Com., Hatfield Papers*, ii. 420, where the letter is conjectured by the editor to be from Sir Henry Cobham, as also Nos. 1031 and -2, although No. 1035, known to be from Walsingham, refers to his interview with the Queen-Mother mentioned in No. 1032.
[2] Digges, p. 422. The order for paying off is in *Lansd. MSS.* xxxi. 83.
[3] It is the story of this diamond ring given as security to Walsingham,

Still chafing at what he considered his faithless treatment, the now desperate exile resolved to leave England at once, but before sailing he attempted to arrange for the surreptitious despatch to his headquarters in France of two vessels that he had bought, in company with two or three others which he had been able to charter. Horsey sent up information of the attempt from the Wight, and on their putting into Plymouth they were arrested there by the queen's order.[1] Eventually, however, it would seem they were permitted to sail to a Norman port where Don Antonio under the auspices of the French court was fitting out a fresh expedition. With this in 1582 he sailed for the Azores, where his fleet was encountered at St. Michaels by Santa Cruz with a powerful force, was outmanœuvred and completely defeated. The greater part of his ships deserted him; his most capable supporters were

combined with the version of the affair which Mendoza wrote home (see esp. his despatches *Spanish Calendar* 1580, &c., pp. 158 and 165), that appears to have raised in Mr. Froude's mind the impression of the affair which he relates; viz. that Don Antonio brought over the Braganza jewels, with which, of course, he had nothing to do; that Elizabeth promised to lend 30,000*l.* upon them; that on his depositing them in her treasury, an instalment of the amount was advanced to him; that she afterwards refused to give them up till the instalment was repaid; and that when with difficulty this was done, actuated by an ungovernable desire to possess them, she finally kept them, on the pretence that she must have security that he would do no harm to any power with whom she was at peace. (*Hist. of England*, xi. 183 and 196.) The story which reached the Venetian Ambassador's ears in Madrid has a somewhat closer resemblance to Mr. Froude's than that which appears in the Burghley-Walsingham correspondence. 'Don Antonio,' he wrote, 'has bought two ships and intended to equip twenty more, but those who found the money for the expedition wished to be sure of their interest; accordingly the jewels Don Antonio had with him were valued, but did not pass 36,000 crowns. Without sufficient security the vessels will not sail. Don Antonio has applied to the Queen of England. As yet no resolution has been taken.' (*Venetian Calendar*, No. 47, Madrid, September 15, 1581.) On October 29, he writes again, 'You will have heard that Don Antonio has arrived at a port in Normandy with some English ships which he raised in that island by pawning his jewels to the Queen' (*ibid.* No. 51). Later he writes that Don Antonio 'has left many jewels in pledge' at Tours (*ibid.* No. 89, June 15, 1582).

[1] *S.P Dom. Cal.* p. 28. 'Horsey to Walsingham,' October 12, 1581, and *ibid.* p. 43, 'E. Tremayne to same,' February 19, 1582.

killed; he himself escaped with nothing but his life; the following year Terceira and the rest of the islands fell into Santa Cruz's hands, and Philip's seizure of the Portuguese dominions was complete.

So ended the second attempt of Walsingham, with Drake's assistance, to force on the inevitable war with Spain. Had the scheme gone forward, had Drake succeeded, as almost certainly he must have done, in establishing at the Azores a kind of pirate kingdom akin to that which Prince Rupert for a time established at Scilly and the Channel Islands, there seem no bounds to where the results would have reached. England would have entered upon the great war, with Parma still helpless in the Netherlands, and with a naval base in the very track along which flowed the mass of Philip's resources. Instead of a defensive war, it would have been what Drake always wished to make it, an offensive war directed against the well-springs of Spanish finance, and it is difficult to see what could have then prevented a complete collapse of Philip's unstable empire. In the later years of the war, as will be seen, when Elizabeth was roused from her dreams of a peaceful solution and took the offensive, it was above all things the want of such an advanced base that served to paralyse each naval campaign at the moment when there seemed nothing to do but reap the fruits of victory.

The 'First Enterprise' being forbidden, Leicester fell back upon the second, and endeavoured out of the wreck of the expedition to organise an attempt to follow up Drake's lead in the East Indies. The outcome was one of the most miserable adventures of Elizabethan times. In failure and disgrace, marked by every bad quality which brought the Spanish power to decay, the first step was taken towards our Eastern empire. Unhappy as is the story, it cannot be omitted, for no one can measure the greatness of the Elizabethan age who does not know through what a world of shame and disaster it marched to its successes. It was the Muscovy Company, now in despair of reaching

Cathay by the North-east, that Leicester persuaded to back his scheme. Drake's services were not available, apparently because in view of the warlike outlook it was thought unwise to let him leave the country. Frobisher, however, accepted the command, and Drake, at Leicester's request, not only subscribed, but furnished a bark or pinnace and some of his ablest officers and men. How completely Drake's exploit had occupied the field, we may see in this attempt to unite the three great schools of English commercial enterprise in order to follow it up. That Leicester could conceive so good an idea and succeed even so far as he did, should entitle him to be remembered amongst the fathers of the Indian Empire. That the great scheme ended in disaster was no fault of his: it lay deeper in the inherent forces of the time, and in the unhappy jealousies which affected like a disease almost every undertaking of Elizabeth's reign.

From the first his well meant attempt led to considerable friction. The Muscovy Company being the largest subscribers claimed the appointment of the second-in-command. The man they were unfortunate enough to pitch upon was Edward Fenton, a pushing and incompetent soldier of fortune whom we have seen Drake dismiss from the First Enterprise. He was a kinsman of Hawkins, and had been Frobisher's second-in-command in his last voyage, but he had quarrelled with the great explorer, and had the impertinence to say openly he was not the sailor men took him for. Frobisher naturally objected to the appointment, and Leicester it would seem suggested Captain Christopher Carleill, a very capable Irish officer and son-in-law to Walsingham. The Muscovy Company however insisted, and finally the city influence proving stronger than that of the Court, Frobisher threw up his appointment, and Fenton the soldier was given the command as admiral in his place.[1]

[1] It is conceivable that the city had also the support of Burghley, who was always the embodiment of their ideas. Mendoza says that Burghley

There was still fortunately the Drake party to temper the new commander's incompetence. Drake, to oblige Leicester, had nominated two of his best men, his old master and his boatswain, as pilots for the voyage. John Drake also volunteered, and was given the command of his kinsman's bark the 'Francis.' Young William Hawkins did the same, and was made lieutenant-general and second-in-command, much to Fenton's disgust, for there was no love lost between them. Besides these there was Luke Ward who had won already a high reputation under Frobisher and in the service of the Muscovy Company. The squadron was a powerful one. For 'admiral' there was the 'Bear' or 'Leicester galleon' of 400 tons; for 'vice-admiral,' the 'Edward Bonaventure' of 300 tons; and besides the 'Francis' of 40, there was also a frigate of 50 tons called the 'Elizabeth.' By its chief promoters it was undoubtedly intended as a purely commercial venture for trade and the establishment of factories in the Moluccas by virtue of Drake's treaty with Ternate. Merchants accompanied it and formed the majority of Fenton's council, and a number of carpenters and brick-layers testified to its colonising character. The instructions drawn up by the Government directed Fenton to proceed to the Moluccas by way of the Cape, 'not passing by the Strait of Magellan, either going or returning, except upon great occasion incident,' and the strictest injunctions were formulated against violence or hostilities of any kind being committed. Fenton was also empowered if possible to make a new attempt under the direction of Drake's men to find a northern passage to New Albion. He was given power of life and death, subject to a procedure modelled on that which Drake had used in Doughty's case, but Hawkins and the other chief officers were made irremovable.

The commercial aspect of the venture the Spanish ambassador believed to be a mere blind to attract the

subscribed 200*l.* to the venture; and this he may have done to secure admission to its secrets. *Spanish Calendar*, 1580, &c., p. 297.

capital of commercial men; and whatever may have been Leicester's idea it is inconceivable that Drake's men had perfectly innocent intentions. Fenton himself seems to have believed (with how much reason cannot be said) that Hawkins and his fellows had been attached to him with the intention of bringing about a new South Sea raid.[1] Drake's men on the other hand suspected Fenton of having received a bribe from Spain, and Mendoza certainly told the king he had been secretly fomenting the quarrel about his appointment, and taking many other steps to delay the voyage. All we know is that either in pursuance of some secret influence, or moved merely by a childish jealousy of Hawkins, Fenton began boldly with an attempt to sail without the Drake contingent, but they were too smart for him and John Drake brought them all on in the 'Francis.'[2] Their contempt for their leader was hardly disguised. They laughed openly at his ignorance of their art, and by taking as it would seem an impossible course persuaded the merchants that the prevailing winds made it unavoidable to go by way of Magellan's Straits. That measures were being taken in Spain to bar the passage was known apparently in England before they sailed. But Drake when consulted had only laughed at them, saying he could wish nothing better, for while the Spanish squadron was thus safely out of the way in the Straits, the English vessels could pass unmolested into the South Sea by way of the open sea he had discovered beyond Tierra del Fuego. Frobisher

[1] Mendoza even got hold of a story that the chief of Drake's men, whom he called Winter, carried secret orders to supersede Fenton. *Spanish Calendar*, 1580, &c., p. 357.

[2] There is a curious passage in a despatch of Mendoza's, which suggests that the antagonistic influence may again have been Burghley's. When the ambassador had audience to protest against the voyage being allowed to proceed, the queen, he says, who had been listening quietly, suddenly cut him short, as he thought on a sign from Hatton, who with Leicester at this time was his open enemy. 'I am informed,' he continued, 'that on the day I saw the Council, after I had left, Cecil said that I spoke with much modesty and good sense, which could not be denied, and Hatton was extremely annoyed at it, saying that I had bribed the Treasurer.' *Spanish Calendar*, 1580, &c., p. 304.

seems to have been as anxious to follow this route as Drake, and offered in spite of the start which Fenton had had, to get an expedition to the Moluccas before him. But for all concerned the route by the Straits had come to spell piracy and the other had been preferred. Only in case of necessity was the western route to be taken, and this necessity had now arisen. From a vessel captured on the coast of South America, Fenton learnt that an expedition to fortify the Straits had preceded them, and that communications had been laid across the continent so that warning could be sent overland from the River Plate to Peru the moment an English ship appeared on the coast. Drake's men were for going on in spite of everything. To follow the quarrels that ensued is unnecessary. Suffice it to say that when Fenton decided first to return to the northward on pretence of re-victualling in a Portuguese port, John Drake, being convinced the voyage was going to be abandoned, deserted with the 'Francis' and determined with reckless daring to proceed alone. In the River Plate, however, he was wrecked and subsequently taken prisoner, and it is to this misfortune we owe his valuable deposition. The rest of the fleet having put into Santos were attacked by a Spanish squadron. In the engagement that ensued they sank the Spaniard's flagship, but were themselves somewhat roughly handled owing to Fenton's incompetence and irresolution, and not a little, if we may believe Ward, to the admiral's drawing inexcusably out of action at the moment when a complete victory was assured.

The action was followed by the abandonment of the voyage. Fenton's instructions strictly charged him not to use violence under any pretence except in self-defence, and he was therefore justified by his orders in drawing off as he did and even in returning to England, seeing that, as far as he knew, it was impossible to proceed without fighting his way. For his failure he seems to have incurred no censure. Everyone probably knew it was due to a conflict of the two influences that were at work—

the influence of Burghley and Sussex and the city still clinging to their idea of expansion by peaceful commerce, and the influence of Walsingham and Leicester seeking to carve it out of the sprawling Spanish Empire with the edge of the sword. It was the conflict which Drake had crushed with an iron hand at Port St. Julian: and the same which he was feeling as acutely in public affairs as he had done as a private adventurer. The policy of England was still swaying between the two stools, and for some time yet Drake could do nothing but look on in impatient unrest.[1]

At the end of the year 1581 he was appointed Mayor of Plymouth, and during his term of office an entertainment was given to the Portuguese ambassador and a new compass was set up on the Hoe. In January 1583 his wife died and was buried at St. Budeaux.[2] In this year too he seems first to have conceived his idea of furnishing Plymouth with an abundant water supply, for which his name became a household word in the borough; for he was granted a lease of the town mills, which appears to have been a necessary preliminary to the scheme.[3]

But public affairs did not consume his whole attention, for soon he was courting again. This time it was no simple Devonshire lass, but the daughter and heiress of the knightly house of Sydenham of Combe Sydenham in Somersetshire. She was quite young and the family tradition says it was a love match opposed by the father, and that the ardent admiral by night and through a lattice won his bride like a Spanish prize. But knowing as we do how marriages were made in Tudor times, we may fairly doubt whether a millionaire like Drake, of knightly rank and in high favour at Court, encountered serious

---

[1] For the conflicting authorities for the voyage, which the publication of Mendoza's correspondence makes intelligible for the first time, see Luke Ward's *Narrative* in *Hakluyt*. William Hawkins's in the *Hawkins Voyages*, *Hak. Soc.* Madox's *Diary* in the *Colonial Calendar*, 1582, May 6. John Drake's Deposition in the *Western Antiquary*.

[2] *Sir Francis Drake*, by Dr. H. H. Drake, p. 15.

[3] Plymouth Town Records. *Hist. MSS. Com.* Rep. x. iv. 537.

A PINNACE UNDER FIGHTING SAILS (CIRCA 1586).

Showing 'waist-cloths' and 'nettings.' From the description of Sir Philip Sydney's funeral (British Museum, T. Laut. c. 21 f, slightly reduced).

disapproval of his suit. In any case the match was made, and early in 1585, Mary Sydenham became Lady Drake.[1] As seems only fit for such a man and the daughter of such a house, the wedding bells were mingled with the sound of arms. The strained and battered peace was breaking up. The men who had supported Drake had triumphed, and on him the eyes of the country were confidently fixed. The first period of his life—the time of his struggle through every difficulty and resistance to the front—was at an end. His ideas were the English policy, and he a recognised pilot of the stormy course it was about to steer. Henceforth his career must be followed on a higher plane; for as the Devon seaman carries home his well-born bride, we see him pass from the ranks of the corsairs to take his place beside the admirals and statesmen who gave us the empire of the sea.

[1] The marriage settlement is dated Feb. 10, 27 Eliz.; see *Sir Francis Drake*, by Dr. H. H. Drake, p. 15. The family legend goes on to say that so highly did the family disapprove of the match that once during a long absence of Drake's they persuaded his wife he was dead and induced her at length to marry again. The bridal party had got as far as the church, when a cannon ball burst up from the earth between them and the church door. 'It is from Drake,' said the bride, 'to tell me he is still alive,' and with that she turned back, and nothing would induce her to go on with the ceremony. The shot is still kept, it is said, beneath the hall table at Combe Sydenham, and no matter where it is carried, it always rolls back to its place. This confirmation of the story, however, loses weight when we remember that Drake was never away from England for a whole year together after his second marriage. It would almost seem as though the legend had been transferred from the first wife, and that the shot in question was really fired while he was in the antipodes on his voyage of circumnavigation.

CHAPTER XII

THE NAVY OF ELIZABETH

THE first official recognition of the new position Drake had achieved was his appointment to serve on a Royal Commission to inquire into the state of the Navy. For some years past there had been continual complaints in various quarters that the Navy Office was being improperly and even dishonestly conducted. Foremost of the grumblers was Sir Thomas Cotton, the veteran officer who had been ordered to the relief of the loyal Protestants at Plymouth at the time of the flight of Drake's family. Both under Henry VIII. and in the present reign he had held the ancient and lucrative office of ' Wafter of the Wool Fleet,' and had been employed in police duty with the Channel Guard. He had, however, a genius for quarrelling with his superiors, and had particularly incurred the displeasure of the Admiralty by persistently reporting disorders in the administration and urging their reformation.[1] Special complaints were made that the money assigned for the upkeep of the ships was not properly applied, that many of the ships were rotten and very few fit for service.[2] During the frequent partial mobilisations that had been taking place, various defects in the system seem to have been discovered, and accordingly when in 1583 war with Spain began to loom as a near and real menace, the Government resolved to take the matter seriously in hand. A Royal Commission was issued to report on the whole state of the

[1] *Hatfield MSS.* i. 489.
[2] Recitals of the Commission. *S.P. Dom.* clxii. 50.

Navy, to reform abuses in the dockyards, to superintend the building of new ships, and to inquire into the condition of the stores necessary for a rapid mobilisation.

The names of the members of the Commission sufficiently attest the important position the fleet had attained in the scheme of National Defence. The Commissioners were the Lord Treasurer, the Lord Admiral, the Lord Chamberlain, Sir Francis Walsingham, and Sir Walter Mildmay, Chancellor of the Exchequer.[1] For the purpose of making a complete inspection they were empowered to appoint sub-commissioners. The list from whom these were to be chosen consists principally of sea-captains, and is interesting as showing the men who had already obtained a maritime reputation. They are Sir Thomas Cotton, Sir William Gorges, Sir Francis Drake, Bingham, Frobisher, Fulke Greville, Carew and Walter Raleigh, Henry Palmer, George Beeston and John Ellis. It was specially directed that they were to receive every assistance from 'our four principal officers of our ships,' Wynter, Hawkins, Holstocke and Borough, as well as of 'our chief shipwrights' Pett, Chapman and Baker, and 'our chief masters' Thomas Grey and William Barnes. The special instructions were to inquire into the charges of embezzling stores; the misappropriation of money allotted for dry-docking the 'Hope,' the 'Philip and Mary,' and the 'Antelope' at Deptford in 1578; the new building of the 'Revenge' and the 'Scout' in 1575 at a cost of £4,400, 'built with bad planks and thereby of no continuance;' an offer which had been made to build two similar ships for £2,600; and generally to draw up regulations to prevent the recurrence of such abuses and to report on the cost of keeping the whole fleet fit for immediate service.[2]

---

[1] Mildmay was a veteran public servant who had begun his career in the Court of Augmentations under Henry VIII. The greater part of his life had been spent serving on Commissions, and especially those which concerned questions of revenue and finance. He was married to Walsingham's sister. (Wood, *Athenæ Cantab.* ii. 51.)

[2] *S.P. Dom.* clxii. 50.

The sub-commissioners eventually appointed were Cotton, Gorges, Drake, and the two masters.[1]

Thus at the outset of his public career Drake was afforded an excellent opportunity of measuring the weapon he was to wield. So much misconception has always existed as to the nature of the force at the Queen's disposal, so long have imaginative pens rejoiced to represent the overthrow of the Spaniards as due to an outburst of instinctive and untutored national energy, that at this late hour it is difficult to disinter the truth. It is only by a patient study of what the officers engaged have left to us, that it is possible to reveal the struggle for what it was—the triumph of advanced organisation and science over a maritime system that was dead and service traditions that had sunk into senility.

Since 1569, when Drake left the service at its lowest ebb, much had happened, and he was to find things greatly altered. The unreadiness in which the country had then found itself to cope at sea with the coalition that threatened it, had led to another naval scare like that which followed the loss of Calais, and Sir Thomas Cotton seems to have been particularly loud in complaint at this time.[2] Amongst other results of the alarm was the production of a pamphlet which is of the highest interest, as presenting us with a marked development in naval thought.[3] Though never published, it was circulated privately amongst members of the Council and the chief naval officers by special request. Its teaching has a flavour that

[1] *S. P. Dom.* cli. 20. This paper is in an undated bundle assigned conjecturally to the year 1581; but there seems no room for doubt, after comparing the names of this Commission with the list in clxii. 50, that it belongs to 1583.

[2] See his letter to Cecil, *ubi supra*; and De Guaras, *Spanish Calendar*, p. 261.

[3] A copy and an old transcript of this remarkable paper are in the British Museum (*Add. MSS.* 20042-3). Another copy is among the Hatton Papers (*Hist. MSS. Com.* i. 32), and a third in the Pepysian Library. It is printed in *Censura Literaria*, v. 29, 137, 260. Though the first part is dated 1570 it seems to have been drawn up some time before. A copy was sent to Leicester in 1571; see *Hist. MSS. Com.* i. 60.

is startling in its modernity; nothing nearly so far advanced has come down to us from the time. Of its author, John Montgomery, nothing is known except that since Mary's time he had given special attention to national defence. The paper is not alarmist in tone, though perhaps rather for fear of being thought treasonable than because the situation was not felt to be grave. As it stands it was calculated to restore calm by pointing out the strength which an adequate navy afforded against invasion if properly used, and that England was in a position to have one. His text is that for a maritime state, unfurnished with a navy, the sea, so far from being a safe frontier, is rather a highway for her enemies; but that with a navy it surpasses all other frontiers in strength. In support of this canon, so sound and so strikingly modern in its ring, he cites a number of examples to enforce the consequences both of its neglect and its observance, showing with what broad sagacity naval history could then be studied. The Venetians are his cardinal instance of its success, and he dwells on the precedents of Carausius, Count of the Saxon Shore under Constantius, who by making himself master of the fleet was able to wrest Britain from the Roman Empire; of Edgar, and Richard II., to show more particularly that a good fleet is the only means of rendering the English coasts invulnerable.[1] To achieve such security he makes no extravagant demands on the resources of the country. He does not call in the modern tone for an absolute command of the sea; he considers it unnecessary to maintain a fleet more powerful than any that an enemy is likely to assemble. A fleet strong enough to dispute the command of the sea he holds to be sufficient. The principle he lays down was perfectly sound in its day. Though a fleet, he argues, be not strong enough to 'charge,' that is, to attack, yet, though the enemy be two and even three to one, an attack may be received without fear; 'for in giving charge,' he

---

[1] The case of Carausius has been very recently revived as a cardinal example of the command of the sea in Clerk and Thursfield's *The Navy and the Nation*, 1897, p. 127.

says, 'is a greater danger than in receiving the charge, and especially upon so forcible, worthy, and warlike a navy, as the Navy of England.' In effect it is an insistence on the advantage of the defensive in a naval action. It was the opinion held by the greatest French admirals to the last, and before the practice of breaking the line and of attacking line-ahead was understood, it was indisputable. English guns and gunnery were superior to all others, and, as has been shown, our peculiar practice was to meet an attack with raking broadsides aimed low, so that a superior enemy attacking line-abreast might well be reduced to an equality before he had really got into action at all; and especially if the wind were light and the advance slow. The argument of course presupposes that the fleet which is the weaker in numbers is individually the more powerful, and of the individual superiority of the English warships there seems to have been no doubt. We have seen how the Venetians, who best could judge, had long considered that England was superior to all its neighbours at sea.[1] Montgomery would put it higher. Our ships, he thinks, were 'of mold so clean-made beneath, of proportion so fine above, of sail so swift, the ports, fights and coins in them so well devised, with the ordnance so well placed that none of any other region may seem comparable to them.' If England, therefore, had a Navy of forty sail of queen's ships with an auxiliary fleet of as many large merchantmen, he thinks no two princes would support the cost of often attempting an invasion. For if our fleet were defeated it could only be at such a sacrifice to the enemy, that they would not dare to land and face fresh troops; or if in the temporary absence of our fleet they managed to effect a landing we could still, like Scipio, deliver a counter-attack on their own coasts and by cutting off their communications have them at our mercy. At the same time, while thus isolating the invaders, we should be in a position either to fetch help from our allies or to join them in a counter-attack abroad. It is all very like Torrington's

[1] *Venetian Calendar*, p. 274.

doctrine of a 'fleet in being' acting as a bar to invasion, but seen dimly and without definition. In his general position, however, Montgomery is clear enough, and in elaborating it he gives special prominence, like the most modern authorities, to the important part which the Roman Navy played in deciding the long contest with Carthage.[1]

As yet it will be seen there is but a very dim conception of what we mean by the command of the sea; though Montgomery seems to grasp that without it nothing can be done. His whole argument, indeed, is based on this position—that, if properly handled, our fleet could paralyse offensive action even against large odds; that is to say, that without command of the sea a successful invasion in force is impossible. The strategy he approves is entirely defensive, and does not aim primarily at the destruction of the enemy's fleet. He advises the division of the home force into three squadrons, one to be stationed off Scotland, one in the Channel, and one about Ireland. To our eyes such a disposition has radical faults, but Montgomery supports it by the success of Elizabeth's dispositions in 1559, when, while the Channel squadron held the French fleet in check, a North Sea squadron under Wynter cut off the communications of the French troops who had seized Leith and compelled them to surrender to the army that was besieging them.

Montgomery's paper seems to have had considerable success. In the summer of 1570 Clinton, the Lord Admiral, was ordered to prepare a scheme of mobilisation, by which at any time the queen wished he could put to sea with fifty good men-of-war having 12,000 mariners and soldiers to man them, and reserves of victual and munitions at the necessary points. In reporting this home the French Ambassador explains that the English calculate on fighting their enemy at sea before permitting him to land, being of opinion that though all the world should be in league against them, yet by these precautions they

[1] See especially Captain A. T. Mahan, *The Influence of Sea Power on History*, pp. 13 *et seq.*

would be able to defend themselves. Their idea is, he further explains, that if they win a naval action they will easily be able to prevent an enemy approaching their coast, and even if the battle be drawn, that they still will be able to prevent a landing: and more than this, if they lose, it can only be after they have so completely broken their enemy that he will be compelled to put back to refit.[1] Montgomery's ideas had clearly taken hold. Fénelon indeed must have seen his paper or been informed by one who had. It may be taken therefore that at this time it was not considered necessary to have command of the sea. It was sufficient to be strong enough to prevent its being obtained by any probable alliance of hostile powers, and on this principle the English naval policy continued to be founded until Drake's genius divined that it must be carried further.

To achieve Montgomery's ideal of naval strength an extraordinarily small expenditure was deemed adequate. From a minute of Hawkins's it appears that for the first ten years of his administration, that is from 1569 to 1579, the annual expenditure on the Navy, exclusive of construction, had been about 8,214*l*. The sum allotted by the 'Warrant dormant,' which was issued yearly for ordinary charges, amounted to 5,714*l*., and extraordinary expenses for 'new building and repairing ships in dock' came to 2,500*l*. With this modest provision Hawkins was expected to keep up not only the old ships, but several new ones which were launched during this period.[2]

For Hawkins had not been long at the Admiralty before there were signs of a new programme being on foot, a programme of very special interest; for from it the true Elizabethan Navy may be said to date. While Elizabeth, to dissemble the anxiety which the news of the victory of Lepanto caused her, was ordering a public rejoicing with

[1] Fénelon, *Corr. Diplomatique*, iii. 251.
[2] See *S.P. Dom.* 1587, ccii. 35. Hawkins was not only Treasurer of the Navy, but in accordance with the administrative system of the time, he also had a private contract with the Government for keeping the Royal Ships in a state of efficiency.

bonfires in the streets and thanksgivings in the churches, and while the Spanish ambassador was giving a triumphant display of fire-works before the embassy in honour of his master's glory at sea, on the stocks in the Thames and the Medway dockyards the new era was already beginning.[1] The new ships show plainly how the ideas of the 'Book of Sea Causes' had triumphed;[2] and beyond this they have a peculiar interest of their own. For not only did some of them come to be amongst the most famous ships of their time, but some of them also received names which, like the 'Swiftsure' and 'Dreadnought,' have continued on the Admiralty lists ever since, and so in a certain very direct way may claim to be the real parents of our modern Navy.

They are further notable as having been designed on more scientific principles than as yet had been employed in the dockyards. The improved system seems to have been introduced about the time that Hawkins brought his mathematical mind to the Admiralty. In the Pepysian Library is a curious manuscript treatise of Elizabeth's time on shipbuilding containing solutions of a number of practical problems of every day occurrence in naval architecture. Amongst many others it gives a table for finding the semi-diameter of a circle, 'without which,' it asserts, 'it is impossible to make a perfect ship,' and the second ship ever designed by the new rule, it tells us, was the '"Foresight" of her Majesty's.' This was a galleon of 300 tons, which with two others, the 'Bull' and the 'Tiger' of 200 tons, rebuilt at the same time, were turned out in 1570.[3] Three years later followed the 'Swiftsure'

[1] Fénelon, *Corr. Diplomatique*, iv. 281.
[2] See *ante*, p. 135.
[3] Except where otherwise stated the dates of launches, &c., are taken from Oppenheim, *Administration of the Navy*, p. 120. The dimensions of the 'Foresight' Borough gives (*S.P. Dom.* ccxliii. 111) as, tons 290, length 79, beam 27, depth 14. By his rule, therefore, she was a galleon, for a galleon, he says, has its length by the keel three times its width at the middle, and the depth in hold but $\frac{5}{12}$ or $\frac{2}{5}$ of the breadth. The 'Bull' and the 'Tiger' were Henry VIII.'s old 'galleasses' rebuilt. The 'Tiger' was of roundship type—being 50 feet in length, 24 in beam, and 13 in depth. The

and the 'Dreadnought,' great-ships of 400 tons, and the 'Achates,' a bark of 80 tons on galleasse lines. The alarm of 1574 produced the most famous of Elizabeth's ships, the galleon 'Revenge,' which though she proved an unlucky ship was considered by Drake a masterpiece of naval construction and his ideal of what a great-ship should be. To the same time belongs another galleon of 120 tons, called the 'Scout.'[1]

As to the galleys, a list of the Queen's Navy bearing date July 30, 1570, on which the names of the new ships have been afterwards inserted, shows how the seamen's influence was advancing.[2] The three galleys indeed appear separately on the list, but against their names is written this note: 'The season of the year doth pass away for any service to be had of them, which in time of service requireth 1,000 men for their full furniture.' And again in the margin in another hand, 'If no galleys come what advantage in furnishing our galleys—this to be debated.' Here we have clear evidence of the growing disfavour with which the expense and unseaworthiness of galleys were bringing them, how they had ceased to be regarded as a necessary adjunct to a fleet, and yet how there lingered the idea that galleys could only be met by galleys. The large sized ships like the 'Triumph' were hardly less out of favour. As early as the mobilisation of 1572 they had been found too big for bad weather, and for this reason had been paid off at the approach of winter.[3]

During these years of alarm constant partial mobilisa-

'Bull' was probably a sister ship, but she was rebuilt as a galleasse in 1591, so that we do not know her dimensions at this time.

[1] Their dimensions were as follows—

			length	beam	depth
'Swiftsure'	355 tons	74 feet in length,	30 in beam,	16 in depth.
'Dreadnought'	360 ,,	80 ,,	30 ,,	15 ,,
'Achates'	90 ,,	55 ,,	18 ,,	9 ,,
'Revenge'	441 ,,	92 ,,	32 ,,	15 ,,
'Scout'	120 ,,	60 ,,	20 ,,	10 ,,

Mr. Oppenheim gives the date of the 'Revenge' and the 'Scout' as 1577, citing the Pipe Office accounts. The Commission of 1583 refers to them as having been new built in 1575. The Pipe Office accounts are perhaps the better authority.

[2] S.P. Dom. lxxi. 63.   [3] Spanish Calendar, p. 430.

tions took place beyond the ordinary summer and winter guards, and in 1574, when Menendez was preparing his great expedition for the Narrow Seas, the whole of the fleet except four sail was directed to be put in commission. The order was issued on the last day of April. Six vessels were to be ready in a fortnight, and eighteen four weeks later. The ostensible object of the Spaniards, it will be remembered, was to bring reinforcements to the Governor of the Low Countries, but suspecting what Menendez's real objective was, the English Government resolved, says Fénelon, to send the fleet to sea with instructions to meet the Spaniards and take up a position on their left flank so as to cover the West of England and the route to Ireland; and in case any vessels straggled from the main body to surround and fight them. As a special measure in view of the peculiar constitution of Menendez's fleet orders were also issued to equip at Colchester eighteen small vessels (*pataches*) of from twenty-five to thirty tons, 'like rowing-frigates with guns close to the water.'[1] The mobilisation, however, was never carried out, for Elizabeth, in the spirit that so often marred her naval policy, could not make up her mind to the expense until she was sure it was necessary. In July the Governor of the Low Countries could write to Menendez that 'there was small danger of his being attacked as he passed through the Channel, so great was the irresolution of the English Government. 'Though there have been this year,' he says, 'a thousand changes in that kingdom, ordering an armament one day in a very great fury and the next promptly dismantling, I hold sure letters from London that the armament will not go forward.'[2] His information proved correct, and the Queen's hesitation justified. Menendez's death put an end to the danger, the fleet was not wanted and thus we are unable to measure the capacity of Elizabeth's

---

[1] Fénelon, *Corr. Diplomatique*, vi. 129.
[2] *Nueva Colec. de Documentos Inéditos*, iii. 130.

naval machinery for what at the time would have been a rapidity of mobilisation without precedent.

By the year 1578 the Royal Navy had reached and even passed the ideal of the 'Book of Sea Causes.' It consisted in all, without counting galleys and small oared-craft, of some twenty-five sail with an aggregate capacity of about 11,000 tons, requiring nearly 7,000 hands to man it.[1] Its chief defect in the seamen's eyes would be that though it exceeded the required tonnage, it fell short in numbers. The five largest ships consumed nearly 4,500 tons and 3,000 men, for which they would gladly have seen nine 'Revenges.' The work of the dockyards now tended all in this direction. Two new great-ships were laid down like the 'Revenge,' which Monson describes as 'low and snug in the water like a galliasse'[2] and as fast as possible the older vessels were remade and 'brought into the form of galleasses.' Still it is possible that what the old style of great-ship of the largest size lost in real power it gained in moral effect. Sir Richard Hawkins, a great authority, indeed preferred such ships as the 'Triumph' to those of the new fashion like the 'Victory,' chiefly, as he says, 'for majesty and terror of the enemy,' and also for their superiority when it came to boarding and the heavier weight of artillery and stronger crews they could carry. Two decks and a half he considers to be the least a great-ship should have, and was of opinion that the fashion for galleasse-built ships—or, as he calls them, 'race' ships—in preference to those 'lofty-built' had been pushed too far.

This was the burning question of Elizabethan naval architecture. It was not only the eternal question of large ships against small; but in it was involved the whole question of the development of a sailing 'long-ship,' the transition, in fact, from the mediæval to the

---

[1] See list in Derrick, *Rise and Progress of the Navy*, p. 25, to which the 'Revenge' must be added.

[2] No descriptive name for the type had yet been agreed on even by experts. Wynter calls them 'galleons,' *S.P. Dom.* clxxxvii. 44.

AN ELIZABETHAN GALLEON.

Showing top-armours and secondary armament in the waist. On her starboard bow is a pinnace. From Visscher's series, circ. 1588.

modern type of man-of-war. The warship of the middle ages was typically a deep-waisted, single-decked, wall-sided vessel with castles fore and aft. These castles, which in vessels especially constructed for war came to take the form of a forecastle and a half-deck, were made musket-proof, or as we should say 'protected;' and being closed athwart ship with similarly protected bulkheads, known as 'cubbridge-heads,' were impenetrable to boarders; while at the same time, by means of loopholes and quickfiring pieces in-board, they could enfilade the waist with musketry and murdering shot. Thus a ship of the English pattern, at any rate, could rarely be held even if boarders entered, until her 'cage works' or protected castles were destroyed by gun-fire. When the development of the sailing war-ship had been carried thus far a theory was started that by substituting for the wall-sided lines a line that 'homed-in' (the Elizabethan equivalent of the later 'housing-in' and 'tumbling home') the ship became more weatherly and easier in a sea-way. This narrowing of the ships upwards, however, had the disadvantage, as Richard Hawkins points out, of 'disenabling them for bearing their cage-works correspondent to the proportion and mould of the ship.' It also, he says, made them 'tender-sided.' To give the additional strength that was thus made necessary, as well apparently as to compensate for the reduced covered accommodation in the narrowed cage-works, the practice of 'race-building,' he tells us, was introduced. These 'race-built' ships Monson calls 'flush-decked'; so that we may conclude that what was done was to cover in the waist with a deck running flush fore and aft, and thus was produced a vessel of essentially modern type. The advocates of the older fashion, however, were quickly able to point to a serious defect in the new design. In the old ships the deck hands were gathered for general quarters mainly in the waist, where by means of high musket-proof 'blinders' of elm, that formed temporary bulwarks from poop to forecastle, they were able to work the ship under cover. Hawkins especially dwells on this want of deck protection as a great defect of the 'race-built' ships, and Monson as a defect of 'flush-decked' ships, by which we know the two expressions meant the same thing.[1] There was also the grave defect that the waist no longer afforded a trap for boarders and the deck could not be enfiladed from protected bulkheads. Various devices to overcome these defects were tried, such as movable elm blinders of 'four- or five-inch planks five foot high, and six foot long running upon wheels'; but nothing was so satisfactory in the eyes of Richard Hawkins as 'where the whole side hath one blinder and one armour of proof for defence of those who of force must labour and be aloft'—that is, on deck—and naval opinion continued to be divided on the question throughout the reign.[2]

We can see, however, that by the time James I. had come to the throne, the new ideas had steadily gained ground, and in spite of the conservative views of some of the best practical seamen were approved by the highest authorities. Sir William Monson, writing at the end of the war, goes very fully into the question. 'There are two manner of built ships,' he says, ' the one with a flush deck, fore and aft, sunk and low in the water ; the other lofty and high charged, with a half-deck, forecastle and copperidge-heads.' He considered the first a good ship to fight in, provided always she was a 'fast ship by the wind,' so as to prevent an enemy boarding her ; for having no half-deck or forecastle for the men to retire to or cubberidge-heads

---

[1] In Spain the race-ship seems to have been merely a vessel of low free-board. 'Navio rasso,' says Dr. D. Garcia de Palacio, 'es el que tiene el bordo basso,' *Instrucion Nauthica*, Mexico 1587.

[2] See Richard Hawkins, *Observations*, esp. pp. 286, 287, 292, 306, 307. Monson *Naval Tracts*, pp. 326 *et seq.* As further evidence of the nature of the structural reform, we know that when Borough was seeking to discredit Sir John Hawkins he wrote : ' The cutting down and defacing of the "romthes" and commodious fights made in her majesty's royal ships for the wars and altering them to the manner of merchant ships, hulks and crayers (as the *Hope* &c.) must be accounted a transforming or reforming them to galleasses.' (*Lansd. MSS* xliii. 33.) 'Romthes' or roomths = rooms, here meaning ' deck-cabins.' Cf. modern 'state-room.'

to carry quick-firing guns she was easily taken when once entered. Her great advantage was that being weatherly and low in the water she could range close up to windward of a high-charged ship and within pistol shot fire into her below the water-line without the enemy's ordnance being able to touch her. The advantages of a high-built ship he considers to be 'majesty and terror to the enemy; more commodious for the harbouring of men; she will be able to carry more artillery; of greater strength in-board and make the better defence; she will over-top a lower and snug ship; her men cannot be so well discerned.' A ship of three decks, however, he condemns altogether, as always overgunned and unhandy. Raleigh was even more strongly opposed to large ships and the old lofty superstructures. 'We find by experience,' he says, 'that the greatest ships are the least serviceable, go very deep to water, and of marvellous charge and cumber, our channels decaying every year. Besides they are less nimble, less mainable and very seldom employed. *Grande navio grande fatiga*, saith the Spaniard. A ship of 600 tons will carry as good ordnance as a ship of 1,200 tons; and though the greater have double her number, the lesser will turn her broadsides twice before the greater can wind once.' And again, 'The high charging of ships it is that brings them all ill qualities, makes them extreme leeward, makes them sink deep in the water, makes them labour and makes them overset. Men may not expect the ease of many cabins and safety at once in sea-service. Two decks and a half is sufficient to yield shelter and lodging for men and mariners and no more charging at all higher, but only one low cabin for the master.'[1] He admits higher charging is possible and well enough for hardened mariners, but it makes a ship roll and 'men of better sort and better breeding would be glad to find more steadiness and less tottering cage-work.'[2]

---

[1] I.e. a 'round-house' on the half-deck.
[2] *Observations on the Navy*, Works, viii. 337 and 339. Raleigh, it must

In Drake's time there is no trace of doubt as to the advantages of the reform, and abroad the new ships seem to have been regarded as particularly formidable. Even in 1574 a Spanish agent describes the middle sized ships 'as powerful vessels . . . with little top-hamper and very light, which is a great advantage for close quarters, and with much artillery, the heavy pieces being close to the water.'[1] Some years later a Spaniard on examination deposed that he thought 'the King of Spain to be very weak by the sea, and that it is a strange thing in comparison that they speak in Spain of the Queen of England's strength by sea and that one English ship is worth four of theirs.'[2]

The form of the ships was not the only improvement. Before copper was used the most destructive enemy to shipping was the *Teredo navalis*. All kinds of sheathing were tried against it, till John Hawkins himself invented one that was really effective, consisting of elm boards closely nailed over a layer of felt made of tar and hair.[3] . The Spaniards used lead, which was found costly, and if thick enough to stand, very heavy. The well-known list of improvements, which Raleigh says had been introduced in his time, such as movable top-masts, chain-pumps, capstans and longer cables, do not seem to have been peculiar to the English service, and some of them at least were certainly borrowed from the Mediterranean.[4]

Naval ordnance, too, in sympathy with other branches of the art of war had been making steady progress. In Henry VIII.'s time many of the great-ships still carried the bombard, the typical gun of the middle ages. Though sometimes cast in both iron and bronze, it was normally a wrought-iron cylinder made of longitudinal

be remembered, was very anxious to get a regular establishment of gentlemen for naval officers, and hence his desire to consult their feelings. (See *post*, p. 385.)

[1] *Spanish Calendar*, p. 479.   [2] *S.P. Dom.* clxxix. 15 (3).
[3] Sir Rich. Hawkins, *Observations*, p. 203.
[4] See *Invention of Ships*. Works, viii. 323.

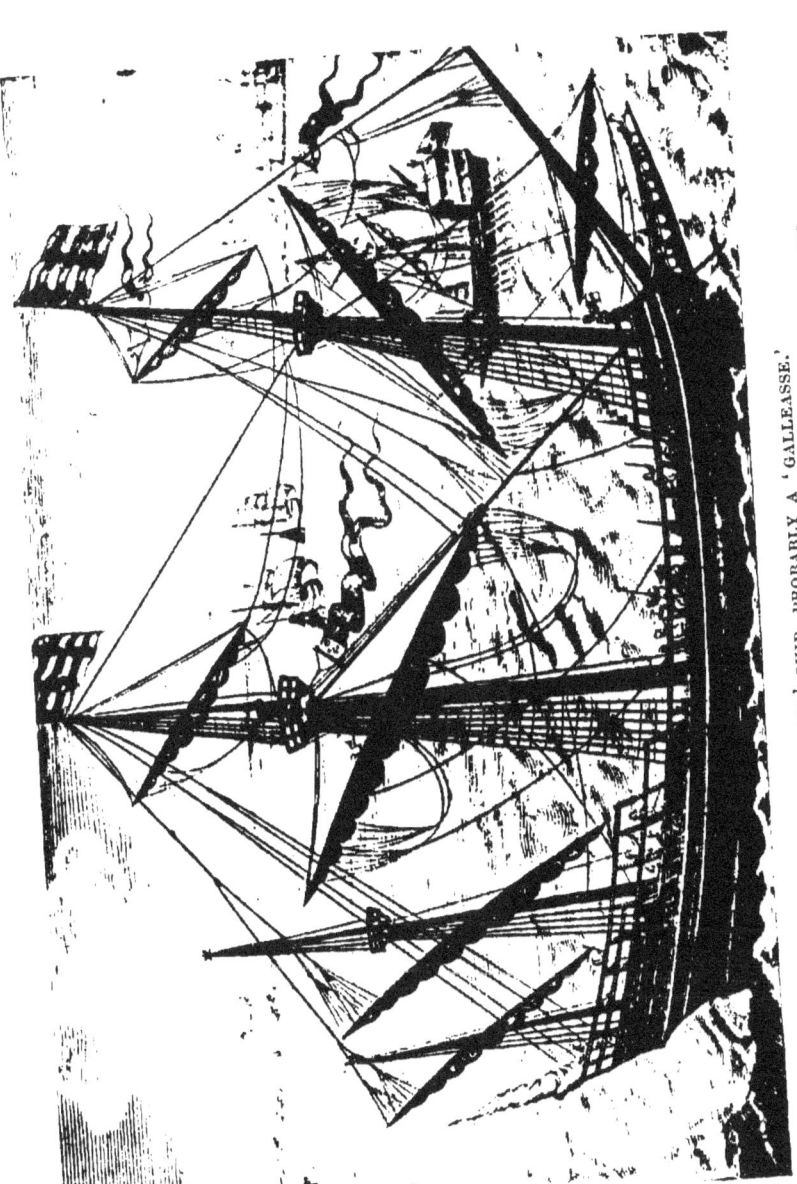

A 'RACE-BUILT' SHIP, PROBABLY A 'GALLEASSE.' From Visscher's Series, circ. 1588.

In the middle distance is a galley, probably the 'Bonavolia.'

bars clamped together with rings forced on red-hot, and it was mounted on a bed made of a solid beam of timber. Loading, as in all early guns, was done at the breech on the system of a removable powder chamber, which was nothing but a shorter cylinder exactly like the barrel, but closed at the hinder end and chamfered at the other. When filled it was laid in its place at the hinder end of the timber bed and wedged up into the breech of the gun. The process of loading bombards is thus described by Cataneo: 'They are charged with iron chambers ('mascoli'), which should be thoroughly well fixed, so that when the time comes to give fire, the bombard shall not blow ('non respiri'); for if this happen it will not do good work and its chamber will be full of powder without burning it. When it [the chamber] has been filled a plug of soft wood should be driven firmly into it, and the plug having been inserted into [the breech of] the bombard, let a disk of very hard wood be placed behind the chamber and driven home as hard as possible with a mallet. The disk will be between the chamber and the bed, but between the chamber and the disk should be placed a pad of lead or a piece of an old boot (in case you have no lead), because this will lessen the shock of the recoil which the chamber would give without it, on account of the wood. But before the chamber be set to the bombard there is put into it [i.e. the breech of the bombard] a wisp of oakum ['sfilacci'] or straw, so that the shot cannot roll out. The shot is then inserted and close to it is put the chamber, then the wooden disk, well forced down and driven home. This done adjust to a hair's breadth and fire when occasion shall arise.'[1]

With so imperfect a system of breech mechanism as the only one in practical use, it is easy to understand how artillerists welcomed the introduction of cast muzzle-loading guns. At first to be of any endurance they could

[1] Girolamo Cataneo, *Dell' Essamini di Bombardieri*, Brescia 1564, p. 79. Brescia at this time had the most famous gun foundries in Italy. See also Ruscelli, *Precetti della Militia Moderna*, Venice 1608, p. 16.

be made only out of bronze and were very costly. The forged bombard therefore continued in use; Cataneo in 1564 even specifies it as a suitable arm in certain cases for galleons and *galee di mercantia*.[1] But when the art of casting iron ordnance began to be understood and a cheap muzzle-loading gun that was thoroughly serviceable could be produced, they rapidly superseded breech-loaders for all the heavier calibres. So much was at once settled, but with the growth of gun founding sprang up a host of problems concerning the relation of length to calibre, the proportion and distribution of metal and the like, which produced so great a multiplicity of types as to be at first sight beyond measure bewildering. Cyprian Lucar,[2] in the appendix to his translation of Tartaglia, the great Italian mathematician and scientific artillerist who dedicated his work on ordnance to Henry VIII., enumerates something like forty different kinds of guns and by no means exhausts the list of those mentioned in contemporary writers. By regarding the confusion, however, in the light of the two main classifications, which the theorists of the time adopted, comparative clearness is obtainable.

The first and most purely theoretical method of classing artillery was on the basis of the proportion and distribution of the metal, of which the gun was formed.[3] A three-fold division was thus obtained into 'Legitimate,' 'Bastard,' and 'Extraordinary' ordnance. In the Legitimate or 'ordinary fortified' the thickness of metal was at the touch-hole, $\frac{7}{8}$ calibre; at the trunnions, $\frac{3}{8}$ calibre; at the muzzle $\frac{1}{4}$ calibre, and the class included all sizes of Cannons, all sizes of Culverins, as well as Sakers, Falcons, Falconets, Robinets and Bases. In Bastard or 'Lessened'

[1] *Dell' Essamini di Bombardieri*, p. 81.
[2] *Three Books of Colloquies concerning the art of shooting in great and small pieces of artillery; written in Italian by Nicholas Tartaglia and now translated into English by Cyprian Lucar; whereunto is annexed a Treatise called Lucar Appendix*. London, 1588, fol. It is dedicated to the Earl of Leicester.
[3] See John Roberts, *The Compleat Cannoniere or Gunner's Guide*, London, 1639, p. 35. Robert Norton, *The Gunner*, London, 1628, cap. vi. *et seq.*, and cf. Sir James Turner, *Palias Armata*, ch. vii.

pieces the thickness of metal was at the touch-hole $\frac{3}{4}$ calibre; at the trunnions $\frac{9}{16}$ calibre; at the muzzle $\frac{3}{16}$ calibre; and the class included 'Basilisks' (Bastard Double-Culverins), 'Serpentines' (Bastard Culverins), Aspicks or Asps (Bastard Demi-Culverins), Pellicans (Bastard quarter-Culverins or Sakers), Bastard Falcons, and Bastard Robinets. In the Extraordinary or Double-fortified pieces, the thickness of metal was at the touch-hole 1 calibre; at the trunnions $\frac{1}{2}$ calibre; at the muzzle $\frac{7}{16}$ calibre, and the class included Flying-dragons, Sirens, Flying-sparrows or *Passovolanti* and Sakers-, Falcons-, and Robinets-extraordinary. This of course represents the ideas of English artillerists at the conclusion of the war. The tendency was continually to increase the weight of metal, and in 1583 guns may have averaged slightly less in weight. Norton, writing in 1628, tells us that a hundred or a hundred and fifty years before his time ordnance was bad and weak because powder was weak; and that in his day they gave guns two or three times more metal to the weight of the shot than formerly. Cannon, he says, once weighed but 80 times their shot, now they weighed 200 times or more, and Culverins 300 times and small ordnance 400 times.[1]

Besides this highly technical classification there was another and more practical one, which had a real meaning to gunners in the presence of an enemy. The basis of it was the proportion of length to calibre. English artillerists formed upon it four great classes, Cannons proper or Cannons of battery, Culverins or long guns, Periers or short guns, and Mortars. Any attempt to tabulate them, however, with accurate measurements can only be misleading. Hardly two tables of the last half of the century will be found to coincide. 'Through an intolerable fault,' laments Lucar, 'of careless or unskilful gun-founders all our great pieces of one name are not of one length, nor of one weight nor of one height in their

---

[1] *The Gunner*, p. 189. Turner's remarks are obviously founded on Norton's, but he makes no acknowledgment of his original.

mouths (calibre), and therefore the gunner's books, which do show that all our great pieces of one name are of an equal length and of an equal weight and of an equal height in their mouths are erroneous.'[1] Foreign ordnance he says was worse, so this to a great extent explains the confusion of the authorities. Keeping in mind, however, the possibility of all kinds of variations from the average type, the Elizabethan guns may be taken to be typically and in round numbers as follows :

Class I. CANNONS PROPER, battering guns from 18 to 28 calibres long.

Double Cannon or *Cannon Royal*, an 8½ inch 65 pdr. M.L. 12 or 13 ft. long.

Whole Cannon, an 8 inch 60 pdr. M.L. about 11 ft. long.

Demi-Cannon, a 6½ to 7 inch 30 pdr. M.L. about 10 ft. long.

Class II. CULVERINS, from 32 to 34 calibres long.

Whole Culverin, 5 to 5½ inch M.L. 17 pdr. about 13 ft. long.

Demi-Culverin, 4½ inch M.L. 9 pdr. about 12 ft. long.

Saker, 3½ inch M.L. 5 pdr. about 11 ft. long.
Minion, 3 inch M.L. 4 pdr. about 8 ft. long.
Falcon, 2½ inch M.L. 3 pdr. about 7 ft. long.
Falconet, 2 inch M.L. 1½ pdr. about 6½ ft. long.
Robinet, 1 inch M.L. 1 pdr.
Bases, 1¼ inch B.L. about 4 ft. long (9 inch chamber).

Class III. PERIERS, from 6 to 8 calibres. These were guns something of the modern carronade or Howitzer type, intended for shooting stone-balls, carcase or case-shot, shell, fire-balls and the like. Abroad they were usually chambered with a bell-mouthed or tapering contraction of

---

[1] Tartaglia's *Colloquies, App.* Cap. 37, p. 33. Cf. Sir Geo. Carew to Sir R. Cecil, *S.P. Dom.* ccxlix. 43, July 31, 1594, where he says he cannot tell the weights of certain demi-culverins without seeing them. 'The founders never cast them so exactly, but they differ two or three cwt. in a piece, but twenty-eight cwt. is sufficient for a ship demi-culverin.'

THE NAVY OF ELIZABETH

the bore at the breech end, but English gunners preferred them not chambered.[1]

Cannon Periers, 6 in. M.L. 24 pdr.

Periers Proper, sometimes called *Demi-Cannon Periers*, probably 5 in. M.L. as they come in the lists between *Demi-Cannon* and *Culverins*.

Port Pieces, $5\frac{1}{2}$ inch B.L. with $3\frac{1}{2}$ inch chamber 16 inch long.

Stock Fowlers, probably about 4 inch B.L.

Whole Slings, $2\frac{1}{2}$ inch B.L. $2\frac{1}{2}$ pdr. length of chamber 22 in.

Three-quarter Slings, ? 2 inch B.L.

Half Slings, ? $1\frac{1}{2}$ inch B.L.

Quarter Slings, ? 1 inch B.L.[2]

Class IV. MORTAR PIECES. These were about $1\frac{1}{2}$ times their extreme calibre and were chambered to about $\frac{1}{8}$ of it. *Petards* were included in this class; also a B.L. piece called a *Murderer*, and a small brass mortar piece to which the obsolete name of *Bombard* was transferred.[3]

It should be noted that these two systems of classifi-

---

[1] Periers had not of course the special characteristics of carronades or howitzers. They are only to be compared with them as relatively light, large calibred, short range guns. Another gun to which the name of 'Curtal' was given, and which possibly more closely resembled a carronade, was known in James I.'s time, but was rejected apparently on the same grounds upon which the introduction of the carronade was opposed. 'What say you,' asks the admiral in Boteler's Fifth Dialogue, 'to the cannons called "Courtaux?"' 'I fear not to say,' replies the captain, 'that in respect of their boistrous reverse, they are both troublesome and dangerous, and in regard of their overshortness are of little or no execution beyond the common mortar piece.' It was probably a new type of gun with the old name revived, for 'Curtals,' though common under Henry VIII., occur in no Elizabethan lists. Another light piece of recent introduction called a 'Drake' Boteler condemns for the same defects. (Cf. p. 26, n.)

[2] Cecil's *Memorandum Book*, 1552-1557 (*Lansd. MSS.* 118, 6, 81), has some notes on iron ordnance in which he puts 'slings' as from $2\frac{1}{4}$ to $4\frac{1}{2}$ inches. But this is little guide to what they were thirty years later. For he puts fowlers 3 to $5\frac{1}{2}$ inches 'shooting stone,' portpieces from $5\frac{1}{2}$ to 12 inches 'shooting stone.'

[3] See 'Charge and Discharge of Brass Ordnance, 1568-1582,' *S.P. Dom.* clxxxvi. f. 23.

cation do not exhaust all the various kinds of artillery in use at the time. Sheriffe's list [1] includes a Cannon-Serpentine and a Bastard Cannon, which have no place in Norton's system. With Norton all bastard pieces are Culverins and the Serpentine is a Bastard Whole-Culverin or 5 in. gun, while Sheriffe has a piece called a Serpentine, which is a 1½ in. gun. In Henry VIII.'s time the same term is applied to some French field guns, 'three feet long or more, firing stone shot as much as a swan's egg or more,' while at Carlisle in 1539 were small ' Serpentines of brass a foot long.' [2] Again in some of the official lists of Elizabeth's appear such pieces as Culverin-, Demi-Culverin-, and Saker-Periers, names which, as crosses between the long and the short types, seem to violate every system of nomenclature and are inconceivable, but as only one of each kind is scheduled they were probably experimental pieces not adopted into the service.[3] Still it is clear that a good deal of confusion continued to prevail in the nomenclature as well as in the dimensions of guns, and that as in the naming of classes of ships no fixed system had yet taken hold.

It will have been noticed that while all the 'great-ordnance' was muzzle-loading, there were several types of guns that were not. For us in these days of a secondary armament of quick-firing and machine guns, this division of Elizabethan artillery, which was very little insisted on by the gunners of the time, is the one most replete with

[1] *S.P. Dom. Eliz.* ccxlii. f. 64, printed by Professor Laughton (*Armada*, App. C. ii. 350). Not much reliance can be placed on Sheriffe's list. From his use of the name *Cannon Pedro* instead of *Perier* it would seem he was not a highly educated man. It is also undated and probably not strictly Elizabethan at all. The small obsolete 'serpentine,' as Sheriffe places it (between 'falconets' and 'robinets'), ceases to appear in ordnance schedules after the inventory taken at the accession of Edward VI., and other similarities between these two lists suggest that they were not widely separated in date. The table given by Sir William Monson (*Naval Tracts*, p. 312) is scarcely more abreast of the times. Indeed, it seems to be but a copy of Sheriffe's list with some of his fanciful quarter-inch gradations of calibre omitted. Monson corrects *Pedro* to *Petro*.

[2] Lord Dillon in *Archæologia*, li. 219, n.

[3] 'Charge and Discharge of Brass Ordnance,' *ubi supra*.

interest. Tudor ships, it must be remembered, had besides their main chasing and broadside batteries a secondary armament in tops and cage-works. Except for the minor characteristic that they did not have fixed ammunition, these pieces, being all breech-loading and mounted on a non-recoil system, corresponded exactly in value and

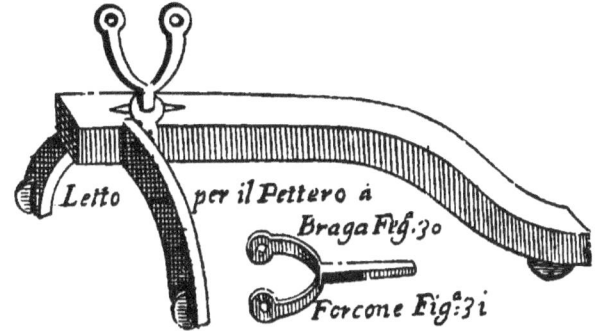

CARRIAGE OF BREECH-LOADING PIECE, SHOWING PIVOT-MOUNTING [1]

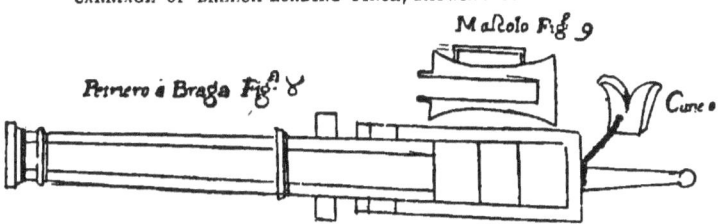

BREECH-LOADING PIECE, SHOWING THE DETACHED CHAMBER (*mascolo*) WITH 'SHOULDERING' OR 'WATER-PIPE' JOINT, AND THE 'WEDGE' OR 'COIN' (*cuneo*) FOR LOCKING IT IN POSITION [2]

From Trattato dell' Artiglieria di Tomaso Moretti. Brescia 1672, 4to. [plate opp. p. 20]

conception to the machine and quick-firing guns which have been so recently introduced into the service. Their

[1] This is not the carriage of the English sea service as described by Norton, see *post*, p. 369.

[2] This is not a true breech-loading perier, as known to English gunners, for it is considerably over 8 calibres in length. Moreover, the English breech-loading periers (portpieces and fowlers) had four square tenons on the chase instead of trunnions. (Norton, *The Gunner*, p. 58.) Its proportions are those of the sling.

breech action was an improvement on that of the bombard. Instead of the chamber being wedged into the bed, the piece was furnished with what was called a 'tail' to receive it. This was a kind of stout stirrup welded on the gun by means of two check-pieces, which enfolded the barrel on each side from the trunnions to the breech. Across the under side of the 'tail' or stirrup a thin curved bar prevented the chamber falling through when laid in its place. In contradistinction to the 'chamber' or powder case, the gun itself thus furnished was called the 'hall,' and in the lists we find scheduled 'port piece-halls' and 'fowler-halls,' with their complement of 'port piece-chambers' and 'fowler-chambers.' The process of loading was very much like that of a bombard, except that the fore-end of the chamber was finished with a 'shouldering,' so that it made what was called a 'water-pipe' joint with the breech, and it was locked in its place by means of an iron wedge driven in behind it or by a 'forelock' which passed through slots cut in each side of the stirrup.[1] 'Every chamber piece,' says Lucar, 'ought to have three chambers, and when a gunner will give fire to a chamber piece he ought not to stand on that side of the piece where the wedge of iron is put to lock the chamber of the piece, because the said wedge may through the discharge of the piece fly out and kill the gunner.' 'Being discharged,' says Norton,[2] 'these chambers are to be taken out and filled again and others to be put in ready charged in the place thereof.' Comparative rapidity of fire was regarded as one of their chief advantages. One kind, called a 'Harquebus-à-croc,' could be fired, Norton tells us, 300 times a day or nearly once every two minutes.[3]

[1] Tartaglia's *Colloquies*, App. chap. 53.
[2] *The Gunner*, p. 58.
[3] It should be noted that in saying this, he is speaking of the endurance of the gun, not of its extreme possibilities in rapidity of fire. It is possible, therefore, it could be fired much more rapidly for a short time. As to the muzzle loading pieces, Turner tells us that the cannon could fire eight times an hour, the demi-cannon ten times, the quarter cannon twelve times, while 3-pdr. field-pieces, which were falcons, could fire 15 times an hour.

The patterns most in use under Wynter's administration were portpieces, fowlers, slings, bases, and murderers, and they were of three main types. Portpieces and fowlers, as we have seen, belonged to the perier class. Portpieces having a 5½ inch barrel and chambers of only 3½ inches must have been intended for stone shot and 'carcases.' Fowlers, the 'Nomenclator Navalis'[1] tells us, fired case. These were the two heaviest patterns, and to secure their non-recoil they had a very elaborate mounting which Norton thus describes : ' Instead of round trunnions there are four square tenons cast, joining with the side of the chase[2] of the piece, on either side two : which being let into the block or carriage holdeth the whole fast therein, leaving the Cornish [that is, the cornice or muzzle reinforce] lying upon the edge of the ship's port and triced up with a rope fastened about the muzzle. The tail of the carriage is to rest, and to be shored up with an upright post or foot full of holes to slide up and down in a square mortise fitted thereunto, having a shiver [that is, a grooved pulley-wheel] at the lower end thereof, with two trestle legs mortised before under the block of the carriage. The foot with holes hath a pin to stay the piece on any monture [elevation] assigned.'[3] Slings and bases, on the other hand, were long pieces of the culverin class, the sling being a 2½ inch 2½ pounder with a chamber 22 inches long, and the base a 1¼ inch piece with an inch chamber 9 inches long carrying a 6 oz. ball ; but they were also used with ' base, burr, musket, and other kinds of murdering shot put up in bags or lanthorns.' These lighter patterns had a simple swivel mounting 'upon a forked prop or pintle [pivot] upon the ends of which the trunnions rest,' and they were aimed similarly to a modern light quick-

[1] *Add. MSS.* 21,575, *anno* 1625.
[2] The 'chase' of a gun is the exterior surface between the ring in front of the trunnions and the ring where the swell of the muzzle begins ; or as a gunner of the time would have said, 'the superficies between the Trunnion Ring and the Cornish ring.' (See John Roberts, *Compleat Cannoniere or Gunner's Guide*, London, 1639, p. 25.)
[3] *Op. cit.* 58.

firer, with 'a long stern-handle of iron' forged in one with the butt of the 'tail.'[1] A double or great base, which seems to have been the pattern preferred in the English service,[2] was probably a 2 or 2½ inch piece. The third type of quick-firing gun was the murderer, which, as we have seen, belonged to the mortar class. Though not in Wynter's list it was certainly used at the time or soon after, if not in the Navy, certainly by English privateers. In speaking of the danger of fire from using the great ordnance after you have laid any enemy aboard both Sir William Monson and Sir Richard Hawkins commend their use. We have seen that an admitted defect of the flush-decked ship, Monson considered, was that she could not carry these pieces. 'As I have said,' Monson writes, 'such a ship that has neither fore-castle, copperidge-head, nor any other manner of defence, hath no fowlers, which are pieces of great importance, after a ship is boarded and entered or lieth board and board; for the ordnance stands her in little stead. . . . but a murderer or fowler being shot out of their own ship, laden with dice-shot, will scour the deck of the enemy and not suffer the head of a man to appear.'[3] Sir Richard Hawkins has a similar passage: 'All that which hath been spoken of the danger of the artillery in boarding is not to be wrested or interpreted to cut off utterly the use of all artillery after boarding, but rather I hold nothing more convenient in ships of war than fowlers and great-bases in the cage-works and murderers in cobridge-heads, for that their execution and speedy charging and discharging is of great moment.'[4] Bourne is particularly explicit on

---

[1] Norton, p. 58.
[2] See Wynter's report (*infra*, p. 372 n.), and Hawkins's *Observations*, p. 293.
[3] *Naval Tracts*, p. 327.
[4] A cobridge-, couperidge- or cubbridge-head was any bulkhead, but especially the bulkhead of the forecastle called the 'cobridge-head afore,' and the bulkhead of the half-deck called the 'cobridge-head abaft.' *Nomenclator Navalis*, 1625, *Add. MSS.* 21,575; *Monson*, p. 316; Nathaniel Boteler, *Six Dialogues about Sea Services*, 1685 (but written temp. Jac. I.).

the point. 'If the enemy mean to enter,' he says, 'give level on the scuttles [hatchways] where the men must come up with your Fowlers, Slings, and Bases, for there you shall be sure to do most good. . . . If you do mean to enter him then give level with your Fowlers and Portpieces, where you do see his chiefest fight [i.e. close-fight or stronghold] of his ship, and especially be sure to have them charged and shoot them off at the first boarding; for then your guns are sure to speed, and furthermore mark where his men have most recourse and there discharge your Fowlers and Bases.'[1]

From these passages it is clear the whole secondary armament was intended primarily for close quarters; the two pieces of the perier type being specially for breaking in the enemy's close-fights and the murderers for clearing the waist of boarders when your own vessel was entered. The culverin types seem to have been mounted chiefly in the tops, and both were much used in arming pinnaces and boats. The whole class of breech-loading guns, however, seems to have soon lost favour. The reason is not clear, but doubtless it was due in a great measure to the growing importance of artillery attack in naval actions, and the general adoption of the new type of vessel in which the best positions for the secondary armament disappeared. Writing after 1593, Sir Richard Hawkins says: 'Many I know have left the use of them and of sundry other preventions as of "shere-hooks," stones in the tops, and arming them, . . . but upon what inducement I cannot relate, unless it be because they never knew their effects and benefit.'[2] Norton in 1628 says 'Portingale or Portugal bases' still lingered in use, but chiefly for small vessels.[3]

Up to the Armada campaign, however, they were freely used and considered essential to a proper armament. Attempts were even made quite early to apply a better breech-loading mechanism for great ordnance. Norton in dealing with obsolete guns speaks of a chambered

[1] *The Arte of Shooting in Great Ordnance*, p. 55.
[2] *Observations*, p. 293.   [3] *The Gunner*, cap. iv. p. 41.

cannon-perier, the chamber of which, he says, 'is made of a piece by itself screwed into the chase and hath trunnions, but by reason of the great trouble to screw it, the same is also out of fashion.'[1]

With this general view of the artillery of the time it is possible, by the light of the various reports on the naval ordnance that exist, to get a fairly clear idea of the types of guns in ordinary use for the sea-service of Elizabeth.[2] The following table taken from the ordnance report of 1585

Name	Class	Tons	Battery			Q.F.	Composition of Heavy Battery [3]
			Heavy	Light	Total		
Elizabeth Jonas	great-ship	900	34	16	50	26	D.C., C.P., Cl., D.Cl.
Triumph . . .	„	1,000	34	8	42	26	,,
Bear	galleon	900	44	12	56	26	,,
Victory . . .	great-ship	800	30	6	36	28	,,
Hope	,,	600	20	8	28	22	,,
Marie Rose . .	,,	600	20	8	28	12	,,
Nonpareil . .	galleon	500	16	14	30	22	,,
Lion	,,	600	22	8	30	22	,,
Revenge . . .	,,	500	22	12	34	12	,,
Bonaventure .	great-ship	600	20	10	30	22	,,
Dreadnought .	,,	400	16	8	24	18	C.P., Cl., D.Cl.
Swiftsure . .	,,	400	14	12	26	16	,,
Antelope . . .	galleon	400	10	10	20	18	,,
Swallow . . .	,,	360	6	16	22	18	,,
Foresight . .	,,	300	12	12	24	12	Cl. & D.Cl.
Aid	,,	250	2	17	19	19	D.Cl.
Bull	,,	200	6	11	17	8	,,
Tiger	great-ship	200	7	12	19	4	,,
Scout	galleon	120	—	18	18	8	—
Achates . . .	pinnace or galleon	100	—	16	16	6	
Merlin . . .	pinnace	20	—	8	8	4	—

[1] *The Gunner*, cap. iv. p. 41.
[2] See 'Charge and Discharge of Brass Ordnance,' *ubi supra*, and especially Sir William Wynter's report, March 23, 1586. *S.P. Dom.* clxxxvii. 44; also 'Brass ordnance remaining XIV^{mo} of Her Majesty's reign in the Tower of London, Her Highnesses ships, on Chatham wharf, at Upnor Castle and Woolwich, with a note what Brass Ordnance have been provided and bought and cast of her Majesty's metal from the year aforesaid unto XXV^{mo}, [i.e. 1572-3 to 1582-3]. This paper may have been an outcome of the commission on which Drake was sitting.
[3] D.C. = Demi-cannon, 30-pdr. C.P. = Cannon perier, 24-pdr. Cl. = Culverin, 17-pdr. D.Cl. = Demi-cuvlerin, 9-pdr.

shows the guns which some years previously Sir William Wynter had considered necessary for the armament of the Navy as it then existed. For simplicity the various types of guns which he specifies have been grouped into three classes. Demi-cannons, cannons-perier, culverins, and demi-culverins are classed as 'Heavy Battery Guns : ' sakers, minions, falcons, and falconets as 'Light Battery Guns.' The quick-firing pieces form the third class, but it must be borne in mind that this classification is quite arbitrary and was not recognised in Tudor times.

In the first place it is to be noted that the heaviest piece carried is the 30-pounder demi-cannon, and this only by vessels of 500 tons and upwards. The cannon has been condemned for the sea-service ; and henceforth this rule was seldom departed from, for Monson tells us that in his time no ship commonly carried greater pieces than a demi-cannon. In the next place we see the cannon-perier (the equivalent of a 24-pounder carronade) still retaining its favour and allowed to vessels of over 350 tons burden. The 300-ton class has nothing heavier than the 17-pounder culverin, while the smallest class of capital ship is restricted to the 9-pounder demi-culverin. The secondary armament comprises in all the vessels the two quick-firing periers (port-pieces and fowlers) and the quick-firing culverin or base. Whether Wynter's scheme of armament was ever carried out we do not know, but in 1585 all the ships show a departure from his recommendations and most of them show a gun power considerably under his ideal. This no doubt was not entirely due to neglect,·but in part at least to the decision which seems to have been taken about this time to re-arm the whole of the Navy with brass guns. A report of 1582 tells us how far the process had gone by that time. Large purchases of brass battery guns had been made since 1569, and nearly all are in the culverin class, as though there was a growing tendency towards guns of long range and high penetration. Of iron battery guns little more than fifty remained, while the brass pieces numbered 632. Turning to the secondary armament, it appears that the gun-founders' energies had been devoted almost entirely to producing fowlers. Iron pieces of this class number 69 to 110 brass; portpieces 70 to 10. No bases or slings had been made at all. The increasing importance of battery guns, or in other words the tendency towards preferring artillery attack to boarding, which had been in progress since Henry VIII.'s time, is further emphasised by Wynter's report that in 1567 he returned to the Tower as unserviceable no less than 334 iron quick-firing pieces of which 232 were bases, and a few years later as many more of which 175 were bases. The proportion, therefore, of secondary to battery pieces must have been very high at that time.

As to the actual form of armament eventually decided on, as the result of the Commission on which Drake was sitting, we unfortunately have no definite knowledge. Wynter's original scheme seems to have been taken at least as the basis; for the report of 1585 contains a return of the guns wanting to bring the figures up to his estimate. The only change distinctly recognised is in the case of the 'bases.' These are returned as obsolete, 'not in use,' and there is a suggestion that 'muskets' should be substituted.[1] Brass bases, however, were subsequently turned out successfully, and the quick-firing culverin was restored as a recognised arm of the service.

Still the original scheme can only have been taken as a basis; for in the same report Wynter gives a scheme for arming certain new and rebuilt ships which shows he was

---

[1] These 'muskets' were not small arms, but recognised pieces of breech-loading artillery. They are thus classed by Cataneo, who calls them *moschetti da bracca* or 'muskets with a breech-piece.' He says they fired a one pound ball with half a pound of powder, and gives an elaborate description of the method of loading them. The system was very like that of portpieces and bases. The *bracca* or 'tail' was of 'stirrup' type. They were mounted on some non-recoil principle, probably a mere pivot, and Cataneo contrasts them with M.L. pieces on wheeled carriages. They were probably akin to Norton's Harquebus-à-croc, if not identical with it

AN ELIZABETHAN GREAT-SHIP OR GALLEON.

Showing secondary armament in the cubbridge-heads fore and aft. From Visscher's Series, circ. 1588

tending to an increased weight of battery. In the 'Tiger,' which was new building, the comparison is as under.

—	Culv.	d-culv.	Saker	Minion	Falcon	Q.F.
Estimate of 1569 . . .	0	6	10	2	2	8
Armament in 1585 . . .	0	7	7	4	1	4
Estimate of 1586 . . .	4	8	8	0	2	8

For two new galleons he proposes 8 demi-cannon, 10 culverins, 14 demi-culverins, 4 light pieces, and 18 quick-firing. These vessels were the 'Vanguard' and 'Rainbow,' much of the same dimensions as the 'Lion,' though of the new low free-board type, and they were rated like her at 500 tons. Wynter's armament for the 'Lion' was 4 demi-cannon, 4 cannon-perier, 6 culverins, 8 demi-culverins, 8 light pieces, and 22 quick-firing pieces. The new galleons, therefore, were to be given a heavy battery of 32 pieces against the old one's 22 and their secondary armament reduced to suit their design. A new 'bark' or small galleon (the 'Tramontana') of 150 tons is to have 4 heavy guns and 8 light ones against the 18 light pieces of the older 'Scout,' which was only 30 tons smaller. Even the new pinnaces, which registered over 50 tons, were given a demi-culverin. The tendency then is clearly towards increasing the weight of the battery. Wynter's estimate of 1569, we may therefore presume, was much under the complement with which the war was actually fought, and as we advance, evidence that this was certainly the case will increase upon us.

If a broad picture be desired of the force of the Elizabethan war-ships, we may think of the largest class of great-ships, like the 'Triumph,' as from 40 to 45-gun ships with a secondary armament of 25 to 30 guns; of the second-class galleons, such as the 'Lion' and 'Revenge,' as, say, 34-gun ships with a secondary armament of 20 guns; of the 200-ton type, like the 'Tiger,' as of 20-gun ships with 10 secondary pieces; and of the pinnaces either as gun-boats with one long chaser and two smaller guns, or as 8-gun sloops, all well furnished with 'quick-firers.' Comparing, then, the ships of Drake with the ships of Nelson, we find them on the whole considerably smaller but more heavily armed for their size. Elizabeth's largest great-ships, such as the 'Bear' and the 'Triumph,' were about the same tonnage as the 44-gun frigate of George III., and none were as large as his smallest ships-of-the-line. The first 'Victory' was the size of a 36-gun frigate. Yet even before the increase of armament the 'Bear' had 56 guns in battery and the 'Victory' 36, besides their powerful secondary armament. The 'Elizabeth Bonaventure,' which before the Armada became a 38-gun ship, was no bigger than a 28-gun frigate; and in Nelson's time there was no frigate so small as the 'Revenge.' [1]

Of projectiles for the sea-service there was great variety. The plain iron round-shot was that most generally employed, but for close quarters free use was made of stone balls, 'carcasses' or iron frames like lanterns filled with stones or bullets, case-shot, chain- and bar-shot, and many other kinds. To what were called fireworks the English attached great importance, and the text-books of the time give a large variety of directions for making shells or grenades, both plain and shrapnel, to be shot out of great ordnance or mortar-pieces and to explode by means of a fuse; illuminating shells for detecting an enemy's movements at night; shells containing 'wild-fire' of all kinds that would burn in water and was only extinguishable with sand or ashes; besides a number of other devices for damaging and firing an

[1] How little gunnery had advanced since Elizabeth's time until the quite recent introduction of rifled ordnance is shown in the armament of the 'Prince Albert,' a four-decker of 110 guns and 3,760 tons, which was launched in 1854 and was considered the most heavily gunned ship of her time. Her armament was mainly of 32-pounders, which were about equivalent to the Elizabethan demi-cannons. She had but sixteen 8-in. guns, equal to whole cannons, and one 5-ton, 69-pounder bow-chaser with an extreme range of three miles. A cannon-royal, which was the Elizabethan 65-pounder, weighed a little over $3\frac{1}{2}$ tons and had a random range of nearly two miles. The 15-pounder basilisk had a random range of 3,000 paces or 3 miles (1,000 paces = 1 mile. Monson, p. 311). What improvement there was in power seems due entirely to the better quality of the powder and improved boring.

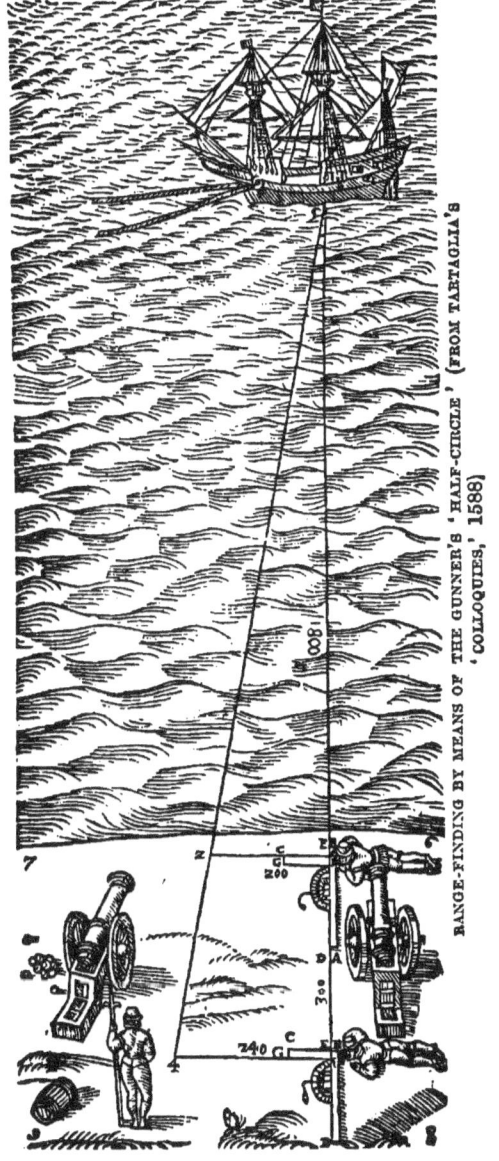

RANGE-FINDING BY MEANS OF THE GUNNER'S 'HALF-CIRCLE' (FROM TARTAGLIA'S 'COLLOQUES,' 1588)

enemy's rigging. A curious kind of projectile for smal arms should also be mentioned, since it was in great favour with English seamen, and apparently a secret of our service. This was a short arrow fired from a musket. A wooden plug or 'tampkin' was driven in on the top of the powder and the arrow then inserted. Thus used they had extraordinary penetration and easily passed through musket-proof defences.[1]

As great guns were not bored, but simply cast round a core, which the English gun-founders seem to have been specially accurate in adjusting, and as a quarter inch windage was allowed between the diameter of the shot and that of the bore, shooting cannot have been very accurate. Still gunnery was taught on thoroughly scientific principles. Guns were not usually sighted at the foundries, but the treatises contain rules for what was called 'disparting' or finding the true sighting. The degree of elevation was ascertained by means of an instrument called a 'gunner's quadrant.' It was like a carpenter's square with one long arm which was put down the barrel of the gun while the shorter arm was left to hang downwards. From the angle of the square hung a plumb-line, and by this means the gunner could read off the elevation of his piece upon a graduated quadrant fixed between the two arms. These quadrants and a similar instrument called a gunner's 'half-circle' could also be used as range-finders both afloat and ashore.[2]

So scientific, indeed, was the system that a supply of gunners was one of the chief difficulties of the Admiralty. Shortly before the Navy Commission was appointed particular attention was drawn to this serious flaw in the scheme of mobilisation. In 1582 a petition was presented to the Privy Council praying for a renewal of the Charter of the Fraternity of Artillery, with additional powers

[1] Hawkins, *Observations*, sec. lxvi. Drake had 1,000 of them on the 'Revenge' in 1588. See Laughton, *Armada*, i. 126, and *Accounts, &c.* (*Exch. Q.R.*) Bundle lxiv. 9, April 30.
[2] Tartaglia's *Colloquies, Appendix*, chap. 117.

and privileges in order to enable them to deal with the
question. Power was asked to examine all candidates
for the rank of Master-Gunner in the Navy. One gunner
to every twenty tons the petitioners considered a proper
proportion, and to ensure an adequate supply of trained
men they proposed that at every sea port an official

DEPRESSION RANGE-FINDING (FROM TARTAGLIA'S 'COLLOQUIES,' 1588)

register should be kept of men qualified or desiring to
serve as gunners and that copies of these registers should
be deposited with the Fraternity every Easter. They
further recommend that merchantmen, for every two
guns aboard, should be ordered to carry one seafaring
man who was a scholar, in order that he might be
instructed in the art of gunnery, and that an allowance
of powder should be made from the Government Stores

for the purpose of his training.[1] Whether the petition was granted, is not known, but Raleigh tells us that in 1588 the supply of gunners was still lamentably deficient. Forty-gun ships, he says, were fought with no more than twenty gunners, though each piece required four to handle it properly.[2] Still the existence of the petition goes to show the methodical way in which the sea-officers were going about the organisation of the Navy, though the only permanent establishment for the naval ordnance seems to have been a master-gunner and four under-gunners.[3]

The general manning of the Navy was done on the same system which obtained when an army was required. It was known as 'Pressing' or 'Taking-up,' and on the whole it worked very smoothly. It had nothing akin to the 'press-gang' of the eighteenth century, but was rather a system of compulsory naval service enforced on all seamen by a kind of conscription. The procedure was to issue from the Admiralty precepts to local officers directing them to summon all seamen before them and to serve so many of them as the precept required with notice to proceed by a certain day to the headquarters of the fleet, usually Gillingham. For this purpose each of the conscripts was furnished with money for his outfit and journey, called 'coat and conduct money,' and also with a detailed itinerary of the most direct road to the rendez-vous, with the proper sleeping places and other necessary information.[4]

The pay of seamen, though often received irregularly, was good. Up till 1585 every man received six and eight-pence a lunar month, or nearly threepence a day, equivalent to about two shillings of our 'money. As they were only engaged for a short period there was of course no pension; but they had a free kit, ample rations, and

---

[1] *S.P. Dom.* clvii. f. 42.
[2] *Observations on the Navy,* 'Of Great Ordnance,' Works, viii. 342.
[3] *S.P. Dom.* clvii. f. 42.
[4] Robert Humphrey's *Naval Miscellany.* MS. in the Pepysian Library.

certain clearly defined rights of loot aboard prizes. Seeing that an able seaman's pay is now one and sevenpence, this was fairly generous. Yet so great was the demand for seamen by the merchants and so attractive service aboard privateers, that it did not prove enough to attract or keep the best men, who bribed themselves clear or deserted at the first opportunity. In 1588 therefore Hawkins proposed an increase to ten shillings a month. He argued that twenty-five high class men, ' such as can shift for themselves, keep themselves clean, without vermin and noisomeness which breedeth sickness and mortality,' and who knew their duty, were worth thirty 'tag and rag,' and that the proposed increase would therefore cost no more, especially as then the admiralty could insist upon each man bringing his own sword and dagger.[1]

His suggestion was therefore adopted; but even this high rate of pay did not long suffice. Both Monson and Raleigh complain that the queen's ships were worse manned than any, and that privateering was so much more profitable and popular than service in the Royal Navy, that all officials concerned from captains to mustermasters were able to make money ' by putting the best and ablest men in their pockets.'[2]

The method of manning the galleys is more obscure. The punishment of condemning criminals to the benches was unknown to the common law, and the tenderness everyone felt in meddling with so sacred an institution probably had a good deal to do with the fact that no regular system of galley slaves was ever established. That criminals were sometimes employed, however, there is some reason to believe. In 1513, after the disastrous attack on Prégent's galleys at Conquêt, Sir Edward Howard dispatched a pressing demand for convicts to be employed in the fleet. Again on February 30, 1551, the Council ordered the Lord Admiral to report on the

[1] Laughton, *Armada, App. D.* ii. 352, and *Introduction,* I. lxx.
[2] Monson, *Naval Tracts,* p. 343 ; Raleigh, *Observations on the Navy,* ' Ot Mustering,' Works, viii. 346.

money that was due 'to galley men and touching the galleys, that the same may be discharged out of hand, considering they are of great charge to the King and serve indeed to little purpose,' and accordingly on March 30 a warrant was issued to Sir Edward Peckham 'to pay unto Mr. Gunstone £231 12s. for the charge of the galleys and £55 to be divided equally among the "Forsatts."'[1] But these men appear to have been captured French *forçats* or galley-slaves, and they therefore afford no real evidence one way or the other. If the system had ever regularly existed it had certainly fallen into desuetude; for in this reforming year 1582 there is evidence of an idea of re-establishing it. It is a draft order intended apparently to be addressed to the Justices in Eyre, 'Trusty and well beloved,' it reads, 'we greet you well. Forasmuch as we have occasion for service in our galleys to have certain numbers of men to remain and row in the said galleys, the labour whereof is very great and painful and therefore in many other countries is appointed for a great penalty; we have thought meet at this present to require you, that at such gaol delivery as shall at the next assizes be made before you, you shall use such considerations that such as you shall think for the quality of their crimes or offences neither meet to be put to death nor yet to full liberty may be reprieved and committed to the gaol, with charge to the Sheriff and keeper of the gaol to stay them until we or our Privy Council may be certified thereof and by the advice of the Admiral the same may be sent for to be committed as prisoners to our galleys; And amongst them we do not mean to have any stayed that have committed wilful murder, burglaries, sacrilege or divers and manifest robberies, thinking it very meet that no reprieve be had for the saving of such from execution &c.'[2] Whether

---

[1] *Extracts from the Council Book relating to Naval Affairs*, MS. in the Pepysian Library.

[2] *S.P. Dom. Eliz.* clvii. 38. The paper is assigned to 1582, but there seems no internal evidence of its date beyond the fact that Burghley has

this curious order was ever put in force we cannot tell, but in any case there can be no doubt that as a rule galleys in England on the rare occasions when they were put in commission were rowed by free labour. In most if not all the Navy estimates that we have, the galley crews are calculated on the same scale as the others, and in Drake's time, when the Queen had but one galley, it was called the 'Bonavolia,' a name which seems to have no signification except as an indication that its rowers were free men, *rematori di bonavoglia* being the technical term in the Italian services for men who had voluntarily enlisted for the benches.[1]

The bulk of the officers were provided in much the same way as the men. As yet there was no regular establishment as we understand it. In James I.'s time Raleigh was urging vainly, that young gentlemen who were the king's sworn servants should be sent to sea to be trained, but even this was only with a view to providing capable captains. From time immemorial the subordinate officers such as the master, master-gunner and boatswain had been chosen like the seamen from hand to mouth, and except in cases where seamen had raised themselves to an exceptional position the command of ships was given to noblemen and gentlemen, who often had little knowledge of the naval art. With the exception possibly of the lieutenant, a rank introduced about the end of Elizabeth's reign[2] for large ships, all his subordinates were rather warrant- and petty-officers, than what we understand by commissioned officers to-day. They were regarded as seamen and paid the same wage, only that to each ship was given a certain number of 'dead-shares,' or pay for men who did not exist, and to the warrant- and petty-officers these 'dead-shares' were

been trying a pen on the back of it. The scheme is again referred to in Burghley's State Paper on national defence which he drew up in February 1584. (*S.P. Dom.* clxviii. 3.)

[1] *Gugli*motti, iii. 283.

[2] Monson, p. 307. The master, however, was a quarter-deck officer; that is, his place was 'abaft the mast' (*ibid.* 312).

allotted in various proportions, as pay for the office they exercised. The master and master-gunner—and this is eloquent of the importance attached to the guns—were placed on a footing and each received one 'dead-share.' The boatswain's share is unknown. Quartermasters had a half-share, ordinary gunners a third. All these officers had one or two mates who probably also received something above common pay. Besides the 'dead-shares' the officers were also allotted 'rewards' on some elastic system that is not clear, and had special rights of plunder attached to their several ranks.

As to uniforms, there were no prescribed regulations, and as coat money was issued instead of a free-kit men were able to dress as they liked. Still at a time when costumes were more regarded than in modern times, some degree of uniformity was probably attained. It was in any case the custom for the crew of the cock-boat and the coxswain to be 'able and handsome men well-clothed and all in one livery,' and for the trumpeter to have a tabard and trumpet-banner of his commander's colours.[1]

The interior discipline of the ship, as Sir Richard Hawkins describes it,[2] was much what it remained in the English service down to our own times—purely maritime and without a trace of military influence. Under the captain the chief officer was the master, whose general duties were 'the guide and disposing of the sailors with the tackling of the ship and the works that belong thereto within board and without;' he was, in short, the captain's lieutenant, when no lieutenant was specially appointed. In small vessels he commanded, and in most cases, and probably always where there was also a lieutenant, he was the navigating officer. In other cases a special navigating officer was appointed called the pilot, whose duty was 'to look carefully to the steerage of the ship: to be watchful in taking the heights of sun and star, to note the way of his ship, with the augmenting and lessening of the wind,

[1] Monson, p. 318.   [2] *Observations*, p. 275.

&c.' The next in degree of the seaman-staff was the boatswain, whose special charge was the rigging and boats. His duty was to see 'his ship kept clean; his masts, yards and tacklings well coated, matted and armed; his shrouds and stays well set; his sails repaired, and sufficiently prevented with martnets, blayles and casketts [that is, leach-lines, brails and gaskets], his boat fitted with sail, oars, thwarts, tholes "danyd," windles and rother [windlass and rudder]; his anchors well buoyed, safely stopped, and secured.' There was a steward, who had charge of the provisions and served out rations. In cases where there was a purser, the steward was his deputy. The carpenter's special duties were 'to view the masts and yards, the sides of the ship, her deckes, and cabins, her pumps and boat.' The other petty officers were the four quartermasters, each with his 'squadron of the watch,' the cooper, the coxswain, and the trumpeter. Independent of all these and ranking, as we have seen, as one of the chief officers of the ship was the gunner, who was responsible for the guns, small-arms, ammunition, and fireworks, and was instructed to have special regard to the 'britching and tackling of his artillery': for when small ships were so heavily armed the danger from guns breaking loose was a captain's great anxiety in bad weather.[1] In action the gunner seems to have been entitled to a certain extent to control the ship. Monson tells us, 'a principal thing in a gunner at sea is to be a good helmsman and to call to him at helm to loof or bear up to have his better level and to observe the heaving and setting of the sea.' Every officer was directly responsible to the captain for his own department and supreme in it. To them a good captain addressed all his orders personally, and never gave an order to a subordinate except in cases of urgency, and all orders as far as possible were secret and in writing. These were the strict rights of the various officers, but everything seems to have been subject to the admirable understanding that each must be ready

[1] Cf. Monson, *Naval Tracts*, p. 458.

to sacrifice his privileges to the will of his superior officer and cheerily to undertake any duty outside his office that was put upon him. The same readiness to be useful was expected of the soldiers or marines aboard. They too were under a non-commissioned officer with the rank of corporal, except of course in mixed expeditions where their numbers were large. But as marines they were considered in every way as part of the ship's crew and subject to the orders of the superior sea-officers.

To this excellent tradition born of the practical necessities of the sea the English service no doubt owed much of its efficiency. With the Spaniards all was different. Their sea discipline was cast in a military form and hidebound with limitations that, excellent as they were on land, were fetters afloat. A Spanish ship was organised like a fortress and its company divided into three distinct bodies—soldiers, mariners, and gunners—with the soldier element supreme. 'The soldiers,' says Sir Richard Hawkins, ' ward and watch and the officers in every ship [make the] round as if they were ashore. This is the only task they undergo except cleaning their arms, in which they are not over curious.' In like manner the gunners were especially exempted ' from all labour and care except about the artillery.' 'The mariners,' he goes on, ' are but as slaves to the rest, to moil and toil day and night, and those but few and bad and not suffered to sleep or harbour themselves under the decks. For in fair or foul weather, in storms, sun or rain, they must pass void of covert or succour,' or in other words they are exactly in a soldier's eyes on the level of galley-slaves. Of the officers, he says, 'there is ordinarily in every ship of war a captain, whose charge is that of masters with us ; and also a captain of the soldiers, who commandeth the captain of the ship, the soldiers, gunners and mariners in her. . . . They have their *maestros de campo*, sergeant, and master-general or captain of the artillery, with their *alfere* major and all other officers, as in a camp.'[1] 'If they come to fight with

[1] *Maestro de campo* at this time was the rank of the man who com-

another *armado* [ship-of-war] they order themselves as in a battle by land; in a vanguard, rearward, main-battle and wings, &c. In every particular ship the soldiers are all set upon the decks; their forecastle they account their head-front or vanguard of their company; that abaft the mast the rearward; and the waist the main-battle, wherein they place their principal force and on which they principally rely; which they call the *plaza de armas* or place of arms, which taken their hope is lost. Their gunners fight not but with their great artillery: the mariners attend only to the tackling of the ship and handling of the sails, and are unarmed and subject to all misfortunes; not permitted to shelter themselves, but to be still aloft, whether it be necessary or needless. So ordinarily those which first fail are the mariners and sailors of which they have greater need. They use few close-fights or fire-works; and all this proceedeth, as I judge, by error of placing land-captains for governors and commanders at sea; where they seldom understand what is to be done or commanded.'

The picture is no doubt coloured adversely by the professional contempt that Hawkins felt for the system, yet in its main lines it is true. It was the military system of the galley applied to the sailing ship, and again serves to indicate the radical and organic difference between the two methods which were now nearing their great trial of strength. In organisation, as in form, the English war-ship was a development of the round-ship; the Spanish betrayed in every feature its descent from the galley. Each had the defects and qualities of its parentage, and even Hawkins admits that in discipline

manded a *tertia*, as a Colonel commanded a regiment. Before it was so specialised it meant the chief of a staff, at this time called *Maestro de campo generale*. *Sergente* or sergeant was also a staff rank equivalent to adjutant. The rank was afterwards called 'sergeant-major' (whence our 'major'), when the word 'sergeant' was taken for the non-commissioned rank. *Alfiero* before the introduction of lieutenants was the second officer of a company (Shakespeare's 'ancient'; Modern, 'ensign'). *Alfiero major* indicates a staff rank.

the Spanish service was superior to his own. In the stirring sense of individual responsibility, in initiative, and adaptability it was inferior.

In organisation, then, the Spaniards were as far behind the English as they were in comprehension of the naval art and in the material for its exercise. Elizabethan literature constantly sounds the note of sturdy contempt with which Englishmen regarded the newly introduced rapier, when they saw it reduce their honest old swordplay to a farce. Yet they hardly recognised that when England stood face to face with the adversary on whose disasters she was to build her greatness, it was she who held the rapier. Nor is it just to a warlike nation that had nothing but the time honoured weapon to bring into the field, not to remember that Spain entered upon the contest at a technical disadvantage that no height of chivalry or courage or devotion could countervail.

APPENDICES

APPENDIX A

BIRTH, PARENTAGE, AND EARLY YEARS

I

THE evidence for the date of Drake's birth is as follows:
1. The dates on the portraits.
The Buckland Abbey portrait has the inscription 'Ætatis suæ 53, A.D. 1594,' giving 1540-1.
Lord Derby's miniature has 'Ætatis suæ 42, A.D. 1581,' giving 1538-9.
The Dutch engraving, has 'Ætatis suæ 43.' The original is generally supposed to have been painted when he visited Holland in the autumn of 1586, which would give 1542-3. The inscription, however, refers to no exploit later than 1580, though in 1586 he had just returned from his famous 'Indies Voyage.' There is evidence, too, that he paid a later visit to Holland before his last expedition, so that even if the original was painted there, the portrait proves nothing.
Another Dutch Portrait, published in 1596, has the legend 'Ætatis suæ 46,' giving 1539-40. (See 'Western Antiquary,' iv. p. 236.)
2. A passage in Stowe's 'Annals': 'At the age of eighteen he was made purser of a ship to Biscay; at twenty years of age he went to Guinea; at twenty-two he was made captain of the 'Judith' at Saint Juan de Ulloa.' This last appointment was made between January 1568, when according to Hartop's narrative of the expedition (Arber's 'English Garner,' vol. v.) Drake was still in command of the 'Grace of God,' a Portuguese

prize, and August of the same year, at which time Hawkins's squadron was at San Juan de Ulua. If he was twenty-two in 1568 he was born in 1545-6.

3. A passage in 'Sir Francis Drake Revived' (see *post*, App. D) according to which he and all his crew, except one, were under thirty in May 1572 when his expedition to Nombre de Dios sailed. This would put the date of his birth after May 1542.

The evidence as to the portraits then is conflicting and valueless, and contradicted by the family narrative. Stowe, who on all matters connected with Drake's early life is very accurate, is quite explicit, and there seems no adequate reason to reject his statement. On the other hand it is in some way confirmed by the fact that Sir Francis Russell, who was his godfather, was only seventeen years old in 1545. Had Drake been born much earlier Russell would have been quite a boy when he was christened, and it does not seem to have been usual for boys to stand as sponsors. The only reason for fixing on an earlier date seems to be a statement in the 'Inquisitio post mortem' that Thomas his youngest brother was 'forty or more' when Drake died in 1596, but this is too vague to weigh against Stowe's explicit statement.

II

The evidence as to his parentage and early years is as follows:

1. A passage in Camden's 'Annals,' *sub anno* 1580. 'This Drake (to relate no more than what I have heard from himself) was born of mean parentage (*mediocri loco natus* in the Latin edition) and had Francis Russell (afterward Earl of Bedford) for his godfather, who according to the custom gave him his Christian name. Whilst he was yet a child (*dum adhuc in annis teneris*) his father, Edmund Drake, embracing the Protestant doctrine was called in question by the law of the Six Articles made by Henry VIII. against the Protestants, fled his country and withdrew himself into Kent. After the death of Henry he got a place among the seamen in the King's Navy to read prayers to them; and soon after was ordained deacon and made vicar of the Church of Upnor.' (*sic.*)

2. The 'Advertisement to the reader' in 'Sir Francis Drake Revived,' written by his heir and nephew, has this passage: 'His father suffered in it (a religious persecution) being forced

to fly from his house near South Tavistock in Devon, into Kent; and there to inhabit in the hull of a ship, wherein many of his younger sons were born. He had twelve in all.' Of these we know the names of four, John and Joseph, who died during the Nombre de Dios voyage; Edward, who is mentioned in their father's will and was buried at Upchurch; and Thomas, the youngest, who became Sir Francis's heir.

3. Stowe says that he was 'son of Edmund Drake, sailor,' and that ' he was the eldest of twelve brethren brought up under his kinsman Sir John Hawkins.'

4. A note in Stowe's handwriting (Harl. MSS. 540 f. 93, Stowe MSS. iv.) contains this passage, ' for fraunces Drake Knyght, sone to Sir . Drake Vickar of Upchurche in Kent.'

5. An entry in the Lambeth registers (Add. MSS. 6088 Plut. CLXXII.) : 'Upchurch. Cant. dioc. vicar. 25 die Mensis Jan. A.D. 1560 apud Lambehith. Dns admisit Edmund Drake cleric'ad. v. pr. (*sic*.) Eccl. p'och' de Upchurche, Cant. &c.' On March 3, 1567 Edmund Drake was dead and his successor was admitted.

6. Edmund Drake's will made December 22, 1566, and proved January 16, 1566-7). In this he describes himself as vicar of Upchurch.

There is a pedigree which gives Drake's father as 'Robert Drake, third son of John Drake of Otterton,' but upon the above authorities we may safely conclude that he was certainly the son of Edmund Drake who was vicar of Upchurch. Camden's 'Upnor' is clearly nothing more than a slip of memory. There was no church of Upnor.

As a slip of memory, too, we must put down his difficult assertion that Edmund Drake was driven from Devonshire during a persecution under the Six Articles Act of 1539. In the first place the persecution that followed the passing of that Act was at once stopped by Cromwell. At his fall in 1540 it was renewed, but not, as far as we know, in Devon. What persecution there was seems to have been hottest in London and the neighbourhood; so that Drake would hardly have bettered himself by flying from the protection of the Russells and the Hawkinses to Kent. Secondly, the balance of evidence makes it pretty certain that Francis Drake was not born before 1540, and Camden's expression ' dum adhuc in annis teneris' seems to imply that he was two or three years old at least when the flight took place. Thirdly, the Lay Subsidy Rolls of 37 Henry VIII. include Edmund Drake's name as an inhabitant of Tavistock, showing that a man of that name was still living there in 1545.

The easiest and most natural way out of the difficulty is that Camden had forgotten what Drake had told him about the Six Articles, and that the troubles he alluded to were those that occurred in the Catholic Insurrection in the West, under Edward VI. One of the most important demands of the insurgents was for a restoration of the Law of the Six Articles, which had been repealed, so that the confusion in Camden's memory is very natural. We know that everyone, whether gentle or simple, who would not signify his adhesion to the doctrine of the Six Articles, had to fly for his life, that Plymouth had been surrendered by its mayor to the rebels and was no safe refuge for Protestants, that William Hawkins, the elder, was barely holding a footing there, and that the Channel Squadron was ordered to its relief. ('Somerset and Council to Lord Russell' in Cam. Soc. 1885, p. 33, and *ib.* pp. 46, 59 and 61, and 'List of Ships ready to serve in the Narrow Seas.' S.P. Dom. Ed. VI. vol. vii. f. 9.) Indeed the whole circumstances of this insurrection tally so exactly with the ascertained facts of Drake's early years, that it seems almost impossible to resist the conclusion that it was this and not the persecutions of 1539 or 1540, which was the cause of his father's flight.

At any rate it would seem that in this year the Crowndale Drakes disappear from Tavistock. For in the Lay Subsidy Rolls of 2 and 3 Ed. VI. their names are no longer included. ($\frac{9\,9}{3\,2\,0}$ 2-3 Ed. VI.) The insurrection took place at Whitsuntide 1549.

APPENDIX B

AUTHORITIES FOR HAWKINS'S THIRD VOYAGE

MOST of the English documents are collected in Arber's 'English Garner,' vol. v., to which for convenience the references in the text are made, as far as possible. Discrimination, however, must be used in accepting the Editor's explanatory notes.

First.—There is Hawkins's own account. It was published in pamphlet form the same year he returned, and has the air of having been designed to stir public opinion on the subject against Spain. Mr. Payne, in his 'Voyages of the Elizabethan Seamen' ('Clar. Press, 1893, Introd. xliii.') is of opinion that it 'is largely made up from the narrative of Philips,' overlooking the fact that Hakluyt's edition of it was only a reprint. The original pamphlet was 'Imprinted at London in Paul's Churchyard, by Thomas/Purfoot for Lucas Harrison/dwelling at the sign/of the Crane/anno 1569.' It is entitled 'A true/declaration of the/troublesome voyage of/Mr. John Hawkins to the/parts of Guinea and the/West Indies in the/years of our Lord/1567 and 1568.' Philips did not return from captivity till 1583, and his narrative is subsequent to that date. The fact, then, is that he used Hawkins's tract in constructing his narrative and not the converse as Mr. Payne supposed.

Secondly.—A MS. volume in the Record Office ('S. P. Dom. Eliz.' LIII.) entitled, 'Sir John Hawkins's Voyage 1568.' It contains an official record of the proceedings at the inquiry instituted by the Lord High Admiral before Dr. Lewes, Judge of the Admiralty Court, and mainly consists of the depositions sworn in answer to eleven interrogatories, and of declarations as to the value of the property lost through the action of the Spaniards at San Juan de Ulua. The deponents are Jean Turren, the trumpeter of the 'Jesus'; Clerk, one of the super-cargoes or merchants; Hampton, captain of the 'Minion'; Hawkins himself; Tomes, his servant; Fones, steward of the 'Angel'; and Fowler, a skilled witness as to Spanish values. Of these only Hawkins's affidavit is printed in full by Arber.

At the end of the record follows the queen's proclamation announcing Alva's embargo on English ships in the Netherlands, and enjoining retaliation upon Spanish subjects by embargo and reprisal, together with an official account of the circumstances which had led to her taking action. The proclamation is followed by three affidavits of merchants that the embargo had been extended to Spain by February 16." The whole volume must of course be taken as an *ex parte* statement of the case of the English government against Spain, but the main facts are indisputably true. It is only in its omission that it puts the English case too high. The exact purpose of this collection of documents is not clear. The title-page of course is subsequent to 1588, the date of Hawkins's knighthood. It may have been used in the peace negotiations that were proceeding when the Armada sailed.

Thirdly.—A letter from Hawkins to Cecil written from the 'Minion' the same day he arrived in Mount's Bay. It contains a short abstract log of the voyage, which gives a few facts not appearing elsewhere. This letter seems to have been overlooked by Arber.

Fourthly.—Three narratives by survivors of the fight, who were made prisoners by the Spaniards; all reprinted by Arber.

1. David Ingram's, which relates almost entirely to his own adventures in captivity and was thought untrustworthy by Hakluyt.

2. Miles Philips, who adds many details, and was at least careful to refresh his memory with Hawkins's tract.

3. 'The rare travels of Job Hartop, an/Englishman who has not been heard of / in three and twenty years' space'/ &c., London, 1591, which though written so long after the event has the air of a careful compilation, though of course coloured by what he had suffered at the hands of the Inquisition. It was dedicated to the queen.

Fifthly.—There is Herrera's account contained in his 'Historia General,' Part I., lib. xv. cap. 18, which though written some years after the event, and not very accurate in detail, admits all the chief points in the English case, and presents the treachery of the Spaniards in even a worse light than do the English authorities.

Lastly.—Philip, feeling sure, as he said, that the English would put their own construction on the affair, sent to Alva 'a true statement of what happened,' to be forwarded to the Spanish minister in London. This, however, Alva for some reason thought best to suppress (see 'Spanish Calendar': 'The King to Alva,' February 18, 1569, and Alva's answer). Captain Duro's indefatigable industry has succeeded in unearthing what seems to be a copy of this report in the 'Coleccion Navarrete.' With ready courtesy he furnished me with his transcript, a translation of which is appended in view of its great importance as the Spanish official account of the incident out of which the great war eventually grew.

APPENDICES

ANNO 1568.—REPORT OF THE ACTION OF THE ARMADA AND
FLEET OF NEW SPAIN IN THE PORT OF SAN JUAN DE LUA,
WITH THE CORSAIR JUAN DE AQUINES IN THE MONTH OF
SEPTEMBER, 1568.

'News having been received in Vera Cruz on September 15, 1568, that on the 14th of the said month eight ships had been sighted under sail off Villa Rica la Vieja, they were supposed to be the fleet of Spain which was hourly expected. And therefore that night the representatives of the royal officers of Vera Cruz came to the port to receive it. And on Tuesday after midday they saw approaching ten ships, and supposing them to be the said fleet, they launched a boat to meet it in order to receive the letters and dispatches of his majesty. And those that went in her did not succeed in recognising that the ships were foreign and English, until they found themselves in their midst, when they were suddenly seized and carried before Juan Aquines, general of the said Armada. Here they met Captain Francisco Maldonado, whom they had taken with his ship sailing with a cargo of wine, with others they had picked up on those coasts.

'The said general asserted that he had sailed from England bound for La Mina of Portugal, and that through foul weather he had not reached it before he was forced to seek fresh stores (*venir á rehacerse*), and thus he went in search of a port in order to revictual for his money; that he desired no other thing than what he had had in the other ports where he had touched; and that he would immediately release the persons he had detained. Accordingly he released some though not all; whereupon, because those of the port knew him so little until he was inside, without any gainsaying he came in and anchored; and immediately released those he had detained except the Deputy of the Treasurer, Francisco de Bustamante.

'Next day, the 17th, in the morning there were sighted three ships of the fleet of Spain coming straight for the port, who on being informed of what was going on by Captain Delgadillo in a boat, hove-to about three leagues from the port. And when the Englishman saw the fleet, he said to the captain of the said port, that in order to make a good agreement for peace, it was necessary that he should have possession of the island, and that therefore all who were upon it should leave, as was done; and that Delgadillo should treat with the general of the Fleet, that they might be given such stores as they required for their money, and that so long as they were there, no one should be allowed to land or take arms upon the island, and that he likewise would take none. That officer having gone to the fleet returned in the evening with the decision that orders should be given that he (Hawkins) should be at once allowed what was necessary for his voyage, and should immediately leave the port. But he would not agree unless he had effective possession of the island, which no one must enter with arms, and each side must give ten persons as hostages.

'With this resolution the said captain returned to the Viceroy of the Armada with an officer [1] of Aquines who spoke Spanish. Against the morrow he (Hawkins) landed, and with much diligence set to cleaning and loading the artillery, which he found on the island and in the ships which were in the port, and placed them in position ashore at its entrance. And he drew his people together, and his *capitana* and the *almiranta*, placing all in very warlike order, and thus he occupied the entrance of the port.

'Of all this Captain Delgadillo gave intelligence to the Viceroy and the Armada; whereupon, having called a council, and in order that the fleet might not be lost, he determined to accept the terms, very onerous as they were, although he had a sure report of the many injuries and insults which he (Hawkins) had committed on those coasts, and that he was in fact deemed a pirate and corsair, and though he understood how little he could trust his word, and that the fleet would be placed in danger of that man burning it, in case that was his aim.[2] And the said fleet not having been able to enter the port before for want of a wind, it anchored about an arquebus shot from it on the Monday night, September 20, expecting to go in the next morning.

'Meanwhile the people from Vera Cruz arrived, who were about 120 men, and embarked in the ships by night without being seen, and next day, in the morning, being Tuesday, St. Matthew's day, the fleet entered the port as it could. Some ships were placed close to those of the English, but they made them move away together with a hulk, because they seemed to interfere with the fire of the artillery in case they might desire to use it. The Viceroy, without leaving the *capitana*, in which

[1] *Criado* = a gentleman attached to his person.
[2] *Cuando viese la suya*, perhaps, 'in case he saw his way to it.'

he still was, having considered the matter on Tuesday and Wednesday, determined to chastise the corsair as best he could. To this end he that night caused 130 arquebusiers to go on board the hulk which the English had had moved away from close to their ships, and then the Viceroy, in order to make it serve as a kind of cover for what he intended to do farther, had it berthed in the midst between the two fleets.

'Next day, in the morning, the Englishman, suspicious of what was going on and with intent to understand it, sent his trumpet to the Viceroy with the master of his ship to understand what was happening. The general having entertained him so that he should not be spoken to, or perceive the preparations, between eight and nine the admiral held up his hand with a white napkin, which was the signal he had given, and immediately upon the *capitana*, wherein was the Royal standard and the Viceroy, a trumpet sounded: To arms! In a moment, before the Spanish Armada fired a shot, the Englishman began to discharge his guns with much damage to the *capitana* and *almiranta*; for the first shot killed a gunner, and the *almiranta* received two bad hits on her broadside in such wise that she began to take in water. Then came into her a perier-shot, which fired a barrel of powder, and then she was entirely consumed with more than fifteen or twenty men, without saving more than one boat load of clothes out of all that was in her. Meanwhile, with great celerity, the Vera Cruz people sprang ashore and rushing upon the two batteries gained them both, killing some of the English, who immediately abandoned them to fly to their ship. Because the hulk, by reason of the great resistance which was made to it, could not be got as close as was needful and had fouled the *almiranta* of the corsair, our people leaped out of their ships, leaving the Viceroy in the *capitana*, almost alone with the Royal standard, which fell into great danger; and the general of the Armada from one of the batteries began to discharge the guns that were in it, in such wise that he did great damage to the enemy, and set fire to a vessel, which he caused to be set adrift, and directed it against the English *Capitana*, whereby the enemy were seized with panic and began to leap out of her to abandon her. And from the other battery Captain Delgadillo put many shot into the English ships, killing much people. Whereupon the Englishman, having lost much people, and amongst them most of his gunners and petty officers, drew off and left the port.'

APPENDIX C

DRAKE'S DESERTION OF HAWKINS

WHETHER justly or unjustly, Drake was much blamed at the time for parting company after the disaster at San Juan de Ulua; and even long after in 1587 Vice-Admiral Borough, whom Drake was charging with mutiny, raked up the accusation. Hawkins certainly considered himself injured. Still with a fine dignity he does not even mention Drake's name in his report. All he says is: 'So with the " Minion" only and the "Judith," a small bark of fifty tons, we escaped; which bark the same night forsook us in our great misery.' There is no evidence that Drake after this was in Hawkins's service, although he certainly commanded expeditions, in which Hawkins was alleged to have been interested.

Miles Philips alters 'forsook' to 'lost.' Hartop has nothing on the point. 'He' (Hawkins), he says, 'willed Master Francis Drake to come in with the " Judith," and to lay the " Minion" aboard and take in men and other things needful; and to go out. And so he did.' Both these men it must be remembered, however, were writing, when Drake was rich, famous, and powerful.

Herrera largely embellishes the story, accusing Drake not only of disobeying Hawkins's orders, but of embezzling the gold that was saved from the 'Jesus,' 'and this,' says he, 'was his beginning.' For this offence the Queen, he relates, imprisoned him for three months, but on intercession being made in his behalf he was pardoned, and so the matter rested. These assertions are supported by no English authorities, and may safely be rejected together with so many other Spanish stories, as an invention to Drake's discredit.

For us, with this information, it is difficult to understand wherein Drake's alleged offence lay. Nothing was more natural than that the two ships should part company in the night. On the morrow of the action a northerly gale sprang up, which Hawkins rode out under the lee of an island till next morning. After that he 'wandered in an unknown sea (the Gulf of Mexico) by the space of fourteen days.' How he expected Drake to rejoin is hard to say. The 'Judith' herself must have been overcrowded with the men she had taken from the 'Minion,' no rendez-vous seems to have been given, and it was out of Drake's power to assist the 'Minion' even if he could have found her. In the absence of further knowledge we can only admire the seamanship and skill of the young captain in navigating his vessel home alone, and applaud his decision.

APPENDIX D

THE AUTHENTICITY OF 'SIR FRANCIS DRAKE REVIVED'

IT is to this work we owe nearly all we know of Drake's early exploits on the Spanish Main and Central America. Its authority has never been questioned until in his 'English Seamen' (p. 84) Mr. Froude, without giving any reasons, characterised it as 'obviously mythical, in parts demonstrably false and nowhere to be depended on.'

The work was published by Sir Francis Drake the younger at London in 1626, when Charles I. and Buckingham were stirring the country into their lamentable travesty of the Elizabethan policy. It is entitled ' Sir Francis Drake/reviv'd;/ calling upon this dull or effeminate Age/to follow his noble steps for gold and silver,/&c.' and purports to be 'faithfully taken out of the report of Master Christopher Ceely, Ellis Hixom and others who were in the same voyage with him, by Philip Nichols, Preacher.' It is also said to have been revised by Drake himself 'before his death, and much holpen and enlarged by divers notes, with his own hand here and there inserted.' The book was dedicated by Sir F. Drake, Bart., to Charles I., but also contains a dedication by Sir F. Drake, Knight, to Elizabeth, dated January 1, 1592-3, as though, according to the custom of the Court, he had presented the MS. to her as a New Year's gift. The date makes the fact of the revision probable, because, since 1590, Drake had been in disgrace and unemployed at sea, and 1593 was the year he was taken into favour again. Further, the admiral gives as his reason for drawing up the original MS. narrative, that garbled fragmentary and incorrect accounts of his voyages and actions had been published, and speaks of it as the first-fruits of a complete relation of his life that he had in contemplation. He probably had Hakluyt and Ryther's translation of Ubaldino's version of Howard's account of the Armada chiefly in view.

The first edition of Hakluyt's 'Collected Voyages' was published in 1589, Ryther's book in 1590, and Drake may well have been discontented with the meagre account of his exploits these works contained, and with the poor figure they make him cut.[1]

As to the credibility of the work, the fight in Nombre de Dios (on the improbability of which Mr. Froude's doubts seemed chiefly to rest), as well as the capture of the mule-trains, the sack of Venta Cruz and several minor points are confirmed from Spanish authorities. The capture of the mule trains, with the burial and loss of the silver, and the fruitless pursuit by the Spanish launches are also confirmed by Lope de Vega in the first canto of the 'Dragontea.'

The most convincing confirmation, however, is to be found in a paper (' S.P. Spain, XVIII.') dated January 1580 (O.S. i.e. 1581) and headed 'Memoria de los Cossarios Ingleses que han hecho robas en las Indias,' &c., which was sent to the Queen by Philip apparently to support his case against Drake after the voyage round the world. After relating his exploit at Cartagena, it goes on 'The same Francis Drake entered by night into Nombre de Dios and killed eighteen persons, and gave out that he was making war on behalf of her Highness, the Queen of England, and carried off from the harbour a ship of Francis Gallego's laden with wine,' which practically disposes of Mr. Froude's objection. The remainder of the paper deals with the sack of Venta Cruz, and the havoc Drake made with the West Indian shipping, giving in many cases the names of the owners.

As to the details of the adventures, difficulties, failures and successes, of which the Authorised Narrative is full, from the point of view of purely literary criticism, they certainly bear the stamp of genuineness. The most extraordinary incidents, such as Drake's cruise on the raft, the death of his brothers, the scuttling of the ' Swan,' and many others, are such as a Stevenson to-day might have invented, but are entirely foreign to the fiction of Elizabeth or the early Stuarts. De Foe had yet to conceive the novel of adventure.

Hakluyt has only an extract from the 'Discourse of the West Indies and the South Sea, written by Lopez Vaz, a Portugal . . . which was intercepted with the author thereof at the River of Plate by Captain Withrington and Captain Christopher Lister in the fleet set forth by the Right Hon. the

[1] Cf. Appendix B, vol. ii.

Earl of Cumberland for the South Sea in 1586.' The extract, however, confirms Drake's own narrative at all the chief points. Captain Duro ('Armada Española,' ii. p. 506) calendars a MS. as 'relating with curious details the attack which Drake, in company with the Cimaroon negroes of Vallano, delivered upon the Peru silver recua on the march near Nombre de Dios,' but I have been unable to obtain a transcript.

APPENDIX E

AUTHORITIES FOR THE VOYAGE OF CIRCUMNAVIGATION

THE greater part of these are collected in the volume of the Hakluyt Society, entitled ' Drake's World Encompassed,' which was edited in 1854 by Mr. W. S. W. Vaux, Keeper of the Department of Coins and Medals at the British Museum, an antiquarian of wide range, but without special qualification apparently, for dealing with maritime questions or a conflict of evidence ; so that in his preface he seems almost perversely to miss the significance of his important discovery of the Cooke manuscript.

The special authorities are as follows :

1. 'The World Encompassed by Sir Francis Drake, being his next voyage to that to Nombre de Dios, formerly imprinted; carefully collected out of the notes of Master Francis Fletcher, Preacher in this employment and divers others his followers in the same, offered now at last to publique view both for the honour of the actor, but especially for the stirring up of heroick spirits, to benefit their countrie, and eternise their names by like noble attempts, London, 1628 :' a small quarto.

This work, which is quoted in the text as the 'Authorised Narrative,' is apparently what it purports to be, a narrative which Sir Francis Drake, Bart., the admiral's heir and nephew, caused to be drawn up in continuation of his ' Sir Francis Drake Revived ' (see App. D). Fletcher's notes, which still exist, and are printed in full by Vaux, are clearly the foundation of the work as far as they go. Where they cease, Pretty, one of Drake's gentlemen-at-arms, takes Fletcher's place. There is internal evidence, too, that other material was before the editor. Dates, courses, and latitudes, for instance, seem to have been corrected from a detailed log, which is now lost. Some minor incidents too must have come out of MSS. such as Fortescue's quoted by Fuller in his 'Holy State,' or from the notes of 'divers others his followers.' The whole work, however, loses weight from having been very freely edited in Drake's favour, and in the Doughty affair must be practically rejected except where confirmed from hostile sources.

2. A MS. (Sloane 61) entitled 'The first part of the second voyage about the world attempted continued, &c., by Mr. Francis Drake.' Copy.

In the body of the work it is stated to be by Fletcher, and without doubt is the 'Notes' on which the 'World Encompassed' was founded. As such it is printed by Vaux. It ends unfortunately with the incident at Mocha Island, just before the great raid on the Pacific coast began. Of the second part nothing is known. What we have was written after Cavendish's voyage in 1588. It was very likely the fact of this work's being in progress that Hakluyt had in his mind when he wrote that he had refrained at first from publishing anything about Drake's great voyage for fear of spoiling another man's labour. Fletcher was an ardent Protestant, objecting to the Romish tendencies of some of his comrades, and having a perfect horror of idolatry. The notes are much swollen by pious digressions and comments. He was also a bit of a scientist, dealing largely with cosmographical questions, as well as with the fauna and flora observed. This was probably his special duty; for the MS. contains a number of sketches of the more curious specimens. It also has two highly interesting charts to illustrate the discovery of Cape Horn. On the Doughty episode he is hostile to Drake, but always in a shrinking kind of way, as though he had not forgotten being fastened by the leg to the hatchway off Celebes. His fear and admiration of Drake are both apparent throughout.

3. A MS. (Harl. 540, f. 93) in Stowe's handwriting, and endorsed by him 'For frauncis Drake, Knight, sone to Sir Drake, vickar of Upchurche, in Kent,' as though he had transcribed it as material for his history, but he does not appear to have used it. It has the name 'John Cooke' at the foot and extends to the desertion of Wynter, on whose ship Cooke was sailing. For the Doughty affair it is invaluable, being written by a violent partisan of his, red-hot with the sense of a great

crime having been committed upon his friend, and with the undisguised intention of making the affair as black for Drake, as it seemed to be to him. His sincerity is obvious. He was clearly taken in by Doughty, and believed he was advocating the cause of a noble gentleman foully murdered by a tyrannical sea-captain at the instigation of worthless ruffians, who were jealous of the accused man. Still, in spite of his animosity, where Doughty is not concerned, he cannot withhold his admiration of Drake's powers, and in his heat he continually blurts out admissions which in his infatuation for Doughty he cannot see tell in Drake's favour. This is especially the case when he innocently records Doughty's confession that he had betrayed the voyage to Burghley. Vaux has been blamed for attaching too much importance to the MS.; he should rather have been blamed for using it without discrimination. Its bias is so obvious that as evidence against Drake it is inadmissible except where confirmed by the friendly narratives; but as evidence against Doughty it is of as high a value as an historical document can well be. The general correctness of Cooke's facts is amply borne out by the confirmation his narrative obtains from other sources, and especially from the Articles and Depositions (vide *infra*). He is always scrupulous to distinguish what was hearsay to him from what he had at first hand. It is only his inferences that need be suspected. As for his sincerity one case will suffice. He begins his narrative by saying, what Doughty always gave out and had probably persuaded him was the truth, that Drake, Wynter, and Doughty sailed 'as equall companions and friendly gentlemen' (Vaux, p. 187); yet he does not shrink from recording (at p. 214), without comment, Wynter's admission, that he held his command unconditionally at Drake's pleasure.

4. A set of papers (Harl. MSS. 6221) in a clerkly hand entitled 'Sir Francis Drake's Voyage with his proceedings against Thomas Doughty, R. St. 1615.' The 'Voyage' is that of 1585, but the 'proceedings' relate to the 'Voyage Round the World.' They consist, apparently, of the Articles and Depositions upon which Doughty was tried, and may possibly be copies of the 'Writings about Sir F. Drake's Voyage' referred to by Dr. Lewes of the Admiralty Court in a letter to Walsingham ('S.P. Dom. CLIV. 62, 1582'). They were certainly not drawn up after Drake's return, for Articles 9, 10, 11 (Vaux, p. 169) were signed by Thomas Flood and John Brewer, who

were the two men killed at Mocha (see *ante*, pp. 261, 262). There is therefore no reason for doubting that they are what they purport to be, the record of the actual proceedings at the court martial. They were all printed by Vaux, except one, 'Thomas Doughty's Oration,' which is in f. 7, and which he seems to have overlooked. It is given in full in the text (*ante*, p. 223). These documents are chiefly valuable for the admissions they contain against Doughty by Fletcher, Cooke, and other of his friends, and also for the general confirmation they give of the correctness of Cooke's account of the trial.

5. The well-known narrative printed by Hakluyt, which was drawn up by Francis Pretty, one of Drake's gentlemen-at-arms, and is entitled 'The Famous Voyage of Sir Francis Drake into the South Sea and thence about the whole Globe of the Earth.' It is chiefly valuable as being reserved and impartial in tone on the Doughty affair, and as being the main original source from the point where Fletcher's notes end. He seems, however, to have been a soldier who took little interest in navigation or seamanship. Whenever he attempts to be detailed on these points he is almost invariably wrong. It is his muddled account of the movements of the squadron after first entering the Pacific, that had cast doubt on Drake's discovery of Cape Horn. He is similarly entirely wrong about the order of events off Guatemala and Nicaragua, as the Spanish documents clearly show. As an instance of his confusion of mind may be taken his statement that on leaving Guatemala Drake sailed *northerly* to get a wind, whereas of course he sailed *westerly*; a northerly course would have run him immediately on the coast of Mexico. This narrative was reprinted by Vaux.

6. The official narrative of Nuño da Silva, the Portuguese pilot, which extends from his entering Drake's service at the Cape Verde Islands to his being set ashore at Guatemala. It was drawn up by the command of Don Martin Enriquez, Viceroy of Mexico, and this is probably why he held his tongue about the discovery of an open sea south of Tierra del Fuego. He was not likely to give up to the Spaniards gratuitously so valuable a secret. A translation of his narrative was printed by Hakluyt in his collection of Voyages, and was reprinted by Vaux. The original is calendared by Captain Duro, as in ' Colec. Sans de Barutell, vi. 75.' (See ' Armada Española ' II. 506, App. ii. 'Noticias relativas al corsario inglés Francis Drake.')

APPENDICES 407

7. 'The Voyage of M. John Wynter into the South Sea, &c.' This is the third account given by Hakluyt. It was written by Edward Cliffe, mariner, who went home with Wynter. Though short, it is of value on all questions of navigation and seamanship, and seems carefully and impartially written. It also is in Vaux's volume.

8. 'A Discourse of the West Indies and the South Sea,' by Lopez Vaz. This work has been noticed under Appendix D. For the voyage of circumnavigation its chief interest is for the effect Drake's raid had upon the Spanish-Americans and the measures taken in consequence.

9. 'A Discourse of Sir Francis Drake's jorney and exploytes after he had past ye Straytes of Megellan into Marc de Sur, &c.,' printed by Vaux. It is in Harl. MSS. 280, f. 23, closely written on both sides of the paper. It gives several details not appearing elsewhere, but its authority is doubtful, and in places it is very incorrect. It is written by someone with a grievance against Drake. The words 'pirate,' 'thief,' and 'robbery' are freely used, and Drake is accused of defrauding one of his men called Legge, who, there can be little doubt, was the author, and under his name the document is quoted in the text. In the original is an erased passage, which Vaux has omitted. It comes between the words 'Grand Capitayne' and 'So hee carying' (Vaux, p. 180, line 10), and relates how Legge found gold in searching a chest and gave it to Drake, 'who promised to reward him for his true dealing, but Drake arrested Legge afterwards on an action for debt whereas he (Drake) was in Legge's debt 200*l.* by promise for his voyage whereof no whit is yet performed.' He also relates in detail every case where Drake received presents from his prisoners, as though to show how his crew had been defrauded of their rights, whereas Tremayne, an impartial witness, goes out of his way to praise the generosity with which Drake had treated his men (see *ante*, p. 313). On the whole it is impossible to attach much importance to the document, as, whether true or not, these are the kind of vulgar slanders a dissatisfied seaman would naturally invent.

10. John Wynter's deposition before the Lord Admiral (in ' S.P. Dom. Eliz.' CXXXIX. 44). This would seem to have been made in consequence of the demand of the Portuguese ambassador for satisfaction on account of the capture of the 'Mary' at the Cape Verde Islands. It relates to this incident

alone, and the shifting of part of her cargo to Wynter's ship in St. Julian's Bay. The document is not of much value as being obviously designed to throw the whole responsibility for piracy upon Drake's shoulders.

The chief Spanish authorities are:

1. The examination of San Juan de Anton, master and owner of the 'Cacafuego,' taken before the chief judge of the High Court of Panama and forwarded to England in support of the Spanish claims for compensation. This and the rest of the evidence are in S.P. Spain (bundle 8). A translation of Anton's deposition is also amongst the Burghley Papers (Lansd. MSS. cxxii. 4), but Vaux seems to have missed it. It gives many interesting details not found elsewhere.

2. The despatches and reports of various American officials and prisoners, which are collected by Peralta in his 'Costa Rica, Nicaragua y Panama en el siglo XVI.,' Madrid and Paris, 1883.

3. 'Relación del viaje que hizo Francisco Drake al mar del Sur, hecha en la ciudad de Santa Fé, pór John Drake, sobrino de dicho capitan.'—' Colec. Navarrete,' xxvi. 18.

This is the examination of John Drake, Sir Francis's page, who fell into the Spaniards' hands during Fenton's voyage. Another taken at Lima is *Ibid*, No. 22. A not very accurate translation of this was published anonymously in the 'Western Antiquary.' It is of great value, and supplies many details not given elsewhere. John Drake's actual degree of relationship to Francis is disputed by Devonshire genealogists.

4. 'Relacion de lo que el corsario Francisco hizo y robo en la costa de Chile y Peru' &c., written by Pedro Sarmiento de Gamboa, the navigator.

It is the official report, which he made as sergeant-major of the South Sea Squadron sent in pursuit of Drake by the Viceroy of Peru. It is printed in the 'Coleccion de Documentos Inéditos,' xciv. pp. 432–458.

APPENDIX F

AMOUNT OF DRAKE'S PLUNDER

1. TREMAYNE's official return of what he sent up to the Tower from Saltash Castle ('S.P. Dom. 1580, cxliv. 17') shows forty-

six parcels of treasure averaging over 2 cwt. each, i.e. nearly five tons. The exact amount registered was 4 tons, 15 cwt. 4 lbs. This was after Drake had been authorised secretly to abstract a large amount for himself and his crew, besides several horse-loads of gold and silver, and some of the most precious items of his booty, which John Drake says he himself took with him to London.

2. Another account of all silver bullion that was brought into the Tower by Sir Francis Drake, dated December 26, 1585, in Murdin's 'Burghley State Papers' (p. 539), puts the total at over 10 tons.

The figures are as follows:

	Lbs.	Ozs.
650 ingots of silver fine and coarse	22,899	5
Sundry pieces of 'corrento' coarse	512	6
Total	23,411	11

Out of this there had been coined under Royal Warrants or refined the following amounts:

Coined for Sir Christopher Hatton	£2,300		
„ „ Sir F. Walsyngham	4,000		
„ „ Earl of Leicester	4,000		
	10,300		
Refined into clean ingots	29,625	15	9
Total	£39,925	15	9

Remaining in the vault, 243 ingots and the 512 lbs. corrento.

Besides the silver there were ingots and cakes of gold which had been coined into £205. More than a third therefore remained uncoined, so that we may safely place the total value of such part of the silver as reached the Tower at 55,000*l*., or 440,000*l*. of our money.

3. Purchas gives what purports to be a complete account of all he carried from the coast of Peru, as follows:

866,000 pesos of silver, = 866 quintals = 86,000 lbs.
866 quintals at 1,200 Spanish ducats the quintal = 1,039,200 ducats.
100 quintals of gold at 1,500 ducats   = 150,000
                               Total   .   . 1,189,200 ducats.

A Spanish ducat was worth at the time from 5*s*. 6*d*. to 5*s*. 10*d*. ('S.P. Dom. Eliz. 1582, cliii.'), which gives the total at 326,530*l*., or about two millions and a half of our money, and this Purchas says was not counting unregistered treasure such as money and jewels.

4. Lewis Roberts in his 'Merchant's Map of Commerce,' 1682, quoted by Barrow, says he had seen an account signed by Drake's own hand, showing a profit after payment of all charges and outgoings of 47*l*. for each 1*l*. invested. The accounts of Hawkins's voyage of 1567 show the initial cost of its outfit to have been about 15*l*. per ton. Drake's expedition was about 275 tons, so that the initial cost would be approximately 3,625*l*. The amount divided then after compromising Spanish claims, &c., would have been about 170,000*l*., or considerably more than a million of our money. The queen's private share on her investment of a thousand crowns would be 11,750*l*., which, being equal to nearly 90,000*l*. of our money, goes far to account for the favour she showed Drake.

5. The copy of the register of the 'Cacafuego,' which was sent to England to substantiate the Spanish claims, is totaled up in a marginal note of Burghley's at 363,333 *pesos* ('S.P. Spain,' 1580, xviii.). The plunder of another vessel is claimed at 14,000 *pesos* of gold. The *peso* was usually taken at 6*s*. 8*d*., which gives, say, 1,090,000*l*. The *peso d'oro* was worth 8*s*., giving for the other ship 56,000*l*. The total of the two prizes is therefore 1,146,000*l*., or more than nine millions of our money, which clearly must have been an exaggeration, and suggests that the Spanish calculations of damage were as heroic as those afterwards applied in the case of the 'Alabama.'

APPENDIX G

DRAKE'S ARMS

THE achievement of arms stamped upon the cover of the present work is neither what Drake generally used, nor what was granted to him at his knighthood, but a combination of the two, which has been adopted for the following reasons.

The exact form of the arms granted in respect of the knighthood is a subject attended with difficulty, which the College of Arms seems unable to clear up. The data, as far as I have been able to disentangle them from the confused information obtainable from the Heralds' College, with the help of outside material, are as follow.

With regard to the arms proper—that is, the shield--granted in 1581, there is no difficulty. It was *sable, a fess wavy between two stars argent*. It is in the crest that the uncertainty lies. In the original patent which is preserved at Nutwell Court, the blazon continues 'the helm adorned with a globe terrestrial upon the height whereof a ship under sail trained about the same with golden haulsers by the direction of a hand appearing out of the clouds, all in proper colours, with these words, *Auxilio divino*.' But in many early representations of the crest, notably in that which surmounts the cocoanut cup given to Sir Francis by the queen and in the heraldic mantelpiece put up by his brother Thomas at Buckland Abbey, a demi-wyvern appears in the ship. In a sketch preserved at the College of Arms (*Vincent*, 184, p. 54), it is a whole wyvern, but so badly drawn that it appears to be hanging by the neck from the rigging, and here, perhaps, we have the origin of Prince's joke (see *ante*, p. 61).

On the other hand, there are early examples with no wyvern at all. There is still in the possession of the family a fine silver seal mounted in ivory and inscribed about the neck with the words: 'The arms given unto Sir Francis Drake by the Queen's Matie for the voyage round about the world. Anno Dom. 1580.' In this the wyvern is absent, nor is it discoverable in the achievement painted on the Buckland Abbey portrait (vol. i., frontispiece). Still, it is certain that Sir Francis's immediate successors always used the crest with a wyvern or demi-wyvern in the ship. Sir Francis's own views are unknown, for reasons to be mentioned later.

Under these circumstances it becomes a matter of considerable doubt whether the wyvern should appear in the ship or not. The fact of its appearance on the cup and its use by Drake's heirs is, however, not difficult to explain, in spite of there being no mention of it in the existing patent. Indeed the explanations are various. Some incline to the view that it is an emblematical representation of Sir Francis himself in the characteristic fashion of the time. It was thus the queen loved to symbolise herself by a phœnix. Others again regard it as an assertion by Sir Francis's family of their right to bear the ancient cognisance of the house, a wyvern gules.

Continuing to examine existing data we find in the Ashmolean MSS. (834, fol. 44) a draft with the date blank in which the arms are *sable a fess wavy argent between two stars or*, and in the ship and globe crest is 'the upper half of a red dragon.' But at the head of the document is noted : 'This draft took none effect ; it was never used.'

Further on (at fol. 37*b*) is another draft, dated June 21, with the arms and crest the same as above, and at the head of this is noted : ' This draft was abridged and made shorter according as it is set down on the next leaf following.' Turning to this leaf (fol. 38) we find the following memorandum :

'This instrument above written was abridged and made shorter in form hereafter expressed and delivered unto Sir Francis Drake under the hand of Robert Cooke, Clarencieux.

'And after being the second time newly made and fair written for the said Sir Francis, this clause following was added next before the witness [i.e. the witnessing clause] of Clarencieux, and the latter end of all in place where this mark * is placed, viz :

'"Notwithstanding that the said Sir Francis Drake, being well-born and descended of worthy ancestors such as have of long time borne arms, as tokens and demonstrations of their race and progeny, which likewise to him by just descent and prerogative of birth are duly derived, may for the arms of his surname and family bear *argent, a waver dragon volant gules* with the difference of a third brother, as I am credibly informed by the testimony of Bernard Drake, [blank] in the county of Devon, Esquire, chief of that coat armour, and sundry others of that family of worship and good credit. In witness whereof," &c.'

Then follows the abridged draft, also dated June 21. In this not only is the preamble abridged, but the blazon is altered. The shield is now *sable a fess wavy between two stars argent*—that is, the stars are changed from *or* to *argent*, being thus given the same tincture as the fess. In the crest the 'red dragon' is changed to a 'red dragon volant.' At the head of the draft the whole is sketched in trick. Although in the draft there is nothing to indicate the position of the dragon volant, a wyvern, which presumably was regarded as the same thing, is placed in the ship, 'displayed' and looking up at the hand in the clouds, while at the mainmast head is a golden star of which nothing whatever is said in the draft. In the Buckland Abbey portrait this star appears. In the silver seal it does not.

Returning to the College of Arms, we find this last draft entered in a book under title ' A Confirmation to Sir Francis

Drake,' thereby implying that this was a supplementary grant made in addition to or in substitution of the original patent at Nutwell Court.

The inference, then, from this entry and Cooke's notes on the Ashmolean drafts read with the additional clause, is that Drake was dissatisfied with the original patent on the ground that it did not recognise his right to bear the family arms as well as those granted him by the queen, and that on his protesting Clarencieux made a new draft or confirmation, inserting the above clause, and further recognising his right by adding the 'red dragon volant' to the new crest.

The patent as finally issued with the amendments is unfortunately missing. The original draft by which Clarencieux sought to satisfy Drake's objections exists at the College of Arms (F 12, 163-4), and explains the fair copies in the Ashmolean MSS. It is full of corrections and erasures. For instance, he first wrote the 'upper half of a red dragon sheweth itself,' and then erased the words 'upper half of,' perhaps because Drake insisted on having the complete charge. It is also shortened by a long passage in the preamble being cut out, for the simple reason perhaps, as Dr. Drake has pointed out, that the old grant was found too long to go into an ordinary skin of parchment with marginal decorations, the result being that the original patent is a very clumsy and untidy piece of penmanship. On the back of the same draft is Clarencieux's note on which, almost in identical words, the additional clause declaring Drake's right to the family arms was founded.

Taken with this new clause the addition to the blazon clearly is intended as a recognition of Drake's ancient gentility. The difficult question, however, remains, What did Clarencieux mean by the amended clause? The blazon in the final draft runs thus : 'The helm adorned with a terrestrial globe in the height whereof a ship in sail trained about the same with two golden haulsers by the direction of a hand appearing out of the clouds all in their proper colour, a red dragon volant sheweth itself regarding the said direction with the words *auxilio divino*.' Here, as has been said, there is nothing about the dragon volant being in the ship, or indeed any indication of his position. Yet it is certain that on the fair copy of the draft Cooke drew a wyvern in the ship. On the other hand, the sketch contains an obvious error in the addition of the star at the masthead. Further, it does not appear beyond dispute that the winged monster in the ship is a dragon volant. I have endeavoured at the College of Arms to set this point at rest, but on the generic distinctions or resemblances of dragons, dragons volant, waver dragons, waver dragons volant, and wyverns feeling seems still to run high.[1] On the whole we seem as far as ever from knowing how Clarencieux finally made up his mind to interpret his own obscure blazoning.

It is possible that Drake was still dissatisfied, and, being unable to get Cooke to do what he wanted, washed his hands of the whole thing, and after his manner went his own way, content with the recognition of his ancestral rights. What Drake wanted, I would suggest, is that the new arms should be expressly granted as an augmentation of honour upon his family coat, and that the patent should clearly recognise his right to *two* crests—one the preposterous new one, and the other the old wyvern gules of his house—and that when Cooke insisted on combining the wyvern with the globe and ship, Drake would have nothing more to do with it.

As to what he did there is no doubt. The parvenu heraldry of globe and ship and hand and clouds and haulsers he discarded altogether, and the fess and stars he used as an augmentation of honour upon the old coat.

Many examples of his seals exist, and as far as is known he never used anything but a shield with the old and new arms quarterly, the old taking precedence, as shown on the cover, and for a crest, a birdlike device which is usually regarded as an eagle displayed. But since it has a dragon-like tail, it is more probably a wyvern displayed, or, in other words, 'a dragon volant shewing itself.' Its head, moreover, is always turned to the right—that is, it is regarding the direction of the hand. Examples of these arms as thus used habitually by Drake may be seen on the Dutch engraved portrait, where he also has a wyvern in the front of his helmet, and on seals in Lansdowne MSS. 70, and Harleian MSS. 4762, fol. 132. It is also to be seen thus carved upon a mantelpiece in the oldest part of Buckland Abbey, in what was once one of the principal rooms, but is now a lumber loft.

Under these circumstances it has been thought best to show

---

[1] It may also be mentioned for the guidance of students that some confusion appears to exist at the College between a draft, a copy, and an original of a document.

the shield as Sir Francis always used it, and in lieu of the doubtful crest he used, the crest that he ought to have used as having been expressly granted to him by patent. The red dragon volant is, however, omitted, as it is impossible to know where and how it was eventually placed in the final patent.

END OF THE FIRST VOLUME

AT THE BALLANTYNE PRESS
PRINTED BY SPOTTISWOODE, BALLANTYNE AND CO. LTD.
COLCHESTER, LONDON AND ETON, ENGLAND

www.ingramcontent.com/pod-product-compliance
Lightning Source LLC
Chambersburg PA
CBHW020545300426
44111CB00008B/801